THE MASONIC BOOK CLUB

VOL. 9

Anderson's Constitutions of 1738

Lewis Edward & W. J. Hughan

Westphalia Press
An Imprint of the Policy Studies Organization
Washington, DC

Anderson's Constitutions of 1738

All Rights Reserved © 2025 by Policy Studies Organization

Westphalia Press
An imprint of Policy Studies Organization
1367 Connecticut Avenue NW
Washington, D.C. 20036
info@ipsonet.org

ISBN: 978-1-63723-541-6

Daniel Gutierrez-Sandoval, Executive Director
PSO and Westphalia Press

Updated material and comments on this edition
can be found at the Westphalia Press website:
www.westphaliapress.org

The Masonic Book Club

The *Masonic Book Club* (MBC) was formed in 1970 by two Illinois Masons, Alphonse Cerza, 33°, and Louis L. Williams, 33°. The MBC primarily reprinted out-of-print Masonic books with scholarly introductions; occasionally they would print additional texts as "bonuses" (though none were marked specifically as such on the title pages); sometimes a reprint would be marked "Masonic Book Club Edition"; often an unnumbered bonus was published jointly with the Illinois Lodge of Research or the Supreme Council, 33°, NMJ, USA.

Most of the MBC volumes indicated on the title page, "Volume [*Number*] of the Publications of the Masonic Book Club," some were misnumbered, and some were unnumbered. Indeed, the numbering of the early volumes was inconsistent. For example, *A Serious and Impartial Enquiry* is "Volume Five" (1974) but *Masonic Membership of the Founding Fathers* is "The Masonic Book Club Edition" (1974). Then, *Masonry Dissected* is "Volume Eight" (1977), *The Trestleboard* is "Volume 8A" (1978), and *Anderson's Constitutions of 1738* is "Volume Nine" (1978). If nothing else, MBC books keep bibliophiles on their toes.

The first volumes had deckle-edged paper and pages of slightly different sizes, though eventually the MBC settled into a 6″×9″ trimmed-page format for their books. The books were bound in a dark blue fabric with gold lettering. Listed below are the fifty-nine MBC volumes published 1970–2010 with bonuses. N.B.: A number and letter, e.g. "Volume 8A," is a numbering for this reprint series.

The club originally was limited to 333 members, but the number grew to nearly 2,000, with 1,083 members when it dissolved in 2010. In 2017 MW Barry Weer, 33°, the last president of the MBC, transferred the MBC name and assets to the Supreme Council, 33°, SJ, USA. Under the editorship of Arturo de Hoyos, 33°, G∴C∴, and S. Brent Morris, 33°, G∴C∴, the revived Masonic Book Club has the goal of publishing classic Masonic books while supporting Scottish Rite, SJ, USA philanthropies.

Publications of the Masonic Book Club, 1970–2010

1	1970	*The Regius Poem*	Masonic Book Club
2	1971	*The Constitutions of the Free-Masons*	Benjamin Franklin
3	1972	*Ahiman Rezon*	Laurence Dermott
4	1973	*Illustrations of Masonry*	William Preston
5	1974	*A Serious and Impartial Enquiry into the Cause of the Present Decay of Free-Masonry in the Kingdom of Ireland*	Fifield D'Assigny
5A	1974*	*Masonic Membership of the Founding Fathers*	Ronald E. Heaton

6	1975	*The Signers of the Declaration of Independence*	David C. Whitney
7	1976	*The Signers of the Constitution of the United States*	David C. Whitney
7A	1976*	*Masonic Symbols in American Decorative Art*	Louis L. Williams & Alphonse Cerza
8	1977	*Samuel Prichard's Masonry Dissected, 1730*	Harry Carr
8A	1978*	*Trestle-Board (A facsimile of the original Trestle Board by the Baltimore Masonic Convention of 1843)*	Dwight L. Smith
9	1978	*Anderson's Constitutions of 1738*	Lewis Edward & W. J. Hughan
10	1979	*Sufferings of John Coustos*	Wallace McLeod
11	1980	*The Revelations of a Square*	George Oliver
11A	1980	*Biblical Characters in Freemasonry*	John H. Van Gorden
11B	1980*	*A Masonic Reader's Guide*	*Guide* Alphonse Cerza & Thomas Warden
12	1981	*Three Distinct Knocks and Jachin and Boaz*	Harry Carr
13	1982	*Masonic Almanacs and Anti-Masonic Almanacs*	Plez A. Transou
13A	1982*	*Stephen A. Douglas: Freemason*	Wayne C. Temple
14	1983	*The Beginnings of Freemasonry in America*	Melvin M. Johnson
14A	1983*	*Bespangled, Painted & Embroidered: Decorated Masonic Aprons in America, 1790–1850*	Scottish Rite Masonic Museum & Library
14B	1983*	*Making a Mason at Sight*	Louis L. Williams
15	1984	*Masonic Concordance of the Holy Bible*	Charles Clyde Hunt
15A	1984*	*By Square and Compasses: The Building of Lincoln's Home and Its Saga*	Wayne C. Temple

16	1985	*The Old Gothic Constitutions*	Wallace McLeod
16A	1985*	*Modern Historical Characters in Freemasonry*	John H. Van Gorden
17	1986	*The Rise and Development of Organised Freemasonry*	Roy A. Wells
17A	1986*	*Ancient and Early Medieval Historical Characters in Freemasonry*	John H. Van Gorden
18	1987	*The Lodge in Friendship Village and Other Stories*	P. W. George
18A	1987*	*Masonic Charities*	John H. Van Gorden & Stewart M. L. Pollard
18B	1987*	*Medieval Historical Characters in Freemasonry*	John H. Van Gorden
18C	1987*	*George Washington in New York*	Allan Boudreau & Alexander Bleimann
19	1988	*Records of the Hole Crafte and Fellowship of Masons*	Edward Conder, Jr.
20	1989	*A Candid Disquisition of the Principles and Practices of the Most Ancient and Honourable Society of Free and Accepted Masons*	Wellins Calcott
20A	1989*	*Freemasonry and Nauvoo, 1839–1846*	Robin L. Carr
21	1990	*Masonic Odes and Poems*	Rob Morris
22	1991	*Lessing's Masonic Dialogues*	Gotthold Lessing
22A	1991*	*ABC of Freemasonry: A Book for Beginners*	Delmar D. Darrah
23	1992	*The Folger Manuscript*	S. Brent Morris
24	1993	*Freemasonry and Christianity: Lectures from Two Ages*	T. De Witt Peake & John J. Murchison
25	1994	*The Constitutions of St. John's Lodge*	Robin L. Carr
25A	1994*	*The Mystic Tie and Men of Letters*	Robin L. Carr
26	1995	*Recollections of a Masonic Veteran*	S. Brent Morris

27	1996	*The Freemason's Monitor or Illustrations of Masonry in Two Parts*	Thomas Smith Webb
28	1997	*The Masonic Ladder or the Nine Steps to Ancient Freemasonry*	John Sherer
28A	1997*	*Freemasonry and Democracy: Its Evolution in North America*	Allen E. Roberts & Wallace McLeod
29	1998	*The Masonic Harp: Collection of Masonic Odes, Hymns, Songs*	George Wingate Chase
30	1999	*Symbolic Teachings of Masonry and Its Message*	Thomas Milton Stewart
31	2000	*Freemasonry Its Meaning and Significance, An Exposition of its Ethics, Religion and Philosophy*	Otto Caspari
32	2001	*K. R. Cama Masonic Jubilee Volume*	Jivanji Jamshedji Modi
33	2002	*Caementaria Hibernica*	W. J. Chetwode Crawley
34	2003	*A Daily Advancement in Masonic Knowledge*	Wallace McLeod & S. Brent Morris
35	2004	*The Craftsman, and Templar's Textbook and, also, Melodies for the Craft*	Cornelius Moore
36	2005	*The Text Book of Freemasonry*	Retired Member of the Craft
37	2006	*Orations of the Illustrious Brother Frederick Dalcho Esq., M.D.*	Frederick Dalcho
38	2007	*Antiquities of Freemasonry Comprising Illustrations of the Five Grand Periods of Masonry from the Creation of the World to the Dedication of King Solomon's Temple*	George Oliver
39	2008	*Diogenes' Lamp or an Examination of our Present-Day Morality and Enlightenment*	Adam Weishaupt
40	2009	*Proofs of Conspiracy Against All the Governments of Europe*	John Robison
41	2010	*The Evolution of Freemasonry*	Delmar Darrah

* indicates a bonus book

ANDERSON'S CONSTITUTIONS OF 1738

ANDERSON'S
CONSTITUTIONS OF 1738

ANDERSON'S
CONSTITUTIONS OF 1738

A facsimile of
the original text with commentaries
by Lewis Edwards and W. J. Hughan

VOLUME NINE
of the publications of
THE MASONIC BOOK CLUB

Published by
THE MASONIC BOOK CLUB
A Not-for-Profit Corporation of Illinois
Bloomington, Illinois
1978

This volume has been published
solely for the Members of
The Masonic Book Club
and this edition limited to
1,200 copies
of which this is

No._____

© 1978, by The Masonic Book Club
Printed in the United States of America

Contents

	Page*
PREFACE	
FACSIMILE OF THE LEWIS EDWARDS COMMENTARY OF 1928	. 357
FACSIMILE OF QUATUOR CORONATORUM ANTIGRAPHA MASONIC REPRINT OF 1890	
Introduction, by W. J. Hughan	v
Dedication	iv
Table of Contents	vii
Part I—The History of Masonry from Creation throughout the known Earth; till true old Architecture was demolished by Goths and at last Revived in Italy	1
Part II—The History of Masonry in Britain from Julius Caesar, till the Union of the Crowns, 1603	55
Part III—The History of Masonry in Britain from the Union of the Crowns to these times	97
The Old Charges	. 143
The General Regulations	. 152
The Constitutions of the Committee of Masons Charity	. 178
A List of Lodges	. 184
Deputations of Grand Masters	. 190
Approbations	. 199
Songs	. 200
A Defense of Masonry	. 216
Brother Euclid's Letter	. 226
BIBLIOGRAPHICAL NOTE	
COLOPHON	

*(The page numbers are those of the original printing.)

Preface

The Constitutions of the Freemasons by Dr. James Anderson, published in 1723, is the most famous Masonic book in the world. It has been translated into many foreign languages, has been the subject of considerable examination and comment over the years, and has been reproduced many times. With the passage of time it has become universally recognized as the basic law book of Freemasonry. It is significant that the first Masonic book to be published in the Western Hemisphere was the 1723 edition of Anderson's book, by Benjamin Franklin, in 1734. A facsimile of Franklin's book was the second volume to be published by The Masonic Book Club, in 1971 together with the differences listed between the original and Franklin's edition.

It is worthy of note that the 1723 and the 1738 editions of the Constitutions were issued by Anderson as a private venture, and were not the official publications of the Grand Lodge of England. On February 24, 1735 the Grand Lodge of England acknowledged that the book belonged to Anderson. It has been stated on several occasions that both editions were a private financial project of Anderson. But the Grand Lodge did lend some authority to the volumes, since the 1738 edition stated that on January 25, 1738, the Grand Master, the Deputy Grand Master, and the Wardens ordered Anderson, the author, to print and publish "our new Book of Constitutions, which they recommend as the only Book for the use of the Lodges."

Original copies of the 1723 edition of this book exist in far greater number than the 1738 edition. Furthermore, the 1723 edition has been reproduced many times; it became easily accessible to Masons in the United States when it was reproduced in facsimile form in the various editions of the Little Masonic Library. Volume 7 of the Quatuor Coronatorum Antigrapha contains a facsimile of the 1738 edition with an introduction by William J. Hughan. But this volume has been out-of-print for many years and is very rare in the United States. In 1977 Quatuor Coronati Lodge published a volume with facsimiles of both Constitutions; this was the first time that the 1723 and the 1738 editions have appeared in the same volume.

Aside from its scarcity there are other reasons why this volume was selected for distribution to our members. We do not have the Minutes of the Grand Lodge of England prior to June 24, 1723. The 1738 edition of Anderson's Constitutions has what purports to be a summary of what took place at the Grand Lodge meetings during these six years. Unfortunately, at that time Anderson was sick, was approaching the end of his days, (he died on May 29, 1739), and was overwhelmed with many personal problems, and as a result did not do a careful job in reporting the Grand Lodge meetings. We do not know whether he was present at these meetings or was relying on reports given to him by others. The Pocket Companion of 1754 points out some defects in the 1738 Constitutions and attributes this to the ill health of Anderson. Comparison with other available written records such as diaries, newspapers of the day, etc. do not support some of the statements made by Anderson. But to have the report is better than nothing of a contemporary nature. Also the 1738 edition elaborates and gives additional details on the history of the Craft as set forth in the 1723 edition, and this is of interest even though the history is almost completely fanciful and imaginative in nature. Another reason is that when Prichard's *Masonry Dissected* was published in 1730, (this book being the 1977 volume issued by The Masonic Book Club), an answer was published under the title *Defence of Masonry*. It was reproduced in the first volume of Quatuor Coronatorum Antigrapha, but this volume also is rare and not readily available. This famous item was reproduced at the end of the 1738 edition of the Anderson book, and, of course, is reproduced in the present volume.

This book has been reproduced from Volume 7 of Quatuor Coronatorum Antigrapha, published in 1890. Both Brother Jerry Marsengill, of Des Moines, Iowa, and Brother Harry Carr, of London, England were fortunate in having copies of this book, and both have graciously loaned their volumes to us for reproduction. On behalf of all the members of our Book Club we thank them for this generosity in sharing these valuable volumes with us.

In order to make the 1738 edition of Anderson's book meaningful, we have reproduced the fine commentary on this book prepared by Brother Lewis Edwards in which he calls attention to the specific differences between the first and second editions of the Constitutions as prepared by Anderson. This has been done with the special permission of Quatuor Coronati Lodge. On behalf of our members we thank the lodge for this permission, thus adding materially to the value of this volume to our members.

At the end of this volume there is a bibliographical note which will assist any member who wishes to make a further study of this subject.

ALPHONSE CERZA
LOUIS L. WILLIAMS

FACSIMILE REPRINT OF

Commentary

BY LEWIS EDWARDS

REPRODUCED FROM THE

Transactions of the Quatuor Coronati Lodge

VOLUME 41, 1928

ANDERSON'S BOOK OF CONSTITUTIONS OF 1738.

BY BRO. LEWIS EDWARDS.

N attempting any appreciation or criticism of a book written at a past date, however recent that date may be, it is necessary in order fairly to judge it, to consider it both in the light of the time and circumstances in which it was composed and also having fully in one's mind the characteristics of the author, his intellectual make-up, his social, religious and political *milieu*, desires, and aversions.

The age in which James Anderson wrote was one of political inquiry, of scientific inquisitiveness, of increasing social amenities. The first is connoted by the names of such political theorists as Hobbes (an early influence), Filmer, Locke, and Bolingbroke. The institution and influence of the Royal Society is the outward and visible sign of the scientific spirit, while the growing popularity of the coffee houses, of social gatherings, and the general spirit of clubability are evidence of the growth of the social spirit, of amenity, of urbanity. Moreover, the rise and prevalence of Deism and of ideas of toleration make the period one of considerable interest in the history of religious opinion. This side, however, may perhaps be more conveniently dealt with in discussing the somewhat tantalising phrasing of the First Charge and its variations in the 1723 and 1738 Editions.

Yet in spite of all this, however much the renascence of Freemasonry may have been influenced or even inspired by these currents of opinion, it cannot be said that either the form or content of the *Book of Constitutions* show many effects of the spirit of inquiry, of rationalism, or of modern historical method. Indeed, though the first two editions of the *Constitutions* stand at the parting of the ways between the old Freemasonry and the new, and despite the claims of their author, yet it seems that they look backward in form and in spirit to what is popularly considered mediævalism rather than forward to eighteenth century enlightenment and method.

For, consider their characteristics. The reverence for antiquity, for precedent, for the great names of sacred and profane history, the claim to universality, the marks of a *pièce à thèse*, the jumble of facts and dates, the lack of proportion. It cannot be too often emphasised that while the modern mind cherishes material antiquities and tends to scorn old institutions, valuing them merely for their suitability or adaptability to modern needs, the mediæval mind, while accounting material antiquities as mere stocks and stones fitted only for the rude foundations of its own structures, valued ancient institutions as sacred by reason of their very age, and would use age and consonance with precedent as the criterion of perfection, proclaiming for anything new its derivation from the old, and not its novelty, as its title to regard. The smallness of the mediæval world, the idea of a Catholic Church and a Catholic State, was still impressed on men's minds when the conditions and institutions from which they derived had long since passed away. The writing for a purpose, rather than the inquiry without prejudice into the subject matter of the work, *e.g.*, to demonstrate the greatness and the wide extent of architecture, is another characteristic of the mediæval as opposed to the modern mind. The jumble of facts and dates, the lack of proportion, or what seems so to us, is due, not so much to a lack of a sense of chronology and of geography as to the fact that being viewed under a different aspect and from a different angle, events, times, and processes seem to our ideas curiously foreshortened and otherwise distorted.

THE AUTHOR.

The chief facts in the life of Dr. James Anderson, thanks to the studies of Bros. Crawley, Thorp, Robbins, and Miller, are well-known to the members of this Lodge, and it is unnecessary here to do more than briefly recapitulate them. But there are a few which either from their direct connection with the *Book of Constitutions*, or from the light which they throw on our author's character and opinions, require somewhat detailed treatment.

[1] His father, James Anderson, glazier, was a substantial burgess of Aberdeen, for many years secretary, and for some fifty years a member, of the Lodge of Aberdeen. James the younger was baptised on January the 19th, 1679, and was educated at the Marischal College there, becoming Johnston Bursar of Divinity, and probably leaving on the completion of his studies in 1702. There is no evidence of his presence at Aberdeen after this date, nor of his being licensed by the local Presbytery, but it would seem that he preached for some time thereafter in Scotland without having any definite living, probably being licensed by some other Presbytery. Save for this his history between 1702 and 1709, when he appears in London, is unknown to us. To close this account of his connection with Aberdeen it may be said that he took the degree of Doctor of Divinity there in 1731.

A question which has not yet been settled is the date and place of his initiation. As has been said, his father was a prominent member of the local Lodge (his Mason's Mark has been preserved), and Anderson himself introduces into the *Book of Constitutions* one or two Scottish Masonic terms; although there is nothing in the Lodge records to show that he was a member, yet these records are incomplete for the years during which his initiation may have taken place. And further we may compare two passages, one from the *Book of Constitutions* of 1738 (page 91):—

> "The Fraternity of old met in Monasteries in foul Weather; but in fair Weather they met early in the Morning on the Tops of Hills, especially on St. John Evangelist's Day, and from thence walk'd in due Form to the place of Dinner, according to the Tradition of the old Scots Masons, particularly of those of the Antient Lodges of Kilwinning, Stirling, Aberdeen, etc.";

and the other from the Aberdeen Lodge Rules of 1670 (*A.Q.C.*, xxxvi., 102 to 103):—

> "no Lodge be holden within a dwelling where there is people living in it, but in the open field, except it be ill weather."

> "all entering Prentices be entered in our ancient outfield Lodge."

The Rules of 1670 enacted that every apprentice and fellow craft, on admission, should provide a dinner, and that, on St. John's Day, twelve shillings should be collected from each member, the money to be spent as the Lodge should think fit for the honour of the Day, which was to be kept as one "of rejoicing and feasting."

On the other hand, had Anderson been 'made' in Scotland, one would have expected him to have interested himself in English Freemasonry earlier than in fact he appears to have done, and it must be admitted that the circumstances just related are quite consistent with his not having been initiated until after he had taken up residence in England. Still, whatever other inference can be drawn, it is quite clear that he grew up with Freemasonry all about him and that whether from within or from without many of the practices and terms of the Freemasons were known to him.

[1] *A.Q.C.*, xxxvi., p. 86.

[1] Coming to London, as has been said, in 1709 Anderson became the ritualistically inclined minister of a Scotch congregation meeting in Swallow Street, St. James's (opposite the Wren Church in which some 100 years later Gilkes was to be buried) and continued his ministerial duty apparently until his death in 1739, although after a secession or schism he and a part of his congregation removed to another meeting-house in Lisle Street, Leicester Square. He published a few sermons and theological treatises, a voluminous compilation on "Royal Genealogies" (in effect a translation with additions of a German work by Hübner) and two editions of the *Book of Constitutions*, while his "News from Elysium" was published posthumously. He held for a time the position of Chaplain to the Earl of Buchan, a member of a family closely associated with the early days of the Craft.

To his writings cannot be attributed any considerable literary qualities, and his readers generally are agreed that dullness and prolixity are their most characteristic features. In political opinions a staunch Hanoverian, and indeed one who received favours from the reigning House, in religion "a Defender of the Faith," and a foe to "Idolaters, modern Jews and Anti-Trinitarians"—to quote the smiting epithets of his pamphlet on "Unity in Trinity." One whose Masonic origins are—subject to what has been said above—obscure, whose interest in the Craft was seemingly intermittent and not free from motives of profit and glory. One who was careless and inaccurate in his facts and unattractive in his style and who sought that patronage of the great which is so useful an aid to the ambitious journeyman of letters.

This enumeration is not given as what modern jargon calls a mere pen-portrait, but is necessary to a full appreciation of the *Book of Constitutions*, and in particular in any attempt to answer or even to pose certain interesting questions arising thereout. Is there a political bias or basis? Is there a religious? How deep was Anderson's knowledge of the Craft, how large his experience, how sound the basis of his opinion? How far is his treatment affected and either improved or vitiated by qualities or defects of matter or manner?

On the eve of the Jacobite Rebellion of 1715, Anderson delivered and published the sermon entitled "No King-Killers," in Dr. Crawley's words, [2] "A vigorous repudiation of the charge that the Scottish nation had permitted its commercial instincts to get the better of its loyal sentiments, in selling its King to the Parliament," the Dedication of which is addressed to the Reverend Daniel Williams, D.D., as "a professed and firm friend to Monarchy and Presbytery, and [as one who] ever asserted them to be highly consistent." The *Royal Genealogies* and the second edition of the *Constitutions* are dedicated to the Hanoverian Prince of Wales. [3] In October, 1735, he was granted by the Queen-Consort-and-Regent the sum of £200. Anderson was a loyal and firm adherent and admirer of the Duke of Montagu, a staunch supporter of the ruling house. Clearly then his own sympathies were definitely Hanoverian. On the other hand, there is clear evidence, even to the distortion and misrepresentation of facts, of what in 1738 had become our author's dislike of the Duke of Wharton, the notorious Jacobite. The subject cannot be fully discussed in this paper, nor the evidence considered of the Jacobite Lodge in Rome, or of the suggested political imagery of the legend of the Third Degree. But taking what little has been here said and the description of the Masonic gathering at Stationers' Hall given by the author of the *Praise of Drunkenness*, where "no mention [was] made of Politics or Religion . . . And when the Music began to play, 'Let the King enjoy his own again,' they were immediately reprimanded by a Person of great Gravity and Science," would it be wrong to assume that at about the time Anderson published his first edition there were in the Craft

---
[1] A.Q.C., xxiii., p. 6.
[2] A.Q.C., xviii., p. 30.
[3] A.Q.C., xxiii., p. 17.

conflicting political currents, and that the recollection of these was yet in his mind at the time he published the second? Point is added to this assumption by the fact to be noted later, that to the second Charge of the 1738 edition (page 144) while inculcating respect and loyalty toward the civil magistrate, he yet adds that "tho' a *Brother* is not to be countenanced in his *Rebellion* against the State; yet if convicted of no other Crime, his Relation to the *Lodge* remains indefeasible." Is this an attempt at a *modus vivendi* between the two parties?

The question of the religious basis of Freemasonry after the Revival is one peculiarly difficult to decide. Begemann would see as its basis, Christianity in the form of the national Church of England. The other school is not unfairly represented by a recent French clerical writer, the late Mgr. E. Jouin,[1] who states that "the dogma is simple: it is that of a universal religion. In its own phrase, it is called Deism. The person who applies the term is certainly not yet an atheist but is travelling on the path of atheism."

In his first edition (p. 50), Anderson says: "A *Mason* is obliged by his Tenure, to obey the moral Law: and if he rightly understands the Art he will never be a stupid Atheist, nor an irreligious Libertine [*i.e.*, Freethinker]. But though in ancient Times Masons were charg'd in every Country to be of the Religion of that Country or Nation, whatever it was, yet 'tis now thought more expedient only to oblige them to that Religion in which all Men agree, leaving their particular opinions to themselves; that is, to be good Men and true, or Men of Honour and Honesty, by whatever Denominations or Persuasions they may be distinguish'd; whereby Masonry becomes the Center of Union, and the Means of conciliating true Friendship among Persons that must have remain'd at a perpetual distance."

In the second edition (p. 143), he puts the matter thus: "A Mason is obliged by his Tenure to observe the Moral Law, as a true *Noachida*; and if he rightly understands the Craft, he will never be a Stupid Atheist, nor an Irreligious Libertin, nor act against Conscience."

"In ancient Times the *Christian Masons* were charged to comply with the *Christian* Usages of each Country where they travell'd or work'd: But *Masonry* being found in all Nations, even of divers Religions, they are now only charged to adhere to that Religion in which Men agree, (leaving each Brother to his own particular opinions), that is, to be Good Men and True, Men of Honour and Honesty, by whatever Names, Religions, or Persuasions they may be distinguish'd; For they all agree in the three great *Articles* of Noah, enough to preserve the Cement of the Lodge. Thus *Masonry* is the Center of their Union and the happy Means of conciliating Persons that otherwise must have remain'd at a perpetual Distance."

Obviously the *prima facie* import of the passages cited is to show a society free from dogma, in which are inculcated only general Theistic and moral doctrines. But what evidence is there either to strengthen or to rebut this *prima facie* view?

It is noticeable, it is perhaps significant, that while many of the Old Charges open with a Trinitarian invocation, as does even the *Roberts* printed version of 1722, there is no such passage in either of Anderson's editions. In 1732 a Jew was initiated, and in the list of early Grand Stewards there occur many Jewish names. [2] The members of the Order are attacked in the First "Letter to a Friend concerning the Society of Freemasons" of 1725 in regard to those "who write themselves S.T.P., which some are apt to imagine, stands for Sacrosanctæ Trinitatis Persecutores," and there are the "dust and scandal," unknown but imaginable, referred to in the Preface to the *Roberts* Constitutions. [3] Stukeley in his Diary refers to Martin Folkes as "in matters of religion an

[1] *Livre des Constitutions Maçonniques* (Paris, 1930), p. 69.
[2] Gould, iii., p. 480.
[3] Diary, i., p. 100.

errant infidel and loud scoffer . . . [who] believes nothing of a future state, of the Scriptures, of revelation . . . perverted Duke of Montagu, Richmond, Ld. Pembroke, and very many of the nobility, who had an opinion of his understanding, and who made 'the infidel System' fashionable in the Royal Society." Stukeley's language is so strong as to make us rather doubtful of the truth of his allegation, but it is rather a matter of wonder that within forty years of Bothwell Bridge and "The Killing Time," a society could constitute itself under so non-sectarian and so tolerant a banner as that of the Freemasonry of the Revival.

On the other hand, there seems to be nothing of the sceptic about Anderson himself. We have his Christian references, and even his mention of Jesus as "the Great Architect or Grand Master of the Christian Church." His pamphlet against "Idolaters, modern Jews, and Anti-Trinitarians" has been adduced to show that he would give no countenance to any non-Christian society, particularly one with Jewish members, but is it not plain that the reference is merely a controversial one, more or less synonymous with Anti-Trinitarians, and that there is no necessary inconsistency between such a reference in a theological controversy and meeting Jews in such a society as those who take the non-sectarian view hold Freemasonry to have been? Begemann [1] quotes the decidedly fervent Christianity of the Preface to *Long Livers* in support of the sectarian view, but the enthusiasm and expectancy of its author are much more apparent than any detailed knowledge of the Order.

Such, then, is a *résumé* of the chief evidence on each side, and it is open to anyone to decide this most interesting and most important question for himself. One may say of this as of other conflicts of evidence that we may have occasion to refer to hereafter, that in these trials by written evidence we are under the very great disadvantage of not being able to see the witnesses and note their demeanour, advantages which tell so strongly in a *viva voce* trial since it is often the *imponderabilia* which finally help in a decision. Here the *imponderabilia* are the peculiarities and unconscious predilections of those who judge, which is not nearly so satisfactory. Omitting these, and feeling that whichever side one takes one has some worthy names to support one, it is thought not unfair to put the position thus. As compared with the words of many of the Old Charges, Anderson's First Charge—in both versions—marks a great change of phraseology in a most important particular. It is more reasonable to suppose it deliberate than accidental, and were it accidental and opposed to contemporary feeling in the Craft, however slight may have been the control to which Anderson was subjected, we could scarcely expect it to have passed unchallenged and unamended by Grand Lodge and its advisers.

Perhaps it is possible to suggest a view intermediate between these two extremes. I have particularly in mind what Anderson says on page 23 in speaking of the Zoroastrians: "They are here mention'd, and not for their Religious Rites that are not the subject of this Book: For we leave every Brother to Liberty of Conscience. But strictly charge him carefully to maintain the *Cement of the Lodge*, and the three Articles of Noah." Might it not be that the First Charge attempts only to define not the whole body of religious belief of the members, but that part of the religion of each which is common to all, the highest common factor. Freemasonry admits those of many religions if its adherents admit the necessary minima of the common belief. Their additional articles of faith are irrelevant and indeed should not be discussed, lest an attempt to travel outside should create dissension.

What were Anderson's qualifications as the first Masonic historian? How long was his Masonic experience? How large his acquaintance with Grand Lodge and its proceedings? Much of the answer to this is doubtful. We do not know

[1] Begemann, *Vorgeschichte*, ii., 93.

where or when he was initiated. True he uses Scottish Masonic terms, like Entered Prentice, but he may just as well have learnt them outside the Lodge of Aberdeen as within. Begemann thinks that he did not associate himself with the English Order until it was becoming popular with noblemen and persons of consideration, and it is very probable that had Anderson been a member in the early days of the revival he would have been offered and (can we doubt?) have accepted office in Grand Lodge earlier than his own statements show him to have done. In the matter of his attendance at Grand Lodge, a fair index of his enthusiasm, we are on much surer ground. We have his version of his attendances and that in the Minutes.

As the latter begin only on the 24th of June, 1723, our sole guide—if guide it is—is [1] Anderson's own account of his earlier connection with Grand Lodge, and according to this in September, 1721, he was ordered to digest the Old Constitutions; in December, 1721, a Committee was appointed to examine the work; in March, 1722, they reported that they had perused his manuscripts, and in January, 1722/3 he produced the *Book of Constitutions* and it was again approved. A full discussion of the credibility of these assertions will be found in Bro. Vibert's paper, and I need only say here that Anderson has attempted to make out that what was in reality a private undertaking was the carrying out of the spontaneous orders of Grand Lodge.

[2] Anderson states that on the 17th of January, 1722/3, the Duke of Wharton appointed him as (Junior) Grand Warden, apparently according to him in place of William Hawkins, "for Hawkins demitted as always out of town," at the same time as Desaguliers was made Deputy Grand Master. But the Approbation of the 1723 edition drawn up about the beginning of December, 1722, gives Desaguliers as Deputy and Hawkins as Junior Grand Warden. [3] Further, the earliest extant Minute, that of the 24th of June, 1723, has by Bro. Songhurst been found to have been tampered with. It originally read (as Junior Grand Warden): "The Reverend Mr. James Anderson who officiated for Mr. William Hawkins," but the last six words have been erased, leaving Anderson as Warden *simpliciter*. [4] Moreover, in the list of Grand Wardens for 1722, after the name of Hawkins is added in what is clearly Anderson's handwriting the words "who demitted and then James Anderson A. M. was chosen in his place." Therefore, if one leaves out what Anderson has written and restores what has been erased (and who other than Anderson could have had a motive for erasing it and an opportunity withal to erase as well as to add?), we find that from the Minutes Anderson's only claim to the rank of Junior Grand Warden is his acting as substitute for Hawkins. Further, in the 1756 edition of the *Constitutions*, although Hawkins is given as Grand Warden under date the 24th of June, 1722, his name is omitted altogether on the 17th January, 1722/3, his demission not mentioned, and "James Anderson A.M." is given as (Junior) Grand Warden. By the time the *Freemasons' Calendar* is published in 1775, no mention at all is made of the unfortunate Hawkins in the list of Past Grand Wardens. However, whether or not we can consider Anderson's claim to the Warden's chair as established, there can be no doubt that the subsequent Minutes recognise it, since after Grand Lodge had on the 10th of May, 1727, resolved that Past Grand Wardens should be admitted at all Quarterly Communications, he not only attended, but is noted as a former or late Grand Warden and on several occasions officiated in that capacity. He does not appear to have availed himself of the privilege extended to him in May, 1727, for some three years, although in fairness it must be admitted that the other Past Grand Wardens as a rule do not appear to have been assiduous or

---

[1] 2nd Edition, pp. 113-115.
[2] p. 114.
[3] *Q.C.A.*, x., p. 49 and plate on p. 48.
[4] *Q.C.A.*, x., p. 196 and plate.

even frequent in their attendances after the expiration of their periods of office. Anderson attended Grand Lodge once in 1730, twice in 1731 (once speaking on a Charity Petition), twice in 1732, and once in 1733. Now if we bear in mind the fact that in 1732 appeared the *Royal Genealogies* with a distinguished array of Freemasons as subscribers or encouragers, we can not unfairly guess the reason of his renewed interest in the Craft. On the 24th of February, 1735, Anderson presented a memorial regarding a new edition of the *Book of Constitutions* and his objection to what must have been Smith's *Pocket Companion*, and after that we find him attending on two other occasions in that year, twice in 1736, once in 1737, and twice in 1738, the year before his death.

It is therefore quite clear that except when concerned to get authority for his literary work or to obtain patronage for his publications, Anderson, if the attendances at Quarterly Communications be a criterion, was no more disinterestedly concerned in the affairs of the Craft than other past Wardens, and Begemann's view that his interest in Freemasonry was that of the discoverer of a remunerative field for literary employment can hardly be said to be unfair.

The Second Edition of the *Book of Constitutions* (1738) consists of :—

I. Frontispiece and title-page.

II. Anderson's Dedication to the Prince of Wales (iii.-vi.).

III. "The Author to the Reader," containing a short introduction and explanation, and a table of contents (vii.-x.).

IV. The Sanction, with on the reverse the arms of Lord Carnarvon.

V. The Constitutions (1-139).
   This is divided into three parts, each part being again divided into chapters.
   Part I. The History of Masonry from the Creation throughout the Known Earth; till true old architecture was demolished by the Goths and at last revived in Italy (1-55).
   Part II. The History of Masonry in Britain, from Julius Cæsar, till The Union of the Crowns, 1603 (55-96).
   Part III. The History of Masonry in Britain, from the Union of the Crowns to these Times (97-139).

VI. List of Grand Masters or Patrons of the Free Masons in England, from the Coming in of the Anglo-Saxons to these Times, who are mentioned in this Book (140-142).

VII. The Old Charges (143-149).

VIII. The Antient Manner of Constituting a Lodge (149-151).

IX. The General Regulations (152-178).
   [The "Old" and the "New" Regulations are set out in an attempt at parallel columns.]

X. The Constitution of the Committee of Masons Charity first proposed at the Grand Lodge on 21 Nov. 1724 (178-184).

XI. A list of the Lodges in and about London and Westminster (184-190).

XII. Deputations of several Grand Masters to Wales, the Country of England and foreign Parts (followed by an historical and rhapsodical appreciation) (190-198).

364   *Transactions of the Quatuor Coronati Lodge.*

XIII. The Approbation (199).

XIV. Some of the usual Free-Masons Songs (200-215).

XV. A Defence of Masonry, published A.D. 1730. Occasioned by a Pamphlet called Masonry Dissected (216-226).

XVI. Brother Euclid's Letter to the Author against unjust Cavils (226-228).

XVII. Names of Brethren and Lodges who "kindly encouraged" the Author (229-230).

XVIII. A page (un-numbered) of Corrigenda, with on the reverse the publisher's announcements.

I. FRONTISPIECE AND TITLE-PAGE.

Unlike the first edition, that of 1738 has no half-title. The frontispiece is the same in both editions, save that in the later the Engraver's name and address do not appear. The title-page of the 1738 edition is printed partly in red, and Anderson's name appears thereon for the first time. "James Anderson, D.D." The title itself is much longer, and may be compared with that of 1723 :—" The | Constitutions | of the | Free-Masons | containing the | History, Charges, Regulations etc. | of that most Ancient and Right | Worshipful Fraternity. | For the use of the Lodges. | " (1723). " The | New Book | of Constitutions | of the | Antient and Honourable Fraternity | of | Free and Accepted Masons | containing | Their History, Charges, Regulations, &c. | Collected and Digested | By Order of the Grand Lodge from their old Records, | faithful Traditions and Lodge-Books. | For the Use of the Lodges. | " (1738). We may note the appearance of the description of the Craft which has now become time-honoured, the claim " By order of the Grand Lodge," and the variations of spelling, "ancient" and "antient" in the two editions. The new imprint is that of "Brothers Cæsar Ward and Richard Chandler," of the "Ship, without Temple Bar," Coney Street York and "Scarbrough-Spaw."

It is to be noted that the account of the proceedings of Grand Lodge closes with the Meeting of the 28th of June, 1738; that he mentions the Lodge at Halifax meeting at the Black Bull being constituted on the 1st of August; that he dates his Preface the 4th of November, and that Brother Euclid's letter is dated the 9th of November. From this it is clear that the various parts of the *Book of Constitutions* were completed by Anderson at different dates, but it would appear nevertheless that these were printed consecutively in view of the fact that from the evidence of the catch-words the book was printed as a whole. The probable date of publication we should suggest in common with other authorities to be somewhere in or about February, 1738/9.

With regard to the publishers, Mr. Richard Chandler was a member of the Lodge meeting at the Sun in Fleet Street in 1731.

II. THE DEDICATION.

The Dedication is addressed to Frederick Lewis, Prince of Wales, "a Master Mason, and Master of a Lodge," by Anderson himself, and not as before by a third person, *i.e.*, Desaguliers, and the author states that he does so by order of the Grand Master and the Fraternity and in their name, although there is no record of the facts in the Minutes of Grand Lodge. It is interesting to note Anderson's reference to the Royal Art, and his allusion in the spirit of the Old Charges, to respect for the civil magistrate and to liberty of conscience.

Anderson records under date the 5th November, 1737, that an "Occasional Lodge" was held at the Prince of Wales's Palace at Kew, at which, there being present Desaguliers "(formerly Grand Master) Master of this Lodge," William

Gofton and Erasmus King, Senior and Junior Grand Wardens (neither of these brethren being Wardens of Grand Lodge and not even finding a mention in the Q.C. edition of the earlier Minutes), and others, the Prince of Wales " was in the usual Manner introduced, and made an Enter'd Prentice and Fellow Craft, and that he was made a Master Mason by the same Lodge, that assembled there again for that Purpose." There is no reference to Frederick's initiation in the Minutes, but that is accounted for by the fact that what was held appears to have been a meeting of a private Lodge, probably summoned especially for the purpose, and on the lines of the pre-1717 meetings, e.g., that at which Ashmole was initiated. The influence of Desaguliers, who was Chaplain to the Prince, was, we may suppose, not without effect in beginning the connection between the house of Hanover and the Craft.

IV. THE SANCTION.

Bro. Vibert takes the view that the Approbation of the 1723 edition was written by Anderson himself, and the same would seem to be the case with regard to the Sanction of the 1738 edition.

There we find his expression in " ample form " which is not given in the Minutes. He states that on 25th November, 1723, Grand Lodge resolved " That no alterations shall be made in their printed Book of Constitutions without leave of the Grand Lodge." It did no such thing, and certainly on no such date. [1] The official record informs us that on the 24th June, 1723, the Sanction of the first edition (at the end of page 91) having been read, it was moved (on the main question) " That the said General Regulations be confirmed so far as they are consistent with the Ancient Rules of Masonry," but that then the question was moved and put, whether the words " so far as they are consistent with the Ancient Rules of Masonry," be part of the question, and this latter resolution was carried. But the main question was not put, and the question was moved " That it is not in the power of any person or body of men to make any alteration or innovation on the body of Masonry without the consent first obtained of the Annual Grand Lodge," which last question was resolved in the affirmative. That is the nearest we can get in words to Anderson's statement. We find that the words are incorrectly given, the version garbled, and the date erroneous, and the whole spirit of the resolution transformed. The condemnation of Smith's *Pocket Companion* in 1735 is fairly represented in the second paragraph of the Sanction, but in the third Anderson goes on to say that Grand Lodge " order'd " him to print the book, whereas what took place was that on his desiring the Grand Master's Commands and the approbation of Grand Lodge, this request was granted him.

The Sanction concludes with a recommendation of the book as the only *Book of Constitutions,* and a rather exhaustive warning against any other books, the compilations of Smith or of any imitators he might have, being no doubt implied.

It is instructive to compare this Sanction with that of the Grand Officers given to Preston's *Illustrations,* where it is much more accurately stated that Preston having compiled his book " has requested our Sanction for the publication thereof " and that having perused the said book, and finding it to correspond with the ancient practices of this Society, the undersigned Grand Officers " do recommend the same."

V. THE CONSTITUTIONS.

A criticism of the Constitutions will be attempted later when the whole book has been considered, but, before we consider them in any detail, it will be both fairer and more convenient if we endeavour to adjust ourselves to that angle

[1] *Q.C.A.*, x., pp. 50-1.

of vision, however false, it may seem to modern ideas, from which Anderson saw the things of which he wrote.

He states (p. vii.) that the MS. Constitutions contained not only the "Charges and Regulations, but also the History of Architecture from the Beginning of Time; in order to show the Antiquity and Excellency of the Craft or Art, and how it gradually arose upon its solid Foundation the noble Science of Geometry, by the Encouragement of Royal, Noble and Learned Patrons in every Age and in all polite Nations." He, to continue his explanation, was ordered to digest the old Constitutions "with a just Chronology" in the 1723 edition, and had now published his new edition "about twice as large, having many proper Additions," including the transactions of Grand Lodge since that date. "It had been tedious, and of no great use" to have given his authorities, particularly as most of the facts were to be found in other histories—"only some Authors are quoted as more necessary Vouchers." "But the Omission is well enough supply'd by an exact chronology . . . Some few Genealogies are put in the Margin . . . But the History here chiefly concerns Masonry, without meddling with other Transactions, more than what only serves to connect the History of Masonry, the strict subject of this Book." Such is Anderson's intention. Masonry for him connotes architecture, and his aim is to trace its rise and progress, and to detail its glories and its distinguished patrons and practitioners in every age and in every clime. He has his dislikes and preferences. His ideal architecture is Augustan; the purer and now greatly preferred Greek he has no such esteem for. It is noteworthy that that epoch of all others in English history to which the term Augustan is generally applied should have seen the revival of Freemasonry and in its first historian so great a lover of the Augustan style. As has been pointed out before, Anderson failed to observe that the Gothic period when individual craftsmanship counted for so much, and when classes and crafts were such individualized entities, is that in which the spirit of Masonry probably had its greatest success as an *esprit de corps* among the Operatives.

In order to give an idea of how little originality there was in Anderson's ideas and how these were in strict conformity with contemporary thought it is useful to quote the following passages from a book of reference which had a wide circulation at the time — the *Dictionarium Britannicum or . . . English Dictionary* by N. Bailey (Second Edition 1736). (It is noted on the title-page that the Etymological part is by T. Lediard, whom we know as the translator of *Sethos*):—

Geometry

Geometry originally signified the art of measuring the Earth, or any distances or dimensions on or within it: but it is now used for the science of quantity, extension or magnitude abstractedly considered, without any regard to matter.

It is very probable, that it had its first rise in Egypt where the river Nile, every year overflowing the country, and leaving it covered with mud, laid men under a necessity to distinguish their land one from another by the consideration of this figure; and to be able to measure the quantity of it, so that each man after the fall of the waters might have his portion of ground allotted and laid out to him. After which, it is very likely, a further contemplation of these draughts and figures helped them to discover many excellent and wonderful properties belonging to them, which speculation continually was improving and still is to this day.

Out of Egypt Thales brought it into Greece, and there it received its chiefest proportion. For the geometry of the antients was contained within narrow bounds, and extended only to right lines and curves of the first kind or order: whereas new lines of infinite orders are receiv'd into geometry which orders are defined by equations, involving the ordinates and abscisses of curves.

The subject of Geometry is the length, breadth and height of all things. It is divided into Speculative and Practical. The former treats of the proportion of Lines and Figures, such as Euclid's Elements, Appollonius's Conicks, etc., and the latter shows how to apply those Speculations to use in life.

. . . . . .

Geometry is painted as a lady with a sallow face, clad in a green mantle fringed with silver, and holding a silver wand in her right hand.

Gothick Building.
A manner of building brought into use after those barbarous people, the Goths and Vandals, made their irruptions into Italy; who demolished the greatest part of the ancient Roman architecture, as also the Moors and Arabs did the Greeks; and instead of those admirable and regular orders and modes of building, introduc'd a licentious and fantastical mode, wild and chimerical, whose profiles are incorrect, which altho' it was sometimes adorn'd with expensive and costly carvings, but lamentable imagery, has not that augustness, beauty and just symmetry, which the ancient Greek and Roman fabricks had: However, it is oftentimes found very strong and appears rich and pompous, as particularly in several English cathedrals.

Free Masons { a very antient Society or body of men, so-called, *Accepted* Masons { either for some extraordinary Knowledge of masonry which they are supposed to be masters of; or because the first founders of that Society were persons of that profession. There are now in all or most nations of Europe; what the end of this society is, yet remains in some measure a secret, unless that they tend to promote friendship, society, mutual assistance and good fellowship.

And Bailey was not alone in his contempt for Gothic, as witness the following quotation from that arbiter of taste, the *Spectator*:—

Let anyone reflect on the disposition of mind he finds in himself at his first entrance into the Pantheon at Rome, and how the imagination is filled with something great and amazing; and at the same time consider how little, in proportion, he is affected with the inside of a Gothic cathedral, though it be five times larger than the other; which can arise from nothing else but the greatness of the manner in the one and the meanness in the other.

Spectator, vi., No. 415.

The Old Constitutions had been lax in their chronology, and many versions are not uninfluenced by the historical or literary predilections of the individual scribe, and in their faults Anderson excelled them. Flushed with the success of the first edition and his enlargement on his anonymous predecessors, and conscious of his authorship of the *Royal Genealogies*, Anderson gave free rein to his own fancy and his newly-acquired Chronology. Interpreting the directions of Grand Lodge as he did, as including the patrons of the art, he found himself free to fling his net over every age and over the great names of the civilised world, for all could be brought in, either as Grand Masters, or officers, or as patrons.

And indeed, a whole chapter might be written on Anderson's use of the term "Grand Master" (or "Deputy" or "Wardens") and another on his use of the word "Lodge." There are in the 1738 edition considerably over one hundred instances of the employment of one or other of these words in reference to conditions before 1717, when according to modern usage and with anything like a close regard for exact nomenclature such a use would be at once ludicrous and unpardonable. To take only a few instances, we have:—

The Israelites . . . having many expert artists in every Tribe that met in Lodges and Societies (p. 9).

Hiram Abbif . . . who in Solomon's absence fill'd the Chair as Deputy Grand Master and in his presence was the Senior Grand Warden, or principal Surveyor and Master of Work (p. 12).

The High Priests of Jerusalem had been Provincial Grand Masters there, under the Kings of Egypt (p. 38).

Herod . . . marshalled them in Lodges under 1000 Priests and Levites that were skilful Architects, as Masters and Wardens of the Lodges, and acted as Grand Master himself with his Wardens Hillel and Shammai . . . (p. 40).

Laurentius I. . . . of Florence stiled the Magnificent Grand Master of the Revivers (p. 50).

(cf. *Laurentius* II. . . . Patron of the Revivers) (p. 50).

James Sansovino constituted a Lodge of Architects (or Masters) at Venice . . . and fortify'd the whole Republic as Grand Master of Masons (p. 54).

We may conclude our list with Anderson's statement, on p. 81, of a rule, found nowhere else, "Here it is proper to signify the Sentiment and Practice of the old Masons, viz.: That Kings and other Male Soveraigns, when made Masons, are Grand Masters by Prerogative during Life, and appoint a Deputy, or approve of his Election, to preside over the Fraternity with the Title and Honours of Grand Master; but if the Soveraign is a Female, or not a Brother, or a Minor under a Regent, not a Brother; or if the Male Soveraign or the Regent, tho' a Brother, is negligent of the Craft, then the old Grand Officers may assemble the Grand Lodge in due Form to elect a Grand Master, tho' not during Life, only he may be annually rechosen while he and they think fit." If we were here criticising we should have to ask not only what is Anderson's authority for the rule, but also whether the latter portion is not inconsistent with paragraph xix. of both the Old and the New Regulations.

We may discern in Anderson's use of the term at least three meanings of the word "Grand Master," *i.e.*, chief architect, patron of architecture, and prince or ruler. More space may have been given to this point than it seems worthy of, but if it be remembered how often the list of Grand Masters beginning with St. Alban has been found in works on English Freemasonry, and that it is on Anderson's assertions that the list is founded, perhaps justification may be pleaded.

There is a constant tendency, both in the Old Charges and in Anderson, to represent events in contemporary dress or in that of the mediæval operatives. For example, some of the great historical figures are said to have given charges or founded lodges, and if an analogy is sought for this, it may be seen in what was for centuries the universal habit of artists of dressing Biblical or historical characters in the habiliments of the painter's epoch. And the analogy supplies also a warning. One must no more think that because an historical personage is represented as giving charges or founding a lodge that he in fact did so in the form that we would think of or even that Anderson would think of as an historical fact, than we should be justified in thinking of the Madonna as having the features and wearing the dress of a Flemish *bourgeoise* or of an Italian *contadina*.

If my general observations on the Constitutions may seem rather finedrawn or what is popularly called special pleading, it is because I have in them attempted, as has been said, to see things from Anderson's point of view. If sense and eye have been strained, it has been but to obtain an unusual angle of vision.

V. PART I. THE HISTORY OF MASONRY FROM THE CREATION THROUGHOUT THE KNOWN EARTH: TILL TRUE OLD ARCHITECTURE WAS DEMOLISH'D BY THE GOTHS AND AT LAST REVIVED IN ITALY.

In view of Bro. Vibert's detailed treatment of the sources of the historical portion of the first edition, it is unnecessary here to do more than to compare and contrast this with the second.

It is a small point, but one significant of the carelessness of Anderson, that even the heading of Part I. as given on page vii. differs slightly from that on page 1, e.g., " good old Architecture," as compared with " true old Architecture." In the second edition Anderson seems to have followed the Scriptures more closely and indeed makes his early account more or less a masonic, that is, an architectural commentary on the earlier portion of the Book of Genesis. The tentative tone of 1723, " Adam must have had the Liberal Sciences, particularly Geometry, written on his Heart . . . No doubt Adam taught his Sons Geometry," becomes in 1738 quite positive, "till his Sons grew up to form a Lodge, when he [i.e., Adam] taught Geometry and the Great Use of it in Architecture." Whereas Anderson had formerly, after mentioning the crafts of Tubal Cain, Jubal and Jabal, added " which last [i.e., Tent Making] is good Architecture," this phrase is now omitted, and we may wonder whether this omission is in deference to the strictures of the " Briscoe " Secret History (p. 30) or is just another meaningless variation. In a footnote to page 3 of the earlier edition Anderson had mentioned Enoch's erecting the large pillars (" tho' some ascribe them to Seth "); but he now adds a new footnote to the effect that " some call them Seth's Pillars, but the old Masons always called them Enoch's pillars, and firmly believed this tradition." Yet, as Begemann points out, in the old versions the children of Lamech are given as the builders according to Masonic tradition. Anderson's apparently meaningless alteration and the vague but misleading statement by which he supports it are but one of many instances to be found throughout the work. Further, in this same footnote our author gives Josephus as the authority for a statement that the Stone Pillar still remained in *Syria* in the latter's time. What Josephus wrote was *Syna* (i.e., Upper Egypt), but the letters as printed in italics in the 1675 edition of the Jewish historian might easily have been misread as Syria.

We are then told that "after the Flood, Noah and his 3 Sons, having preserved the knowledge of the Arts and Sciences, communicated it to their growing off-spring . . . they found a Plain in the Land of Shinar, and dwelt there together as Noachidæ, or Sons of Noah," and Anderson adds as a note to Noachidæ that it is " the first name of Masons, according to some old traditions." The story in the Old Charges of the recovery of the two pillars with the inscriptions thereon is thus dropped, and Anderson gives his own version of the oral transmission of the knowledge of the Craft.

We have also here the first printed use of the term Noachida afterwards so extensively used in Continental Freemasonry, which is also found in Krause's so-called York Constitutions. At a Grand Lodge held on 13th December, 1733,[1] at which Anderson does not appear to have been present, Captain Ralph Winter, Provincial Grand Master of East India, was announced to have sent a chest of arrack for its use and 10 Guineas from the members of his province as a contribution to the Charity, and at the meeting of the 31st March, 1735,[2] which our author attended, the Minutes state that Lord Crauford, G.M., ordered the arrack to be made into punch and distributed among the brethren.

Bro. Chetwode Crawley[3] has discovered in the Rawlinson Collection at the Bodleian a letter of thanks from Lord Weymouth, Crauford's successor

[1] Q.C.A., x., p. 237.
[2] Q.C.A., x., p. 252.
[3] A.Q.C., xi., pp. 35-6.

as Grand Master, addressed to the giver of the present, in which the fourth paragraph runs as follows:—" Providence has fixed your Lodge near these learned Indians that affect to be called Noachidæ, the strict observance of his Precepts taught in these parts by the Disciples of the great Zoroastres, the learned Archimagus of Bactria, a Grand Master of the Magians, whose Religion is much preserved in India (which we have no concern about) and also many of the Rituals of the Ancient Fraternity used in his time, perhaps more than they are sensible of themselves. Now if it was consistent with your other Business, to discover in those facts the Remains of Old Masonry and transmit them to us, we would all be thankful . . ." Now on p. 23 our author has a long paragraph dealing with Zoroaster:—

> "In his Reign Zoroastres flourished, the *Archimagus* or *Grand Master* of the *Magians* (who worshipped the *Sun* and the *Fire* made by his Rays) who became famous everywhere, call'd by the *Greeks the teacher of all human and divine Knowledge*: and his Disciples were great Improvers of *Geometry* in the liberal Arts, erecting many *Palaces* and *Fire Temples* throughout the Empire, and long flourish'd in Eastern *Asia*, even till the *Mahometans* prevail'd. Yet a Remnant of 'em are scattered in those Parts to this Day, who retain many of the old Usages of the *Free Masons*, for which They are here mentioned, and not for their Religious Rites that are not the Subject of this Book: For we leave Every Brother to Liberty of Conscience; but strictly charge him carefully to maintain the *Cement of the Lodge*, and the three Articles of Noah."

The striking similarities, not only of diction but of thought, between the Grand Master's letter and Anderson's text strongly suggest that the same individual wrote both. It is the case that the original letter is not in Anderson's handwriting. At the very least, Anderson must have seen the letter, in the Grand Secretary's office presumably, and used its ideas and phraseology, including this word Noachidæ, which he also uses in the First Charge. In that case the letter not only takes the use of the word back to some undiscovered originator, but it shows that others at this time shared with Anderson his historical haziness, his desire to prove Masonry universal, and his laxity of nomenclature in the use of the title Grand Master. But the simpler explanation, to my mind, is that the Grand Master's letter to Captain Ralph Winter was drafted for him by Anderson himself.

On page 8 there is a misprint which is corrected in the Corrigenda. The reference for the appointment of Aholiab and Bezaleel as Grand Wardens is given as Exodus xxxii., 6, whereas it is in the thirty-first chapter that these two are named and their qualifications and duties described (although needless to say they are not given as Wardens), and the sixth verse of this latter chapter refers to Aholiab "given with him" (*i.e.*, Bezaleel). The Bible gives Aholiab as the assistant, or at any rate the junior in point of mention, which order is followed in the 1723 edition at page 8, but reversed in the footnote on page 12, whereas in 1738 he comes as the senior, whether for alphabetical reasons or by chance, and it is curious how Masonic ritual always speaks of Aholiab and Bezaleel, reversing the Scriptural order.[1]

---

[1] R. E. Swartout in "The Monastic Craftsman" (1932) notes that a comparison with Bezaleel was "A common compliment to metal-workers, lay and monastic, in the Middle Ages" (p. 44, n. 4). Mortet in his *Receuil de Textes relatifs à l'Histoire de l'Architectture* (p. 38) gives the following passage (1005-1030)—" Rursus Rodulfus, in omni arte fusoria peritissimus, velut alter Beseleel," and adds in a note that this surname was given in the Carolingian Palace to Eginhard, the superintendent of buildings under Charlemagne. Dermot in *Ahiman Rezon*, with his not unusual accuracy, in his frontispiece gives Bezaleel a position on the right of Moses as being apparently immediately next to the latter in precedence.

In the 1723 edition the ascription in the Old Charges of the building of the Tower of Babel to Nimrod had been rejected in favour of the posterity of Noah, but in 1738 the old version was restored, for what reason we know not.

In the second, as in the first edition, Anderson gives a long description of King Solomon's Temple, and it is not surprising to find that these descriptions vary one from the other, as they both do from that given in the *Royal Genealogies*.

In view of the fact that to the period between 1723 and 1738 belongs the spread, if not the rise, of the ceremony now known as the Third Degree, it is interesting to compare certain references in the two editions. The earlier (p. 11 and note) states that Hiram or Huram King of Tyre sent his namesake Hiram or Huram "the most accomplished Mason upon Earth," and then gives a long footnote, explaining his origin and that of his name. In 1738 (p. 12 and note), in the corresponding passage the King of Tyre is said to have sent "Hiram Abbif, the most accomplished designer and operator upon Earth, who in Solomon's absence filled the Chair as Deputy Grand Master, and in his presence was the Senior Grand Warden or principal Surveyor and Master of Work," and there follows a footnote to the same effect as before but with verbal variations, in which it is said "as in the Lodge he is called Hiram Abbif, to distinguish him from King Hiram." Our author then goes on to describe the building and completion of Solomon's Temple, and when he comes to the celebration of the Cope-Stone by the Fraternity he says: "But their joy was soon interrupted by the sudden death of their dear master Hiram Abbif, whom they decently interr'd in the Lodge near the Temple according to ancient usage."[1] He describes the consecration "after Hiram Abbif was mourned for," and then adds: "But leaving what must not, and indeed what cannot be committed to writing, we may certainly affirm, that . . . the Royal Art . . . was never perfected till the building of this gorgeous House of God . . .," which passage we may compare with a somewhat similar one in the "Manner of Constitution" and we may wonder whether this is a reference to the esotery of the "Third Degree" or just a piece of pseudo-crypticism.

The vexed question of that name of many aliases and of disputed connotation, Naymus Graecus, Anderson deals with in his own fashion. On page 16, he states that "the old Constitutions affirm, that one called Ninus, who had been at the building of Solomon's Temple, brought the refined Knowledge of the Science and the Art into Germany and Gaul," and at page 61 speaks of "Charles Martel, the Right Worshipful Grand Master of France . . . who had been educated by Brother Mimus Graecus."

It were tedious to follow Anderson through the many pages devoted to the history of Greece and Rome, and his attempts to bring into his narrative the great names in the story of both nations, and we will only quote a few of his more surprising passages and then make some observations which will serve to show his preferences in Architecture or Freemasonry, with him synonymous terms. In Greece (pp. 27-28) many excellent painters and philosophers, we are told, are in the list of ancient architects, openly taught Geometry, and being Gentlemen of good repute, "they were generally at the head of the craft, highly useful to the Fellow Crafts . . . and bred them up clever artists: only by a law in Greece no slave was allowed to learn the 7 liberal sciences, or those of the Freeborn: so that in Greece also they were called Free Masons, and in their many Lodges, the noble and learned were accepted as Brothers, down to the days of Alexander the Great and afterwards for many ages"—for all the world like the noblemen and gentlemen of eighteenth century England! We may note that the catalogue of the liberal arts and sciences formerly so conspicuous with their names and descriptions in the Old Charges is here relegated to a side-note naming them "according to the Old Constitutions."

[1] The death of Hiram Abbif is not mentioned in Anderson's *Royal Genealogies*.

In the Greek section we have more than one instance of Anderson's quoting the old traditions and the old Masons as authorities for his statements. "Ptolemy, Grand Master, with Euclid, the Geometrician, and Straton, the Philosopher, as Grand-Wardens, built his palace at Alexandria," "according to the traditions and the old Constitutions"; Archimedes was "call'd by the old Masons the Noble and Excellent Grand Master of Syracuse." The surviving Old Charges give no support to these assertions.

Augustus Cæsar, "who patronized the Fraternity as their illustrious Grand Master (so call'd always by the old Masons)" and his successors, Anderson looks upon as the patrons of the Craft at its zenith: "Therefore the present remains of ancient Rome in his time [*e.g.*, that of Augustus], and of some following Emperors, are so accurate, that they are the best patterns of true Masonry extant, the epitome of all the old Grecian architecture, commonly expressed by the Augustan stile: and we now wish to arrive at its glorious perfection in Wisdom, Strength and Beauty."

Anderson passes to Judæa and gives a liberal amount of space to the reign of Herod the Great and the building of the Third Temple.

At the conclusion of the Roman Section, we return to the author's views on the general decline of architecture. With the accession of Totila the Augustan style totally departed in Italy and the West, and with that of the Iconoclastic Emperors in the East "the Augustan style was quite lost and the loss was public"; and the conquering Mahometans had no "Grand Design . . . to cultivate Arts and Sciences . . . so that Architecture in Asia and Africa suffer'd by them as in Europe by the Goths." "For when the Gothic nations, and those conquered by them, began to affect stately structures, they wanted both heads and hands to imitate the Ancients, nor could they do it for many ages . . . yet not wanting wealth and ambition, they did their best: and so the more ingenious gradually coalesced in Societies or Lodges, in imitation of the Ancients, according to the remaining traditions that were not quite obliterated, and hammer'd out a new style of their own, call'd the Gothic."

"But tho' this is more expensive than the old style, and discovers now to us the ignorance of the architect, and the improprieties of the edifice, yet the inventions of the artists to supply the want of good old skill, and their costly decorations, have manifested their esteem for the Royal Art, and have rendered their Gothic structures venerable and magnificent; tho' not imitable by those that have the true high taste of the Grecian or Augustan style."

In the last Chapter of Part I., after observing that "the Royal Art lies dead and buried still in the East, by the wilful ignorance of the Mahometan nations," Anderson goes on to deal with the history of the Renascence in Italy and with its great names, with a good sprinkling of Masonic terms. Cimaboius and the Pisans "educated many fine Masters and Fellow Crafts" (p. 48); John de Medicis "became the learned patron of the Revivers, or their Grand Master, and carefully supported the said Lodge, or academy of masters and connoisseurs" (p. 49); "Pope Julius II. the learned patron or Grand Master of Rome retained Bramante as his architect and Grand Warden" (p. 51), and finally we are told that "But from the first Revival, the Masons began to form new Lodges (called by the painters Academies or Schools, as all true Lodges ought to be) far more elegant than the former Gothic Lodges; for instructing disciples or Enter'd Prentices, for preserving the secrets of the Fraternity from strangers and Cowans, and for improving the Royal Art, under the patronage of the Popes and the Italian Princes and States, as could be more amply prov'd" (p. 54).

As an instance of Anderson's incurable looseness in the use of terms, I may mention a small point in this chapter, where although there was obviously no purpose to be achieved by a mis-statement, he deliberately or carelessly makes one. The Medici family since the earliest part of the fifteenth century had become by far the most influential in Florence, and with Lorenzo (d. 1492) had in effect become its rulers, but it was not until the time of Alexander that they were given the title, "Duke of Florence." Yet from the time of John, over one hundred years before, Anderson styles them Dukes of Florence, and to get over the difficulty in Alexander's case states that he was made the first "absolute" Duke.

PART II.

Here again, as in the case of Part I., and also of Part III., the heading in the table of contents on page viii. differs slightly from that in the book itself.

True to his plan of fitting Freemasonry into history, as he had done in the case of the Scriptural and classical periods, Anderson takes his reader through the whole course of English history, beginning with Julius Cæsar, but sparing us, as some non-Masonic chroniclers have not always done, any connection with classic Troy. In his accustomed manner he goes on to tell of Ostorius Scapula being succeeded by several Roman lieutenants "that soon formed Lodges for building castles and other Forts to secure their conquests." In the 1723 edition Anderson makes no mention of the story of St. Alban. According to Hughan (*Old Charges*, 1895 ed., pp. 131-2) he had become acquainted with the *Spencer* text (either the *Inigo Jones* MS. or a later representative) between 1723 and 1738, and to his account of the proto-martyr he adds a passage quoted from the *Spencer* MS. with a considerable amount of accuracy, with the important exception that to the MS. statement that St. Alban "was thereat himself" (*i.e.*, the Assembly) he adds "as Grand Master." On page 60 we get our first mention of Inigo Jones and John Webb in respect of their opinions of Stonehenge, but with no notice here of their being Freemasons.

We are told on p. 61 of the coming of Austin (*i.e.*, St. Augustine) afterwards to be numbered among the Grand Masters of the Order, though nothing is here said of any architectural works of the Apostle of the English, but we are told how he converted the Anglo Saxon Kings and how they started building and "requir'd many Masons who soon form'd themselves into Societies, or Lodges, by direction of foreigners that came over to help them." Can this be a jumbled reminiscence of Benedict Biscop's importation of foreign artisans?

In their account of Freemasonry in Britain the Old Charges jumped from St. Alban to Athelstan and Edwin. Anderson, however, like nature abhorring a vacuum, fills in this gap in the following fashion:—"Ethelbert . . . sent to Charles Martel the Right Worshipful Grand Master of France . . . who had been educated by Brother Mimus Graecus: He sent over from France [about A.D. 710] some expert masons to teach the Saxons those laws and usages of the ancient Fraternity that had been happily preserv'd from the havoc of the Goths: tho' not the Augustan style . . . This is strongly asserted in all the old Constitutions and was firmly believ'd by the old English Masons."

In the 1723 edition is purported to be quoted "a certain Record of Free-Masons, written in the reign of King Edward IV.," which Begemann[1] numbers among those of the Plot family, of which the most conveniently accessible is the *William Watson* MSS. As the question of Athelstan and Edwin is a rather vexed one, and in order to give a good and complete instance of Anderson's method, I shall, following and extending Begemann's example, take the *William Watson* MS.[2] and the relevant portions of the editions of 1723 and 1738, set them out and endeavour to compare and contrast them.

"Which said King Ethelstane and the same Edwin loved well Geometry and applied himself busily in learning that Science and also he desired to have the practice thereof. Wherefore he called unto him of the best Masons that were

---

[1] *op. cit.*, ii., p. 187.
[2] Hughan's Reprint, p. 16. But I have not thought it necessary to preserve the original spelling.

in the realm for he knew well that they had the practice of Geometry best of any craft in the realm and he learned of them Masonry and cherished and loved them well and he took upon him the Charges and learned the manners and afterward for the love that he had unto the craft and for the good grounding that it was found in he purchased a free Charter of the King his father that they should have such a freedom to have correction within themselves and that they might have communication together to correct such things as were amiss within themselves and they made a great Congregation of Masons to assemble together at York where he was himself, and let call the old Masons of the realm to that Congregation, and commanded them to bring to him all the writings of the old books of the craft that they had out of which books they contrived the charges by the devise of the wisest of Masons that were there, and commanded that these charges might be kept and holden and he ordained that such Congregation, might be called Assembly and he ordained for them good pay that they might live honestly the which charges I will declare hereafter and this was the craft of Masonry there grounded and considered." (*William Watson* MS.).

"That though the ancient records of the Brotherhood in England were many of them destroyed or lost in the wars of the Saxons and Danes, yet King Athelstan, (the Grandson of King Alfred the Great, a mighty architect) the first anointed king of England, and who translated the Holy Bible into the Saxon tongue, when he had brought the land into rest and peace, built many great works, and encouraged many Masons from France, who were appointed Overseers thereof, and brought with them the Charges and Regulations of the Lodges preserv'd since the Roman times, who also prevail'd with the King to improve the Constitution of the English Lodges according to the foreign model, and to increase the wages of working Masons."

"That the said King's youngest son, Prince Edwin, being taught Masonry, and taking upon him the Charges of a Master-Mason, for the love he had to the said Craft, and the honourable principle wherein it is grounded, purchased a free Charter of King Athelstan his father, for the Masons having a Correction among themselves (as it was anciently express'd) or a freedom and power to regulate themselves, to amend what might amiss, and to hold a yearly Communication and General Assembly."

"That accordingly Prince Edwin summoned all the Masons in the realm to meet him in a Congregation at York who came and composed a General Lodge, of which he was Grand Master; and having brought with them all the writings and records extant, some in Greek, some in Latin, some in French, and other languages, from the contents thereof that Assembly did frame the Constitution and Charges of an English Lodge, made a law to preserve and observe the same in all time coming, and ordain'd good pay for working Masons etc." (1723 *Constitutions*, pp. 32-3.)

Anderson in the 1738 edition relates that "Athelstan the eldest son [of Edward the Elder] succeeded tho' only the son of a concubine, and at first left the Craft to the care of his brother Edwin, called in some copies his son: for in all the old Constitutions it is written to this purpose, viz.," and he then goes on to repeat with very small alterations the first of the paragraphs of the 1723 edition just quoted, and continues as follows:—

"That Prince Edwin, the King's Brother, being taught Geometry and Masonry, for the love he had to the said Craft, and to the honourable principles whereon it is grounded, purchased a free Charter of King Athelstan his brother, for the Free Masons having among themselves a correction, or a power and freedom to regulate themselves, to amend what might happen amiss, and to hold a yearly Communication in a General Assembly.

"'That accordingly Prince Edwin summoned all the Free and Accepted Masons in the realm, to meet him in a Congregation at York, who came and form'd the Grand Lodge under him as their Grand Master, A.D. 926.

"That they brought with them many old writings and records of the Craft, some in Greek, some in Latin, some in French, and other languages and from the contents thereof, they fram'd the Constitutions of the English Lodges, and made a law for themselves, to preserve and observe the same in all time coming, etc. etc. etc."

Anderson here finishes his quotation and proceeds as follows:—

"But good Prince Edwin died before the King [A.D. 938] without issue, to the great grief of the Fraternity; though his memory is fragrant in the Lodges, and honourably mentioned in all the old Constitutions.

"Some English historians say that Edwin being accused of a plot, the King set him adrift in a boat without sail and oars; that Edwin protesting his innocence, went abroad and jumped into the sea, and that his esquire was drove into Picardy.

"But the historian Malmsbury disbelieves the whole story as grounded only on some old ballad, and because of Athelstan's known kindness and love to all his brothers and sisters; and Huntingdon writes of the loss of Edwin by sea, as a very sad accident, and a great misfortune to Athelstan, who was very fond of him."

Bro. Vibert, in his Introduction to the Facsimile reprint of the 1723 *Book of Constitutions*, pp. xvii., xviii., points out that the passage which occurs in both of Anderson's quotations naming the languages of the old writings and records occurs for the first time in the later versions of the Old Charges, of the Grand Lodge and the Sloane Families, where the mention of Greek is usual. He adds that "some texts [*e.g.*, the Aberdeen of 1670] also mention Hebrew, but Anderson certainly did not come across any of them, for if he had he would not have failed to quote so valuable an addition to his evidence."

But if we consider these portions which deal with the Craft, we are on very uncertain ground. It is obvious how Anderson varied and expanded the *William Watson* version of the Plot Family and how his own two versions differed. The *William Watson* version gives Edwin as the son of Athelstan, the 1723 edition as his youngest son, and the 1738 edition as his brother. Begemann [1] suggests that Plot's objection of 1686 that Athelstan appears to have been unmarried resulted in the change of the Spencer Family to "brother" instead of "son," and that Anderson reading the Cole Constitutions of 1726 (belonging to that Family) made the alteration in his second edition.

We see Anderson again introducing the Masonic terms of the revival into his version of the Old Charges. He changes "Masons" into "Free Masons." The "Charges" of the *William Watson* MS. become the Charges and Regulations of the (foreign) Lodges. The "great Congregation" at York becomes first a "yearly Communication and General Assembly," and then "a yearly Communication in a General Assembly." In the 1723 edition Anderson introduces the phrase Master-Mason. The "Masons" and "old Masons" of the MS. assembled at York, became in 1723 a "General Lodge" of which Edwin is "Grand Master," and in the 1738 edition "the Free and Accepted Masons" constitute the "Grand Lodge" under the former as "Grand Master," with the date A.D. 926 given (without any discoverable authority) for the first, but unfortunately by no means the last, time. It may be noted that, though as Begemann suggests, Anderson read and used Cole's Constitutions, yet he assigns no date to the Charter, although Cole gives it as A.D. 932.

---

[1] *op. cit.*, i., 394, note.

Further discussion of the alleged Grand Lodge at York would be out of place here, otherwise than to quote Begemann's verdict [1] that "it has no other authority than the Legendary history of the Old Charges, and that fact completely demolishes the myth of the Grand Lodge of York and the 'Ancient York Masons' as they styled themselves."

In justice to Anderson it should be mentioned that Bro. Dring [2] makes him an honourable exception to those Masonic writers of the eighteenth century who "not being able to reconcile the legend with history, have had little compunction in asserting that the Edwin mentioned in the legend was not Edwin son of Edward, but Edwin, King of Northumbria 617 to 633."

He attributes the fact that Edwin is described in the Old Charges as the King's son to (1) the writer of the Cooke MS. in his ignorance of history attributing the obtaining of the Charter to the youngest son and (2) to later copyists, noticing the historical inaccuracy or wishing to emphasise the statement by giving the name, seeing in a charter the words "Edwinus Clito" and taking this to mean the son.

Dring also appositely quotes Freeman's *Mythical and Romantic Elements In Early History*, in which that author discussing the legend of Edwin states "that there is no evidence at all to connect Athelstane in any way with the death of his brother."

The earlier mention of Henry Yevell, "the King's Free-Mason, or General Surveyor of his buildings," becomes in 1738 "Henry Yevell" (call'd at first, in the old Records, the King's Free Mason) the "old Records" being Stow.

A matter is dealt with by Anderson on pages 73-74 which deserves a passing mention. He there quotes the Statute 3 Hen. VI., cap I., which is directed against the "yearly Congregations and Confederacies made by the Masons in their General Assemblies" whereby the Statute of Labourers is contravened and rendering the frequenting thereof a felony. He quotes the opinion of Chief Justice Coke (whom in the first edition, though not in this, he had claimed as a Freemason by reason of this opinion) that as the Statute of Labourers was repealed by the Act of 5 Fliz: cap 4, *cessante ratione legis cessat ipsa lex*, any act, including the Statute of Henry VI., passed against the contravention of the Statute of Labourers, became by the repealing act, of no effect. He adds that the Statute of Henry VI. was never effective, that the Masons always laugh'd at it, and, with a flourish, that "they ever had, and ever will have their own wages, while they coalesce in due form, and carefully preserve the cement under their own Grand Master; let Cowans do as they please." Begemann took the view [3] that 3 Hen. VI., cap I., did not prohibit the ordinary meetings of the Craft, but was only directed against irregular assemblies, outside the formal organisation, which were aimed at raising wages in breach of the Statute of Labourers. Dr. Cunningham, however, in his *Notes on the Organisation of the Mason's Craft in England* (pp. 6 and 7), was of the opinion that it was the regular assemblies which were rendered illegal under Henry VI., though "there is no reason to suppose that they may not have formed a sort of national organisation of masonry under public patronage in the fourteenth century."

In his *Notes on the Craft Guilds of Norwich* Tingey [4] states that: "The Masons again attracted the attention of the Assembly in 1491 when it appears that no Masters were sworn to make any search for defects of workmanship, and it is stated that by a recent statute masons were merely accounted labourers, and forbidden to cause any gathering for forming regulations upon such defects. Therefore it was agreed, that the mayor, with two or more discrete men of the craft, should have authority to correct such defects, assess fines, and so forth. What statute is here understood is uncertain, but probably an Act of Parliament, for it was unusual to call the local enactments by that name."

[1] op. cit., i., 462.
[2] A.Q.C., xxii., 11.
[3] op. cit., i., 326.
[4] A.Q.C., xv., 197.

But as in Rye's *Extracts from the Records of the Corporation of Norwich* we find that in the fifteenth year of Elizabeth the Corporation granted the Petition of Masons to hold an assembly and approved their regulation it would seem that they had recovered their former rights.

Anderson follows the passages just referred to by a statement that "even during this King's (*i.e.*, Henry VI.'s) minority, there was a good Lodge under Grand Master Chicheley held at Canterbury . . . in which are named Thomas Stapylton the Master and John Morris Custos de la Lodge Lathomorum or Warden of the Lodge of Masons, with fifteen Fellow Crafts, and three Enter'd Prentices all named there. And a Record in the reign of Edward IV. says, the Company of Masons, being otherwise termed Free Masons, of ancient standing and good reckoning, by means of affable and kind meetings divers times, and as a loving brotherhood use to do, did frequent this mutual assembly in the time of Henry VI. in the twelfth year of his most gracious reign, viz. A.D. 1434, when Henry was aged thirteen years." We may note in passing the usual anachronistic use of the term "Grand Master" in the case of Archbishop Chicheley. With regard to the contents of the first sentence of the passage just cited, we may quote Begemann's comments. Anderson in the margin quotes as his authority for his statement about Chicheley a document entitled "Liberatio generalis Domini Gulielmi Prioris Ecclesiae Christi Cantuariensis Erga Festum Natalis Domini 1429."

Begemann[1] states that the actual document is in the Bodleian among the Tanner MSS., but that the contents differ materially from Anderson's account, and that he gives the names incorrectly. Nothing is said therein about Chicheley forming any Lodge; and it is merely a list of the Lathomi of the Loygge who were given clothing by the Priory. There were sixteen Lathomi (not fifteen) and Three Apprenticii, and there is not a word about Fellow-Crafts or Enter'd Prentices. Mapylton (not Stapylton) is styled Magister Lathomorum and Johannes Morys Custos de la Loygge Lathomorum.[2]

With regard to the second portion of our quotation Stow says: "The Company of Masons, being otherwise termed Free-masons, of ancient standing and good reckoning, by means of affable and kind meetings divers times, and as a living Brotherhood should use to do, did frequent this mutual assembly in the time of King Henry the fourth, in the twelfth year of his most gracious reign." In the 1723 edition, this statement is reproduced and attributed to "an old Record of Masons," but Henry V. is substituted for Henry IV. In 1738, as we see, the passage is again reproduced, but the Record becomes that of the reign of Edward IV. (1461-1483)—Stow's dates were 1525-1605[3]; and by an Andersonian progression Henry IV. now becomes Henry VI., while the addition "viz. A.D. 1434 when Henry was aged thirteen years" is our author's own.

Anderson gives on pages 78 and 79 an account of the levelling of the footstone of Henry VII.'s chapel at Westminster as follows:—"This Royal Grand Master [*i.e.*, Henry VII.] chose for his Wardens or Deputies, the foresaid John Islip, Abbot of Westminster, and Sir Reginald Bray, Knight of the Garter, by whom the King summon'd a Lodge of Masters in the Palace, with whom he walked in ample form to the East end of Westminster Abbey and levell'd the footstone of his famous chapel on 24th June 1502." Scott, in his *Gleanings from Westminster Abbey*, quotes Holinshed's version which Stow repeats, Anderson probably basing himself on the latter, as we have seen him do before, but with what additions Scott's quotation will show:—

---

[1] *Vorgeschichte*, i., p. 94.
[2] See also Knoop and Jones: *Masons and Apprenticeship in Mediæval England—Econ. Hist. Rev.*, Vol. iii., No. 3, p. 362. The authors mention a further entry in 1431 (p. 136) where are named 14 lathomi, 2 apprenticii and 6 cementarii.
[3] Stow (1633 edn.), p. 630; Gould's *History*, ii., p. 177.

"An Reg. 18; *1503* In the eighteenth year, the twenty fourtth day of January . . . the first stone of our lady chapel within the monastery of Westminster was laid, by the hands of John Islip, abbot of the same monastery, Sir Reginald Bray Knight of the Garter," etc. We see how our author embellishes his authority, again adding his usual anachronistic Masonic touches— "Grand Master," "Wardens," "Deputies," the summoning of a "Lodge of Masters," "ample form" (as we shall see later one of his own phrases) and in addition his carelessness in the matter of dates.

In the 1723 edition (p. 38, note) a story is given of how Queen Elizabeth, being jealous of the assemblies of Masons,[1] sent an armed force to break up an annual "Communication" at York, how her emissaries were at once admitted to the Lodge, and how being then satisfied of the honourable character of the gathering, they returned to the Queen with a favourable report and so allayed her fears that she left the Craft unmolested. This account is repeated in a somewhat different form in the second edition, and made more definite. The date is given as the 27th December, 1561, and it is there stated that "Sir Thomas Sackville, Grand Master, took care to make some of the chief men sent Free-Masons." Bro. Vibert says that he knows of no autthority having yet been suggested for the incident just recorded. It is a curious fact that the scholarship of Sir Sidney Lee (and it is in knowledge of the Elizabethan period that this particularly manifested itself) far from affording us any help in the mattetr, here fails us in a peculiarly irritating fashion, for an examination of his account of Sir Thomas Sackville in the Dictionary of National Biography shows him to have included the story of the Lodge at York, but to have included it on the authority of Anderson himself. Our author fortifies himself by saying that his account was "firmly believ'd by all the old English Masons," but as we know this carries us no further. In support of Anderson's story there is quoted in *Mis. Lat.* (ii., 58, 59) a portion of an address given by Archdeacon Freer and reprinted in his *Memoirs* (1866) in which a somewhat similar story is related, but with Archbishop Parker in the place of Sir Thomas Sackville; but one cannot give much credit to this evidence in the absence of the Archdeacon's authority for his statement.[2] Bro. Vibert has further considered the matter in his *York and the Craft through the Centuries*, pp. 12, 13, and feels that Anderson must have had some foundation for his story. Can we believe that Anderson deliberately invented the story or that he so dressed it up that it cannot be recognised in any other authority, or that his is the only record that remains to us of an actual incident? Sharing Bro. Vibert's feelings, I can only say that the story may well be true in substance, if not in fact, but that one cannot corroborate it.

We are further told how in the reign of Elizabeth on the resignation of Grand Master Sackville, the Earl of Bedford was chosen in the North and Sir Thomas Gresham in the South. Preston, of course, repeats this account, but adds no other evidence, and in deciding the truth or falsity of this story we must be guided by whatever idea we may have formed of Anderson's credibility, and by our general view of York Freemasonry. We cannot accept the story as told,

---

[1] In chapter 9 of the rare German book, *Gründliche Nachricht von den Frey-Maurern* . . . Franckfurt am Mayn, 1738, there occurs the following passage, given in the words of the late Bro. J. T. Thorp's translation on page 11 of his Foreword to Leicester Masonic Reprint, xiv.:—"Thus this Samson was at length compelled, by the unshakeable determination of his Delilah, to hand over to her, in order that she might boast of her success in obtaining them, what the great Queen Elizabeth of England had long-ago failed to extort from the Earl of Essex (*sic*)." I have never seen this passage quoted in juxtaposition to Anderson's account, and one would dearly like to know whether the two came from the same source.

[2] In *The Sufferings of John Coustos* (1746 edn.), p. 30, appears the story taken from Anderson, but with "the Archbishop of Canterbury, Primate of her Kingdom," in place of Sackville, so that Freer's source would appear to be Coustos, and Coustos' source his confused recollection of Anderson—so we are once again at a dead end.

but it is open to us to suppose that, however inaccurately, it may be based on some actual York tradition; but if this were so it is difficult to explain why Drake in his famous oration does not mention the tradition.

We need not linger long over our author's account of Freemasonry in Scotland and Ireland, save for two or three points that stand out in his record.

He relates that Claud Hamilton, Lord Paisley, made King James VI. a Brother Mason. It is a curious fact that James VI. was in fact made a Mason (though not in our modern sense), but not as Anderson supposed. Bro. D. Crawford Smith in his *History of the Ancient Masonic Lodge of Scoon and Perth*[1] says "there can be no doubt of the statement made further on in the Minutes that King James the VI. was by his own desire entered Freeman Mason and Fellow-Craft (there being no Master Mason degree in those days). King James made a state visit to Perth 15th April 1601, on which occasion he was made a Burgess at the Market Cross . . . We think that it would be on this occasion that the King was entered by his own desire." Hughan in his Introduction to this work supported Crawford Smith and saw "no reason whatever to question the assertion of the ordinance of 1658, though it would have been still more satisfactory had an actual Lodge Minute, or some other contemporary record been preserved of the occurrence." The facts quoted do not of course support Anderson's credibility. It is obvious that he did not have them before him when he wrote, and that it just happens that he hit upon the truth, or an approximation thereto.

With regard to Ireland, stifling a sigh of regret that Anderson did not think it worth while to enquire into what Bro. Crawley's papers and Bros. Lepper and Crosslé's *History* show to have been the interesting beginnings of Freemasonry in that country, I will content myself with noting just two points in our author's account. He states (p. 96) that: "At last the ancient Fraternity of the Free and Accepted Masons in Ireland, being fully assembled in their Grand Lodge at Dublin, chose a noble Grand Master, in imitation of their Brethren in England, in the third year of his present Majesty King George II., A.D. 1730, even our noble Brother James King Lord Viscount Kingston . . ."

Now Bros. Lepper and Crosslé in their *History of the Grand Lodge of Ireland* (vol. i., pp. 53 ff) take the view that the earliest date assignable for its foundation is 1723, and the latest 1724, and quote Begemann's suggestion (in his *Freimaurerie in Ireland*, p. 16) that it may even have been founded in 1721. In addition, they reproduce the issue of *The Dublin Weekly Journal* No. 13 of Saturday, 26th June, 1725, in which there is a long account of the meetings of the Most Ancient and Right Worshipful Society of Free-Masons, at which it was announced that the Grand Lodge had chosen the Earl of Ross Grand Master for the ensuing year. If Anderson could ignore or rather perhaps did not trouble to inform himself of an event occurring at the most some thirteen years before he wrote, we can gain considerable assistance from this fact in any attempt to estimate the general credibility of our author.

On page 95 Anderson gives an impressive account of the laying of the foundation stone of the Parliament House at Dublin on 3rd February, 1728/9, when "Lord Carteret then Lord Lieutenant, the Lords Justice . . . with many Free Masons . . . made a solemn Procession thither, and the Lord Lieutenant, having in the King's Name levell'd the Footstone at the South side, by giving it 3 knocks with a Mallet, the Trumpets sounded, the solemn crowd made joyful acclamations, a Purse of Gold was laid on the stone for the Masons, who drank to the King and the Craft etc." Bros. Lepper and Crosslé (*Freemasonry in Ireland*, vol. i., pp. 72 and 73) state that the story is a fiction, that Carteret was in London at the time and that in his absence the ceremony was performed in the presence of the Lords Justices and that "the only connexion

[1] Pp. 49-52.

of masons of any description with the ceremony was some money given to the workmen to celebrate the occasion." They add that Pennell who was at the time preparing his *Constitutions* and was probably present, describes on page 37 exactly what happened and that Anderson "got hold of Pennell's story, and, being always ready to adorn a tale, proceeded to make it more picturesque and absolutely misleading."

It must strike the most cursory reader of the second edition how the pages positively bristle, not only with dates, but with long genealogical tables. Anderson has remembered only too well his alleged order to "digest the Constitutions with a just chronology" (p. vii.) and has been far too modest in his statement (p. x.) that "some few genealogies are put in the margin (not to hinder the reader) that are needful for the connection of the history [*i.e.*, in Part I.]. But in Parts II. and III. they show more distinctly how the Craft has been well encouraged in the several periods and successions of the Saxon . . . Kings of England, down to the present Royal Family."

Anderson had issued Proposals for printing by subscription his *Royal Genealogies* which was in fact founded on the work of John Hübner of Hamburg, and had promised that "the subscribers names" would "be printed as the Encouragers of so useful a work."[1] It is characteristic of his curious use of words that when the book came to be published in 1732, he headed the list of patrons with the words "Subscribers to, or Encouragers of this book," which expression if we had not known the terms of the prospectus might lead us to suppose that some of these patrons were merely honorary. But knowing these terms as we do we must suppose that the more than four hundred names printed at the beginning of the book represent actual subscribers, and a very goodly collection it is, representing distinguished members of the nobility, gentry and the professions, and including many of the early officers of Grand Lodge together with two of the author's brothers. Needless to say, much of Anderson's history in the 1738 edition is repeated from the *Royal Genealogies*, *e.g.*, the account of Herod's Temple, although even here there are such considerable variations as to render the two accounts two different versions in many respects. The reference, " John ii., 20," correctly given in the *Royal Genealogies*, is given in the *Book of Constitutions* as John xi., 20. I shall give just one instance for the purpose of showing how Anderson worked up the materials of his *Royal Genealogies* into Masonic history for the 1738 edition. He had written in 1732: " Rome was now adorned with several noble structures by Agrippa, who also at his own charge, finished the famous Pantheon, or Temple of All Gods, (now the Temple of all Saints) and made curious Aqueducts for the City."[2] He had said of Augustus Cæsar that he "proved an excellent magistrate, reform'd the city and army, renewed the great secular games, and obliged the players to be modest and decent"[3]; but had nowhere spoken of any architectural pretensions of the Emperor. But in 1738 he could write (p. 37): "Octavianus, now called Sebastos, or Augustus Cæsar who patroniz'd the Fraternity as their illustrious Grand Master (so call'd always by the old Masons) and his Deputy Agrippa, who adorned the Campus Martius, and built the Grand Portico of the Rotunda[4] Pantheon, with many more charming piles mention'd in history."

PART III.

Anderson commences this part with an account of Inigo Jones. He begins with his birth in 1572 (Mr. Gotch, his latest biographer, says the date was 1573) and his education, and tells how James I., " a Royal Brother Mason, and Royal Grand Master by prerogative appointed Jones his general surveyor" and

---

[1] *A.Q.C.*, xviii., pp. 31-2.
[2] *Royal Genealogies*, p. 294.
[3] *Royal Genealogies*, p. 296.
[4] In original misprinted *Routnda*.

approved of his being chosen Grand Master of England, to preside over the Lodges. Anderson (p. 98) gives a circumstantial account of how "the King with Grand Master Jones and his Grand Wardens (the foresaid William Herbert Earl of Pembroke and Nicholas Stone the sculptor) attended by many Brothers in due form [1] and many eminent persons, walked to Whitehall Gate, and levell'd the footstone of the new Banquetting House with 3 great knocks, loud huzza's, sound of trumpets, and a purse of broad pieces of gold laid upon the stone for the Masons to drink 'To the King and the Craft' A.D. 1607." It is an unfortunate fact that, again according to Mr. Gotch,[2] Jones did not obtain the Surveyorship until 1615, "and during the ten or fifteen years of maturity that preceded this event there is no properly authenticated building by his hand." Queen Elizabeth had built a Banquetting House of wood, which James had replaced in 1607 by another and a better one.[3] The building constructed in 1607 was in fact burnt down in 1619, and it was then that Jones as the King's Surveyor was instructed to prepare plans to replace it. Thus Inigo Jones could have had nothing to do with Whitehall in 1607, and as for the procession, whether or not Jones was in it, we have found no other mention of it whatever. It is a coincidence which has been pointed out to me that the year 1607 is also the date which has been written (but not by Anderson) on the so-called *Inigo Jones* MS.; was it anything more?

Elias Ashmole's connection with Freemasonry is not referred to in Anderson's first edition, but is given considerable attention in the second. Bros. Chetwode Crawley and Shum Tuckett have dealt exhaustively with the variations between the MS. version, the two 1717 editions or issues, the second (1774) edition, and Dr. Campbell's article "Ashmole," in the *Biographia Britannica* 1747, and with the discrepancies between these and Anderson's version. In particular, there is the alteration of "were" to "was" and the variation of "by" before "Sir William Wilson," thereby making it appear as though Ashmole was again made a Mason (which is nonsense) and confusing the admission *of* Wilson with admission *by* Wilson. Anderson's version, although it reads "we" for "were," seems on the whole to follow the MS. more correctly than either the 1717 or 1774 editions so far as the 1682 entry is concerned, although he quotes the printed version of 1717, but he unwarrantably introduces the expression Fellow-Crafts.

Anderson in 1738 gives an account of a General Assembly and Feast of Freemasons held in 1663, and states that Charles II., who had been made a Freemason in his travels, approved of Lord St. Albans as Grand Master and that the latter appointed Denham his Deputy and Wren and Webb Grand Wardens. "According to a copy of the Old Constitutions," this Grand Master held the Assembly on the 27th December, 1663, when certain regulations (set out in full) (pp. 101-2) were made. Roberts in his *Constitutions* published in 1722 had published certain "Additional Orders and Constitutions made and agreed upon at a General Assembly held at . . . on the Eighth Day of December 1663" (pp. 23 ff). Anderson has obviously taken Roberts's account and adapted it in his own fashion. He has changed the date to St. John's Day, 27th December, added the name of the chief English architects of the time as the Grand Officers, and transcribed Roberts's Additional Orders with his customary variations and errors. In Clause one the expression "regular Lodge" is his own, and he replaced "workman" by "craftsman"; in Clause two there is a grammatical error. The change in Clause three is particularly interesting. The Roberts version had said "that no person hereafter, which shall be accepted a Free-Mason,

---

[1] Henry VII.'s procession was "in ample form"; this is "in due form," and yet on both occasions the Grand Master was present in person. I return to the question of this phraseology later on. For the present it is sufficient to say that, at this stage at all events, Anderson would appear not to have understood his own technical terms.
[2] J. A. Gotch: *Inigo Jones*, p. 15.
[3] Gotch, pp. 104-5.

shall be admitted into any Lodge or Assembly, until he hath brought a certificate of the time and place of his Acceptance, from the Lodge that accepted him, unto the Master of that limit or division, where such Lodge *was* kept . . ."[1] Anderson altered the regulation to read "unto the Master of that limit or division where such Lodge *is* kept . . ." Roberts was obviously referring to those occasional Lodges, at which *e.g.* Ashmole was admitted, but Anderson by his slight alteration suggested his idea of a permanent and no doubt regular Lodge. In Clause five the word "Grand Master" is an unauthorised and glaring departure from Roberts, who had merely said "shall be regulated and governed by one Master," not "one *Grand* Master." Clause six agrees with Roberts, but Anderson omits Clause seven with the oath of secrecy. Throughout Anderson uses the word "Acceptation" for Roberts's "Acception," of the use of which former word Begemann[2] says it would be hard to find another instance. Almost all the changes from Anderson's authority as we might by now have been sure are in the direction of showing Freemasonry as being in 1663 regularly and definitely organised, with officers, dates of meeting, and qualifications of candidates as at the time at which our author was writing.

The question of Sir Christopher Wren's relation to Freemasonry, although so often debated, is one which must be touched on however inadequately, in an account of Anderson's *Book of Constitutions* as it seems in many respects a crucial test of the author's merits.

In the first edition, the only references to Wren are as the "ingenious architect" who "conducted" the foundation of St. Paul's Cathedral (p. 41), and as "the King's architect" who designed and conducted the Sheldonian Theatre (p. 43 note). But in 1738 things are quite changed. Wren is mentioned as Grand Warden in 1663; Deputy Grand Master in 1666, 1669 and 1673, and apparently from 1674 to 1679 or possibly 1685; as Grand Master in 1685 (and being confirmed in his office by William III.) until 1695, when the Duke of Richmond and Lennox[3] was chosen Grand Master and he became Deputy again until in 1698 he became Grand Master once more. "Yet still in the South the Lodges were more and more disused, firstly by the neglect of the Masters and Wardens, . . . and the annual Assembly was not duly attended. G. M. Wren . . . celebrated the Capestone [of St. Paul's] . . . in July A.D 1708. Some few years after this Sir Christopher Wren neglected the office of Grand Master: yet the Old Lodge near St. Paul's and a few more continued their stated meetings . . . after the Rebellion was over A.D. 1716 the few Lodges at London finding themselves neglected by Sir Christopher Wren, thought fit to cement under a Grand Master . . .," and then follows the account of the Revival by the four original Lodges. Now Anderson's statements and opinions are quite clear. Wren according to him was intimately and continuously associated with the Craft for some fifty years and it was through his ultimate neglect of his duties that the necessity arose for a revival. Is his statement acceptable and credible? Now we have the fact that although we have Wren playing a great part in the Society, and occupying a pivotal position, Anderson in 1723 while mentioning his architectural authorities and writing a sketch of Freemasonry in England does not think it worth while to connect the two. In spite of many allusions to the Craft in the periodical Press of the time and in pamphlets and other literary forms, we have no reference to Wren as a Freemason (with the exceptions to be mentioned) and nothing in the *Parentalia or Memoirs of the Family of the Wrens.* The exceptions are

---

[1] Begemann, *op. cit.*, i., 418.
[2] id., 419.
[3] The well-known petition of Edward Hall recommended by the Second Duke of Richmond, which according to the Minutes (*Q.C.A.*, x . 216 and note (*a*)) was read on 2nd March, 1732, will be remembered in this connection, as Hall was said to have been made a Mason by the late (*i.e.*, the first) Duke 36 years before that date.

Aubrey's *Memoires of Naturall Remarques of the County of Wiltshire* and two newspapers of the period. In the former occurs the following passage:—

                1691   after Rogation Sunday
Mdm. this day [May the 18th being Monday] is a Great Convention
                                Accepted
    of St. Paules church of the Fraternity of the   F̶r̶e̶e̶-Masons: where
    Sr. Christopher Wren is to be adopted a Brother: and Sr. Henry
                                      divers
        Goodric:————————of ye Tower, and   s̶e̶v̶e̶r̶   others————————
There have been Kings, that have been of this Sodalitie.

Objection has been taken to the acceptance of this note on the ground of Aubrey's credibility, and the absence of contemporary corroborative evidence, and the great authority of Gould is against it.[1] But Crawley[2] puts the case, it is suggested, not unfairly, by saying that although Gould's argument has demolished Wren's alleged Grand Mastership, yet when his arguments are extended to exclude the possibility of Wren's acceptance they become inconclusive. "Something more than the silence of contemporaries who might have known or ought to have known, or even must have known, is required to invalidate Aubrey's clear report. Aubrey was a gossip; but all the better reporter. His testimony is unexceptionable on the points of honesty of purpose, habitual veracity,[3] and adequate means of knowledge. The MS. was revised by himself, and the particular paragraph was remodelled, as will be seen from the version quoted by Mr. Halliwell. If he had seen any reason to correct the statement, he had an opportunity of doing so. The MS. was submitted to, and annotated by Ray, Evelyn, and Tanner, men conversant with Wren and his associates. If they had thought it worth while to correct the statement, they had an opportunity of doing so."

Among all the newspaper notices of Wren's death there are only two which refer to him as a Freemason. One is in the *Postboy*, No. 5,245, from March 2nd to March 5th: "London, March 5, this evening the corpse of that worthy Free Mason, Sir Christopher Wren, Knight is to be interr'd under the Dome of St. Paul's Cathedral," and the other in similar terms in the *British Journal*, No. 25, March 9th, the latter possibly copied from the former. But it seems on the whole most likely that these two newspapers (and these alone) were not referring to membership of the Society, but were merely using the term as applying to one who was an architect and builder.

Now the position is this. It seems probable that Wren was in fact made a Freemason as in Aubrey's account, which is accepted by Crawley and Begemann, but rejected by Gould. If, however, we accept this account, we cannot credit Anderson's story of the Grand Wardenship in 1663 of a person not admitted until 1691, nor reconcile the silence of Press and literature alike with our author's claim of a fifty years' prominent association with the Craft. As in the case of King James I., Anderson seems by accident to have stumbled on a part of the truth, but in such a way as to throw doubts on rather than to strengthen his own credibility.

The account of the other Grand Masters contemporary with Wren's association with the Craft—Rivers, Arlington and the rest—is altogether unsupported by any other authority (with a possible exception in the case of Richmond) and for this reason we can in no wise accept it, particularly in view of our author's garbled version of the Roberts *Constitutions*. Anderson has

---

[1] Gould, ii., pp. 4 ff.
[2] *A.Q.C.*, xi., p. 11.
[3] If we think that Crawley's attribution of "habitual veracity" is too flattering in view of Aubrey's credulity, we may still well ask who can have had any object in imposing on the latter?

blundered rather badly in his account of the laying of the foundation-stone of St. Paul's. According to him (p. 103), Charles with a numerous retinue "in due form levell'd the footstone of the New St. Paul's, designed by D.G.M. Wren A.D. 1673, and by him conducted as Master of Work and Surveyor with his Wardens Mr. Edward Strong, Senior and Junior . . ." Valentine Strong had six sons who all followed their father's occupation of builder [1] of whom Thomas the eldest, and three others, including Edward, the fifth son (who compiled a Family Chronicle which, though not published until 1815, was in fact written in 1716), went to London in 1667 to take part in its rebuilding. Now Edward Strong states that it was his brother Thomas who laid the foundation stone; Edward himself was only 23 at the time, so that his son Edward, Junior, being either a baby or yet unborn, could not have been present at the ceremony. Moreover, according to the Family Chronicle, the elder Edward only took up his duties on the work after Thomas's death in 1681. The foundation was in fact laid in June, 1675. Begemann's comment on these facts seems fully justified: "This is one of the innumerable instances of Anderson's fertile imagination, and of the way in which later authors [he refers especially to Preston] have blindly accepted and improved on his assertions. They know nothing at all of the true layer of the foundation stone, Thomas Strong, the Family Chronicle not having been as yet published. But that is no excuse for these fictions, for both the Edward Strongs, father and son, were still alive in Anderson's days."

With the year 1717, we now come to perhaps the most important date in the history of the Craft, and it is at this point that Anderson's narrative should be of extreme value, if we could be at all sure whether it is accurate, or at least, how much of it is accurate.

Anderson says that what were later to be known as the Four Time Immemorial Lodges "finding themselves neglected by Sir Christopher Wren, thought fit to cement under a Grand Master as the center of union and harmony." We have seen that there is no evidence save his earlier statement of Grand Masters before 1717, and how little that statement is to be believed, and how, if we neglect his account of Wren (as we feel bound to do) and rely on Aubrey, there is nothing to connect Wren with either the neglect or the revival of the Craft. So that whatever truth there is in the record of the establishment of Grand Lodge, Anderson's record cannot be accepted nor his preamble admitted.[2] He then goes on to tell how the Four Lodges and some old Brothers met and having put into the Chair the oldest Master Mason (now the Master of a Lodge) they constituted themselves a Grand Lodge pro tempore in Due Form, and forthwith revived the Quarterly Communication of the Officers of Lodges (call'd the Grand Lodge) resolved to hold the Annual Assembly and Feast, and then to choose a Grand Master from among themselves, till they should have the honour of a noble Brother at their head.

Accordingly on S. John Baptist's Day in the third year of King George I. A.D. 1717, the Assembly and Feast of the Free and Accepted Masons was held . . . and the Brethren by a majority of hands elected Mr. Antony Sayer Gentleman, Grand Master of Masons . . . Capt. Joseph Elliot, Mr. Jacob Lamball, Carpenter, Grand Wardens.

Sayer, Grand Master, commanded the Masters and Wardens of Lodges to meet the Grand Officers every Quarter in communication . . . He adds two marginal notes:—

> "N.B. It is call'd the Quarterly Communication, because it should meet quarterly according to ancient usage. And when the Grand Master is present it is a Lodge in Ample Form; otherwise, only in Due Form, yet having the same authority with Ample Form" (pp. 109-110).

---

[1] Begeman, op. cit., i., 47 note; Gould, ii., pp. 40 ff.
[2] op. cit., ii., 37.

It is unfortunate that Anderson did not consider it necessary to set out these facts in his first edition. It is generally accounted a matter of suspicion when an historian omits to mention circumstances which should be fresh in his memory until a later date when that freshness has been lost. But it is perhaps possible to excuse him in this case, because by 1738 his plan had been enlarged. Even accepting this, there is much to be doubted in his narrative. He again pursues his favourite plan of reading past events in the light of their successors. He does not make the real organisation of 1717 a new thing as in fact it was, but makes out that it was a revival of the old Masonic administrative system. As we have seen, the office of Grand Master was a new one; and moreover the system of a centralised and permanent Grand Lodge was really an innovation to those who had been accustomed to the spasmodic and occasional meetings of local Lodges having little connection one with the other.

It is probable that the new movement was not universally approved; Sadler has demonstrated that there were probably Lodges in existence in 1717 which did not join in. Anderson's mention of the four Lodges and some old Brothers seems to suggest that there might have been other members of the Lodges to which the old Brothers belonged who did not approve. As far as we know, the distinction between "Ample Form" and "Due Form" is Anderson's invention, since there is no evidence in the Minutes of Grand Lodge up to the date of his second edition of any such distinction as he noted. We see that, in regard to most of the points on which Anderson's narrative can be checked, they find contradiction instead of confirmation, and there is much to be said for Begemann's conclusion that the whole story of the election of the first Grand Master is a myth of Anderson's invention, that the actual choice was made in a much more simple fashion, and that the single fact remaining as established is that Sayer was chosen Grand Master on 24th June, 1717, with Lambell and Elliot associate with him as Wardens.[1] We can perhaps accept the fact and the date of the re-organisation, but in the absence of corroboration reject Anderson's details.

I shall now proceed briefly to comment on Anderson's account of the subsequent assemblies.

24th June, 1718. Payne G.M. is stated to have recommended the strict observance of the Quarterly Communication. This would appear to corroborate what has already been said regarding these, *i.e.*, that they had not yet been regularly established. Payne desired the Brethren to bring "any old writings and records concerning Masons and Masonry," "and this year several old copies of the Gothic Constitutions were produced and collated" (p. 110.) There is no other evidence of this, and conversely, when, according to Stukeley,[2] Payne produced an old MS. of the Constitutions (the Cooke text) on 24th June, 1721, Anderson makes no mention of this fact. But it would be unfair not to point out that apparently the old records had not begun to be interesting and that there is no antecedent possibility against Anderson's statement.

24th June, 1719. "Some noblemen were also made brothers and more new Lodges were constituted." This is at best unlikely, otherwise one of the noblemen would probably have been made Grand Master; and we have no record of so early a series of constitutions.

24th June, 1720. "This year, at some private Lodges several very valuable Manuscripts (for they had nothing yet in print) concerning the Fraternity . . . were too hastily burnt by some scrupulous Brothers, that these papers might not fall into strange hands." Many theories have been built on this note, into

---
[1] *op. cit.*, ii., 39.
[2] Diary, i., 64.

which we cannot here enter. Begemann notes, for example, that we have no confirmation of this, but that on the contrary many MSS. have come down to us, that there is nothing in them which is secret, and indeed in 1722 Roberts published one of them. It is just conceivable of course that an unreasoning panic seized on some private Lodges, and that through fear and ignorance, the great enemies of written literature, such a holocaust may have been consummated, but it is unlikely. It is however possible that Begemann's view is too severe. With the discovery of such writings as the *Chetwode Crawley* MS., and the later MSS. whose finding has been chronicled in *A.Q.C.*, it is becoming clear that there were written records of esoteric working, and that it is necessary to distinguish these from the Old Charges which dealt chiefly with the historical and administrative sides of the Craft, and in regard to which Begemann's remarks are apt. But it may be that Anderson was referring to Rituals, and in that case what he stated to have occurred may quite well in fact have happened.

"It was agreed, in order to avoid disputes on the Annual Feast-Day, that the new Grand Master for the future shall be named and proposed to the Grand Lodge sometime before the Feast, by the present or Old Grand Master . . ."

Anderson at the end of his book prints what he calls the Old and the New Regulations, and No. xxix. and the following Regulations deal with this point. The so-called "Old" Regulations say that at the Annual Feast the Master and Wardens of the private Lodges are to consult about the new Grand Master for the ensuing year (if they had not done so the day before) and if the old Grand Master is not to be continued in office, he shall nominate his successor. The "New" Regulation xxix. sets out the resolution of 24th June, 1720 (with the customary inaccuracy).

Prima facie it is curious to find that if the resolution so-called of 1720 was passed in that year, the Old Regulation as printed in 1723 does not incorporate it, but is to a different effect and that it only, according to Anderson, becomes part of the system some years after a different regulation had been approved. Further we find that on 24th June, 1723, according to the official Minutes, Wharton is desired to name his successor (in accordance with the old Regulations), in spite of the resolution of 1720. We are therefore forced to the conclusion that Anderson's date of 1720 as given on page 111 is wrong, and that the so-called Regulation of 1720 is really only a New Regulation introduced by Anderson in 1738.[1]

"Also agreed that for the future the new Grand Master as soon as he is installed, shall have the sole power of appointing both his Grand Wardens and a Deputy Grand Master . . ." (p. 111). Old Regulation xxxv. however directs that the in-coming Grand Master shall nominate and appoint his Deputy, and also his Wardens, but that if his choice is not unanimously approved by Grand Lodge, then they shall be balloted for (p. 173). From the Minutes of 24th June, 1723 [2] we see that the nominees of the new Grand Masters for all three offices were put to the Lodge and carried, though that of Desaguliers as Deputy only by a majority. At the next meeting of 25th November, 1723, it was expressly put to Grand Lodge and carried that: (1) the Grand Master had power to appoint his Deputy; (2) Desaguliers be Deputy as from the last meeting; (3) that the Grand Wardens appointed at that meeting be confirmed in their office; and on 28th April, 1724, that the Grand Master has power to appoint his Wardens. Thus we see that Anderson's version in his history differs from that in his Regulations, and that moreover as in the preceding quotation he has again antedated events.

[1] I have argued in this from Anderson's own statements and from the subsequent official Minutes. But as we have only Anderson's account of Payne's Old Regulations, which he admits he has recast, the whole matter is very doubtful.
[2] *Q.C.A.*, x., 51-2.

25th March, 1721. "Payne Grand Master observing the number of Lodges to encrease" (p. 112). This passage Begemann alleges is another case of ante-dating. He quotes Stukeley's diary under date 6th January, 1721, when the latter was made a Freemason,[1] and the Doctor's comment, "I was the first person made a free mason in London for many years. We had great difficulty to find members enough to perform the ceremony. Immediately after that it took a run, and ran itself out of breath through the folly of the members,"[2] and also his entry in the third person, "that his curiosity led him to be initiated into the mysteries of Masonry suspecting it to be the remains of the mysteries of the Ancients, when with difficulty a number sufficient was to be found in all London. After this it became a public fashion not only spread over Britain and Ireland, but all Europe."[3] This passage it must be added is, from what we know of the contemporary conditions of the Craft, not altogether clear in its implications. It is scarcely to be taken literally for there must have been in London several Lodges and an appreciable, if an uncertain, number of Masons. It is likely that what Stukeley means is that there could only with difficulty be collected a sufficient number of his own class or that there was a difficulty in assembling a quorum of those qualified to attend the ceremony which we now know as the Third Degree.

Begemann[4] finds it hard to believe that as early as March 25th, 1721, there had been a noticeable increase of Lodges and is doubtful whether the Duke of Montagu was admitted as early as this, since he thinks that his initiation would have been chronicled in the Press, as was his installation on the 24th June. He thinks that Montagu had been initiated only a very short time before his installation. I suggest that here Begemann presses Anderson too hardly. Stukeley says that after 6th January, Freemasonry immediately took a run, and in view of this, and of its becoming "a public fashion," it is not unlikely that enough had occurred in the space of twelve weeks to bring about a considerable increase in the number of members of the Craft, although perhaps not to increase the number of Lodges. No doubt the installation of the Duke of Montagu increased the popularity of the Craft, but it is very probable that the admission of Montagu was also a result as well as a cause of that popularity.

Under date the 24th June, 1721, Anderson gives a long account of a meeting of Grand Lodge, several passages of which are open to comment (pp. 112-3): He says that they made some new brothers including Lord Stanhope. Stukeley in his Diary[5] under the same date notes that the "Masons had a dinner at Stationers Hall, present, Duke of Montague, Lord Herbert, Lord Stanhope, Sir Andrew Fountain etc. etc. Dr. Desaguliers pronounc'd an oration." Now had these persons been initiated at that meeting it is almost certain that Stukeley would have mentioned the fact. Moreover, we have no other instance of an initiation being performed at a Grand Lodge instead of a Private Lodge (the Occasional Lodge of 5th November, 1737, which Anderson mentions, could hardly have been a meeting of Grand Lodge). Anderson further states that the Grand Officers, Past Grand Officers and Master and Wardens met the Grand Master elect at the King's Arms Tavern and marched on foot to Stationer's Hall, and that the old Grand Master made the first and the new Grand Master made the second procession round the hall. In regard to this, as Begemann points out,[6] this statement is inadmissible for two reasons; firstly, because according to the Minutes of Grand Lodge the earliest occasion on which a procession was combined with the formal fetching of the Grand Master was the Duke of Norfolk's installation in 1730, and, secondly, because although the holding of the Feast is mentioned in the contemporary newspapers, there is no mention of a procession which, had it in fact taken place, must have drawn to itself much attention. Further, the processions of the outgoing and incoming Grand Masters round the

---

[1] Diary, i., 62.
[2] Diary, i., 122.
[3] Diary, i., 51.
[4] op. cit., ii., 68.
[5] Diary i., 64.
[6] op. cit., ii., 50.

Hall are not referred to in the Minutes until several years later, and the old Regulations dealing with the Installation made no allusion to any procession. Here again we have Anderson antedating.

With the mention of the name of the Duke of Wharton, we enter upon a famous episode in the history of Grand Lodge, and as it is also one with which Anderson's veracity, or at least his credibility, is closely connected, it is here necessary briefly to summarise the matter, referring those interested for a full treatment to Bro. Gould's paper (*A.Q.C.*, viii., pp. 114 ff).

Our author tells us that "Grand Master Montagu's Good Government inclin'd the better sort to continue him in the chair for another year [he had occupied it from June, 1721, to June, 1722]; and therefore they delayed to prepare the feast.

"But Philip Duke of Wharton lately made a Brother, though not the Master of a Lodge, being ambitious of the chair, got a number of others to meet him at Stationer's Hall, 24th June, 1722, and having no Grand Officers, they put in the chair the oldest Master Mason (who was not the present Master of a Lodge, also irregular) and without the usual decent ceremonials, the said old Mason proclaimed aloud Philip Wharton Duke of Wharton Grand Master of Masons and Mr. Joshua Timson, Blacksmith } Grand Wardens, but his Grace appointed Mr. William Hawkins, Mason } no deputy, nor was the Lodge opened and closed in due form.

"Therefore the noble Brothers, and all those that would not countenance irregularities, disown'd Wharton's authority, till worthy Brother Montagu healed the breach of harmony by summoning the Grand Lodge to meet on the 17th January, 1722/3," when on his promising to be true and faithful, he was proclaimed Grand Master.

Now in contradiction of Anderson's account there are the following facts:—

1. Stukeley's Diary under date May 25th, 1722, notes that he "met Duke of Queensborough, Lord Dumbarton, Hinchinbroke, etc., at Fountain Tavern Lodge to consider of Feast on St. Johns."

2. The public Press contained announcements of the forthcoming Feast of the Freemasons.

3. The 24th June, 1722, fell on a Sunday, and the Feast was accordingly held on Monday, 25th.

4. The Press records the Election of the Duke of Wharton either unanimously or without referring to any dissent.

5. The author of *The Praise of Drunkenness*, in an account referring probably to the Feast of June, 1722, gives no colour to any suggestion that the installation was without the usual decent ceremonies.

6. Stukeley's mention under date 3rd November, 1722, of the Duke of Wharton and Lord Dalkeith (who in fact succeeded Wharton as Grand Master) visiting his Lodge at the Fountain, shows that at least one of the "noble Brothers" had not "disown'd" Wharton's authority.

7. Desaguliers is mentioned by the *Daily Post* of 27th June, 1722, as having been chosen Deputy Grand Master, and had in fact signed the Dedication of the first edition of the *Book of Constitutions* as Deputy Grand Master, before it was presented to Grand Lodge in January, 1723, and the Approbation of the 17th January, 1722/3, is signed by Wharton as Grand Master and Desaguliers as Deputy, while the Frontispiece shows Wharton and a clergyman (presumably Desaguliers) in those respective positions.

In face of these matters of disproof it seems clear that Anderson was wrong in his account of the proceedings. But there are certain newspaper extracts given by the late Bro. Robbins (*A.Q.C.*, xxii., 67 ff) which tend to show conclusively that there were some discussions among the Masons, but what they were in effect is not clear. We leave the subject with an uneasy suspicion, not for the first time, that although our author has made an untrustworthy entry in his chronicle, although his facts are wrong, yet he is probably dealing with an actual occurrence, even though his method of treatment helps us little in determining its circumstances. However distorted by Anderson's prejudice, fancy, or faulty memory, we still have the smoke, and must presume the fire.

Anderson's account of the meeting of 25th April, 1723, again contains many statements open to challenge. He begins by stating that the Lodge was opened in ample form; as has been said before that was a distinction known at that date only to Anderson himself. Then according to his story there being no Secretary yet appointed (this is probably true, as the first Minute of Grand Lodge informs us that Cowper was not appointed until 24th June, 1723) Grand Warden Anderson called the roll. I have already discussed his claim to be Grand Warden; whether he called the roll may or may not be true—some have doubted it. Then Wharton "proposed for his successor the Earl of Dalkeith (now Duke of Buckleugh) Master of a Lodge, who was unanimously approv'd and duly saluted as Grand Master Elect." But the Minutes of 24th June, 1723, inform us "Then the Grand Master [Wharton] being desired to name his successor and declining to do so, but referring the nomination to the Lodge The Right Honourable the Earl of Dalkeith was proposed to be put in nomination as Grand Master for the year ensuing . . . accordingly the Earl of Dalkeith was agreed to be put in nomination as Grand Master for the ensuing year. The Lodge was also acquainted that (in case of his election) he had nominated D^r. Desaguliers for his Deputy." Desaguliers' appointment as Deputy was then put to Grand Lodge and carried by a majority of one. After dinner Dalkeith was declared Grand Master, and Wharton stating that he had doubts about the number on the division for Deputy proposed that this question be again put, and he and several others withdrew as voting against Desaguliers. In their absence, a written authority from Dalkeith was produced to the effect *inter alia* that he appointed Desaguliers his Deputy, and protest was made on his behalf and on that of the whole fraternity against Wharton's proceedings. On Wharton's return and his being made acquainted with what had taken place during his absence, "the late Grand Master went away from the Hall without any ceremony." If Wharton declined to name his successor in June it is not likely that, as reported by Anderson, he had proposed Dalkeith in April. But further let us see what is Anderson's version of the proceedings in June of which we have just given the official account. He states that Wharton came into the Lodge Room with his Deputy and Wardens and sent for the Masters and Wardens of Lodges and formed Grand Lodge. It was then pointed out to him by some that as Dalkeith was still in Scotland, he should name another successor, but Dalkeith's Wardens declared that he would soon be returning. Then they adjourned to dinner, and afterwards Wharton made the first procession round the tables and proclaimed Dalkeith Grand Master, the Deputy and Grand Wardens being appointed in the latter's name. Grand Warden Sorell was then ordered to close the Lodge. Not a word to suggest the dispute about Desaguliers, and Wharton's resentment. The probably unveracious statement of the Grand Warden's closing the Lodge (there is no mention whatsoever of any such procedure in any of the Minutes) fittingly closes Anderson's achievement in suppressing the true and suggesting and even expressing the false. Anderson's offence is made the more rank by the fact that we chance to have a letter written by him to the Duke of Montagu on the 29th June, 1723, which includes the following passage:—" Your Grace's company would have been useful, because, though with unanimity they chose the Earl of Dalkeith the Grand Master, represented by his proxy, the D[u]ke of W[harto]n endeavoured to divide us against Dr. Desaguliers (whom the Earl named for Deputy before his Lordship left London), according to a concert of the said D[u]ke and some he had persuaded that morning to join him; nor will the affair be well adjusted until the present Grand Master comes to London." [1]

Under date the 24th June, 1725, Anderson records a meeting (during Richmond's Grand Mastership) saying that the Grand Wardens were continued 6 months longer (p. 119). The Minutes state that Martin Folkes, Deputy Grand Master, was present (suggesting inferentially that the Grand Master was absent) and that Desaguliers declared for the Grand Master that "it was his Grace's pleasure to continue the Deputy and Grand Wardens in office for the next 6 months" (*Q.C.A.*, x., 62). The hitherto unsuspected explanation of this is to be found in a letter from Richmond to Folkes, dated 27th June, 1725, which is now available in its original form since the recent dispersal of the Folkes Correspondence [2] and which is given only in an incomplete version on page 120 of the present Duke of Richmond's *A Duke and His Friends*, in which the Grand Master apologises to Folkes for the fact that " St. John's Day, being the *great and important day*, was entirely out of my head, so much that I have never since cast an eye upon the report of the Committee upon charity; which I ought to have returned a week ago," that is, Richmond had apparently forgotten to attend Grand Lodge, and Folkes and Desaguliers had to cover his absence as best they could.

A few minor errors of Anderson's may be mentioned parenthetically. Under date the 24th June, 1724, George Payne and Francis Sorell are given as Grand Wardens (p. 118), whereas the Minutes of Grand Lodge gives them in the reverse order.[3] In his account of the procession of the 29th January, 1730 (p. 126), he gives the names of several Grand Masters present, together with those of Desaguliers, Payne, and Sayer. The Minutes of Grand Lodge omit the last three,[4] and if only by reason of the fact that the unfortunate Sayer's mention in the Minutes is only for the recording of disciplinary or charitable action, there is no reason to think that Anderson here again was other than inaccurate. He records under date the 27th March, 1731, the appointment of Brother George Moody [5] as Sword-Bearer (p. 128). But on the 29th May, 1733, the Minutes [6] stated that a memorial on behalf of the Master of the Lodge at St. Paul's Head in Ludgate Street relating to his carrying the Grand Sword at the annual feast being offered to be read, the Deputy Grand Master replied that the Grand-Sword Bearer being an officer of Grand Lodge was therefore to be appointed by the Grand Master, and that the then Grand Master had appointed Moody to that office, and that Brother is in fact given as Sword-Bearer in the Minutes of the following meeting. Anderson therefore is some two years out in his dates. Begemann,[7] who points out this mistake, then goes on to say: " In his description of the procession of 29th January 1729/30 he describes the Book of Constitutions as carried by the Master of the Senior Lodge in contradiction of the minutes themselves "; but Begemann's attempted correction is itself wrong, as the Minutes clearly state "The Book of Constitutions carried on the velvet cushion by the Master of the Senior Lodge." Either Begemann had overlooked this point or wishing to challenge Anderson's account of his alleged procession on 24th June, 1724 (which the Minutes of that date justify his doing), he has

---

[1] *A.Q.C.*, xii., 106.
[2] *A.Q.C.*, xliii., 255.
[3] *Q.C.A.*, x., 58.
[4] *Q.C.A.*, x., 116.
[5] Anderson had previously mentioned (p. 127) under date the 29th January, 1730/1, that Moody, the King's Sword-Cutler, had been ordered to engrave the scabbard of the sword of Gustavus Adolphus.
[6] *Q.C.A.*, x., 229-31.
[7] *op. cit.*, i., 444 2.

mistakenly given the wrong date 1729/30, instead of 1724. In effect, what Anderson did was to give an account of a procession in 1729/30 correctly, but also and incorrectly to give one as having taken place in 1724.

There are some general points arising out of Anderson's treatment of contemporary history which require some mention. Begemann[1] deals at length with the figures of Lodges given for the earlier years which by reason of the regular order of their progress, and for other reasons, he finds suspicious, i.e., 12, 16, 20, 24. Bro. Vibert has dealt with the point in his paper to which I have referred,[2] so that it is not necessary again to consider it in detail. He points out in Anderson's favour that with regard to the critical date 1722, Begemann's estimate does not greatly differ from our author's, and that even Begemann's estimate which is based on the list of Lodges signing the approbation of the 1723 edition is not necessarily reliable since that list may not be a chronological one. Briefly to summarise the position, Anderson's figures may be somewhat round, but they are possible, at any rate as a rough estimate; Begemann's objections are not very firmly based, and even if successfully upheld, would not greatly affect Anderson's version at the critical date.

If we examine the dates of the meetings of Grand Lodge as given in the *Book of Constitutions* for its quarterly assemblies from 1720 until June, 1722, we find them to be as follows:—

24th June 1720.   27th December 1720.   25th March 1721.
24th June 1721.   29th September 1721. 27th December 1721,
25th March 1722. 24th June 1722.

That is, all the meetings given above were held either on the legal quarter-days or on the 27th December, St. John the Evangelist's Day, which was for a time the date of the yearly assembly of the Scottish Lodges, and of those in the North of England. But Begemann[3] points out that an analysis of the dates of meetings as given in the official Minutes shows that on very few occasions did Grand Lodge meet on the quarter day, and that although from 1725-1729 (with one exception) it met on 27th December, yet it did not do so previous to the former year. Moreover, we ought to note a fondness for the 27th December which Anderson has shown in his historical portion. It will be recollected that to that date have been rather arbitrarily assigned by him both Queen Elizabeth's attack on the Order in 1561 and the Earl of St. Alban's Grand Lodge of 1663. (Although Roberts dates the general Assembly as the 8th December.) With regard to the alleged meeting of 27th December, 1721, at which Grand Master Montagu is stated to have appointed "14 learned Brothers" to examine and report on Anderson's MS., and which "was made very entertaining by the lectures of some old Masons," Stukeley[4] has the following notice in his Diary under that date: "We met at the Fountain Tavern Strand and by consent of Grand master present, Dr. Beal [Deputy Grand Master] constituted a new Lodge there, where I was chose Master:" If Stukeley's entry is correct—and there is no reason in the circumstances to doubt it—it is scarcely likely that both the Grand Master and his Deputy would have arranged to attend the consecration of a private Lodge on the day of meeting of Grand Lodge, going from one to the other.

Anderson's historical portion makes use of two famous phrases for which Grand Lodge Minutes afford no authority, which were probably his own invention, and of which one at any rate has been adopted by the Craft, and the other by the 'side' degrees:—

"Brother Payne having invested his Grace's Worship with the Ensigns and Badges of his office and authority, install'd him in Solomon's chair . . . ." 1721, p. 113.

[1] op. cit., ii., 65, et. sqq.
[2] A.Q.C., xxxvi., 64-6.
[3] op. cit., ii., 64.
[4] Diary, i., 60.

"The Duke [of Richmond and Lennox] having bow'd to the Assembly, Brother Dalkeith invested him with the proper Ensigns and Badges of his office and authority, install'd him in Solomon's Chair . . ." 1724, p. 118.

"and having invested him [i.e., the Duke of Norfolk] and install'd him in Solomon's Chair." 1729/30, p. 126.

"John Beal, M.D. as his Deputy Grand Master, whom Brother Payne invested, and install'd him in Hiram Abbiff's chair . . ." 1721, p. 113.

"Martin Folkes, Esq. his Deputy Grand Master invested and install'd by the last Deputy in the Chair of Hiram Abbif." 1724, p. 118.

I do not know of any instance of earlier references to these Chairs, and if there is none, Anderson's references are of considerable interest in view of the spread of what we know as the Third Degree.

With regard to the meeting of the 27th November, 1725, Anderson in the historical portion gives it a very short notice, merely mentioning that Lord Paisley was proposed as the new Grand Master, and that "no Stewards being appointed," Brother Heidegger was desired to prepare the feast (p. 119). As a matter of fact, the meeting according to the Minutes[1] was of considerable importance as Grand Lodge then dealt with the arrangements for the Festival, the restoration to private Lodges of the power to make "Masters," the Committee for Charity, and the giving of security by the Grand Treasurer; and though many of these points are dealt with by Anderson in the administrative portion of his Book, we feel that some reference to them might have been made in the historical portion. There is no reference in the Minutes to Heidegger under the date given, but at the next meeting it is recorded that the healths were drunk of the Grand Steward J. J. Heidegger and his two Deputies, Potter and Lambert. Anderson gives the meeting of the 27th December, 1728, as taking place at Mercer's Hall (p. 123); the Minutes[2] as at Stationer's Hall—Preston of course copies the former. Anderson records under date the 25th November, 1729, that Kingston G.M. presented several articles of masonic furniture, a "curious pedestal," a cushion for its top, and a velvet bag and a badge of two gold pens for the Secretary. It is somewhat strange that although mention is made in the Minutes both of the Duke of Norfolk's gifts and of the famous consignment of arrack, Lord Kingston's generosity passed apparently unregarded therein: one wonders whether there is any trace of the gifts in the other records of Grand Lodge. Anderson's accounts of the meetings of the 28th August and the 15th December, 1730 (p. 127), both very short in view of the many matters which the Grand Lodge Minutes show to have been discussed there, make no mention of the attacks on and exposures of Masonry which had been published. Desaguliers at the August meeting[3] had stood up and taking notice of a certain exposure had "recommended several things to the consideration of Grand Lodge" for preventing the admission of false brethren into Lodges, and Blackerby, Deputy Grand Master "seconded the Doctor and proposed several rules to the Grand Lodge to be observed in their respective Lodges for their security against all open and Secret Enemies to the Craft." In December[4] Blackerby took notice of Prichard's *Masonry Dissected* and condemned it, proposing that measures should be taken for the strict vouching of any persons visiting a Lodge. It is a remarkable fact that Anderson does not interrupt what by this time has become a perfunctory abstract of Grand Lodge meetings to deal with or even to mention these facts. It cannot be accounted unto him for righteousness that when it comes to matters which in the opinions of many led to a considerable alteration in the Masonic Secrets he apparently ignores them, and this in spite of the fact that at the August meeting he was actually present and acting as Senior Grand Warden.

[1] Q.C.A., x., 63 ff.
[2] Q.C.A., x., 93.
[4] Q.C.A., x., 125 ff.
[3] Q.C.A., x., 131 ff.

Anderson says that the Duke of Lorraine (afterwards husband of Maria Theresa and Emperor of Germany) was made an Enter'd Prentice and Fellow Craft at the Hague, and then he adds, putting this second statement between circumstances related under date respectively the 14th of May and the 24th of June, 1731, that he was made a Master Mason at Walpole's "house of Houghton-Hall in Norfolk," at an Occasional Lodge, by Lovel, Grand Master. According to Bro. Daynes, the Duke did not arrive in England until October and he did not got to Houghton until November. Bro. Daynes was of the opinion that Desaguliers conferred all three degrees at the Hague and that the Royal Mason was not raised at Houghton. Anderson, probably having in mind the introduction into Free Masonry of the Prince of Wales, has either assimilated or confused the two incidents.

VI. LIST OF GRAND MASTERS OR PATRONS OF THE FREE MASONS IN ENGLAND.

We have already seen that what Anderson was desired to do by Grand Lodge was "to print the names . . . of all the Grand Masters that could be collected from the beginning of time, together with a list of the names of all Deputy Grand Masters, Grand Wardens, and the Brethren that have served the Craft in quality of Stewards."[1] These recommendations he cannot be said to have carried out; his sins were both positive and negative. Grand Lodge had made no mention of patrons in its instructions, but Anderson has, in form at least, extended those instructions, although in spite of not being told to do so, he has limited the list to England. That he has extended them in spirit is not so clear. A body which eighteen years after the formation of Grand Lodge and the first use of the term Grand Master asks an author to produce a list of all the Grand Masters who can be "collected from the beginning of time" is to all intents and purposes asking to be supplied with some such fantastic mixture of history and legend, fact and fiction, misnomer and anachronism as that which Anderson so obligingly compiled.

A minor fault of Anderson's is that though he has in the historical portion mentioned the other Grand Officers, yet he has compiled no such list of them as Grand Lodge had ordered him to do.

There is no occasion to deal in detail with the list given on pp. 140-142. Some of the names have been dealt with in considering the historical portion. Suffice it to say, that the list (except of course from 1717) is chiefly one of those whom either history or legend have handed down as patrons of the building art, together with a few craftsmen whose connection with anything like Freemasonry in the modern sense is far from being established.

Although the *Constitutions* of Anderson as has been said found general acceptance, yet even from early days there was an under-current of objection. As far back as the *Briscoe* MS. its author takes serious objection to Anderson's history, points out that he makes the term Freemasonry cover too wide a ground, and as a matter of historical detail points out that there is no record of either Charles II. or William III. having been Freemasons.

And Dermott, in the *Ahiman Rezon* states his view as follows:—

"Query, whether such histories are of any use in the secret mysteries of the craft" p. i.

". . . I immediately fancied myself an Historian, and intended to trace Masonry, not only to Adam, in his sylvan lodge in Paradise, but to give some account of the craft even before the Creation. And (as a foundation) I placed the following works round about me, so as to be convenient to have

---

[1] *Q.C.A.*, x., 251.

recourse to them as occasion should require, viz: Doctor Anderson . . . immediately before me.

". . . I tied up in the public *Advertiser* of Friday, October 19, 1753, and threw them under the table" p. ii.

VII. THE OLD CHARGES.

It is proposed only to deal here with the differences between these as given in 1723 and in 1738.

In view of the changes which have taken place in the head-lines, for purposes of comparison I set out those in the two editions and trace the subsequent changes.

First Edition: "The | Charges | of a | Free-Mason, | extracted from | the ancient Records of Lodges | beyond Sea, and of those in England, Scotland, | and Ireland, for the use of the Lodges in London : | to be read | at the making of New Brethren, or when the | Master shall order it."

Second Edition: "The old | Charges | of the | Free and Accepted Masons, | collected by the author from their old Records, at the | Command of the Grand Master the present Duke of | Montagu.

"Approved by the Grand Lodge, and order'd to be printed in | the first Edition of the Book of Constitutions on 25 March 1722."

1756 Edition as in 1738, save that the words "by the author" and "the present Duke of Montagu" are omitted.

1767 Edition. Same as in 1756.

1784 Edition has merely "Antient Charges : | Collected from Old Records."

1815 and 1819 Editions return to a slightly modified form of the 1723 edition :—

"The | Charges | of a | Free-Mason | extracted from | the Antient Records of Lodges beyond Sea | and of those in | England, Scotland, and Ireland | For the Use of Lodges | To be read | at the making of New Brethren, or when | the Master shall order it.

"Now republished by Order of the Grand Lodge."

All the subsequent editions follow the 1819 save that that of 1827 is the only one of them to have the words "Now republished [etc.]" That of 1841 and its successors have merely "published." The expression "old" used in connection with the Charges in 1738 and ever afterwards is something of a misnomer. In the form given they were no older than the first edition, and are in fact nothing more than Anderson's version of the genuine "Old Charges." Each of his two versions, the 1723 and 1738 contains the same seven charges, the "Finally" of the earlier being split up, part becoming a (new) Section Seven of the Sixth Charge, and part a separately numbered and headed Charge "Concerning Law-suits" in the later, but the wording and arrangement are altered in many places.

We have already discussed the religious question arising out of the First Charge, and suggested an origin for the expression Noachida, occurring in the later edition. The statement that in ancient times Masons were charged in every country to be of the religion of that country is amended to Christian Masons complying with the Christian usages. Begemann [1] sees in this only one more of Anderson's myths, since the latter knew no more of foreign Masonry than was to be found in the old texts, or than he had heard of its spread since 1723. He sees in the alteration only a recognition of the practice which had grown up of

---

[1] *op. cit.*, ii., 206.

admitting non-Christians. With regard to the reference to the "3 great Articles of Noah" which follows, the same authority, working from the reference to Brotherly Love or Love and Friendship in both editions, the emphasis laid on Charity in early Freemasonry, and the frequent references to Truth, and quoting "The Grand Mystery of Free-Masons Discovered" of 1724, and Drake's Oration of 1726, considers these to be the famous Masonic triad of Brotherly Love, Relief and Truth.

Bro. Vibert's view [1]— a much simpler one—is that we can deduce from Anderson's text "that there was a stock phrase in use in the Lodges; the mason is to be a good man and true and strictly to obey the moral law, and that it is this sentence which is an echo of the text in Genesis 'Noah was a just man and perfect and walked with God' that constituted the Grand Articles of Noah." I confess I prefer this explanation.

Bro. Crawley [2] says that "the subsequent modifications of their language, particularly in that of the Second Charge will serve as an index to the spirit that actuated the Brotherhood. The Grand Lodge of England (Moderns) abandoned the version of 1738 throughout the remainder of the century, and reverted to the version of 1723, which formed the groundwork of the Irish version of 1730. The Grand Lodge of Ireland on the other hand, abandoned the original version of 1730 and adopted, in 1751, Anderson's later version of 1738. This, in its turn, entailed the adoption of the Irish form by the Grand Lodge of the Antients, whose *Ahiman Rezon* follows the Irish *Book of Constitutions* of 1751. The first two editions of the *Ahiman Rezon* reproduced the Charge without comment, but, in the third edititon, 1778, Laurence Dermott appended the following pithy note:—

> "That is, he [the Brother convicted of disloyalty] is still a Mason, though the Brethren may refuse to associate with him: However, in such case, he forfeits all benefit from the Lodge."

Immediately after the suppression of the Rebellion of 1798, the Grand Lodge of Ireland, by solemn resolution, decided to omit for the future the concluding clause of the Charge "beginning with the word 'but,' and ending with the word 'indefeasible.' This Resolution continued in force during the nineteenth century. In June, 1899, the Grand Lodge of Ireland reverted to the Old Charges which they had adopted in 1730 . . ."

In the later version the Second Charge is less than one-half that of the earlier, although the effect is much the same. In 1738 the Third Charge is much extended on the whole, though some portion of the earlier version is dropped. The latter had spoken of particular and general Lodges, which would be best understood by attendance, "and by the Regulations of the general or grand Lodge hereunto annexed"; the former omits the reference to general lodges. The 1738 version is much more operative in character. To the qualifications are added, "hail and sound, not deformed or dismember'd at the time of their making . . . no eunuch," and then follows a new paragraph, still with a reminiscence of the old operatives, and a not unskilful mingling of operative and speculative: "When men of quality, eminence, wealth and learning apply to be made, they are to be respectfully accepted, after due examination: For such often prove good lords (or founders) of work, and will not employ cowans when true Masons can be had; they also make the best officers of Lodges, and the best designers, to the honour and strength of the Lodge: Nay, from among them, the Fraternity can have a noble Grand Master. But those Brethren are equally subject to the Charges and Regulations, except in what more immediately concerns operative Masons."

---

[1] Somerset M.L. *Trans.*, 1927, 110-1.
[2] *A.Q.C.*, xxiv., 56.

The Fourth Charge is half as long again in 1723 as in 1738. A comparison of the two versions is interesting as showing the now established position of the Master Mason. Previously Anderson had spoken of a candidate becoming an Apprentice and then a Fellow-Craft, so that if qualified he may be capable in succession of becoming Warden and then Master of a private Lodge, and Grand Warden and, if worthy, Grand Master. He could not become a Warden until he had been a Fellow-Craft, Master until he had been Warden, nor Grand Master until he had been Master. Anderson now says that a Prentice may when of age and expert, become an Enter'd Prentice and on "due improvements" a Fellow-Craft and Master Mason; the Wardens are chosen from among the Master-Masons, and (save in extraordinary cases) every Master must have served as Warden and every Grand Warden as Master. Whereas in 1723, as Anderson states, a Grand Master must have been a Fellow Craft before election and of noble or gentle birth or of personal distinction, in 1738 it is laid down that he must have served as Master of a Lodge. But Anderson's statements with regard to the necessary qualifications for a Master Mason seem not altogether borne out by certain facts we know of. Hughan in *The Origin of the English Rite*, p. 58, says that "There was a disinclination to proceed to the Third Degree manifested by many brethren during the early part of the 18th century, and there seems to have been some little truth, at least, in the assertion made in 1730: 'There is not one Mason in a hundred that will be at the expense to pass the Master's part.' As late as 1752, when the first Provincial Grand Master of Cornwall was installed, the Brother who presided was only a Fellow Craft." Further to our argument, Hughan states (p. 46) that "The two Wardens who were 'passed' as Masters in 1729, had been elected as Wardens previously," so the "Third" was not a prerequisite for office at that time, neither was it for years later, many brethren being content with their status as Fellow Crafts (p. 48). At a lodge meeting on the 3rd December, 1734, Sir Cecil Wray was re-elected Master and nominated his Wardens, but as these and several other Brethren worthy of the Master's degree had not been called thereto, Wray directed that a Lodge of Masters should be held on the 30th inst. at which they were admitted.

The Fifth Charge differs in the two versions, but chiefly in the recognition in the later of the trigadal system, and in the use of new Masonic terms which have since become part and parcel of the Craft. For "the most expert of the Fellow-Craftsmen" from whom the Master is to be chosen, we have "a Master Mason"; "nor shall Free Masons work with those that are not free" becomes "Free and Accepted Masons shall not allow Cowans to work with them."

In the Sixth Charge the second paragraph of the first section is abbreviated in 1738, but on the other hand the second half of the second Section of 1723 is cut off and made a third paragraph to the first Section of 1738. In both editions we get a reference to { The Catholic religion above-mentioned / the oldest Catholic religion above hinted, *i.e.*, to "that Religion in which all men agree" of the First Charge. Sections three to six are substantially the same in both, but differ in phraseology and in length.

The forbidding of the forcing a Brother to eat or drink beyond his inclination in Section two gives Anderson an opportunity of referring it to "the Old Regulation of King Ahasuerus" quoted by him from the first chapter of the Book of Esther on page 24 of the historical portion.

As has been stated, the concluding paragraph of the 1723 version is split up. The exhortation to observe the Charges which begins it is taken out and made the conclusion in 1738, more logically, perhaps. The next portion becomes Section seven of the Sixth Charge, and the remainder is divided and becomes two paragraphs of a new Seventh Charge—in most cases, as we might expect, with many verbal alterations.

VIII. THE ANTIENT MANNER OF CONSTITUTING A LODGE.

As the 1738 version of this does not greatly differ from that of 1723, and as the "Manner" has been fully treated in Bro. Vibert's paper,[1] there is little that it is necessary to say here. With regard to the later edition he points out that the reference to Wharton in the heading is now omitted, not to be included again until the first post-Union edition in 1815. It is noteworthy that although the Charges, as has been pointed out, show signs of the trigadal system, yet this portion still retains the Fellow-Craft's as, so to speak, the qualifying degree for constitution and installation. Bro. Vibert states that neither "in the Manner nor in the Regulations is it anywhere laid down that the Master shall have served the office of Warden." This is as it stands correct, but one might usefully add that in the Fourth Charge—1723 edition (p. 52)—it is stated that a Brother cannot be a Master until he has acted as a Warden, and in the 1738 edition (p. 145) this is repeated, subject to exception in "extraordinary cases," or when "a Lodge is to be formed where none can be had," for then three mere Master Masons may be constituted Master and Wardens of the new Lodge.

The later edition has a new conclusion (p. 151): "This is the sum, but not the whole ceremonial by far; which the Grand Officers can extend or abridge at pleasure, explaining things that are not fit to be written: though none but those that have acted as Grand Officers can accurately go through all the several parts and usages of a new Constitution in the just solemnity."

This is one of those rather cryptic observations in which Anderson seems occasionally to delight. Bro. Speth[2] has however accepted it as conclusive evidence of a ceremonial and held that to doubt the ceremony of Constitution is "to cast a doubt on the origin of our present system."

IX. THE GENERAL REGULATIONS.

In view of the lengthy treatment which the earlier version has received at the hands of Bro. Vibert,[3] all that need be done here is to compare the version given in 1738 with that given in 1723.

Once again we see considerable verbal and indeed substantial changes in the headings of the two versions. In particular the later omits the limiting phrase "for the use of the Lodges in and about Westminster" in view of the great extension of the Craft that had taken place meanwhile. Anderson's object was to set out the Old Regulations and to add in a distinct opposite column, as he says, "the New Regulations, or the alterations, improvements and explications of the Old, made by several Grand Lodges, since the first edition." Now the left-hand column should according to this be a verbatim reprint of those published in 1723, but so far from this being the case, throughout the whole thirty-nine I have found only one instance, that of No. 30, where there has not been some variation, even if often only a slight one, between the original and what in effect purports to be an exact reproduction. Moreover, the so-called "New Regulations" are not regulations at all. The Old Regulations were a code, or at least a digest. The New are little more than a jumble of resolutions of Grand Lodge (sometimes appositely quoted in extension, qualification, or amendment of the Old, and sometimes not), foot-notes and pious hopes, their insertion in many cases obviously dictated by the typographical necessity of placing some attempt at a New Regulation in the right-hand column opposite to one of the "Old."

In an Appendix I have brought together the more important changes introduced by Anderson in his 1738 version of the "Old Regulations."

[1] *A.Q.C.*, xxxvi., 62-3.
[2] *A.Q.C.*, viii., 214.
[3] *A.Q.C.*, xxxv., 56-62.

We have now within the limits of our space to consider the alleged "New Regulations."

Old Regulation One had laid it down that the Grand Master had a full right to preside at a private Lodge at which he was present, but that if the Grand Wardens were also present he need not ask them to act as Werdans, but might ask the Wardens of the Lodge or any other Master-Masons: in 1738 Anderson amends this by saying that the Grand Wardens must act, if present. In view of the scantiness of the early Minutes of private Lodges it is difficult to find out exactly what the practice was, but I shall quote two instances which may guide us in our conclusion. On 24th June, 1730, the Duke of Norfolk, Grand Master, and his officers attended the Lodge of Antiquity,[1] and "the Grand Master was received with the Honors of Masonry and every respect shewn to him and his company by the Right Worshipful Master in the chair *who presided during the whole evening.*" (The italics are mine.) Bro. Dixon, in the extracts from the Minutes of Lodge No. 28 given in his *History of Freemasonry in Lincolnshire* (p. 13), quotes the following passage:—"There were present also the Rt. Worshpl. Sr. Cecil Wray Bart. late Deputy Grand Master and the Rt. Honble the Lord Loudon Grand Master did this Lodge the Honour of a visit and they favoured the Society with their company to midnight when the Lodge was closed by the officers of the Lodge." We see that in neither of these cases did the Grand Officers apparently occupy their corresponding chairs in the private Lodge.

It would appear that the procedure varied according to whether or not the visit was "in form." Although it is much later than the period under consideration, an extract from a letter of Dr. Manningham, Deputy Grand Master, under date the 13th July, 1757,[2] seems to show the distinction: "Whenever they [*i.e.*, the Grand Master or Deputy Grand Master] honour a private Lodge with a visit, the Master of such Lodge immediately resigns the chair to them, if they choose to accept it, for they have votes and preside over all Lodges by Virtue of their high Office; when they visit in Form, they always take the chair, but if the visit is private, they accept or refuse it as they think proper; the Grand Wardens never act as Grand Wardens, but when the Grand Master or his Deputy presides." It should be borne in mind that at the time Manningham gave his ruling, the only written authority of Grand Lodge governing the point was a textual re-enactment of Anderson's Old and New Regulations.

In an addition to the Second Regulation, it is noted in the margin "but was neglected to be recorded"; and with this we can compare the entry as part of New Regulation xiii., "tho' forgotten to be recorded in the Grand Lodge Book"—25th November, 1723. This entry rather sets one wondering "where." There are no Minutes existing before 24th June, 1723, on which date William Cowper was appointed apparently the first Secretary. Were there in fact rough notes of the meetings in existence before this date from which Anderson obtained his account of the earlier meetings, or did he rely on his own and his friends' recollection, and if so why does he single out this particular item as omitted from the record? And were they not signed at the time? Bros. Lane[3] and Rylands[4] think it probable there were lists and notes accessible to Anderson or he may have used the recollections of his friends.

In the Third Regulation it is stated that during the Mastership of Dalkeith (1723-4) "a list of all the Lodges was engraven by Brother John Pyne in a very small volume." Now Bro. Lane[5] says that "the other List of 1723 was engraved, and was, probably, the first ever published; but no copy is known to be in

---

[1] W. H. Rylands: *History of the Lodge of Antiquity*, i., 11.
[2] *A.Q.C.*, v., 110.
[3] *Handy Book to List of Lodges*, pp. 3 and 4.
[4] *History of Lodge of Antiquity*, i., 37.
[5] *Handy Book to List of Lodges*, p. 5.

existence; for that in Grand Lodge, generally designated as of the year 1723, is actually a List of 1724 . . . in five small pages . . . at the foot of the fourth page is the imprint 'Printed for and sold by Eman. Bowen, Engraver in Aldersgate Street' manifestly indicating that this was the last page of a former List issued in 1723, to which a fifth page was added in 1724." But Lane has overlooked the fact that the ornamental heading of the List contains not only the words " Earl of Dalkeith Grand Master 1723 " but also " J. Pine, Sculp." So that Anderson's statement is perfectly correct, although Bowen may have been responsible for the additional matter in 1724. After this note Anderson gives three resolutions of Grand Lodge, only one of which is even remotely connected with Old Regulation Three.

While the old Fourth Regulation deals with the age of initiation and the number of initiates to be taken at one meeting, the corresponding new Regulation deals with the Number of Lodges a Brother may belong to—quite a different topic.

It may be pointed out that certain resolutions passed by Grand Lodge on the 19th February, 1723, are separated by Anderson, part being given in New Regulation Four, part in Six, and part in Eight.

New Regulation Five is in effect but a note to Old Regulation Five.

New Regulation Six is a revision of Old Regulation Six by making complete unanimity in admitting a new member no longer necessary.

New Regulation Seven contains only a reference to the Account of the Constitution of the General Charity, and a note giving private Lodges power to make their own charitable arrangements.

New Regulation Eight consists of several resolutions concerning clandestine and irregular "makings" and Lodges which cease their functions. We may note this as evidence of the increasing authority of Grand Lodge, and call to mind prosecutions, *e.g.*, that of Sayer, for irregular or clandestine makings.

New Regulation Nine deals with the removal of Lodges, although the corresponding Old Regulation had dealt with ill-conducted and disobedient brethren, quite a different matter.

New Regulation Ten in extension of Old Regulation Ten which limited private brethren to giving their opinion in Grand Lodge through their Master and Wardens, allows them in a "sudden Emergency" to speak on leave being given.

New Regulation Eleven is merely a note to the corresponding Old Regulation.

New Regulation Twelve gives the resolutions extending membership of Grand Lodge to past Grand Officers and also certain resolutions concerning the wearing of jewels.

With regard to New Regulation Thirteen it should be said that Anderson wrongly gives the date of this important resolution as the 22nd instead of the 27th of November, 1725. He states the terms of the resolution as follows:— " The Master of a Lodge with his Wardens and a competent number of the Lodge assembled in due Form, can make Masters and Fellows at Discretion." In fact, as we learn from the reprinted Minutes of Grand Lodge, the real resolution was as follows:—" A Motion being made that such part of the 13th Article of the General Regulations relating to the making of Masters only at a Quarterly Communication, may be repealed, and that the Master of each Lodge with the consent of his Wardens and the majority of the Brethren being Masters may make Masters at their discretion. Agreed Nem Con." Anderson has therefore suggested that there were three classes of Masons instead of two and also, if we take him literally and the old and the new versions together, would have implied that previously the making not only of Masters but also of Fellow Craft was confined to Grand Lodge, which is absurd. Generally it may be said that this

400   *Transactions of the Quatuor Coronati Lodge.*

Regulation is that of the whole series which has given rise to most controversy, and, as Bro. Songhurst[1] has said, is the basis of much that has been written on the subject of degrees. He pertinently adds that the alteration, *i.e.*, the restoration of the power to private Lodges, was made immediately after certain brethren who were members of a regular Lodge as well as of the Philo Musicæ Societas had been summoned for making Masons irregularly.

Anderson states in para. 4 of the same Regulation that Grand Lodge appointed Cowper Secretary, but that since then "the new Grand Master upon his commencement appoints the Secretary, or continues him by returning him the books," but we learn from the Minutes that on 17th April, 1728,[2] the Grand Master having appointed Reid Secretary would not insist on the appointment without their unanimous consent—*i.e.*, of Grand Lodge.

In New Regulation Fourteen Anderson states that it is the right of the Grand Wardens to preside in the absence of the Grand Master and his Deputy and that it has been since found that the Old Lodges "never put in the chair the Master of a particular Lodge unless there were no Grand Wardens present." One asks where and how it had been found, and why? He apparently adopts this method of concealing his previous error or inadvertence.

In the Fifteenth Regulation it is stated that "if no former Grand Wardens are in company, the Grand Master, or he that presides, calls forth whom he pleases to act as Grand Wardens pro tempore." One rather wonders whether, if this was so, Anderson's title to Grand Wardenship was due to this rule or practice, and whether Hawkins being absent on the occasion of the meeting of 24th June, 1723, Wharton asked our author to act as the erased entry suggests.

New Regulation Sixteen is a good instance of Anderson's method and of the fact that many of these New Regulations are used merely to fill up space. It runs as follows:—

1. This was intended for the ease of the Grand Master and for the honour of the Deputy.
2. No such case has happened in our Time and all Grand Masters have governed more by Love than Power.
3. No irregular applications have been made to the Grand Master in our Time.

Even as footnotes these observations would be at best perfunctory, but to constitute them a Regulation is absurd.

The Seventeenth Regulation lays it down that if a former Grand Officer is at the moment an officer of a private Lodge, he still sits and votes in the former capacity, and can depute a member of the private Lodge to act as its representative.[3]

New Regulation Eighteen refers to the custom of appointing the Senior Grand Warden to act as Deputy if the latter is absent, and adds two perfunctory notes regarding cases of dissension between the Grand Master and his officers.

New Regulation Nineteen is a mere 'Heaven forbid' to Old Regulation Nineteen.

We are fortunate in finding confirmation of the Twentieth Regulation, which is to the effect that when the Deputy Grand Master visits a Lodge without the Grand Master, he himself acts in that capacity; the Senior Grand Warden acts as Deputy; the Junior, as the Senior. In Bro. Calvert's *History of the Old King's Arms Lodge*,[4] we find an extract from the Minutes under date

---

[1] *Q.C.A.*, x., 64 note (a).
[2] *Q.C.A.*, x., 85.
[3] There may be mentioned a case where on Lord Weymouth becoming Grand Master, while still the Master of the Old King's Arms Lodge (No. 28), the Chair of No. 28 *ipso facto* became vacant and Sir Cecil Wray was elected in his stead (*A.Q.C.*, xviii., 91).
[4] p. 6.

11th March, 1736, to the effect that a number of Grand Officers including John Ward, Deputy Grand Master, acting as Grand Master; Sir Edward Mansell, Senior Grand Warden as Deputy; Martin Clare, Junior Grand Warden as Senior Grand Warden; and Sir Robert Lawley, Master of the Steward's Lodge acting as Junior Grand Warden pro tempore " did the Society the honour of a visit in form."

New Regulation Twenty-One is an extension of Old Regulation Twenty-One. Regulation Twenty-Two states that on the 25th November, 1723, " it was ordain'd that one of the Quarterly Communications shall be held on St. John Evangelist's Day, and another on St. John Baptist's Day every year . . ." The Minutes[1] put the matter differently and say that the question was put and agreed nem. con. " Whether the Master and Wardens of the several Lodges have not power to regulate all things relating to Masonry at these Quarterly Meetings one of which must be on St. John Baptist's Day." Begemann[2] notes that since 1724, Grand Lodge has kept St. John Baptist's Day, and though a resolution to transfer the Festival to 27th December in accordance with Scottish usage was passed on 20th May, 1725, it has rarely been acted on. It may be added that in 1737 the Grand Lodge of Scotland resolved to hold their Annual Election on St. Andrew's Day, instead of St. John the Baptist's.

Anderson's account in Regulation Twenty-Three of the various resolutions passed regarding the choice, duties, &c., of the Stewards is substantially accurate, but as is not unusual he goes wrong in his introductory passage: " The Grand Wardens were antiently assisted by a certain number of Stewards at every Feast, or by some general undertakers of the whole." He has himself noted under date 25th March, 1721 (p. 112) that " the Grand Wardens were ordered, as usual, to prepare the Feast, and to take some Stewards to their assistance, Brothers of ability and capacity, and to appoint some Brethren to attend the tables; for that no strangers must be there. But the Grand Officers not findng a proper number of Stewards, our Brother Mr. Josiah Villeneau, Upholder in the Borrough Southwark, generously undertook the whole himself, attended by some waiters . . ." It is not until the 27th December, 1725, that the Minutes state[3] that a health was drunk " to the Grand Steward, viz., John James Heidegger, and his two Deputies viz. John Potter and Mr. Lambert with thanks for their handsome and elegant entertainment." Anderson's version (p. 119) is that " no Stewards being appointed, Grand Master Richmond desired our Brother John James Heidegger to prepare the Feast in the best manner." (27th November, 1725.) It would appear from the Minutes that the proper arrangements of the Feast and the choice of Stewards developed gradually, and that, at the earlier meetings of Grand Lodge, the appointing of a Steward was somewhat casual. The " anciently " is a mere flourish of Anderson's, and though according to him we have in Villeneau an instance of " some general undertaker of the whole " it is incorrect for him to state with regard even to the earlier period (if in his favour we may so interpret " anciently ") that " the Grand Wardens were assisted by . . . Stewards at every Feast."

New Regulation Twenty-Five (p. 169) is a mere note. 17th November, 1725, is apparently a misprint for 27th November, 1725.

In New Regulation Twenty-Six Anderson states that " The Tylers and other Servants, within or without Doors, are now appointed only by the Stewards," this being his amendment of the Old Regulation that the Grand Master appointed " Porters and Doorkeepers." His statement receives confirmation from the account of the proceedings in Grand Lodge on 8th June, 1732,[4] when the Stewards made a complaint to Grand Lodge that they having

---

[1] Q.C.A., x., 53.
[2] op. cit., ii., 232 note.
[3] Q.C.A., x., 69.
[4] Q.C.A., x., 220-1.

"employed Brother Lewis as an attendant upon them at the last Grand Feast, he had misconducted himself in his office, and on his publicly asking pardon of the Stewards he was forgiven."

In Regulation Twenty-Eight Anderson states that "In antient times the Master, Wardens and Fellows on St. John's Day met either in a monastery, or on the top of the highest hill near them, by peep of day." For this there would seem to be some authority at any rate in tradition. The practice of the Lodge of Aberdeen has been mentioned in dealing with Anderson's Scottish days, and there is also the legendary gathering at St. Rook's Hill, Goodwood, of which the most substantial evidence is the entry in the *Weekly Journal or British Gazetteer* of the 17th May, 1720 (No. 264):—"A few days since, their Graces the Dukes of Richmond and Montagu, accompanied by several gentlemen, who were all Free and Accepted Masons, according to ancient custom, form'd a Lodge upon the top of a hill near the Duke of Richmond's seat, at Goodwood in Sussex, and made the Right Honourable the Lord Baltimore a Free and Accepted Mason."

New Regulation Twenty-Nine explains that the corresponding Old Regulation regarding the election of the Grand Master was inconvenient, and then gives the arrangements made on the 27th December, 1720, which were carried out at the election on Lady Day, 1721. As the Old Regulations of the first edition are stated by Anderson to have been compiled first by Payne in 1720, approved by Grand Lodge on St. John the Baptist Day, 1721, and digested with explanations by himself, why were not these inconveniences and amendments referred to in 1723? Is it not more probable that, as has been suggested earlier, the so-called resolution of 1720 is merely one formulated by Anderson for his second edition?

New Regulations Thirty to Thirty-Five, some dealing with, *e.g.*, the saying of grace, or the seating arrangements at the Grand Feast, others being mere notes, are briefly dismissed by Begemann as idle additions of Anderson's own. We may note with regard to Thirty-Five, laying it down *inter alia* that a Deputy is appointed when the Grand Master is nobly born, that in Scotland (perhaps Anderson had this in mind when he wrote) an operative mason was appointed as Deputy when the Deacon or Warden was a nobleman or a laird.

New Regulation Thirty-Six deals with proxies.

New Regulation Thirty-Seven is a mere note, as is Thirty-Eight.

Regulation Thirty-Nine is of so remarkable a character in view of the incidents on which it is founded that forgiveness may be had for quoting it in full:—

"On the 24th June 1723 at the Feast, the G. Lodge before dinner made this Resolution, that *it is not in the power of any man or body of men to make any alteration or innovation in the body of Masonry, without the consent first obtain'd of the G. Lodge.* And on 25th November 1723 the G. Lodge in Ample Form resolved that *any G. Lodge duly met has a power to amend or explain any of the printed Regulations in the Book of Constitutions, while they break not in upon the antient Rules of the Fraternity. But that no Alterations shall be made in this printed Book of Constitutions without Leave of the G. Lodge.*

Accordingly:

All the Alterations or New Regulations above written are only for amending or explaining the Old Regulations for the good of Masonry, without breaking in upon the antient Rules of the Fraternity, still preserving the Old Land Marks; and were made at several times, as Occasion offer'd, by the Grand Lodge, who have an inherent power of amending what may be thought inconvenient, and ample authority of making New Regulations for the good of Masonry, without the consent of all the Brethren at the Grand Annual Feast; which has not been disputed since the said 24th June 1721 [?1723] for the members of the G. Lodge are truly the representatives of all the Fraternity, according to Old Regulation X.

And so on 6 April 1736

John Wood Esq. D. Grand Master in the Chair proposed a New Regulation of 10 Rules for explaining what concern'd the decency of Assemblies and Communications; which was agreed to by that Grand Lodge "—and then follow the 10 New Regulations.

Bro. Vibert[1] has set out the account that the Minutes give of these incidents, and we shall adopt his translation of them into the language of a modern meeting. It was proposed (? and seconded) that the General Regulations approved on the 17th January, 1723, " be confirmed so far as they are consistent with the ancient Rules of Masonry." An amendment to omit the words " so far . . . Masonry" was negatived. But in place of the original proposition the following resolution was adopted by a majority:—" That it is not in the power of any person or body of men to make any alterations or innovation in the body of Masonry without the consent first obtained of the Annual Grand Lodge." So that in fact the 1723 Constitutions were never fully sanctioned. Brother Songhurst[2] suggests that the apparent dispute " arose in regard to the power of Brethren at a Quarterly Communication to amend or alter the Regulations, for according to Regulation 39 (old version), this could only be done at the Annual Meeting," when the amendments or alterations had to " be offer'd to the perusal of all the Brethren before dinner in writing, even of the youngest Enter'd Prentice." That is, the question was one of the Annual Grand Feast as against the Quarterly Communication.

With regard to Anderson's account of what he claims was the Resolution of 25th November, 1723, the only entry at all relevant in the reprinted Minutes[3] is as follows:—" Whether the Masters and Wardens of the several Lodges have not power to regulate all things relating to Masonry at their Quarterly Meetings. One of which must be on St. John Baptist Day. Agreed Nem. Con." It is relevant to our point that even this Resolution is suggested by Bro. Songhurst to be directed against the attempted enlargement of the Grand Master's power at the expense of Grand Lodge.

How then do the facts appear from Anderson's version and in what way has he used them? There is reason to believe that there was opposition to or at least suspicion of any changes in the " Old Charges." It was to them that a certain sacrosanctity attached. Anderson so to speak throws forward the dispute. He places the conflict as between the *Book of Constitutions* and its revision, whereas it was rather between the " Old Charges" and their revision in the *Book of Constitutions* itself. So little was his printed *Book of Constitutions* held in veneration that it would certainly seem as though Grand Lodge refused to confirm it. He has disingenuously given such a twist to the facts as to raise doubts of his honesty. Taking the resolution against the making of alterations or innovations which was directly against, or at least in limitation or qualification of his own work, he has quoted it as fortifying that work with the traditional sanctity of the Craft. Moreover, in his version of the November resolution he has added a marked reference and an additional protection to his book by adding words which did not appear and which he must have known did not appear in the Minutes, to a resolution which was probably directed to a point irrelevant to the issue which he raised. It is a device ingenious, but which being discovered recoils on its inventor.

To conclude our examination of the " Old " and the " New " Regulations, Anderson's account of what he calls " a New Regulation of 10 Rules " passed

[1] *A.Q.C.*, xxxvi., 60 ff.
[2] *Q.C.A.*, x., 50 note (*b*).
[3] *Q.C.A.*, x., 53 and note.

on 6th April, 1736, is substantially (though, as might be supposed, not verbally) accurate, save that the official Minutes call them "Laws" (he is still anxious to use his own terms wherever possible) and that they are nine and not ten—our author has divided one of them.

X. THE CONSTITUTIONS OF THE COMMITTEE OF MASONS CHARITY.

On the whole this portion is fairly well and accurately treated by Anderson, and requires little comment.

The fourth resolution of the 31st March, 1734, required only the name of the petitioner [1]; it did not require his calling also, as Anderson states.

Under date the 6th April, 1738, he merely says that "the Treasurer Blakerby, having justly cleared his accounts, and stated the balance, thought fit to demit or lay down his office. . Upon which the Secretary Revis was appointed Treasurer [etc.]," and does not mention the incidents preceding Blakerby's resignation. It appears from the Minutes [2] that the Committee of Charity had recommended that the Treasurer should give security for the moneys in his possession, his own bond to be sufficient, apparently. Some brethren however required that some other person should join the Treasurer in the bond, and this proposal being carried, Brother Blakerby, a faithful servant of Grand Lodge, the Housekeeper to the House of Lords, and a man of substance (perhaps partly as in succession the fortunate husband of two rich widows), feeling not perhaps unreasonably that his retention of the office was not consistent with his dignity, forthwith thanked the Brethren and resigned.

XI. A LIST OF THE LODGES IN AND ABOUT LONDON AND WESTMINSTER.

XII. DEPUTATIONS OF SEVERAL GRAND MASTERS . . .

Anderson prefaces his list by saying that " Many Lodges have by accidents broken up, or are partition'd, or else removed to new places for their convenience, and so, if subsisting, they are called and known by those new places or their signs. But the subsisting Lodges, whose officers have attended the Grand Lodge or Quarterly Communication, and brought their Benevolence to the General Charity within 12 months past, are here set down according to their seniority of Constitution, as in the Grand Lodge-Books, and the Engraven List." It was not until after some years that the precedence of Lodges was settled and it was only on 27th December, 1727,[3] that the four officers of Grand Lodge were asked to report on the matter with a view to its settlement, and on the 17th April [4] following " most of the Lodges present delivered the dates of the time of their being constituted into Lodges, in order to have precedency in the printed book," although even on 25th June, 1728,[5] there were still some who had not given the required information. Bro. Lane [6] points out that these Metropolitan Lodges occupy a separate portion of the List and are numbered consecutively from 1 to 106, so that the numbering does not agree with that of the official Engraved List. The Lodges are arranged in three columns, for the " Signs of the Houses," " Dates of Constitution," and "Days of Forming" (i.e., of Meeting). The Three Lodges at the end of the List have no dates of Constitution, although their days of meeting are given, and to the first of these three " 104, Checker Charing Cross " are added the words " have petition'd to be constituted " (presumably meant to include the second and third also). Now as the Lodge at " the Checker "

[1] Q.C.A., x., 251.
[2] Q.C.A., x., 298-9.
[3] Q.C.A., x., 81-2.
[4] Q.C.A., x., 83.
[5] Q.C.A., x., 87.
[6] Handy Book to List of Lodges, pp. 35-6

was in fact constituted on 27th January, 1739, Lane is of the opinion that Anderson's second edition was not in fact published until that year. But it is at least possible that the added words merely show that it had not yet been formally constituted. The regular dates of meetings are given, and the Lodge may quite well have met—and on those dates—before Constitution, which ceremony frequently followed at some interval the *de facto* forming of the Lodge.

After the List of Metropolitan Lodges comes the "Deputations of several Grand Masters to Wales, the Country [*i.e.*, the Provinces] of England, and foreign parts." It is to be noted that in the English Section (there are only the two Provincial Grand Masterships in the Welsh) there is a separation between those of the "Deputations" which are directed to individuals appointing them to Provincial Grand Masterships, and the other cases in which the Grand Master is said to have granted Deputations "at the request of some good brothers in cities and towns throughout England, for constituting the following Lodges . . ." In the latter case what is meant is that for reasons of distance or otherwise it being inconvenient for the Grand Master or his Deputy to be present in order formally to constitute the Lodge, he has deputed certain other Brethren to attend on his behalf in order to perform that function. But in the section of those "sent beyond Sea," as Lane [1] points out, the two classes are mixed up indiscriminately. The same authority [2] further states:—

(1) that Anderson has omitted from his overseas list No. 126 "Boston in New England";

(2) that the Deputation for Gibraltar was not granted by Inchiquin (Grand Master Feb.-Dec. 1727) but by Kingston (Grand Master 9th March 1728/9);

(3) The Lodge at the Hague did not appear in the Register until 1735, although Anderson states that Lord Lovel (Grand Master 1731-2) granted the Deputation to make the Duke of Lorraine a Mason.

Lane [2] states as against Anderson that although the Lisbon Lodge "is said in the Grand Lodge Minutes to have been constituted on 17th April 1735," Anderson assigns the grant of the "Deputation to Constitute" to Weymouth, Grand Master, who was not installed as Grand Master until the very same day— 17th April 1735—on which the Lodge was constituted at Lisbon. True it is that Weymouth was only installed on the date mentioned, but the Lodge could not have been "constituted at Lisbon" on that date because the Grand Lodge Minutes [3] state that a petition was received from some Brethren "in and about the City of Lisbon" asking for a Deputation to be granted for constituting them into a regular Lodge, that the prayer of that petition was granted, and that it was ordered "that the Secretary make out proper Deputations [*i.e.*, for this and another matter] accordingly." The Grand Lodge record is under date the 17th April, 1735, and the resolution followed Weymouth's installation. So that it would seem that rather unusually Anderson was right and Lane wrong.

There were no written Lodge Warrants under the Moderns until the middle of the century. There was a personal Constitution in London, and there are in existence some two or three authorisations in answer to petitions for Lodges in the Metropolis. For the Provinces and Overseas a Deputation was granted to some local Masonic authority to constitute the Lodge.

We may note among the Deputations one from Lord Weymouth to "noble Brother Richmond for holding a Lodge at his Castle d'Aubigny in France," and

---

[1] *id.*, pp. 36-7.
[2] *id.*, p. 37.
[3] *Q.C.A.*, x., 254.

compare and contrast it with the account of another Lodge or Chapter mentioned in the present Duke of Richmond's *A Duke and His Friends*, as evidence of the Second Duke's Masonic activities.

It may be added that Grand Lodge was then as now rightfully insistent on the notification of the removals of Lodges, though not so formal in its requirements. For example, on 25th January, 1737/8 [1] it was ordered that the Master or Warden of a Lodge changing its place of meeting should send notice thereof to the Grand Secretary, and on the 13th April, 1739,[2] that every Lodge removing should pay 2/6d., and every Lodge changing its times of meeting, 1/- to Brother Pine for his trouble and expense in making the necessary alterations in the Engraved List of Lodges.

As we have mentioned, Anderson at the end of this section indulges in a further historical rhapsody apropos of Masonry abroad. He mentions "the Old Lodge at York City, and the Lodges of Scotland, Ireland, France and Italy" as independent under their own Grand Masters, but with "the same Constitutions, Charges, Regulations etc. for substance, with their Brethren of England, and are equally zealous for the Augustan Style and the secrets of the . . . Fraternity." He singles out for praise the architectural monuments of the "antient nations of Eastern Asia," but forgetting, or probably ignorant of the glories of their architecture, laments "the horrid devastations made by the Mahometans," although perhaps we cannot in fairness expect him to be in advance of his time in artistic appreciation.

Many attempts have been made to derive Freemasonry from what were considered earlier societies or associations, such as the Rosicrucians, or the religious orders of chivalry. But Anderson, while suggesting a connection, reverses it, however; since, if Freemasonry is an institution dating from Adam, it follows that if there is any question of descent, the paternal position must be occupied by the Craft and not by the other associations. As he says, "in process of time, the Orders or Fraternities of the Warlike Knights (and some of the Religious too) borrow'd many solemn usages from our more antient Fraternity that has existed from the beginning: For each . . . have their Grand Master . . . and other Grand Officers, with their Constitutions, Charges, Regulations, their peculiar Jewels, Badges, and Clothings, their Forms of Entrance, Promotion and Assembling, of their Sessions and Processions, their Communications and Secrets . . ." (pp. 196-7.) He then goes on to demonstrate how Masonry has ever been encouraged by "the better sort of mankind," and how "the Masons thus countenanced by their Royal, Princely, noble and learned Brothers and Fellows, did ever separate themselves from the common Croud of Artisans and Mechanics in their well-form'd Lodges under their proper Officers" until now "their Secrets and Usages are wisely preserved and propagated, the Science and the Art are duly cultivated, and the Cement of the Lodge is made so firm, that the whole Body resembles a well-built Arch of the beautiful Augustan Style." I had at first taken this passage to be a slighting and ungrateful reference to the separation of the Speculatives from the Operatives, but I hasten with thanks to accept Bro. Rippon's view, kindly communicated, that what Anderson is referring to is the fact that while the Masons formed Lodges, the artisans and mechanics of other trades did not. If the words from "thus countenanced" to "Brothers and Fellows" are treated as a parenthesis, we clearly get the sense suggested by Bro. Rippon—correctly as I now think. The reference to the well-built arch is one of Anderson's architectural figures of speech and must not be taken to involve any allusion to the Royal Arch Degree.

[1] *Q.C.A.*, x., 293.
[2] *Q.C.A.*, x., 314.

XIII. THE APPROBATION.

[1] According to the Minutes of Grand Lodge, on the 24th of February, 1735, " Br. Doctor Anderson, formerly Grand Warden, presented a memorial setting forth that whereas the First Edition of the General Constitution of Masonry, compiled by himself, was all sold off, and a Second Edition very much wanted: And that he had spent some Thoughts upon Some Alterations and Additions that might fitly be made to the same, which was now ready to lay before the Grand Lodge for their approbation if they were pleased to receive them.

"It was resolved Nemine con that a Committee be appointed consisting of the present and former Grand Officers and such other Masters Masons as they should think proper to call on to revise and compare the same, that when finished they might lay the same before the Grand Lodge ensuing for their approbation.

"He further represented that one William Smith said to be a Mason, had without his privity or Consent pyrated a considerable part of the Constitutions of Masonry aforesaid to the prejudice of the said Br. Anderson it being his sole property.

"It was thereupon resolved and ordered that every Master and Warden present shall do all in their power to discountenance so unfair a practice and prevent the said Smith's Books being bought by any Members of their respective Lodges."

[2] On the 31st of March, 1735: "Then a Motion was made that Doctor James Anderson should be desired to print the Names (in his New Book of Constitutions) of all the Grand Masters that could be collected from the beginning of time, together with a List of the Names of all Deputy Grand Masters, Grand Wardens, and the Brethren that have served the Craft in Quality of Stewards, which was thought necessary Because it is Resolved: That for the future all Grand Officers (except the Grand Master) shall be selected out of that Body." On the 25th January, 1738, " Bro. Anderson informed the Lodge that he had sometime since prepared a New Edition of the Book of Constitutions with several additions and amendments which having been perused and (after some alterations made therein) approved of by several Grand officers was now ready for the Press and he therefore desired the Grand Masters Command and the approbation of this Lodge for printing the same Which request was granted him.

"Bro. Anderson likewise informed the Lodge that he had with the assistance of Bro. Payne L.G.M. prepared a Law or Regulation relating to the removal of Lodges which (in case the same should be approved of) he intended to insert in the said Book of Constitutions as one of the Laws or Regulations of the Craft When the same being delivered to the Grand Master in writing was read by the Secretary and is as follows " and then follows that which Anderson (with a few verbal variations) gives as No. ix. of the New Regulations.

Anderson's version of these proceedings (p. 133) 24th February, 1735, is that "Brother Anderson, Author of the Book of Constitutions representing that a new Edition was become necessary and that he had prepared materials for it, the Grand Master and the Lodge order'd him to lay the same before the present and former Grand Officers; that they may report their Opinion to the Grand Lodge. Also the Book called the *Free Mason's Vade Mecum* was condemn'd . . . ." His account of the proceedings in March states that he was "order'd also to insert in the New Edition of the Constitutions, the Patrons of antient Masonry that could be collected from the beginning of Time, with the Grand Masters and Wardens " etc. He describes the approbation as follows (p. 138): "The Grand Lodge approved of this New Book of Constitutions and ordered the author, Brother Anderson, to print the same, with the addition of the New Regulation ix. See the Approbation below." And in the " Approbation "

---

[1] Q.C.A., x., pp. 244-5.
[2] Q.C.A., x., p. 251.

itself there is recited the "order" of February, 1735, and he then states that he submitted his MS. among others to the Duke of Richmond, Desaguliers, Cowper and Payne, "who after making some corrections, have signified their Approbation," and then to the present Grand Officers as directed, who also approved, and it goes on to say that the Grand Lodge then "agreed to order" the publication of the Book, and that it is hereby approved as the only Book of Constitutions. The Approbation is dated the 25th January, 1738, and is signed by Darnley, G.M., Ward, D.G.M., and Lawley and Graeme, Grand Wardens, although according to the Minutes (p. 290) on that date John Ward, the Deputy Grand Master, was absent and his place was taken by Sir Robert Lawley, the Senior Grand Warden. Now it is here apt to recall that the very fact that there are omissions in it indicates that the Approbation of 1723 was signed in open Lodge. Bro. Vibert considers that it was written by Anderson himself; it seems as clear that the 1738 Approbation was also of his drafting. But here Anderson has gone further. He clearly wishes to give the document the appearance of being signed in open Lodge in 1738, and that by the principal officers, so he gives the signatures of them all, forgetting the absence of the Deputy Grand Master. His cleverness this time has overreached itself.

The main difference between Anderson's account of the publication of the Second Edition and that given in the Minutes is that the former represents the work more or less as an official publication of Grand Lodge, from the very title-page itself where "the Constitutions" are stated to be collected and digested "By order" of the Grand Lodge, to the words of the Approbation, while the Minutes show clearly that the publication was a private venture of the author's. Anderson on 24th February, 1735, complained of Smith's infringement of his right in his "Sole Property," the first edition,[1] while the fact that after his death the remainder copies of the second edition were transferred to another publisher and re-issued with a new title-page, shows this also to be Anderson's "Sole Property." Moreover, while Anderson himself constantly uses the word "ordered," the Minutes say "desired," and show generally that the initiative came from the author as a request, not from the Grand Lodge as a command.

It is perhaps here the place to mention that according to Anderson he was ordered to print the names of the Patrons of ancient Masonry that could be collected from the beginning of Time, as well as those of lower office, but that the Minutes offered no Authority for the names of Patrons, only specifying Grand Masters and certain officers of lower rank, but Anderson took upon himself to enlarge his instructions, and if the result was the marvellous historical narrative of 1738, we may indeed say: "The little more; how much it is."

XIV. SOME OF THE USUAL FREE-MASONS SONGS.

Those given by Anderson are as follows:—

(a) The Master's Song. } By "the Author of this Book."
(b) The Wardens Song. }
(c) The Fellow Craft's Song, by Brother Charles de la Fay.
(d) The Enter'd Prentice's Song, by Brother Matthew Birkhead.
(e) The Deputy Grand Master's Song.
(f) The Grand Warden's Song, by Brother Oates.
(g) The Treasurer's Song.
(h) The Secretary's Song.
(i) The Sword Bearer's Song.
(j) An Ode to the Free Masons.
(k) An Ode on Masonry, by Bro. J. Bancks.

[1] $Q.C.A.$, x., p. 244 note (a).

Anderson's Book of Constitutions of 1738. 409

The Master's Song in the 1738 edition is only one-third the length of that in the earlier, our author modestly saying that the full version was "too long"; for the same reason he now prints only two instead of the thirteen verses of the Warden's Song, at the head of which he omits his former reference to the Duke of Wharton, and in the last verse this name is replaced by that of "Great Carnarvon" (Grand Master, April 1738 to May 1739). The six verses of de la Fay's Song appear in both editions, but "from Adam to Carnarvon" is inserted in place of "from Jabal down to Burlington" in verse 6.[1] Birkhead's poem in this edition has the famous ladies' verse inserted. Smith had already printed it in the "Collection of the Songs of Masons" following his *Pocket Companion* and dated 1734.

Thanks to Bro. Chetwode Crawley[2] the authorship of this verse which Anderson includes without any explanation has been traced to Springett Penn, the first Deputy Grand Master of Munster. It may be added that Birkhead did not compose the music of the Entered Apprentice's Song, but fitted the words to an old Irish air.

Only the first four of these songs appeared in the first edition. The Deputy Grand Master's Song is printed with an "additional stanza" by Brother Gofton, of whom all that we know is that he is presumably the Mr. William Gofton who was one of the Encouragers of Anderson's Second Edition, and that, according to our author, Mr. William Gofton, Attorney-at-Law, was appointed as Senior Grand Warden at the Occasional Lodge of November, 1737, at which the Prince of Wales was initiated. It was written "at the time when the Prince was made a Mason, and while the Princess was pregnant":—

> Again let it pass to the Royal lov'd Name,
> Whose glorious Admission has crown'd all our Fame:
> May a Lewis be born, whom the World shall admire,
> Serene as his Mother, August as his Sire.
>   Chorus.
>
> Now a Lewis is born, whom the World shall admire,
> Serene as his Mother, August as his Sire.

To our Brother Frederick, his Royal Highness the Prince of Wales.
To our Brother, his Royal Highness the Grand Duke of Tuscany.
To the Lewis.

The Prince of Wales was initiated on the 5th November, 1737, and the Princess of Wales gave birth to a son, afterwards George III., on 4th June, 1738.

We cannot trace definitely Brother Oates of the Grand Warden's Song. There was a Mr. Oates, Senior Warden of the Lodge, which met at the Red Lion, Richmond, Surrey, and a Mr. James Oates of that at the Anchor and Baptist's Head in Chancery Lane, Senior Warden of that meeting at the Swan and Rummer, Finch Lane. Bro. Banck's Ode on Masonry appeared in Smith's *Pocket Companion* (2nd edition) 1738, and also in the Collected edition of his verse.

In the Secretary's Song, to the words "In vain would Danvers with his wit our slow resentment raise", is a marginal note "that those who hang'd Capt. Porteous at Edinburgh were all Free Masons, because they kept their own secrets. See Craftsman, 16th April 1736. No. 563." On the 16th April, 1737, not 1736, an article appeared in *The Craftsman*,[3] the pen-name of the Editor of

---

[1] de la Fay was an Irish Member of Parliament, a member of the Lodge at the Horn, and his mother was Godmother to one of Desaguliers' children—this last in itself a small point, but one which illustrates the social and family connections of the Freemasons of the Revival.

[2] *Cœmentaria Hibernica*: The Pocket Companion (1734-5), p. 14.

[3] *A.Q.C.*, xviii., 207 ff. The article also appeared in *The Gentleman's Magazine*.

which was Caleb d'Anvers (in fact Nicholas Amhurst), dealing with the Freemasons. This newspaper was the literary focus of the opposition to Walpole's administration, and among the names of its distinguished contributors were those of William Pulteney and Lord Bolingbroke. In the issue in question appeared an article suggesting that notwithstanding the many influential and well-affected persons who were numbered in the ranks of the Society, yet its manners, customs, and general behaviour strongly suggested that their aims and meetings were of a seditious character, and that in particular the recent lynching of Captain Porteous by the Edinburgh mob was in fact the work of the Freemasons. Although the article prompted a reply and defence by the Abbé Prévost,[1] the author of the *Histoire du Chevalier des Grieux et de Manon Lescant*, in his Journal *Le Pour et Contre*, yet the obvious intention of the writer was satire at the expense of Walpole, and not an attack on the Freemasons. The *Craftsman's* real argument was that the Government like all tyrannies was fearful of sedition and that in its eyes even what appeared to be the most harmless of societies should not be above suspicion. All ordinary persons considered the Freemasons to be a well-conducted and well-affected Society in spite of its secrets; therefore this was the very society for a consistent tyranny to fear and to attack. In effect, the article in d'Anvers' journal was a tribute to the peacefulness of the Craft and to the high standing of its members.

Dr. Crawley has pointed out that the Song and Note dropped out of the English *Book of Constitutions* after 1746, but through Spratt found their way into both the English and Irish *Ahiman Rezon*, the second and later editions of the former having the Note in an expanded form, stating that the Porteous Rioters "all wore white leather aprons, which (by the by) is a certain proof they were not Free-Masons."

XV. A DEFENCE OF MASONRY.

On pages 216 and the following pages, Anderson reprints this *Defence* written in reply to the notorious pamphlet *Masonry dissected* of Samuel Prichard. In October, 1730, one Samuel Prichard had published the latter work as an attack on the Freemasons; it immediately had a large sale and was subsequently many times reprinted.[2] The Minutes of Grand Lodge[3] under date the 15th December, 1730, state the Deputy Grand Master "took notice of a pamphlet lately published by one Prichard who pretends to have been made a regular Mason: In violation of the obligations of a Mason which he swears he has broke in order to do hurt to Masonry; and expressing himself with the utmost indignation against both him (styling him an imposter) and his book as a foolish thing not to be regarded." Anderson, however, makes no mention of this condemnation in his account of the proceedings. Prichard's pamphlet was quite probably no mere bid for notoriety but the symptom of a considerable body of feeling against the now increasingly powerful and much altered institution. He may or may not have been, as he claimed, a member of "a Constituted Lodge." If he were not, he was free to attack the institution: and the substance of the attack demands examination; if he were, he was no doubt perjured, and his perjury may necessitate corroboration, but if no corroboration is forthcoming, his attack may need examination nevertheless. Briefly, his case is this. Masonry had been and should be an ancient institution with its Old Charges, confined in its membership to artificers, what we should call really operative craftsmen, with a simple ceremony of admission, at which "some few catechetical questions were necessary to declare a man sufficiently qualified for an Operative Mason," a body

---

[1] In recent times the article, curiously enough, seems also to have been treated as a serious attack by Bro. Tuckett.
[2] *A.Q.C.*, iv., 33 ff.
[3] *Q.C.A.*, x., 135-6.

of simple men meeting together in simple fashion at small cost. But now all had been changed. The operatives were being overwhelmed by an influx of "Lords and Dukes, Lawyers and Shopkeepers, and other inferior tradesmen." An institution for craftsmen, for those who laboured worthily with their hands, was becoming fashionable and was being appropriated by the idlers of the Court, and by the men of the long robe and of the counter. The new-fangled term of Free and Accepted Masons had been devised, and an administration, not heard of, as Prichard says, before 1691, with Constituted Lodges and Quarterly Communications, foisted on the institution. Even its off-spring, the Gormogons, boasted a remoter origin, and if we admit the claims of one, we must admit those of both. Amid these false claims, surely there is to be preferred a Society like that of the Grand Kaihebar (sic) which has no high pretensions but consists of responsible people discoursing of trade and business and promoting mutual friendship. We may get an idea of how the case looked to Prichard if we can imagine the feelings of a working man trade-unionist who suddenly saw the ranks of his union swollen and its policy directed by some members of the House of Lords, a few millionaires, fashionable lawyers, and West End Tradesmen, under whose direction its meetings would be held at an expensive London restaurant, and whose assemblies would be prefaced by ceremonies based on High Church ritual infused with mediæval philosophy. At the risk of disproportion, it has been thought but justice thus to put Prichard's case, since as far as I know, perhaps in disgust at its advocate, few attempts have been made to re-state it. Prichard's book having been published there appeared in December, 1730, a pamphlet entitled *A Defence of Masonry; occasioned by a Pamphlet called* "Masonry Dissected," published by J. Roberts, of the *Roberts Constitutions*. The work as a separate publication is very rare, the Library of Grand Lodge having a copy, however. The work was reproduced in the *Free Mason's Pocket Companion* for 1738, as well as in Anderson's second edition. It is to be noted that while both the pamphlet and the reprint in Smith have the Latin quotations in their original forms, Anderson's version in most cases gives only the English translations.

The researches of Bros. Gould and Dixon at one time led us to suspect that the author of the *Defence of Masonry* might be Martin Clare, but this theory has been seriously shaken by the considerations adduced by Bro. Wonnacott, so that the authorship is at the moment something of a mystery.

The reply to Prichard's strictures is to the following effect:—Where is the impiety, where the immorality, or folly for a number of men to form themselves into a Society, whose main end is to improve in commendable skill and knowledge, and to promote universal beneficence and the social virtues of human life, under the solemn obligation of an oath? And this in what form, under what secret restrictions, and with what innocent ceremonies they think proper. Every Society requires its Members to keep the secrets of that Society; many have oaths of secrecy, and their Masters and Wardens, Constitutions and Orders. Further, if a thing is not unlawful it is not wrong to take an oath to do it. As for the terror of the penalty, a solemn oath is of no more force than a simple oath—the invocation of the Deity is what renders it binding. Finally, any arguments about an oath come not well from the mouth of a self-confessed perjurer, since even if the subject-matter is trivial, an oath still has its obligations.

With regard to Masonry itself, true it is that its pristine purity may be dimmed, yet still much of the good old fabric remains, and its antiquity demands respect. What we should now term its speculative side finds its likeness in the old philosophies and mysteries of antiquity, and for its symbolism, for its legends, and even for the penalties of its obligations we can find parallels in sacred and profane history.

Has the author convincingly answered Prichard? Prepossessions have frequently inspired the answer. Might we attempt to draw an unbiassed conclusion? The author seems to have satisfactorily disposed of some objections, but I think that one or two not unimportant ones remain. His justification of the objects of Masonry, of its requirement of an oath, of the antiquity and value of its forms and ceremonials, seems adequate. But he does not seem to have answered Prichard's objection that an institution formed for a practical purpose by one social class has been appropriated by another class and used in a different form and with a different object. The unknown author has justified Freemasonry by its spirit, but has not attempted to justify its historical development from Masonry.

XVI. BROTHER EUCLID'S LETTER TO THE AUTHOR.

The *Defence* is immediately followed by a letter with the signature of "Euclid" with at its foot the three squares on the sides of a right-angled triangle as in Proposition 47 of Book I. of that geometrician's work, and as given in the frontispiece of the *Constitutions*. The letter is dated the 9th November 5738 "in the vulgar year of Masonry." Bro. Rylands in a letter to the *Keystone* of Philadelphia, 30th August, 1884, referred to by Bro. Gould, points out that if the date of 4th November, 1738, at the end of "The Author to the Reader" may be relied upon, Anderson's second edition was published probably at the close of the year and that as "Bro. Euclid" in one passage (p. 228) almost quotes Anderson's words and in another refers to Part I., chap. vii. of the second edition in addition to thanking him "for printing the clever *Defence*," these facts can only be explained "by the supposition that the latter, *i.e.*, 'Bro. Euclid,' had the use of the manuscript or proof-sheets of the book, or that 'Brother Euclid' was no other than Anderson himself."

There are several phrases in it which lend colour to this latter suggestion, *e.g.*, "true Noachidae," "though without politics or party cause," and it purports to be written from the Lodge at The Horn of which Anderson was a member. The suggestion made in the *Letter* that the author of the *Defence* was not a Freemason, Gould considers as supporting the view which he deduces from the Minutes of the Lincoln Lodge at the Saracen's Head that an endeavour was made to give it greater force by making out that the *Defence* was not the work of a Member of the Craft, but of an unprejudiced outsider. Brother Euclid supplements the argument of the *Defence* by defending the order against the "unjust cavils" of those who accuse it of Satanism; of misogyny, of a false Equalitarianism, etc. He mentions the wild tales of the old woman and the ladder (*c.f.*, the notorious burlesque print) and of "the cook's red hot iron or salamander for making the indelible character on a new made Mason," an early appearance of an old friend, with which we may compare the still earlier reference in the Dublin Tripos of 1688.

XVII. "ENCOURAGERS."

XVIII. CORRIGENDA.

The list of some 66 names of those who "kindly encouraged" the author includes many of interest, about twelve of whom were also among the Encouragers of the *Royal Genealogies*, among these names being those of the Grand Master and other Officers, seven former Grand Masters, four former Deputy Grand Masters, four former Grand Wardens, and twelve former Grand Stewards. Among the Lodges in the list is that at The Chequers at Charing Cross, the date of whose Constitution has already been discussed. Anderson apparently recognised the possible incompleteness of his Corrigenda, as he has placed at the end of the observation "Accurate reader, pray correct these with your pen, or any others you find."

It would be an interesting task, but one of which the limits of this paper do not allow, to trace in detail the subsequent history of Anderson's Second Edition. Bro. Vibert says with reference to the first edition that it was taken "by the Grand Lodge of Ireland as the model for their Book of Constitutions in 1730. It was reprinted verbatim for use in America by Franklin in 1734. It was printed in London and later in Dublin by Smith in 1735. And its author's reputation was great enough to carry off the History he wrote for his second edition of 1738, and lead the Craft for a century and a half to accept it and reprint it as a serious contribution to the subject." Entick when the edition of 1756 was published dropped altogether the version of the older Charges which Anderson gave in 1738 and reverted to that of 1723, and this version has been reprinted ever since in the various editions as they were published. The last occasion on which the historical portion (with additions bringing it up to date) was given was in the 1784 edition. When after the Union the *Book of Constitutions* was again published, in 1815, the volume purported to be only "Part the Second" and contained the promise that "The First Part containing the History of Masonry, from the earliest period to the end of the year 1815 . . . will be printed with as little delay as possible." It would appear that preparations for the publication of the historical portion in 1815 were considerably advanced—for in fact the Library of Grand Lodge has a copy of the 1815 edition of Part II., to which is prefaced almost the whole of the historical portion of the 1784 edition but with a different pagination from that edition, and also a new frontispiece but no title-page—but it never seems to have been published. The 1815 edition was re-issued with corrected sheets in 1819 and when the 1827 edition appeared that also appeared as Part II., but from 1841 the book appeared as a whole and not as a second part.

It was not until 1829 that the Grand Lodge of Scotland, through a Committee, undertook the task of codifying its enactments, until then not only scattered through its records, but often of a contradictory character,[1] and the task was completed with the publication of its first *Book of Constitutions* in 1836, although Alexr. Lawrie in his *History* (1804) dedicated to the members of the Grand Lodge of Scotland had given in Appendix III. what appears to be its Laws and Regulations, and W. A. Lawrie states in his *History* (1839) at p. 167 that on 30.xi.1819 the draft of the First Edition of the Laws and Regulations was read and unanimously approved of. It seems fairly clear that at any rate in the earlier part of its history, Anderson's *Constitutions* was looked upon as authoritative. Bro. Murray Lyon in his *History of the Lodge of Edinburgh* (1900 edn.)[2] states that this work, *i.e.*, Anderson's *Constitutions*, was in its earlier years regarded by the Grand Lodge of Scotland as an authority on the subjects treated of. Seven unbound copies of Smith's small edition of the *Constitutions* were in 1740 ordered for the use of Grand Lodge, and on page 204 he states that a short time before January, 1724, the Lodge of Dunblane was presented with *The Constitutions of the Freemasons* issued under the auspices of the Grand Lodge of England. D. Crawford Smith in his *History of the Lodge of Scoon and Perth* (p. 88) says that on the 2nd November, 1735, Collector Bethune borrowed a large quarto Book entitled "The Constitutions of the Free Masons, dedicated to the Duke of Montagu."

In view of the use apparently made in the years immediately preceding the formation of the Grand Lodge of Scotland in 1736 of Anderson's *Constitutions*, it is interesting to notice how both in substance and in form the Scottish Regulations follow Anderson with the following as some variations and exceptions:—

(1) Each Grand Master to pay towards the general fund "a sum not under" (amount apparently left blank).

---

[1] *Book of Constitutions* (1836 edn.), Introd., p. vii.   [2] P. 2 note.

In the English Grand Lodge each Grand Master pays 2/6d. at each Quarterly Communication (except at the Grand Feast) and the Grand Master also made a payment in respect of the Secretary.

(2) The Grand Wardens, Treasurer and Secretary to be "fellow craft or master masons."

(3) The Treasurer and Secretary not to speak or vote without permission. In England this disability applies only in the election of the Grand Officers.

(4) If the Grand Master names his Deputy and the other Grand Officers they are not to be members of his own Lodge.

We may contrast this with the preponderance of Members of the Lodge at The Horn in the Lists of English Grand Officers.

(5) The ribbons were to be green.

(6) The Stewards were to be appointed by the Grand Master out of a Committee consisting of one member of each Lodge.

(7) 2/6 to be paid for each entrance and a quarterly return of entrants to be made.

We cannot do more than mention Kuenen's French translation published at The Hague in 1736 and the German translation of this published at Frankfurt and Leipzig in 1741 and de la Tierce's French Editions of 1742 and 1746, all founded on one or both of Anderson's Editions. It is not without interest to notice that although even de la Tierce prints the 1723 version of the Old Charges, Spratt in his Irish Edition of 1751 seems to be the only one who adopted the 1738 version, even copying Anderson's inaccuracies in Irish Masonic history.

THE RE-ISSUE OF 1746.

In 1746, Anderson's Second Edition was re-issued with a new title-page. The author had been dead some years and Chandler and Ward had left the scene. According to Bro. Songhurst, "These enterprising brethren, with branches at York and Scarborough, were amongst the foremost publishers of their day, but it would seem that they allowed their ambition to outrun their prudence. In 1744 Chandler found himself unable to pay his debts, and he committed suicide, while in the following year, Ward was declared bankrupt." Presumably, Robinson bought up the remainder copies and published them with a new, and his own, title-page bearing the new date. It may be mentioned as a matter of interest that there is in existence one copy—and so far as is known only one copy—containing both the 1738 and the 1746 title-pages.[1] Dr. Chetwode Crawley after examining copies of the 1746 issue in the original bindings came to the conclusion that some had been originally issued with frontispieces and some had not. Apparently the remainder copies of the engraving were less numerous than those of the letter-press. Save for the title-page, the 1746 issue is the same as that of 1738, Robinson having kept the advertisements of his predecessors on the last page, possibly because it is the back of that containing Anderson's Corrigenda.

[1] This was exhibited at the meeting.

The new title-page is printed only in black, and is much longer and somewhat more grandiloquent than that of 1738. It begins: The | History and Constitutions | of the | Most ancient and honourable Fraternity | of | Free and Accepted MASONS : | containing | An Account of MASONRY.

The three historical sections are then summarised, and we have next: *To which are added*: and this is followed by eight paragraphs of the further contents. Then comes: By James Anderson, D.D. | London: Printed, and sold by J. Robinson, at | the Golden-Lion in Ludgate-street. | In the vulgar Year of Masonry 5746.

CONCLUSION.

At the beginning of this paper I tried briefly to place Anderson in his historical perspective, and if we wish only to consider him as a human antiquity, this is all that is necessary. But every author who is still read and every author who is still quoted demands further treatment, and for him a further trial is necessary. If after his death, he still remains a living influence, and if that influence still continues, it is necessary to examine its value, its basis, and its usefulness. Of Anderson's influence there can be no question. We have seen how his history of the Craft was so far treated as authoritative that it continued to form part of the (by now undoubtedly official) Book of Constitutions even as late as the currency of the 1784 edition. But though it no longer figured in the official publication, yet its influence still continued. Preston's *Illustrations of Masonry* in the historical portion is based on Anderson, and what is more, some of Anderson's wildest and most unsupported statements are so decked out as to give them a new lease of life, if that were needed. Then Jones edits Preston, as afterwards does Oliver, and if we consider the popularity and the circulation of Preston and Oliver and how much in their time they represented the Craft, we see how great must have been the influence and how strong the authority of Anderson's history in effect up to the time of Hughan and Gould and the rise of that School of Masonic historians who took truth as found by research rather than tradition inspired by sentiment as their guide. And even now only too often the ordinary member of the Craft still gets his ideas of Masonic History from our author. And not only the Freemason. We have seen how in so authoritative a work as the *Dictionary of National Biography*, in a notice by so careful an historian as Sidney Lee, Anderson is quoted as an authority without any attempt at question, and to take another instance at random, Edgecombe Staley in his *Guilds of Florence* quotes the *Constitutions of the Free Masons* which he attributed to Desagulier (*sic*) as an authority in his argument; terming the author "quaint and sententious."

If Anderson's *Constitutions* are to be judged, in whose favour or against whom, as the case may be, is judgment to be entered? As between him and Grand Lodge it cannot be said that he alone is responsible. He wrote the *Constitutions*, no doubt, but it cannot be believed that their contents were printed without some sort of approval by the Craft. We have seen that formal approval was refused, or at least not given, to the first edition, but had that compilation been contrary to the views of the majority, he would not have been entrusted with the preparation of a second. It may be that the Committee of Examination was perfunctory in examining the material for the second edition, as Committees can be, but even so had there been anything seriously in conflict with their views or those of the general body of members, we cannot suppose that the work would have received approval. It has been mentioned before that Anderson was asked to compile a list of Grand Masters that could be collected from the beginning of time, and it must be again emphasized that this is the crucial test as to whether the work was to have a real historical foundation or whether it was to be in the nature of propaganda; it was in fact an invitation to the author to exercise his imagination or at any rate to "collect" indiscriminately.

In the Preface to Scott's *Pocket Companion* of 1754, it is stated that the management of the 1738 edition at the time was left to Anderson "But from whatever cause it might arise, whether from his want of health, or trusting to the management of strangers, the work appeared in a very mangled condition, and the Regulations, which had been revised and corrected by Grand Master Payne, were in many places interpolated, and in others the sense left very obscure and uncertain. Besides its being loaded with long chronological tables, which in another place might have had their use, but here could answer no other end than to render the Book very difficult to read." This is not unfair criticism, but what is of interest is the attempt to assign a reason for the defects of the work; and from this has arisen a theory that Anderson was not in effect responsible, either from pathological causes or from his work having been done by assistants. But after all is there really much in this? The reasons assigned are alternatives and mere suggestions. We have no other grounds for supposing that his mind was affected at the time of the composition of his book. The assembling of materials for this began before February, 1735, the book was probably published by the end of 1738, and Anderson's death did not take place until five or six months later, and there is no mention of any mental weakness in any literary or newspaper accounts of his death. As for the suggestion of his being assisted by strangers, there is nothing to show that there was more than one mind at work on the book, and if he had had their assistance it seems reasonable to suppose that there would have been more freedom from obvious mistakes rather than less.

As to its general character. I have several times had occasion to point out the anachronistic character of many of the incidents. The object was rather to compile a work *ad majorem gloriam latomorum* than to seek the historical origins of the Craft. Moreover, in Anderson's mind masonry was one with architecture; not that he was singular in this view because the latter in an architectural age played a part in the education of the gentlemen of the time, a copy of Vitruvius might be bought for the Lodge, and Batty Langley could advertise that he was ready to teach the art to the men of education and of fashion of the time; but although the identification of the two was quite common, yet it rather confuses us nowadays in our historical view. We look for the origins of masonry on its speculative side, and for the beginning of the present Masonic organization, and we find historical incidents dressed up in post-revival forms and given the post-revival terminology. If Lodges are said to be founded and opened by Scriptural or Classical characters, how are we to find out when the founding of Lodges did in effect begin, how distinguish fact from fiction, tradition from history?

In regard to details, I have pointed out confusion—whether accidental or deliberate—of dates and facts, omissions, distortions. There is a curiously slipshod character in his terminology, sometimes an equivocation, an attempt by giving a word two meanings to combine the past with the present, a kind of mental thimble-rigging. The instances where old texts have been garbled to bring them into line with the new conditions are almost innumerable, and many have been mentioned in their place.

An unfavourable criticism of Anderson is bound to cause some resentment. So many have been brought up from their earliest Masonic years on his work and that of his followers. He tells us so much of that of which otherwise we should know nothing, particularly with regard to the period between the revival and that of the earliest existing Minutes of Grand Lodge. He had so many opportunities; he lived and worked during the most interesting period of the Craft.

But if our attempt to check that which can be checked has shown anything, it has shown how much his version differed from other and more reliable accounts, and if that is so, how can we trust his unsupported testimony? What he tells us may be true, but in the absence of corroboration it is impossible by the ordinary rules of evidence to accept it without suspicion, in effect, to accept it at all. True he is the sole authority for much, true his opportunities were great; but can we on that account accept his word, any more than we can be called upon to admit the scholarship of a Schoolboy who wins a prize for constant attendance? Much of modern Masonic research has had to be carried on independently of Anderson, and we have seen what slender support it affords to his statements. Must we not regret that one with so great an opportunity of knowing so misused that opportunity, that so vast an influence in time and in extent on Masonic thought has been a bad influence, and that it is now perhaps too late to correct that false view of Masonic history so common in the Craft, so much of which is due to what one is tempted to call the fairy-tales of Bro. James Anderson.

APPENDIX I.

Variations in the *Old Regulations* in Anderson's two editions:—

	1723.	1738.
I.	"any true Lodge"	"Every Lodge"
	"any other Brethren he pleaseth"	"any other Master-Masons"
II.	"or in his absence the Junior Warden"	Omitted.
VII.	"which Charity shall be lodged with the Master or Wardens, or the Cashier, if the member think fit to choose one."	"which Charity shall be kept by the Cashier"
VIII.	"with the unanimous consent of that other Lodge to which they go (as above regulated)"	Omitted.
	"in forming a new Lodge"	"in forming a new Lodge to be regularly constituted in good time."
IX.	"and reform what gives them Offence."	Omitted.

XII.	"all the regular particular Lodges."	"all the particular Lodges"
	"A Quarterly Communication about Michaelmas, Christmas, and Lady-day."	"3 Quarterly Communications before the Grand Feast"
XIII.	"Apprentices must be admitted Masters and Fellow-Craft only here."	"Apprentices must be admitted Fellow-Crafts and Masters only here."
	"Who must be a Brother and Fellow Craft."	"who must be a Brother and Master Mason."
XV.	"by two Fellow-Craft"	"two Fellow Crafts or Master Masons."
XVIII.	"May choose any Fellow Craft"	"may choose any Brother."
	"chosen Deputy of the Grand Lodge."	"chosen Deputy at the Annual Feast."
XX.	"The Grand Master, with his Deputy and Wardens."	"The Grand Master, with his Deputy, G[rand] Wardens and Secretary"
XXV.	"Fellow-Craft"	"Brother"
XXVIII.	"4. To receive and consider of any good motion, or any momentous and important affair that shall be brought from the particular Lodges, by their representatives, the several Master and Wardens."	Omitted.
XXXI.	"and must not therefore speak"	"and none of these that are not must speak."
XXXIV-V.	"Proclaim'd, saluted and congratulated"	"proclaim'd, saluted and congratulated."
	"Declar'd, saluted and congratulated"	"proclaim'd, saluted and congratulated."
XXXVII.	"Apprentice"	"Enter'd Prentice."

(It is to be noted that here Anderson leaves the words "Fellow Craft or Enter'd Prentice" without adding Master Mason.)

XXXIX.	"Apprentice"	"Enter'd Prentice."

APPENDIX II.

Andersonian phraseology in the present Book of Constitutions:—

Anderson's Version.	Grand Lodge Minutes Version.	Book of Constitutions, 1926 Edn.
Every Annual Grand Lodge has an inherent Power and Authority to make New Regulations, or to alter these . . . provided always that the Old Land Marks be carefully preserv'd xxxix., p. 175 (O.R.)		The Grand Lodge . . . alone has the inherent power of enacting laws and regulations . . . and of altering, repealing, and abrogating them, always taking care that the antient Landmarks of the order be preserved. 4. p. 17
If the G. Master should abuse his great Power, and render himself unworthy of the Obedience and Subjection of the Lodges, he shall be treated in a Way and Manner to be agreed upon in a New Regulation: Because hitherto the antient Fraternity have had no Occasion for it. xix., p. 165 (O.R.)		If the Grand Master should abuse his power, and render himself unworthy of the obedience of the Lodges, he shall be subjected to some new regulation, to be dictated by the occasion; because, hitherto, the Antient Fraternity have had no reason to provide for an event which they have presumed would never happen. 17. p. 24
every Member shall keep in his Seat, xl., 4. p. 177 (N.R.)	each of the Members be obliged to keep his Seat 4. Q.C.A. x., p. 269	All members shall keep their seats. 67. p. 44
Every one that speaks shall rise and keep standing, addressing himself to the Chair: Nor shall any presume to interrupt him, under the foresaid Penalty; unless the G. MASTER, finding him wandering from the Point in Hand, shall think fit to reduce him to Order; for then the said Speaker shall sit down: But after he has been set right, he may again proceed, if he pleases. xl., 6. p. 177 (N.R.)	Every Member who has anything to offer which may require the Attention of the Assembly, shall rise and keep standing in his Place while he is speaking, always addressing himself to the Grand Master or his Deputy in the Chair Nor shall any person presume to interrupt his Discourse under the penalty before said Unless the Grand Master or his Deputy finding him wandring from the point then under publick Consideration shall think fitt to call him to order In which Case he is to sit down forthwith, and after he has been sett right he may proceed if he sees good. 5. Q.C.A. x., p. 269	Everyone who speaks shall rise and remain standing, addressing himself to the Grand Master, and he shall not be interrupted, unless any Brother shall address the Grand Master on a point of order, or the Grand Master shall himself think fit to call the speaker to order, but after he has been set right, he may proceed if he observe due order and decorum. 70. p. 44

Anderson's Version.

If in the G. LODGE any Member is twice call'd to Order, at one Assembly, for transgressing these Rules, and is guilty of a 3d Offence of the same Nature, the Chair shall peremptorily command him to quit the Lodge-Room for that Night.
xl., 7. p. 177 (N.R.)

That whoever shall be so rude as to hiss at a Brother, or at what another says or has said, he shall be forthwith solemnly excluded the Communication, and declared incapable of ever being a Member of any Grand Lodge for the Future, till another Time he publickly owns his Fault and his Grace be granted.
xl, 8. p. 177 (N.R.)

The Antient Manner of Constituting a Lodge,

A New Lodge, for avoiding many Irregularities, should be solemnly Constituted by the Grand Master with his Deputy and Wardens; Or in the G. Master's Absence, the Deputy acts for his Worship, the Senior G. Warden as Deputy, the Junior G. Warden as the Senior, and a present Master of a Lodge as the Junior.
p. 149.

Grand Lodge Minutes Version.

Should it happen that any Member of a Quarterly Communication shall be twice called to order in any one Night for offending against any of the Rules beforegoing, and should be guilty of a third offence of the same Nature he shall at the peremptory Command of the Grand Master or his Deputy be obliged to quitt the Grand Lodge for that Night.

And that none might plead Ignorance herein it was Resolved that these Rules of Conference shall be audibly read by the publick Secretary at every Quarterly Communication after the opening of the Lodge.
6. Q.C.A. x., p. 269

It was also ordered that whatever Member should be so rude as to hiss at what another says he shall be excluded the Quarterly Communication in form and declared incapable of ever being admitted a Member in any Quarterly Communication succeeding.
7. Q.C.A. x., p. 270

Book of Constitutions, 1926 Edn.

If any member shall have been twice called to order for transgressing these rules, and shall nevertheless be guilty of a third offence at the same meeting, the Grand Master shall peremptorily command him to quit the Grand Lodge for that meeting.
71. p. 45

Whoever shall be so unmasonic as to hiss at a Brother, or at what he has said, shall forthwith be solemnly excluded, and declared incapable of being a member of the Grand Lodge, until, at another time, he publicly own his fault, and grace be granted.
72. p. 45

In order to avoid irregularities, every new Lodge shall be solemnly constituted according to antient usage, by the Grand Master with his Wardens; or, in the absence of the Grand Master, by his Deputy. If the Deputy be absent, the Grand Master may appoint some other Grand Officer or Master or Past Master of a Lodge to act as Deputy *pro tempore*.
120. p. 70

Anderson's Version.	Grand Lodge Minutes Version.	Book of Constitutions, 1926 Edn.
When the Grand Master is present it is a Lodge in Ample Form; otherwise, only in Due Form, yet having the same Authority with Ample Form. Marginal note p. 110.		The Grand Lodge is declared to be opened in *ample form* when the Grand Master or Pro Grand Master is present, in *due form* when a Past Grand Master or the Deputy presides, at all other times, only in *form*, yet with the same authority. 61. p. 42
The G. Master or Deputy has full Authority and Right, not only to be present, but also to preside in every Lodge, with the Master of the Lodge on his Left Hand; and to order his Grand Wardens to attend him, who are not to act as Wardens of particular Lodges but in his Presence and at his Command; For the G. Master, while in a particular Lodge, may command the Wardens of that Lodge, or any other Master-Masons, to act there as his Wardens pro tempore. O.R. I. pp. 152/3		The Grand Master has full authority to preside in any Lodge, and to order any of his Grand Officers to attend him. His Deputy is to be placed on his right, and the Master of the Lodge on his left hand. His Wardens, if present, are also to act as Wardens of the Lodge during the time he presides; but if the Grand Wardens be absent, then the Grand Master may command the Wardens of the Lodge, or any Master Masons to act as his Wardens *pro tempore.* 142. pp. 82/3
That is, only when the G. Wardens are absent: For the G. Master cannot deprive 'em of their Office, without shewing Cause fairly appearing to the G. Lodge according to the Old Regulation XVIII. so that if they are present in a particular Lodge with the Grand Master, they must act as Wardens there. N.R. I. pp. 152/3		Unless the Grand Master be present, the Deputy Grand Master has full authority to preside in any Lodge, the Master of the Lodge being placed on his right hand. The Grand Wardens, if present, are to act as Wardens of the Lodge during the time he presides. 143. p. 83
And also all the Transactions of their own Lodge that are proper to be written, O.R. III. p. 154		Minutes of all such transactions of the Lodge as are proper to be written. 172. p. 94
That the Brothers atesting a Petition for Charity shall be able to certify, that the Petitioner has been formerly in reputable, at least, in tolerable Circumstances. Resolution of Grand Lodge of the 31st March 1735 2. p. 182	That it be a Resolution of the Grand Lodge that the Brethren subscribing any Petition of Charity should be able to certify that they have known the Petitioner in reputable or at least tollerable circumstances. (Q.C.A. x., p. 251)	. . . recommendation . . . by the Master, Wardens, and a majority of the members then present, . . certifying that they know him or have good reasons for believing him to have been in reputable, or at least tolerable, circumstances, 243. p. 129

A hearty vote of thanks was passed to Bro. Edwards for his interesting paper on the proposition of Bro. David Flather, seconded by Bro. W. K. Firminger; comments being offered by or on behalf of Bros. W. J. Williams, C. C. Adams, Geo. W. Bullamore, C. Walton Rippon, and the Secretary.

Bro. W. J. WILLIAMS writes:—

Perhaps the last recorded words penned by our Brother James Anderson were those at the very end of the Corrigenda to the 1738 Edition:—

> Accurate Reader, pray correct these with your Pen, *or any others you find.*

That prayer has at long last been answered. The "Accurate Reader" has now been found and he has used his pen to some purpose and given a larger and fuller response to the petition than the petitioner could have anticipated or perhaps desired or as he might think deserved. Where Dr. Anderson anticipated "motes", Bro. Edwards has detected and exhibited "beams".

The paper prepared by our Brother is a striking example of judicial skill combined with the ministration of patience and assiduity. The work needed to be done, and no one could have done it better.

Although in the process of complying with the expressed wish of Dr. Anderson Bro. Edwards has been compelled to deliver a series of drastic judgments, he has occasionally shown his desire to extenuate the delinquencies of the Author so much, so necessarily, and so thoroughly criticised.

We all who are here present may possibly unite in the statement that no office existed entitled Grand Master of Masons or Freemasons prior to 1717, and yet we ourselves are constantly attributing that title to various dignitaries of past ages, such as Solomon and the two Hirams, and we and our successors will probably continue so to do until time shall be no more. Have we any excuse which would not have availed for Dr. Anderson? How many original Grand Lodges do *we* commemorate, and where were they holden?

We must remember that Dr. Anderson like ourselves was a member of an order which is veiled in allegory and illustrated by symbols. That Society in its development or new creation dating from 1717 claimed an antiquity dating back to antediluvian times. But in so doing it only followed in the paths made by their predecessors who framed the Old Constitutions. It was on those lines, and on behalf of a Society making those claims, that Dr. Anderson prepared his 1723 Edition and expanded it in 1738. Once admit those premises and then carry them out to their logical issue and there was no escape from the kind of result which was attained in the 1738 Edition. As a rough version of architectural history through the ages and in many countries the narrative compiled by our Author does produce in broad outline a result which in the main creates a correct general impression, though marred by many inaccuracies in details and by insupportable allegations and encrusted with the unsound suggestions of the existence of Grand Masters and Lodges and certain paraphernalia associated therewith in the post 1717 era, much of which we now find crystallised in our current rituals. If we had attacked Dr. Anderson on that account he would probably have said that by whatever names they were called in the dialects of their respective countries, there must of necessity have been persons ultimately functioning in the same way as Grand Masters, Wardens, Master Masons, Fellowcrafts and Apprentices. Were our Brethren of the 1738 era so dense as to regard the record of matters of that kind as literally true? They were not entirely devoid of intelligence, and I do not think the members of the Craft who then or since have read the History have ever regarded it as being more than a decorated, distorted and adapted version of plain facts dyed with Masonic tinctures.

Turning to another topic of discussion. It is clear that it frequently happens that the records in the minutes as to new or amended regulations differ from the version given in the 1738 book. It does not necessarily follow that the minutes are precisely correct when these differences occur. Minutes frequently give only what the Recorder considers to be the general effect of what is said or done, and the final form of amendments and new regulations is apt to differ from the minutes in words, though not in substance. The Grand Secretary is not likely to have approved the 1738 version without noticing such variations if they were really unauthorised. The idea that the Grand Secretary and other approvers were mere puppets in the hands of Dr. Anderson is one for which there is no warrant in the evidence.

Dr. Anderson and his co-adjutors must have been at some pains to collect much of the information recorded in the History, even though they paraphrased it on the lines before indicated or mis-copied it. Due credit should be given them for this. Among these items may be mentioned (1) the Register of William Molart in the Bodleian, dated 1429. This refers to Thomas Stupylton as Master whose name should have been recorded as Mapylton. I do not know whether it has previously been noticed that this Thomas Maplyton is almost certainly the same person as the Thomas Mapylton of London who was King's Master Mason at that time as appears by my paper on the King's Master Masons. He is described as late Master Mason of the Works in a Patent granted to Robert Westerley dated 6th January, 1439. Thomas Mapylton's own Patent was issued when the King was at Canterbury.

(2) The reference to Stow as to the Company of Masons. It is noteworthy that Dr. Anderson says so very little about that Company. Its continued existence and operations could hardly have escaped his attention, and the omission seems to have been deliberate.

(3) The new Articles which Anderson incorrectly dates 27th December, 1663, and which ought to be capable of being traced in some City Records unless they were burned in the Great Fire.

(4) The two references to Ashmole's Diary.

(5) The very brief and probably accurate account of the meetings leading to the creation of the 1717 Grand Lodge.

(6) The concise (if occasionally biassed) abstract of the meetings of Grand Lodge up to 1738. This abstract must have been a very important help indeed to the whole Fraternity. No really vital errors have been detected in that narration even when passed through the crucible of our severest tests.

(7) and (8) The statements as to the initiation, passing and raising of Frederick Prince of Wales and as to the initiation, passing and raising of the Duke of Lorraine.

The position occupied by these two items seems to indicate that they were inserted in the MS. at a late stage, and it is not at all improbable that they were so inserted at the suggestion of Dr. Desaguliers, who was one of the principal actors in the events referred to. Desaguliers is mentioned in the Approbation as one of those who after making some corrections had signified approbation.

Bro. Daynes in his paper as to the visit of the Duke of Lorraine produced no evidence whatever to shake the statements of Anderson.

Occasionally Bro. Edwards has adopted a somewhat overstressed method of criticism. For instance, he takes exception to Anderson's phrase that Grand Lodge "ordered" him to print the book, whereas what took place was that on his desiring the Grand Master's commands and the approbation of Grand Lodge this request was granted him.

Thus it appears that he was commanded, but must not call it ordered.

Too little weight is given by our critics to the part taken by such men as Desaguliers, Payne and Cowper in the oversight of the 1738 Edition. It was a matter in which they were greatly interested and all three of them were men of ability.

The fact cannot be gainsaid that Dr. Anderson, with all his faults, was the Father of the authentic school in this sense that he regarded the 1717 Grand Lodge as an off-shoot and development of the old operative Lodges and their non-operative associates.

Bro. WALTER K. FIRMINGER said:—

I rise to propose a vote of thanks to Bro. Lewis Edwards for his admirable paper, which, though too lengthy to admit of it being thoroughly discussed at more meetings than one, has this advantage that when it appears in *Ars.Q.C.* it will present to the reader nearly all the available evidence, together with judgments, which, if not in every case acceptable, are characterised by close insight and matured reflection. In regard to one point, Anderson's account of the meetings of Grand Lodge on 24th June, 1721, and 1722, Bro. Edwards has overlooked the evidence supplied by Bro. Harry Rylands in his *Records of the Lodge Original No. 1, now the Lodge of Antiquity No. 2*. Bro. Rylands describes a volume known as "the E. Book". Some of the contents of this volume he says are of no historical value, and in saying this he is referring to "notes purporting to be either the original minutes or extracts from an older minute book" which appear from p. 125 onwards. I am tempted to believe that this depreciatory estimate has in effect led the reader to suppose that the other documents of the E. Book are of little or no importance. Bro. Ryland most certainly did not wish to make that impression. The following on page 11 of the E. Book he believed to be of early date:—

At
A Generall Assembly of a Great Number of
Freemasons Held at Stationers Hall; London
On the 24th June 1721. The Most Noble
  John Duke of Montague=
  Was then chosen Grand Master
  D^r. John Beale Sub^t. Master
  M^r. Josias Villeneau   } Grand Wardens.
  M^r. Thomas Morris   }
The Most Noble Philip Duke of Wharton
The Right Honble. Ld. Herbert
The Right Honble. Ld. Hitchinbrook
The Right Honble. Ld. Hillsborough
S^r. Willm. Leman Bar^{tt}.
S^r. George Oxenden Bar^{tt}.
S^r. Richard Rich Bar^{tt}.
S^r. Andrew Fountaine, K^{nt}.
John Holt Esqr.
Sackville Tufton Esqr.
Willm. Young Esqr.
Willm. Stanhope Esqr.
Coll. John Cope
Coll. Campbell
P[hilip Lord] Stanhope

Christopher Wren Esq'.
Rich^d. Boult. Gent.
Thos. Sayer.
W. Weston Esq'.
James Bateman. Gent.
Charles Hedges
Jos. Bullock

Dr. Stukeley tells us that "L^d. Herbert" and "S^r. Andrew Fountaine" were present at the Dinner at Stationers' Hall, and this seems to show that the E. Book is here not based on Anderson. Sir Andrew, by the way, was one of the founders of the Spalding Lodge. The E. Book also provides a list of Grand Lodge Feasts from June 24th, 1717, to February 26th, 1724, and this list, as Bro. Rylands believed, was drawn up about 1724. I extract the following :—

In ye year 1721 June ye 24th at Stationers' Hal was a Generall Assembley held by His Grace Grand the Duke of Montague Master
Dup^t. Mas^t. D^r. Beal.
Wards. { Josaias Villenav } Chosen for the Year
{ Thos. Morris. S^t. Gileses } insuing

In ye year 1722. June ye 24th at Merchant Taylors Hall was General Assembley by His Grace the Duke of Wharton the Grand Master
Dupt. D^r. Desauclear
Wards. { John Timson } Chosen for the Year
{ W^m. Hawkin } insuing

You observe that this document contradicts Anderson in two very essential parts:—(1) It assigns the place of meeting at the Merchant Taylor's Hall, and (2) is contrary to Anderson's statement "his Grace appointed no deputy". The *Daily Post* of June 27th announced : "On Monday last was kept at the Stationers' Hall the usual Annual Grand Meeting of the Most Noble and Ancient Fraternity of Free-Masons (where there was a noble Appearance of Persons of Distinction), at which Meeting they are oblig'd by the Orders to elect a Grand and Deputy Master, in persuance whereof they have accordingly chosen his Grace the Duke of Wharton for their Grand Master in the room of his Grace the Duke of Montagu, and Dr. Desaguliers Deputy Master, in the room of Dr. Beal, for the year coming".

It is remarkable that Anderson should have been so negligent of Grand Master Payne's regulation of 1721, "Here also the Master or the Wardens of each particular Lodge shall bring and produce a List of such Members as have been made, or even admitted in their particular Lodges since the last Communication of the Grand Lodge". In what is for convenience called the 1723 Grand Lodge List of Members, Anderson appears as a Member of the Lodge at the Horn. What has become within quite a short time of the Lodge on whose behalf he, as its Master, signed the Approval of his 1723 *Book of Constitutions*? Only as the present Master or Warden of a Lodge could he have attended a Communication of Grand Lodge in 1723.

Bro. Lewis Edwards has not mentioned a curious fact recorded by our Bro. W. J. Hughan in his preface to our Lodge's Edition of the *Constitutions* of 1738. Bro. Rylands discovered attached to the cover of his copy of the 1738 *Constitutions* a cancelled leaf in which appeared a number of errors such as "Stephen" instead of "Francis, *Duke of Lorraine*".

I would like to add that some caution requires to be exercised in dealing with Dr. Stukeley's statements, and I would hesitate to say with Bro. Edwards that if such or such an event occurred "Stukeley would have mentioned the facts". The so-called "Diary" was put together by Stukeley at the close of his life. He died in 1765. No doubt he made use of memoranda recorded about the dates given, but he makes reflection on events long after they had taken place. It was quite possible for a brother attending the Annual Feast not to be aware of what had taken place at the earlier Communication of Grand Lodge beforehand. And as for the procession escaping the attention of the Press, the distance between St. Paul's Churchyard and Stationers' Hall is not very great.

The London Library possesses a copy of

> The | Generous Free-Mason | or, the | Constant Lady | with the | Humours | of Squire Noodle and his Man Doodle | a | Tragi-Comi Farcical Ballad | Opera | in Three Acts. | With the Music prefix'd to each Song. | By the Author of the Lovers' Opera. | London. | Printed for J. Roberts in Warwick Lane and Sold | by the Booksellers of London and Westminster. | MDCCXXXI | [Price One Shilling]. |

The printer is he who printed the Old *Constitutions* in 1722. The Opera is inscribed to the Rt. Wor. the Grand Master, Deputy Grand-Master, Grand Wardens and the rest of the Brethren of the Ancient and Honourable Society of Free and Accepted Masons by "Your most Obedient, and Devoted Servant, the Author, a Free-Mason". The title-page of the *Lovers' Opera* (1729) reveals the name "Mr. Chetwood, Prompter of the Theatre", and the Catalogue of the London Library supplies his Christian names, "William Rufus". From the advertisements at the end of the *Generous Free-Mason* I extract:—

> Proposals | By Printing by Subscription | the Life, Memoirs, Voyages, Travels and Adventures of | William Owen Gwinn Vaughan Esq. - - - - - - - [Subscriptions are taken by the Compiler, at the Thea | tre Royal in Drury Lane.] |

It will be remembered that the XVIIth Lodge, which gave its approval to Anderson's *Constitutions* of 1723, remains unidentified, but that its Officers at the end of 1722 were:—

> James Anderson A.M.
>   The Author of this Book. } Master.
>
> Gwinn Vaughan Esq.
> Walter Greenwood Esq. } Wardens.

Bro. DAVID FLATHER *writes*:—

Our sincere congratulations and our grateful thanks are due to Bro. Edwards for his masterly paper.

Frankly, I find it beyond my power to offer any criticism or to add anything of value to it.

Bro. Edwards while confirming the generally accepted opinion as to James Anderson's want of historical truth, throws much light upon his methods and the sources of much of his matter.

I think that Bro. Edwards is perhaps right in suggesting that Anderson's main object was to produce what to-day we should call a "write up" of the

Craft. I venture to suggest that the origin of this idea may have been a definite instruction to produce a book which would assist in widening the scope of organised masonry. The 1723 *Constitutions* throughout convey the impression that they were applicable to a society limited in its range (as in fact it was), to the Cities of London and Westminster.

The 1738 *Constitutions* give me the impression of being an attempt to claim the world-wide and age-long existence of Freemasonry, and to promote the extension of its borders.

With regard to the power of the Grand Master to preside at any private Lodge he may visit, this reminds me of a regular custom which exists in West Yorkshire and probably in other Provinces. It is perhaps hardly a matter which has bearing upon this paper, though it is of interest particularly as the practice might be considered irregular.

The meetings of our Provincial Lodge in West Yorkshire are always held " under the Banner of a Lodge or group of Lodges ", and the following is the procedure:—(1) The Lodge under whose banner the Provincial Lodge is meeting, having obtained the requisite Dispensation, is opened by the Master in form. (2) The Provincial Grand Master, etc., etc., demands admission and enters in procession with his Officers, Grand Officers, etc. (3) The Master or the Lodge presents his Gavel to the Prov. Gd. Master, who accepts and takes the Chair—in like manner the Provincial Officers displace the corresponding Lodge Officers. (4) When Provincial Grand Lodge is closed, the P.G.M. returns the Gavel to the Master, the Lodge Officers resume their stations, and the procession retires. (5) The Master of the Lodge then closes his Lodge in the usual form. There has, in effect, been a short adjournment of the private Lodge, and the Provincial Lodge meeting held during that adjournment. It works perfectly well and, indeed, adds to the solemnity of the meeting—but I doubt if it is strictly regular.

" Foundation Stones " are an interesting subject which I am trying to work up.

While accepting Bros. Lepper and Crosslé's conclusion that Anderson's record is a fiction, it does show that in Anderson's mind and probably in general opinion, the idea of a Masonic stone laying was definitely a suitable ceremony. I would like here to call attention to the use in the same entry of the two words " Foundation Stone " and " Footstone ", which, I think, will be found to be descriptive of two separate and distinct stones.

With regard to Anderson's initiation, unless the Lodge of which his father was a " prominent member " was exclusively operative, and as he was a glazier, and therefore not an operative mason, it is reasonable to suppose that when James was about to leave Aberdeen his father may, realising the advantages of the Craft, have arranged for his becoming a member of it.

Bro. GEO. W. BULLAMORE *writes*:—

One of my youthful memories is of a Dutch tile which was painted to represent Abraham in the act of offering up his son Isaac. The patriarch brandishes a Turkish scimitar and wears knee breeches and a hat like a Quaker Oat advertisement. As Bro. Edwards suggests, such pictures may be aptly compared with Anderson's writings. There is no desire to misrepresent, but the truth can only be regarded as approximate and must be selected according to our knowledge of the subject.

428   *Transactions of the Quatuor Coronati Lodge.*

But when we use negative evidence it is very easy to throw doubt on statements that could have been very easily dealt with at the time by Bro. Anderson. His right to the use of D.D. is an instance of this. And some of the points made by Bro. Edwards against Anderson I should be inclined to regard as unfounded. For instance, on Regulation xiii. "Anderson implied that previously the making not only of Masters but also of Fellow craft was confined to Grand Lodge, which is absurd". But I believe these Regulations to have a basis in the customs of the Livery Companies of the City of London and to have been perfectly sound with an historical basis.

A Livery Company of the City of London was a Gild or Fellowship which governed a body of yeomen or freemen, and where these freemen were a fraternity the Company furnished them with Ordinances, insisted that the master should be of the livery or Fellowship, and collected quarterage without giving them any voice in the government. There was nothing democratic about them, and the master of the Company itself was not elected by the general body but usually by the reigning master and the past masters. The Worshipful Company of Freemasons of the City of London governed the yeomen or journeymen masons, and I think it very unlikely that they allowed these journeymen to appoint to the Livery or Fellowship which governed them. A revival of the system during the rebuilding of London led to a number of honorary masons becoming masterless men after the rebuilding was finished, and it was an attempt to bring these masterless men into an obedience that led to the formation of Grand Lodge. Fellow craft lodges applied to be "Constituted" and led to the repeal of this Regulation for them, but there is no instance of a lodge of modern or first degree masons making fellows or masters. We do know, however, that the Bury Lodge of modern masons evaded the regulation that the master must be among the fellows, for as late at 1768 their master and two past-masters were fellow crafted and raised by the Bolton Lodge.

Then, again, I fail to find that Aubrey is in opposition to Anderson as regards Sir Christopher Wren's connection with Freemasonry. Aubrey having written that Sir Christopher Wren was to be adopted a Free mason in 1691, afterwards corrects it to read the Fraternity of Accepted Masons. The accepted mason appears to have been a journeyman who having been trained in one place was accepted as a mason at another lodge. London must have been full of them at this time. They were workmen, not masters. Aubrey's manuscript does not show that Free mason and accepted mason are interchangeable terms, but that there was a difference which he did not properly understand. If Wren had been, like Ashmole, a member of the Freemasons for many years, it would not prevent his fraternising with the operative masons who were rebuilding St. Paul's Cathedral. Aubrey does not even say that he was to be initiated. He was to be "adopted", which is a term quite appreciable to his joining them although already in possession of their secrets.

Anderson is said to be two years out where he records the appointment of Bro. Moody as sword-bearer on 27th March, 1731. Bros. Edwards and Begemann, relying on the Minutes of Grand Lodge, state that Moody was not appointed until 1733 so Anderson must be wrong. But the copy of the St. Paul's Head Lodge memorial in the *Rawlinson* MSS. shows that these memorialists used the words: "Ever since a Sword of State has been carried before the R.W. the Grand Master at the annual Feast, this Lodge (St. Paul's Head) has carried the same except when Bro. Moody carried it in 1732". If we regard this year as commencing on April 1st we get an exact agreement with Anderson.

To my mind, the wording of the memorial suggests that the St. Paul's Head Lodge had carried the sword for several years, long enough, in fact, to regard it as a right. But this could not be the case if the first procession was in 1730. It would only give them two occasions to the once of Moody. The names of several of their members as given by Rawlinson occur also in the early list of the Queen's Head, Hollis Street, and I therefore identify them with this lodge which was constituted personally by the Duke of Richmond in 1724. They may have carried the sword from 1725 to 1731.

It is fortunate for the Craft that Bro. Anderson was its early historian, but it is probable that many of his absurdities are due to our lack of knowledge and his own lack of clearness. In passing from the accepted Masons of his first *Book of Constitutions* and identifying them with the Freemasons that governed them he has hopelessly muddled and confused the search for our pedigree.

Bro. CECIL ADAMS said:—

It has always appeared to me that, although a commentary on Anderson's second *Book of Constitutions* has been badly needed, only a brave man would face the task. The book is a troublesome one; Jonathan Scott wrote truly when he stated that it appeared " in a very mangled condition ", but there is no doubt that it is of great importance to the Masonic bibliographer. We must remember that this 1738 edition was taken to Ireland and copied by Spratt in 1751, whose book in turn came back to this country in the guise of *Ahiman Rezon* in 1756, and the later editions of Dermott's work take it on to the end of the eighteenth century.

James Anderson could have nothing good to say for the work of William Smith, and for this reason he could hardly appropriate in his second edition that useful address, first published in the *Pocket Companion*, which is now known as the E.A. Charge. But what about the Songs? It seems likely that Anderson borrowed a few of them from Smith, even as Smith, in his turn, had taken other songs from Anderson's 1723 edition. Of the eleven which are printed, certainly two seem to come direct from the *Pocket Companion* and three others are probably from the same source, although they were first printed elsewhere.

The 1738 *Constitutions* has a very modest supply of songs, and one feels that the author regarded that part of his work as of minor importance. Or was it that he did not wish his own songs, now cut to reasonable dimensions, to be lost in a maze of others? Let us give him the benefit of the doubt, and assume that he considered that the " history " and law of Freemasonry should not be confused with things more frivolous.

We must congratulate Bro. Lewis Edwards on his assiduity in giving us a thorough examination of this book, and, at the same time, thank him for his most useful work.

Bro. EDWARDS *writes*, in reply:—

I do feel most truly grateful to the Brethren who have assisted me with their criticisms and with the additional information they have supplied, no less than for the kindness with which the paper has been received. I have felt all along that one who deals with the many points arising in a commentary on the 1738 *Book of Constitutions*, even if possessed of a learning and a quality of carefulness to which I lay no claim, must, so to speak, from the large extent of territory he occupies and the dissemination of his forces, expose himself to many attacks, and I feel most gratified that my main positions are still held at the end of the discussion. I have tried to put the relevant and so often seemingly contradictory facts before the Brethren, and I do not propose to deal in detail with the additional ones brought out in the course of the debate, contenting myself by asking the reader to weigh those brought forward by me with those advanced by my critics, and if he finds in the light of them all that some of my conclusions seems on balance to be erroneous, boldy so to consider them, and I, without any feeling of personal chagrin, will applaud his decision.

With regard to Bro. Firminger's observations I do admit that his points regarding "the E. Book" and also Dr. Stukeley are important factors in considering Anderson's reliability, but how all the various facts are to be reconciled I cannot see. Once again it is a question of the credibility of the witnesses whose evidence is advanced, and as to that each must form his own conclusions. Bro. Flather's remarks are full of interest, and I note with respectful pleasure that he does not appear to disagree with my main conclusions.

I appreciate that Bro. Williams has realised that although I have been compelled to deliver "drastic judgments", I have occasionally shown a "desire to extenuate the delinquencies of the Author". If I set about my task with any object or any prejudice beyond a desire to seek the truth, it was to rehabilitate Anderson and to gratify my patriotism by showing Begemann's strictures to be unfounded, but quite early I found to my regret that save in those cases which I have been careful to point out, Anderson, though his attitude could in many cases be explained, could not be rehabilitated and patriotism had to make way for truth. If in Bro. Williams' words Anderson was "the Father of the Authentic School", how is the adjective to be reconciled with our Brother's view of the *History* as a "decorated, distorted and adapted version of plain facts dyed with Masonic tinctures"?

With regard to Bro. Bullamore's observation, I note his ingenious theory as to that perplexing period before 1717, when there seem to have been both the operative masons of a lower service order and the speculative or (shall we say?) gentlemen masons. I do not think, however, that if Wren had been already a speculative or honorary mason he would have later become, so to speak, an honorary member of the operative craft, and then why so late as 1691? The question of Bro. Moody and the Sword of State, taking into account Bro. Bullamore's objections, seems to be as follows. The Minutes of 29th January, 1781, state that Moody had finished the Sword by that date and had his health drunk for his services, but do not mention his appointment as Sword-Bearer. From this fact and from the memorial regarding St. Paul's Head Lodge not being presented until 29th May, 1733, it would appear that Moody did not receive his appointment in 1731, but at the meeting on 7th June, 1733, as recorded in the Minutes of that date. The Deputy Grand Master in his observations of 29th May, 1733, does not deny that the St. Paul's Head Sword had been carried in previous years, but says that as the new Sword is the Grand Master's it must be carried by the Grand Master's nominee. The position is not, I admit, free from difficulty. On the one hand, if Moody was appointed in 1731, why did not the Minutes say so, and why did the memorialists delay until 1733? On the other, if the Sword was "finished" in 1731, why was not Moody then or soon thereafter appointed, and who carried the Sword (and which Sword?) between 1731 and 1733?

That the subject of the 1738 Edition of *Anderson's Constitutions* required detailed treatment in our *Transactions* I feel confident, and it is as much a pleasure as a duty for me to acknowledge that the paper would never have been written by me, or if written would have shown even more inadequacy had it not been for the inspiration, encouragement and assistance I have had from Bros. Hills, Songhurst and Vibert. Further, Bro. Vibert has eked out my very insufficient knowledge of German by placing at my disposal his unfortunately as yet unpublished translation of *Begemann*.

FACSIMILE REPRINT OF
QUATUOR CORONATORUM ANTIGRAPHA, VOLUME 7

Masonic Reprints

OF THE

LODGE QUATUOR CORONATI NO. 2076, LONDON

1890

QUATUOR CORONATORUM ANTIGRAPHA.

Masonic Reprints

OF THE

Lodge Quatuor Coronati, No. 2076, London.

FROM THE ISABELLA MISSAL.

BRITISH MUSEUM, ADD. MSS., 18,851,
CIRCA, 1500 A.D.

EDITED BY G. W. SPETH, P.M., SECRETARY.

VOLUME VII.

Margate:
PRINTED AT "KEBLE'S GAZETTE" OFFICE.
MDCCCXC.

VOLUME VII.

THE NEW BOOK OF CONSTITUTIONS,

BY

JAMES ANDERSON, D.D.,

MDCCXXXVIII.,

In the Vulgar Year of Masonry, 5738,

WITH AN

INTRODUCTION

BY WILLIAM JAMES HUGHAN, P.M.,

PAST GRAND DEACON.

THE
HISTORY and CONSTITUTIONS
OF THE
Most ancient and honourable Fraternity
OF
Free and Accepted MASONS:

CONTAINING

An ACCOUNT of MASONRY. I. From the Creation, throughout the known Earth, till true Architecture was demolished by the *Goths,* and at last revived in *Italy.* II. From *Julius Cæsar* to the first Arrival of the *Saxons* in *Britain.* III. From the Union of the Crowns of *England* and *Scotland,* in the Person of King *James* the First, to the present Time.

TO WHICH ARE ADDED

I. A List of the GRAND MASTERS or Patrons of the Free Masons in *England,* from the coming in of the *Anglo Saxons* to these Times, who are mentioned in this Work.
II. The old Charges of the Masons, collected from their earliest Records, at the Command of his Grace the Duke of *Montague.*
III. The Manner of constituting a Lodge.
IV. The general Regulations of the free and accepted Masons, both ancient and modern, in distinct Columns.

V. The Constitution of the Committee of their Charity.
VI. A List of the Lodges in and about *London* and *Westminster*; with the Deputations of several grand Masters for the forming of Lodges in *Wales,* the remote Parts of *England,* and foreign Realms.
VII. The Songs sung at the Lodges.
VIII. A Defence of Masonry, occasioned by a Pamphlet called *Masonry Dissected*: With Brother *Euclid*'s Letter to the Author against unjust Cavils.

By *JAMES ANDERSON* D.D.

LONDON: Printed; and sold by J. ROBINSON, at the *Golden-Lion* in *Ludgate-street.*

In the vulgar Year of MASONRY 5746

INTRODUCTION.

THE first "Book of Constitutions" for the premier Grand Lodge was published in 1723, and was by the Rev. James Anderson. As Dr. J. T. Desaguliers wrote the Dedication, his name has been quoted as the Editor, but in error, for in the list of twenty Masters (with their Wardens) who united with the Grand Master and Grand Officers in their approbation of the volume, the 17th Lodge has conspicuously displayed, "JAMES ANDERSON, A.M., The 𝕬𝖚𝖙𝖍𝖔𝖗 of *this* 𝕭𝖔𝖔𝖐."

The Society then was called the "Right Worshipful FRATERNITY of Accepted Free MASONS," but towards the end of the book the more lengthy and appropriate title is noted of "The Right Worshipful and most ancient *Fraternity* of *Free* and *Accepted Masons*." Another change is observable in the second edition of 1738 by James Anderson, D.D., the words "𝕬𝖓𝖙𝖎𝖊𝖓𝖙 and Honourable" being introduced.

The original Regulations, numbered I. to XXXIX. were "Compiled first by Mr. George Payne, *Anno* 1720, when he was 𝕲𝖗𝖆𝖓𝖉 𝕸𝖆𝖘𝖙𝖊𝖗," but were "digested" and arranged by the "*Author* of this Book, for the Use of the Lodges in and about *London* and *Westminster*."[1] From 1724, Lodges were constituted in the Provinces, and from 1728-9 also abroad, so that the Laws soon needed considerable revision and additions. Accordingly, at the Grand Lodge on February 24th, 1735,

> " Bro. Dr. Anderson, formerly Grand Warden, represented that he had spent some thoughts upon some alterations and additions that might fittly be made to the Constitutions, the first Edition being all sold off. *Resolved.* That a Committee be appointed * * * * to revise and compare the same," etc.[2]

The "*New* Book of *Constitutions*" was approved by the Grand Lodge, and the members "order'd the Author Brother *Anderson* to print the same," on January 25th, 1738. In the work Dr. Anderson is supposed to have reprinted the "𝕺𝖑𝖉 REGULATIONS," and added "the 𝕹𝖊𝖜 REGULATIONS in a distinct opposite Column," but even a cursory examination of the former, side by side, with the first edition of 1723, will reveal the fact that the reproduction was not only carelessly done, but in several instances distinct departures from the original text are to be detected, so much so as to considerably lessen the value of the reprint. The unwarrantable alterations are just those which tend to introduce Masonic terms, *as of* 1723, which were then unfamiliar or unknown, such as "Master Mason" instead of "Fellow Craft;" hence due care must be exercised in accepting any part of the reproduction of these Rules as being in exact accord with the originals.

There is thus no lack of confirmation of the statement in Scott's "Pocket Companion," (1754, etc.), that the "Constitutions of 1738 appeared in a very mangled condition." But whatever may be its merits or demerits, according as we look at the volume leniently or critically, the fact remains that to it, and to it alone, we are indebted for a history of the Grand Lodge of England from its inauguration in 1717 to 1723, when the official Records begin, and from that period for an able extract of the Proceedings; hence the work has been described as the "*basis of Masonic History*" by Professor Robison, and its author is termed by the Rev. A. F. A. Woodford "*the Father of English Masonic History*," both titles being fairly earned in respect to the sketch of the premier Grand Lodge.

The importance of the work, united with its admitted scarcity, sufficiently justify the Committee in selecting it as one of the series of Reprints which are a special feature of the

---

[1] Constitutions 1723, p. 58. (*Lodge Catalogue* No. 1074.)
[2] Bro. Gould's "History of Freemasonry," chapter xii. (*Catalogue* No. 242, etc.)

vi.   *Introduction.*

"Quatuor Coronati" Lodge, and contribute considerably to its usefulness as a Masonic organization.

The major portion of the Historical Chapters "from the Creation" to the "Grand Mastership of Sir Christopher Wren," had better be left in the hands of those brethren who care to test the statement of the compiler that "most of the Facts are generally well known in *Sacred, Civil,* and *Ecclesiastical* Histories," and likewise that the omission of any "necessary vouchers" is supplied by an "*exact Chronology.*"

As to these points, as Dr. Anderson observes, "It is good to know what not to say;" but unfortunately his practice was quite the reverse of the advice he gave, "from his *Study* in 𝕰𝖝𝖊𝖙𝖊𝖗 𝕮𝖔𝖚𝖗𝖙, *Strand,* 4th November, 1738," on completing the Address "to the Reader."

The extracts from the "Old Charges" of the mainly operative *régime* in the two editions of the "Constitutions" call for a few words of explanation. The first excerpt, relative to St. Alban, p. 57 edit. 1738, was not in the original issue, and seems to have been taken from "A Book of the Antient Constitutions of the Free and Accepted Masons," engraved and published by B. Cole, 1728-9, and also in 1731. Very few of the Scrolls have the wages noted at so low a rate as "*two shillings a week and three pence to their chear,*" and it is probable that only one or two of these, which agree with Cole and Anderson, were known to the latter Brother. Not one, however, of all the versions of the "Old Charges, etc.," traced and collated of late years and numbering over fifty (ranging from the 14th to the present century), confirm the pernicious interpolation of that modern title, "*Grand Master,*" made by Dr. Anderson, who was lamentably prone to modernize the phraseology of ancient documents, and alter them to suit his whims, whenever he had occasion to cite their testimony.

The second extract (page 63) is somewhat after the style of the 1723 edition, only that now Edwin is described as the "King's Brother," according to the "Inigo Jones'" and "Cole's" texts; whereas formerly that Prince was termed the "King's youngest son," thus favouring the reading of "Roberts' MS.," 1722, "Briscoe's MS.," 1724-5, and most other texts, manuscript and printed. Possibly Anderson preferred to follow the lead of Dr. Plot in his "History of Staffordshire," 1686, which work may not have been known to him in the year 1723. In this garbled extract the "General Lodge" of 1723 is altered to "Grand Lodge," and the year 926 is added. The "Inigo Jones MS." has 932; no more evidence existing for the one than the other, as the MSS. generally are silent as to the date.

The third quotation (page 71) immediately follows the foregoing citation, in the 1723 edition; nothing being said about "*the glorious Reign of* KING EDWARD III." The fourth and two succeeding paragraphs in the 2nd edition occur in a foot note in the senior publication, with the intimation that they were taken from "another transcript more ancient."

The document thus noted was probably one of the "old Copies of the *Gothic Constitutions* produced and collated" in 1718[1]; possibly the "Matthew Cooke MS.,"[2] which in 1728 was copied by Grand Secretary Cowper, who styled it "a very ancient Record of Masonry."[3] This handsome transcript, known as "Woodford's MS.," is now the property of our Lodge, No. 2076.[4] On June 24th, 1721, Dr. Stukeley states in his Diary, "Grand Master Pain [Payne] produced an old MS. of the Constitutions," and exhibited it to the members of Grand Lodge. Dr. Stukeley copied the opening sentences, which are still preserved, and from these we know that it was the "Cooke MS.," or a similar text.[5] The most important extract from the "Old Charges" occurs at page 101, but is not in the 1723 edition. The first typographical reproduction of these Regulations was by Roberts in 1722, in which rare pamphlet they are entitled,

"Additional Orders and Constitutions made and agreed
upon at a General Assembly held at . . . . . .
on the Eighth Day of December, 1663."

I daresay Roberts supplied the above title, but in what may fairly be classed as the original text, viz., the "Harleian MS., No. 1942" (British Museum) these Rules are simply termed "The New Articles,"[6] and are peculiar to that Codex. Dr. Anderson apparently was not satisfied with the date selected, so changed it to "St. John's Day, 27th Dec., 1663," in order to give it a Masonic flavour! This, however, is far from being the most serious of

---

[1] *Constitutions,* 1738, p. 110.   [2] Vol 2 "Quatuor Coronatorum Antigrapha."
[3] Hughan's "Old Charges of British Freemasons," 1872, p. 4. (*Catalogue* No. 239.)
[4] No. 253 in *Catalogue.*   [5] Bro. T. B. Whytehead, "Freemason," 31st July, 1880.
[6] O.C. p. 56, and Q.C. Antigrapha, Vol. 2.

the alterations and departures from the "Harleian MS."[1] or of the "Roberts'" pamphlet. Clause 1 has added, "*unless in a regular Lodge,*" and in the 5th "*Master*" is transformed into "*Grand Master*," whilst the 7th is omitted!

Into the larger question of the actual age of the "Harleian MS., No. 1942," or of the "Inigo Jones MS.," I must not now enter, save to state that the latter part of the 17th century appears to me a very safe estimate. The period of fifty years earlier has been assigned to the former by a very eminent paleographist, but Dr. Begemann favours a much later date for both these MSS. At present, however, I can only refer my readers to the arguments of that industrious Masonic student,[2] and to a careful consideration of the texts of both documents.

Dr. Anderson undoubtedly consulted several copies of the "Old Charges" whilst preparing the 2nd edition of his "Book of Constitutions." These or similar versions are still preserved, and are well known to Masonic experts. To them may possibly be added the "Aberdeen MS." of A.D. 1670 (the unusual reference to "Ninus," page 16, agreeing with that document), and also the missing York MS. of A.D. 1630.[3]

The author did not think enough of the Abraham-Euclid legend to cite it (both of these old worthies, however, are incidentally alluded to), though common to all the regular MSS. except the "Lansdowne" and "Antiquity." The order of the "Seven Liberal Sciences" accords with nearly all the complete Masonic MSS. known, and so does the paragraph concerning CHARLES MARTEL and his Teacher *Mimus Græcus* (with variations), the few exceptions as to the latter legend ("Inigo Jones" family or group) scarcely requiring particularization.

Happily, in due time, the whole of the valuable copies of the "Old Charges" of English and Scottish Freemasons (which communicate light and information during centuries when the minutes of Lodges are silent), will be reproduced, with scrupulous exactitude, by the "Quatuor Coronati" Lodge, and then intelligent and earnest Craftsmen throughout the "wide, wide world" will be able to study those ancient documents for themselves, both in relation to this work of 1738, and to the much more important and extensive question of the usages and customs of the Freemasons during the past five centuries and still earlier times. We are already being prepared to welcome such extensive publications and reproductions by the scholarly labours of Bro. R. F. Gould in relation to the "Regius MS."[4] (the venerable senior of the series), and the able services of Bro. G. W. Speth in relation to the second oldest document, the "Matthew Cooke MS."[5]

"The Charges of a Free-Mason," which introduce the "General Regulations" of 1723, are mainly to be found in the 2nd edition of 1738, but again the insatiable desire of Anderson to modernize and alter is conspicuously manifest. Strictly speaking, the second issue is not the same as that "Ordered to be printed in the first Edition of the Book of Constitutions on 25 March 1722," though the compiler says otherwise. The first charge, concerning "God and Religion," is an old favourite, and substantially remains to this day, save in the vexatious alterations in the 1738 edition. No better exposition, in brief, of the true basis of the Fraternity, or description of its aims and tendency, has ever been written.

Of course, these Charges, which preface the Laws from 1723 onwards, were not actually "collected by the Author from the old Records of the Free and Accepted Masons," but were the composition of Dr. Anderson, who thus produced, in modern verbiage, a more or less accurate digest of the Laws that formerly governed the Lodges.

The Dedication to H.R.H. the Prince of Wales, "A *Master* MASON, and *Master* of a LODGE," was by order of the Grand Master and the Grand Lodge. The Author had the honour of an introduction to the Prince early in 1739, and in the name of the Fraternity presented a copy of the new Book of Constitutions to His Royal Highness, which was graciously accepted.

It is remarkable that "the geniuses to whom the world is indebted for the memorable invention of Modern Masonry" *in* 1717, according to Bro. Thomas Grinsell (*cited by Bro. Laurence Dermott* in the "Ahiman Rezon," 1778, etc., and declared to be "a man of great veracity") were the brethren who were present at the palace of Kew, and formed the

---

[1] Vide Reproduction of the Harleian MS., No. 1942, Vol. 2 "Quatuor Coronatorum Antigrapha."
[2] "Freemason," July 9th and 16th, 1887. Transactions, Vol. 1.
[3] Hargroves "History of York," Vol. 2, 1818, pp. 475-480.
[4] Commentary, Vol. 1, "Masonic Reprints."
[5] Introduction to the "Matthew Cooke MS." etc., Vol. 2, M.R.

viii.   *Introduction.*

"occasional Lodge" for the initiation of H.R.H. Frederic, Prince of Wales, *on 5th Nov.*, 1737 ! From 1778 to 1881 no one seems to have detected the anachronism, but in the latter year Bro. Gould ably exposed the treacherous memory of Dermott's friend and completely shattered the pretentious declaration.[1]

When and where Dr. Anderson was born we know not, and we are in like ignorance as to his initiation. Bro. Gould thinks he may have first "seen the light" at Aberdeen, and there is much to favour that supposition, though no actual facts. Anderson certainly was familiar with Scottish phraseology, and in all probability the visit of Dr. Desaguliers, F.R.S. to Edinburgh in 1721 for scientific purposes contributed also to the same result. Of "the creationist school of Masonic Historians he is the *facile princeps*,"[2] but those who would discard his labours on that account would commit a grave error, as it is not difficult to distinguish between his facts and his fancies, and the value of the former to a great extent counterbalances the frequency of the latter.

The Rev. James Anderson was the minister of the Scottish Presbyterian Church, Swallow Street, Piccadilly, and known to fame as the author of the "Royal Genealogies," 1732 (2nd edition, 1736). He was Master of a Lodge as early as 1722, was appointed J.G.W. by the Duke of Wharton, G.M., on 17th January, 1723, and was a member of the Lodge known as "Original No. 4" (*now* No. 4), with his friends Grand Masters Payne and Desaguliers. As the author of the Constitutions 1723-38, and for his devotion to the Fraternity his name will be gratefully remembered so long as Freemasonry exists. Dr. Anderson's last appearance in Grand Lodge was on April 6th, 1738, when he acted as J.G.W., and his death occurred on May 28th, 1739. He was described in the latter year as "a gentleman of uncommon abilities and most facetious conversation."[3] Dr. Desaguliers was equally devoted to the Craft, his last attendance in Grand Lodge being on Feb. 8th, 1742, his death occurring just two years later (Feb. 29th). The third of the zealous trio, George Payne, was present in Grand Lodge so late as November 29th, 1754, and was appointed on the Committee for the revision of the Constitutions 1738, (April, 1754), preparatory to the publication of the 3rd edition of 1756. He died soon afterwards, viz., on Jan. 23rd, 1757.

Bro. Gould's noble *History* should be consulted as to the period 1717-38, particularly in relation to these three respected Masonic veterans, for, much as I should wish, any attempt to dwell on that interesting subject must resolutely be deferred.

It only remains for me now to say a few brief words on the bibliographical aspect of the question. First of all, the edition of the "Book of Constitutions" for 1723 claims attention.[4] It became the model or standard of all the Laws of the Craft promulgated by other Grand Lodges, was reprinted in Philadelphia, U.S.A., so soon as 1734, by Bro. Benjamin Franklin, and also reproduced in other Regulations abroad, being accepted almost as veritable "Old Landmarks." An excellent reprint of this very scarce book is to be found in Bro. Kenning's "Archæological Library," Vol. I., which includes a reproduction of one of the "Phillipps' MSS." of the 17th century.[5] Another capital reissue of the work forms one of Bro. Spencer's "Old Constitutions,"[6] 1871, which also contains the "Roberts' MS." of 1722, "Spencer's" 1726 *circa* ("Cole's" text), and the Laws of the Grand Lodge of Ireland for 1730.

The 2nd edition of 1738 *has never been reprinted in this country*, and the reproduction by Bro. Hyneman in America was poorly and imperfectly done, so that virtually this is the first of the kind worthy of the name. It is in *exact facsimile*, by Charles Praetorius, Clareville Grove, Hereford Sq., S.W. The process is so perfect that had it been printed on paper of the period it would almost pass as the original work.

As a few were left on hands of the publishers in either 1742 or 1746, but most likely the latter year ("Year of Masonry, 5746"), a new title page was inserted in lieu of the one of 1738, of rather an elaborate character, which by my desire Bro. Speth has had reproduced, and which faces p. v., supplied from Bro. John Lane's copy, who fraternally placed it at the Editor's disposal. Save in this respect, through possibly a change of publishers, the 1738 and 1746 are one and the same work, the latter being the rarer of the two. I have only succeeded in tracing twenty-six of the original issue, and nineteen of the one with the new title page, making forty-five in all, (about one-third "large paper" and two-thirds "small paper,") of which eleven of each have been reported as having Frontispieces the same

---

[1] "Freemason," Feb. 12th and April 9th, 1881. [2] Gould, Vol. 1 p. 105.
[3] "Scot's Magazine," 1739, Vol. 1, p. 236.
[4] One of the original edition, with Frontispiece, is in the Library of the "Quatuor Coronati" Lodge (*Catalogue* No. 1074).   [5] Cat. No. 1085.   [6] Cat. No. 944.

as those of 1723, only without the lettering at foot.[1] These are located in England and the United States, so that probably there are a few more in existence elsewhere.

Bro. John E. Le Feuvre (who has a complete set of the Constitutions 1723-1888),[2] kindly lent his copy of A.D. 1738, having the Frontispiece, for reproduction in our series of Reprints, and I feel assured this tangible proof of his interest in the spread of Masonic literature will be warmly appreciated by all the members of the "Inner" and "Outer" Circles of the "Quatuor Coronati" Lodge.

From internal evidence, I do not think this edition was out of the hands of the printers until early in 1739.[3]

Bro. W. H. Rylands has directed my attention to the leaf pp. 129-30, which was substituted for one cancelled in consequence of its errors. I had not noticed it, neither has anyone else to my knowledge. In his copy, curiously enough, he found, attached to the cover, the central part of the confiscated leaf, which shows some of the errors, such as "STEPHEN," instead of "FRANCIS, Duke of *Lorrain*," and also some other mistakes.

Bro. Rylands tells me that in the "History of the Works of the Learned for the year 1739," (issued in November) vol. II., pp. 317-352, is a long series of extracts from this Book of Constitutions, but not a review proper. It is headed "An incorrect Sketch of this Article was communicated to us by Dr. Anderson himself, a little before his Decease."

The "Defence of Masonry," in answer to Prichard's "Masonry Dissected," is supposed to have been originally published in 1730, but no copy of that date is known. The edition reprinted in the first volume of the "Quatuor Coronatorum Antigrapha" was taken from the "Pocket Companion" of 1738, which was doubtless printed and circulated in the year named, and consequently prior to the publication of the "Constitutions" of 1738. As to its authorship, which is uncertain, I must again forbear extending the limits of this introduction, but evidently Dr. Anderson did not write it, though he has been credited with so doing. Neither do we know who wrote Euclid's letter.

The 3rd edition of the "Book of Constitutions" edited by the Rev. John Entick, was published in 1756, and the 4th in 1767, both having a frontispiece by B. Cole, the Arms of the Grand Lodge forming a special feature of the design. In 1776 an Appendix was issued, written by Bro. William Preston, but now rarely met with. An unauthorized edition was published in 1769 (8vo.) by G. Kearsly, London, and, with another title page and plates, by Thomas Wilkinson, Dublin, in the same year.

The 5th edition is a volume of noble proportions, and though published in 1784, the plate by Bros. Bartolozzi, Cipriani, etc., does not appear to have been ready before 1786. It was edited by Bro. John Noorthouck, and is the last that contains either the long Historical Introduction, or the Transactions of the Grand Lodge and other particulars.[4]

The 6th edition of 1815[5] was the first after the "Union" of December 27th, 1813, and with the 7th of 1819 (corrected sheets) and 8th of 1827 were entitled "Second Part," the first portion containing the Historical Summary, being deferred, but ultimately was dropt, so that the 9th edition of 1841 began the regular series, since continued, with the plates of jewels, etc. The year 1819 saw the last of the quarto series. The 10th, 11th, and 12th editions were published in 1847, 1853, and 1855, respectively, the last mentioned being also issued in 32mo., termed "a Pocket Edition,"—but is very rare now.

The 13th of 1858, and 14th of 1861 are still often to be met with, the junior of the two commencing their sale at the reduced price of 1/6 each. The 15th, of 1863, is now difficult to procure, especially in the larger size, though 2000 were published in 8vo. and 4000 in 32mo. Two editions in 32mo., of 1865 and 1866, (16th and 17th) are very scarce, particularly the former, only two having been traced quite recently. In 1867 the 18th, and in 1871 the 19th appeared, followed in 1873 by the 20th. An entirely new issue began in 1884, being the 21st; the "Book of Constitutions" having been thoroughly revised and re-arranged, after considerable labour was bestowed on its compilation by the Board of General Purposes, and a draft of the proposed revision was circulated by order of the Grand

---

[1] *Vide* letter by Bro. Le Feuvre, "Freemason," Oct. 9th, 1886.
[2] Exhibited at the Plymouth Masonic Exhibition, June 27th, 1887 (*Catalogue* No. 109).
[3] See Bro. Lane's "Handy Book to the Lists of Lodges, 1723-1814" (pp. 35-8) as to this point, and also concerning the Roll of Lodges given by Dr. Anderson, pp. 185-196. (*Catalogue* No. 901).
[4] I gave a brief sketch of the "Constitutions 1723-1888" in the "Freemason," Sept. 15th, 1888, and at more length in a series of articles in that paper for 1886. (*Catalogue* No. 582).
[5] Reprinted in Hughan's "Memorials of the Union," (1872).

Introduction.

Lodge, June 7th, 1882. Meetings of that Body were held on June 29th and August 8th, 1883, and on 5th December following the revision was settled to the complete satisfaction of the many concerned. Although 10,000 were printed of the 8vo. and 20,000 of the 32mo. sizes, another edition was soon demanded, and was issued A.D. 1888, in 32mo., (slips were inserted in those that remained of the 8vo. edition) thus making twenty-two editions in all from 1723 to 1888. I have already alluded to a complete set being owned by Bro. Le Feuvre; another was also exhibited by Bro. George Taylor at the Masonic Exhibition, Shanklin, September 1886.[1] I am not aware that any other brethren have been so fortunate.

It may be as well to state that the Regulations published for the "Ancient" Grand Lodge or "Atholl Masons," and known as the "Ahiman Rezon," were eight in number, viz., I. 1756; II. 1764; III. 1778; IV. 1787; V. 1800; VI. 1801; VII. 1807; VIII. 1813; the last two having Lists of Lodges.

W. J. HUGHAN.

[1] *Lodge Catalogue* No. 324

THE NEW BOOK
OF
CONSTITUTIONS
OF THE
𝔄ntient and *Honourable* FRATERNITY
OF
FREE and ACCEPTED MASONS.

CONTAINING

Their *History, Charges, Regulations,* &c.

COLLECTED and DIGESTED

By Order of the GRAND LODGE from their old *Records,* faithful *Traditions* and *Lodge-Books,*

For the Use of the LODGES.

By JAMES ANDERSON D. D.

L O N D O N:
Printed for Brothers CÆSAR WARD and RICHARD CHANDLER, Bookfellers, at the *Ship* without *Temple-Bar*; and fold at their Shops in *Coney-Street,* YORK, and at SCARBOROUGH-SPAW.

M DCC XXXVIII.
In the *Vulgar* Year of 𝔐𝔞𝔰𝔬𝔫𝔯𝔶 5738.

TO THE
Most *High*, *Puissant* and most *Illustrious* PRINCE

FRIDERICK LEWIS,

Prince *Royal* of GREAT-BRITAIN,
Prince and 𝕾𝖙𝖊𝖜𝖆𝖗𝖙 of SCOTLAND,
PRINCE of *WALES*,
Electoral Prince of 𝕭𝖗𝖚𝖓𝖘𝖜𝖎𝖈𝖐-𝕷𝖚𝖓𝖊𝖇𝖚𝖗𝖌,
Duke of *Cornwall*, *Rothsay*, and *Edinburgh*,
Marquis of the *Isle of Ely*,
Earl of *Chester* and *Flint*, *Eltham* and *Carrick*,
Viscount *Launceston*,
Lord of the *Isles*, *Kyle* and *Cunningham*,
Baron of *Snaudon* and *Renfrew*,
Knight of the most noble Order of the 𝕲𝖆𝖗𝖙𝖊𝖗,
Fellow of the *Royal* Society,
A *Master* MASON, and *Master* of a LODGE.

GREAT SIR,

DEDICATION.

GREAT SIR,

HE *Marquis* of CAERNARVON our Right Worshipful GRAND MASTER, with his 𝕯𝖊𝖕𝖚𝖙𝖞 and 𝖂𝖆𝖗𝖉𝖊𝖓𝖘, and the *Fraternity*, have ordered me their Author humbly to dedicate, in their Name, this their Book of 𝕮𝖔𝖓𝖘𝖙𝖎𝖙𝖚𝖙𝖎𝖔𝖓𝖘 to Your ROYAL HIGHNESS.

It was perused and approved by the former and present *Grand* Officers, and was order'd to be publish'd by our late *Grand Master* the Earl of DARNLEY with his 𝕯𝖊𝖕𝖚𝖙𝖞 and 𝖂𝖆𝖗𝖉𝖊𝖓𝖘, and by the GRAND LODGE in his *Mastership*.

Your ROYAL HIGHNESS well knows, that our *Fraternity* has been often patronized by *Royal* Persons in former Ages; whereby *Architecture* early obtain'd the Title of the 𝕽𝖔𝖞𝖆𝖑 𝕬𝖗𝖙: And the *Free-Masons* have always endeavour'd to deserve that Patronage by their Loyalty.

For

DEDICATION.

For we meddle not with Affairs of State in our *Lodges*, nor with any Thing that may give Umbrage to Civil *Magistrates*, that may break the Harmony of our own *Communications*, or that may weaken the *Cement* of the LODGE.

And whatever are our different Opinions in other Things (leaving all Men to Liberty of Conscience) as *Masons* we harmoniously agree in the noble *Science* and the *Royal Art*, in the *Social* Virtues, in being *True* and *Faithful*, and in avoiding what may give Offence to any Powers round the Globe, under whom we can peaceably assemble in *Ample Form*; as now we happily do in these Islands under Your *Royal Father*, and our Sovereign *Lord*
King GEORGE II.

The *Fraternity* being All duly sensible of the very great Honour done them by your becoming their ROYAL *Brother* and *Patron*, have commanded me thus to signify their Gratitude, their brotherly Love to your *Royal* Person, and
their

DEDICATION.

their humble Duty to Your *Royal* PRINCESS, wishing her to be the happy Mother of many *Sons*, whose Descendants shall also prove the Patrons of the *Fraternity* in all future Ages.

In this the *Free* and *Accepted* 𝔐𝔞𝔰𝔬𝔫𝔰 are unanimous, and none can more heartily wish it, than in all Humility,

GREAT SIR,

Your ROYAL HIGHNESS's.

True and *Faithful*

James Anderson.

The *Author* to the *Reader*.

THE Free-Masons had always a Book in *Manuscript* call'd the *Book* of 𝕮onſtitutions, (of which they have ſeveral very antient Copies remaining) containing not only their *Charges* and *Regulations*, but alſo the Hiſtory of *Architecture* from the Beginning of Time; in order to ſhew the Antiquity and Excellency of the *Craft* or *Art*, and how it gradually aroſe upon its ſolid Foundation the noble *Science* of Geometry, by the Encouragement of *Royal*, *Noble* and *Learned* Patrons in every Age and in all polite Nations.

But they had no *Book* of 𝕮onſtitutions in Print, till his *Grace* the preſent Duke of Montagu, when *Grand Maſter*, order'd me to peruſe the old *Manuscripts*, and digeſt the 𝕮onſtitutions with a juſt *Chronology*.

This *new* Book is above twice as large, having many proper Additions, eſpecially the principal Tranſactions of the *Grand Lodge* ever ſince.

The Hiſtory is now in three Parts, and each Part in ſeven Chapters, *viz.*

PART I.

The *Hiſtory* of Masonry from the *Creation* throughout the known Earth, till good old *Architecture*, demoliſh'd by the 𝕲oths, was revived in *Italy*.

Chap.		Page
I.	From the Creation to *Grand Maſter* Nimrod.	1
II.	From NIMROD to *Grand Maſter* Solomon.	5
III.	From SOLOMON to *Grand Maſter* Cyrus.	11
IV.	From CYRUS to *Grand Maſter* Seleucus.	22
V.	From SELEUCUS to *Grand Maſter* Augustus Cæsar.	29
VI.	From AUGUSTUS till the *Havock* of the 𝕲oths.	37
VII.	The Revival of good old *Architecture* in *Italy*.	47

The *Author* to the *Reader*.

PART II.

The *History* of MASONRY in 𝔅𝔯𝔦𝔱𝔞𝔦𝔫 from JULIUS CÆSAR's *Invasion*, till the *Union* of the *Crowns* on the Death of Queen ELIZABETH, A. D. 1603.

CHAP. I. From JULIUS CÆSAR Page
till the first Arrival of the SAXONS. ———— 55
II. From the Arrival of the SAXONS
to WILLIAM the *Conqueror*. ———————— 59
III. From King WILLIAM the *Conqueror*
to HENRY IV. ——————————————— 67
IV. From King HENRY IV. to the Royal *Tewdors*,
or HENRY VII. ————————————————— 73
V. From King HENRY VII.
till the *Union* of the *Crowns*, A. D. 1603. ———— 75
VI. *Masonry* in SCOTLAND till the said *Union*. ——— 82
VII. *Masonry* in IRELAND till *Grand Master* KINGSTON. 91

PART III.

The *History* of MASONRY in 𝔅𝔯𝔦𝔱𝔞𝔦𝔫 from the *Union* of the *Crowns*, A. D. 1603. to our present *Grand Master* CAERNARVON.

CHAP. I. The AUGUSTAN STILE from the said UNION Page
till the *Restoration*. ——————————————— 97
II. From the RESTORATION till the *Revolution*. — 101
III. From the REVOLUTION to *Grand Master* MONTAGU. 106
IV. From MONTAGU to *Grand Master* RICHMOND,
including WHARTON and BUCKLEUGH. 112
V. From RICHMOND to *Grand Master* NORFOLK,
including ABERCORN, INCHIQUIN, COLERANE
and KINGTON. 117
VI. From NORFOLK to *Grand Master* CRAUFURD,
including LOVEL, Viscount MONTAGU, and
STRATHMORE. 124
VII. From CRAUFURD to our present *Grand Master*
CAERNARVON, including
WEYMOUTH, LOUDOUN, and DARNLEY. 132

NEXT,

The *Author* to the *Reader*.

NEXT,

	Page
— A List of the GRAND MASTERS of *England* that are mention'd in this Book.	140
— The old CHARGES of the *Free Masons*.	143
— The antient Manner of CONSTITUTING a *Lodge*.	149
— The General REGULATIONS, *Old* and *New*, in opposite Columns.	152
— The **Constitution** of the COMMITTEE of *Masons Charity*.	178
— A *List* of the LODGES in and about *London* and *Westminster*.	184
— **Deputations** of several *Grand Masters*, to WALES, to the Country of ENGLAND, and to Parts beyond Sea.	190
— The APPROBATION of this *Book*.	199
— Some of the usual *Masons* SONGS.	200
— A *Defence* of MASONRY, in Answer to a Pamphlet call'd *Masonry Dissected*.	216
— Brother **Euclid**'s Letter to the *Author* against unjust Cavils.	226

Most regular Societies have had, and will have, their own *Secrets*; and, to be sure, the *Free-Masons* always had theirs, which they never divulged in *Manuscript*; and therefore cannot be expected in *Print*: Only, an expert Brother, by the true Light, can readily find many useful Hints in almost every Page of this Book, which *Cowans*, and Others not Initiated, cannot discern.

It had been tedious, and of no great Use, to have pointed at all the *Authors* consulted and collated in compiling the *History* of this Book; especially as most of the Facts are generally well known in *Sacred*, *Civil* and *Ecclesiastical* Histories: Only some Authors are quoted as more necessary Vouchers. But the Omission is well enough supply'd by an exact *Chronology*, viz.

The *Author* to the *Reader*.

The *Hebrew* Chronology before the *Christian Era*, according to Usher, Spanheim, Prideaux, and other such accurate *Chronologers*. And after the *Christian Era* begins, the *History* is here deduced according to the Vulgar *Anno Domini*, or the Year of the *Christian Era*; as on the Margin of Page 2.

Some few *Genealogies* are put in the Margin (not to hinder the Reader) that are needful for the Connection of the History. But in Part II. and III. they shew more distinctly how the *Craft* has been well encouraged in the several Periods and Successions of the *Saxon*, *Danish*, *Norman*, *Plantagenet*, *Welch* and *Scots* Kings of *England*, down to the present Royal Family.

But the *History* here chiefly concerns Masonry, without meddling with other Transactions, more than what only serves to connect the *History* of Masonry, the strict Subject of this Book. It is good to know what not to say! Candid *Reader*, farewell.

From my *Study* in
Exeter-Court, *Strand.*
4 Nov. 1738.

James Anderson.

The SANCTION.

WHEREAS on 25 *Nov.* 1723. the *Grand Lodge* in *ample* Form resolved, *That no Alterations shall be made in their printed Book of* Constitutions *without Leave of the Grand Lodge:*

And *whereas* some have written and printed Books and Pamphlets relating to the Fraternity without Leave of the *Grand Lodge*; some of which have been condemn'd as pyratical and stupid by the *Grand Lodge* in *Ample* Form on 24 *Feb.* 173¾. when the Brethren were warned *not to use them nor encourage them to be sold:*

And *whereas* on 25 *January* 173⅞. the last *Grand Master* the Earl of Darnley, with his *Deputy* and *Wardens*, and the *Grand Lodge*, after due Approbation, order'd our Brother *Anderson*, the Author, to print and publish this our *new Book* of Constitutions, which they recommended as *the only Book for the Use of the* Lodges, as appears by their Approbation, Page 199.

Therefore we also, the *present* Grand Master, Deputy and Wardens, do hereby Recommend this our *new printed Book* as the *only Book of* Constitutions, to the *Free* and *Accepted* Masons; and disclaiming all other Books, that have not the Sanction of the *Grand Lodge*, we warn all the Brethren against being employ'd or concern'd in writing and spreading, printing and publishing *any other Books* relating to *Masons* or *Masonry*, and against using *any other Book* in any *Lodge* as a *Lodge-Book*, as they shall be answerable to the Grand Lodge.

John Revis,
Secretary.

CAERNARVON, Grand Master,
John Ward, *Deputy* Grand Master,
George Graham, ⎱ Grand
Andrew Robinson, ⎰ Wardens.

Frater J. Thornhill Eq. pinx.   I. Pine Sculp.

The Right Honourable
the Marquis of Carnarvon
Gentleman of the Bed-Chamber to His
Royal Highness the Prince of Wales
and K.t of the most Hon.ble Order of the Bath.

A.D.1738. **Grand Master** A.L.5738.

THE CONSTITUTIONS

OF THE

Right Worshipful FRATERNITY

OF THE

Free and *Accepted* MASONS.

Collected from their old *Records* and faithful *Traditions.*

TO BE READ

At the Admission of a NEW BROTHER, when the *Master* or *Warden* shall begin, or order some other Brother to read, as follows.

PART I.

The History of Masonry *from the* Creation *throughout the known* Earth; *till true old* Architecture *was demolish'd by the* Goths *and at last Revived in* Italy.

CHAPTER I.

From the Creation *to* Grand Master NIMROD.

THE ALMIGHTY Architect and *Grand-Master* of the Universe having created all Things very Good and according to *Geometry,* last of all formed ADAM after his own Image, ingraving on his Heart the said noble Science; which *Adam* soon discover'd by surveying his Earthly Paradise and the Fabrication of the *Arbour* or Silvan Lodgment that God had prepared

B   for

for him, a well proportion'd and convenient Place of Shelter from Heat, and of Retirement, Reſt, and Repaſt after his wholeſome Labour in cultivating his Garden of Delights, and the firſt *Temple* or Place of Worſhip, agreeable to his original, perfect and innocent State. *A. M.* or Year of the World   1
* *B. C.* or before the Chriſtian Era 4003
But tho' by Sin *Adam* fell from his original happy State, and was expell'd from his lovely *Arbour* and Earthly *Paradiſe* into the wide World, he ſtill retain'd great Knowledge, eſpecially in GEOMETRY; and its Principles remaining in the Hearts of his Offspring, have in Proceſs of Time been drawn forth in a convenient Method of Propoſitions, according to the Laws of Proportion taken from *Mechaniſm:* and as the *Mechanical* Arts gave occaſion to the Learned to reduce the Elements of *Geometry* into Method; ſo this noble *Science*, thus reduced and methodized, is now the Foundation of all thoſe Arts (eſpecially of *Architecture*) and the Rule by which they are conducted and finiſh'd.

ADAM, when expell'd, reſided in the moſt convenient natural Abodes of the Land of *Eden*, where He could be beſt ſhelter'd

---

* The firſt *Chriſtians* computed their Times as the Nations did among whom They lived till *A. D.* 532. when
Dionyſius Exiguus, a Roman *Abbot*, taught them firſt to compute from the Birth of *Chriſt:* but He loſt 4 Years or began the *Chriſtian* Era 4 Years later than juſt. Therefore, tho' according to the *Hebrew* Chronology of the old Teſtament and other good Vouchers, CHRIST was truly born in ſome Month of the Year of the World or *A. M.* 4000. yet theſe 4 Years added make ——— 4004
Not *before the Birth of Chriſt*, but *before the Chriſtian Era*, viz. ——— 1737
For the true *Anno Domini* or Year after *Chriſt's* Birth is ——— 1740.
But the MASONS being uſed to compute by
the Vulgar *Anno* Domini or Chriſtian *Era*   1737   and ſo theſe Letters *A. M.*
and adding to it not 4004 as it ought, but   ſignify *Anno Mundi* or Year
the ſtrict Years before *Chriſt's* Birth, viz.   4000   of the World: and here
                                                         B. C. is not *Before Chriſt*
They uſually call this the *Year* of MASONRY 5737   but *Before the Chriſtian*
Inſtead of the accurate Year   ——— 5740   *Era.*
and we muſt keep to the Vulgar Computation.
The *A. M.* or *Anno Mundi* is the ſame follow'd by *Uſher* and *Prideaux*, &c.

from

from Colds and Heats, from Winds, Rains and Tempests and from Wild Beasts; till his Sons grew up to form a *Lodge*, whom he taught *Geometry* and the great Use of it in *Architecture*, without which the Children of Men must have liv'd like *Brutes*, in Woods, Dens and Caves, &c. or at best in poor Huts of Mud or Arbours made of Branches of Trees, &c.

Thus KAIN, when expell'd * with his Family *A.M. 130.* and Adherents from *Adam*'s Altars, built forthwith a strong City, and call'd it DEDICATE or CONSECRATE, after the Name of his eldest Son *Enoch*; whose Race follow'd the Example, improving the Arts and Sciences of their Patriarch: for TUBAL KAIN wrought in *Metals*, JUBAL elevated *Musick*, and JABAL extended his *Tents*.

Nor was his Brother SETH less instructed, the Patriarch of the other half of Mankind, who transmitted *Geometry* and *Masonry* to his late Posterity, who were the better skill'd by *Adam*'s living among them till he died. *A. M. 930.*

ADAM was succeeded in the Grand Direction of the *Craft* by SETH, ENOSH, KAINAN, MAHALALEEL and JARED, whose Son *Godly* ENOCH died not, but was translated alive, Soul and Body, into Heaven, aged 365 Years*. He was expert and bright both in the *Science* and the *Art*, *A. M. 987* and being a Prophet, He foretold the Destruction of the Earth for Sin, first by *Water*, and afterwards by *Fire*: therefore ENOCH erected *Two* large PILLARS*, the one of *Stone* and the other of *Brick*, whereon he engraved the Abridgment of the Arts and Sciences, particularly *Geometry* and *Masonry*.

* Some call them SETH'S *Pillars*, but the old *Masons* always call'd them ENOCH's *Pillars*, and firmly believ'd this Tradition: nay *Josephus* (Lib. i. cap. 2.) affirms the *Stone-Pillar* still remain'd in *Syria* to his Time.

JARED liv'd after his Son *Enoch* Years 435. and died aged 962 *A. M.*——1422. the oldest Man except his Grandson METHUSELAH the Son of *Enoch*, who succeeded *Jared*; but *Methuselah* ruled not long: for the Immoral Corruption universally prevailing,

METHUSELAH, with his Son LAMECH and Grandson NOAH, retired

retired from the corrupt World, and in their own peculiar Family preserved the good old Religion of the promised *Messiah* pure, and also the *Royal Art*, till the *Flood*: for LAMECH died only five Years before the *Flood*, and METHUSELAH died a few Days before It, aged 969 Years: and so He could well communicate the Traditions of his learned Progenitors to *Noah*'s 3 Sons; for JAPHET liv'd with him 100 Years, SHEM 98, and HAM 96.

At last, when the World's Destruction drew nigh, God commanded NOAH to build the *great* ARK or floating Castle, and his 3 Sons assisted like a *Deputy* and two *Wardens*: That Edifice though of Wood only, was fabricated by *Geometry* as nicely as any Stone Building (like true *Ship-Building* to this Day) a curious and large Piece of *Architecture*, and finish'd when *Noah* enter'd into his 600 Year; aboard which he and his 3 Sons and their 4 Wives passed, and having received the Cargo of Animals by God's Direction, they were saved in the *Ark*, while the rest perish'd in the *Flood* *   * B. M. —— 1656. for their Immorality and Unbelief.   A. C. —— 2348.

And so from these MASONS, or four *Grand Officers*, the whole present Race of Mankind are descended.

After the *Flood*, NOAH and his 3 Sons, having preserved the Knowledge of the Arts and Sciences, communicated It to their growing Off-spring, who were all *of one Language and Speech*. And it came to pass, * as they journeyd from the East (the Plains of Mount *Ararat*,   * Gen. XI. 1, 2. where the *Ark* rested) towards the *West*, they found *a Plain in the Land of* SHINAR, *and dwelt there* together, as NOACHIDÆ *, or Sons of *Noah*: and when *Peleg* was born there to   * The first Name of *Heber*, after the Flood 101 Years, Father *Noah* partition'd the *Earth*, ordering them to disperse and take Possession; but from a Fear of the ill Consequences of Separation, they resolved to keep together.

CHAP.

CHAP. II.

From NIMROD *to* 𝔊𝔯𝔞𝔫𝔡-𝔐𝔞𝔰𝔱𝔢𝔯 SOLOMON.

NIMROD the Son of *Cush*, the Eldest Son of *Ham*, was at the Head of those that would not disperse; or if they must separate, They resolved to transmit their Memorial illustrious to all future Ages; and so employed themselves under *Grand Master* NIMROD, in the large and fertile Vale of 𝔖𝔥𝔦𝔫𝔞𝔯 along the Banks of the *Tygris*, in building a great and stately *Tower* and *City*, the largest Work that ever the World saw (described by various Authors) and soon fil.'d the Vale with splendid Edifices; but They over-built it, and knew not when to desist 'till their Vanity provoked their Maker to confound their *Grand Design*, by confounding their *Lip* or Speech. Hence the City was called 𝔅𝔞𝔟𝔢𝔩 *Confusion*.

NIMROD signifies a *Rebel*, the name that the *Israeltes* gave him; but his Friends call'd him 𝔅𝔢𝔩𝔲𝔰 LORD.

Thus they were forced to disperse about 53 Years after they began to build, or after the Flood 154 Years, * when

* A. M. 1810. ⎫
   B. C. 2194. ⎭

The General MIGRATION from 𝔖𝔥𝔦𝔫𝔞𝔯 commenced.

They went off at various Times, and travell'd North, South, *East* and *West*, with their mighty Skill, and found the good Use of it in settling their Colonies.

But NIMROD went forth no farther than into the Land of *Assyria*, and founded the *first* Great *Empire* at his Capital 𝔑𝔦𝔫𝔦𝔳𝔢𝔥, where he long reign'd; and under him flourish'd many learned Mathematicians, whose Successors were, long afterwards, called *Chaldees* and *Magians*: and though many of them turned Image-Worshippers, yet even that Idolatry occasion'd an Improvement in the *Arts* of 𝔇𝔢𝔰𝔦𝔤𝔫𝔦𝔫𝔤: * for NINUS King of *Nineveh* or *Assyria*, ordered his best Artists to frame the *Statue* of 𝔅𝔞𝔞𝔩, that was worshipped in a gorgeous *Temple*.

viz. * *Architecture, Sculpture, Statuary, Plastering and Painting.*

From

(6)

From SHINAR, the *Science* and the *Art* were carried to the diftant Parts of the Earth, notwithftanding the *Confufion* of *Dialects*: That indeed gave Rife to the *Mafons* Faculty and univerfal Practice of converfing without fpeaking, and of knowing each other by *Signs* and *Tokens* (* which they fettled upon the *Difperfion* or Migration, in cafe any of them fhould meet in diftant Parts, who had been before in *Shinar*) but It hinder'd not the Propagation of *Mafonry*, which was cultivated by all the firft Nations; till the Negligence of their Chiefs, and their horrid Wars, made them turn ignorant, and lofe their original Skill in Arts and Sciences.

* This old *Tradition* is believed firmly by the old *Fraternity*

Thus the *Earth* was again planted and replenifh'd with MASONS from the Vale of SHINAR, whofe various Improvements we fhall trace.

MITZRAIM or *Menes*, the fecond Son of HAM, led his Colony from *Shinar* to EGYPT (which is *Mitzraim* in *Hebrew*, a dual Word, fignifying both *Egypts*, Upper and Lower) after the *Flood* 160 Years, and after the *Confufion* fix Years, *A. M.* 1816. where they preferved their original Skill, and much cultivated the *Art*: for antient Hiftory informs us * of the early fine Tafte of the *Egyptians*, their many magnificent Edifices and great Cities, as *Memphis*, *Heliopolis*, *Thebes* with 100 Gates, &c. befides their *Palaces* and *Sepulchres*, their *Obelisks* and *Statues*, the Coloffal *Statue* of SPHINX, whofe Head was 120 Foot round, and their famous Pyramids, the greateft * being reckoned the firft or earlieft of the feven *Wonders* of *Art* after the general *Migration*.

* *Diod. Sicul.* lib. 1.

* Some fay it was built of Marble Stones brought from the Quarries of *Arabia*; for there is no Veftige of a Quarry near it. Others call them artificial Stones made on the Spot, moft of them 30 Foot long. The *Pile* at Bottom was 700 Foot fquare, and 481 Foot high; but Others make it much higher: And in rearing it 360,000 *Mafons* were employ'd for 20 Years, as if all the People had join'd in the GRAND DESIGN.

The *Egyptians* excell'd all Nations alfo in their amafing LABYRINTHS, One of them cover'd the Ground of a whole Province, containing many fine Palaces and

100 *Temples*, difpofed in its feveral Quarters and Divifions, adorned with Columns of the beft *Porphyre*, and the accurate *Statues* of their Gods and Princes; which *Labyrinth* the *Greeks*, long afterwards, endeavour'd to imitate, but never arrived at Its *Extenfion* and *Sublime*.

The Succeffors of Mitzraim (who ftiled themfelves the *Sons of antient Kings*) encouraged the *Royal Art* down to the laft of the Race, the learned King AMASIS. See Chap. IV.

But Hiftory fails us in the South and Weft of *Africa*. Nor have we any juft Accounts of the fair and gallant Pofterity of *Noah*'s eldeft Son *JAPHET*, that firft replenifh'd vaft *old Scythia*, from *Norway* Eaftward to *America*; nor of the Japhetites in *Greece* and *Italy*, *Germany*, *Gaul* and *Britain*, &c. 'till their original Skill was loft: But, no doubt, they were good Architects at their firft *Migration* from *Shinar*.

SHEM, the fecond Son of *Noah*, remain'd at UR of the *Chaldees* in *Shinar*, with his Father and great Grandfon HEBER, where they liv'd private and died in Peace; but *Shem*'s Off-fpring travell'd into the South and Eaft of Great *Afia*, viz. ELAM, ASHUR, ARPHAXAD, LUD and ARAM, with SALA the Father of *Heber*; and their Off-fpring propagatd the *Science* and the *Art* as far as CHINA and Japan: while NOAH, SHEM and HEBER diverted themfelves at *Ur*, in Mathematical Studies, teaching *Peleg* the Father of *Rehu*, Father of *Serug*, Father of *Nachor*, Father of *Terah*, Father of ABRAM, a learned Race of Mathematicians and Geometricians *.

* The old *Conftitutions* affirm this ftrongly, and expatiate on ABRAM's great Skill in *Geometry*, and of his teaching it to many Scholars, tho' all the Sons of the *Freeborn* only.

Thus ABRAM, born two Years after the Death of *Noah*, * had learned well the *Science* and the *Art*, before the GOD of GLORY call'd him to travel from *Ur* of the *Chaldees*, and to live a Peregrin, not in *Stone* and *Brick*, but in Tents erected alfo by *Geometry*. So travelling with his Family and Flocks through *Mefopotamia*, he pitched

* *A. M.* 2008.

at

(8)

at *Charran**, where old TERAH in 5 Years died and then ABRAM aged 75 Years, travell'd into the Land of the *Canaanites**: but a Famine soon forced him down to *Egypt*; and returning next Year, he began to communicate his great Skill to the Chiefs of the *Canaanites*, for which they honour'd him as a Prince.   * *A. M.* 2078.
    * *A. M.* 2083. }
    B. C. 1921. }

ABRAM transmitted his *Geometry* to all his Off-spring; *Isaac* did the same to his two Sons, and JACOB well instructed his Family; while his Son JOSEPH was 𝕲𝖗𝖆𝖓𝖉-𝕸𝖆𝖘𝖙𝖊𝖗 of the *Egyptian* Masons, and employ'd them in building many Granaries and Store-Cities throughout the Land of *Egypt* before the *Descent* of *Jacob* and his Family.

Indeed this *peculiar Nation* were chiefly conversant in *Tents* and *Flocks* and military Skill, for about 350 Years after *Abram* came to *Canaan*, till their Persecution began in *Egypt*, about 80 Years before the *Exodus* of *Moses*: But then the 𝕰𝖌𝖞𝖕𝖙𝖎𝖆𝖓𝖘 having spoil'd and enslaved the *Hebrews*, train'd them up in *Masonry* of 𝕾𝖙𝖔𝖓𝖊 and 𝕭𝖗𝖎𝖈𝖐, and made them build two strong and stately Cities for the Royal Treasures, *Pithom* and *Raamses*. Thus the divine Wisdom appeared in permitting them to be thus employ'd, before they possess'd the promis'd Land then abounding with fine *Architecture*.

At length, after *Abram* left *Charran* 430 Years, MOSES marched out of *Egypt* at the Head of 600,000 *Hebrew* Males, marshall'd in due Form; for whose sake God divided the *Red Sea*, to let them pass through, and drowned *Pharaoh* and the *Egyptians* that pursu'd them.   *A. M.* ——— 2513. }
    B. C. ——— 1491. }

While marching through *Arabia* to *Canaan*, 𝕲𝖔𝖉 was pleased to inspire their 𝕲𝖗𝖆𝖓𝖉 𝕸𝖆𝖘𝖙𝖊𝖗 *MOSES*, *Joshuah* his Deputy, and *Aholiab* and *Bezaleel* } 𝕲𝖗𝖆𝖓𝖉 Wardens. } with Wisdom of Heart; and so next Year they raised   *Exod* XXXII. 6.

the curious TABERNACLE or *Tent* (where the divine 𝕾𝖍𝖊𝖈𝖍𝖎𝖓𝖆𝖍 resided

resided, and the holy *Ark* or *Chest*, the Symbole of God's Presence) which, though not of *Stone* or *Brick*, was framed by *Geometry*, a most beautiful Piece of true symmetrical Architecture, according to the Pattern that GOD discover'd to *Moses* on Mount *Sinai*, and it was afterwards the Model of SOLOMON's Temple.

Moses being well skill'd in all the *Egyptian* Learning, and also divinely inspired, excell'd all *Grand Masters* before him, and ordered the more skillful to meet him, as in a *Grand Lodge*, near the Tabernacle in the *Passover*-Week, and gave them wise *Charges, Regulations,* &c. though we wish they had been more distinctly transmitted by Oral Tradition. But of this enough.

When MOSES King of *Jessurun* died *A. M.* 2553.

JOSHUAH succeeded in the Direction, with *Kaleb* as Deputy, and *Eleazar* with his Son *Phineas* as *Grand Wardens* He marshall'd his *Israelites*, and led them over the *Jordan* (which God made dry for their March) into the promis'd Land: and *Joshuah* soon found the *Canaanites* had so regularly fortified their great Cities and Passes, that without the special Intervention of EL SHADDAI, in behalf of his *Peculiar*, They were impregnable and invincible.

JOSHUAH having finish'd his Wars in 6 Years, *A. M.* 2559. fixed the Tabernacle at *Shiloh* in *Ephraim*, ordering the *Chiefs* of *Israel* not only to serve JEHOVAH their God, and to cultivate the Land, but also to carry on the *Grand Design* of Architecture in the best Mosaic Stile.

Indeed the *Israelites*, refined in Cities and Mansions, having many expert Artists in every *Tribe* that met in *Lodges* or Societies for that Purpose, except when for their Sins they came under Servitude; but their occasional Princes, call'd *Judges* and *Saviours*, revived the *Mosaic Stile* along with Liberty and the *Mosaic Constitution*; and only came short of the *Phenicians* and *Canaanites* in sacred Architecture of *Stone*; for the *Phenicians* had many Temples for their many Gods: and yet the one *Temple* or Tabernacle of the one true God at *Shiloh*, exceeded them all in *Wisdom* and *Beauty*, though not in *Strength* and *Dimensions*.

C

Mean

(10)

Mean while, in *Leſſer Aſia*, about 10 Years before the *Exodus* of *Moſes*, Troy was founded and ſtood ſublime till deſtroy'd by the emulous *Greeks*, about the 12th Year of *Tola* Judge of *Iſrael. A. M.* 2819.

And ſoon after the *Exodus*, the famous *Temple* of Jupiter Hammon in *Libian Africa* was erected, that ſtood till demoliſh'd by the firſt Chriſtians in thoſe Parts.

The Sidonians alſo, expert Artiſts, firſt built *Tyre*, and a Colony of *Tyrians* firſt built Carthage; while the *Greeks* were obſcure, and the *Romans* exiſted not yet.

But the *Phenicians* improved in their *ſacred* Architecture; for we read of the *Temple* of 𝕯𝖆𝖌𝖔𝖓 in *Gaza*, very magnificent and capacious of 3000 People under its *Roof*, that was artfully ſupported only by *Two Columns*, not too big to be graſped in the Arms of Samson, who tugg'd them down; and the large *Roof*, like a Burſt of Thunder, fell upon the Lords and Ladies, the Prieſts and People of the *Philiſtins*; nay *Samſon* was alſo intangled in the ſame Death that he drew upon his Enemies for the Loſs of Liberty and Eyes. After the *Exodus* of *Moſes* 379. Before the *Temple* of Solomon 101 *.

Abibalus, King of *Tyre*, beautified that City; and ſo did his Son King Hiram who built 3 ſtately *Temples* to 𝕵𝖚𝖕𝖎𝖙𝖊𝖗, 𝕳𝖊𝖗𝖈𝖚𝖑𝖊𝖘, and 𝕬𝖘𝖙𝖆𝖗𝖙𝖊, the *Tyrian* Gods, and aſſiſted *David* King of *Iſrael* in erecting his *Palace of Cedar*.

Many Monuments of the primitive Architecture are obſcured with Fables; for the true old Hiſtories are loſt, or worn out by the Teeth of Time, and alſo the *oral* Tradition is darkened by the Blending of the Nations.

---

* The *Tradition* of old Maſons is, that a learned *Phenician* called Sanconiathon was the *Architect*, or *Grand Maſter*, of this curious *Temple*: And that Samson had been too credulous and effeminate in revealing his Secrets to his Wife, who betray'd him into the Hands of the *Philiſtins*; for which he is not numbered among the antient *Maſons*. But no more of this.

CHAP.

CHAP. III.

From SOLOMON *to Grand Master* CYRUS.

BUT the most magnificent Structures of *Gaza, Gath* and *Askelon, Jebusi* and *Hebron, Tyre* and *Sidon, Egypt* and *Assyria*, &c. were not comparable to the *Eternal*'s 𝕮emple at *Jerusalem*, built by that wisest mere Man and most glorious King of *Israel*, SOLOMON, (the Son of *David*, who was denied that Honour for being a Man of Blood) the Prince of Peace and Architecture, the GRAND MASTER MASON of his Day, who performed all by divine Direction, and without the Noise of Tools; all the Stones, Timbers and Foundings being brought ready cut, fram'd and polish'd to *Jerusalem*.

It was founded in the 4th Year of SOLOMON, on the second Day of the second Month of the Year after the *Exodus* ——— 480 and SOLOMON employ'd about it, tho' not all *A. M.* 2993. ⎫
upon it, the following Number of Operators, *viz.*   *B. C.* 1011. ⎬
1. 𝕳arodim, Rulers or *Provosts*, call'd also   See 1 *Kings* V. 16.18.
   𝕸enat𝔷chim, Overseers and Comforters   2 *Chron.* II. 18.
   of the People in Working, that were expert *Master Masons*, in Number ————— 3600
2. 𝕲hiblim, *Stone-Cutters* and *Sculptors*, and 𝕴𝖍 𝕮hot𝔷eb, *Men of Hewing*, and 𝕭onai, *Setters*, Layers or Builders, or bright *Fellow-Crafts*, in Number ———— 80000
3. The Levy of Assistants, under the noble ADONIRAM — 30000 who was the *Junior* 𝕲rand-𝖁𝖆rden.

   In all *Free-Masons* —————————— 113600
Besides the *Labourers* called, 𝕴𝖍 𝕾abbal, or *Men of Burden*, ⎫
who were of the Remains of the old *Canaanites*, and ⎬ 70000
being *Bondmen*, are not to be reckoned among *Masons*, ⎭

In all — 183,600

SOLOMON had the *Labourers* of his own; but was much obliged to HIRAM King of *Tyre*, for many of the 𝕲𝖍𝖎𝖇𝖑𝖎𝖒 and 𝕭𝖔𝖓𝖆𝖎, who lent him his best Artists, and sent him the Firs and Cedars of *Lebanon*: But above all, he sent his Name sake * HIRAM ABBIF, the most accomplish'd Designer and Operator upon Earth, who in *Solomon*'s Absence fill'd the Chair as *Deputy* 𝕲𝖗𝖆𝖓𝖉 𝕸𝖆𝖘𝖙𝖊𝖗, and in his Presence was the *Senior* 𝕲𝖗𝖆𝖓𝖉 𝖂𝖆𝖗𝖉𝖊𝖓, or principal Surveyor and *Master* of *Work*.

SOLOMON

---

* In 2 *Chron.* II. 13. HIRAM King of *Tyre* (called there HURAM) in his Letter to King SOLOMON, says, *I have sent a Cunning Man* le Huram Abbi; which is not to be translated, like the Vulgate *Greek* and *Latin*, HURAM *my Father*; for his Description verse 14 refutes it; and the Words import only HURAM *of my Father's*, or the Chief *Master Mason* of my Father ABIBALUS. Yet some think that King HIRAM might call the Architect HIRAM his Father, as learned and wise Men were wont to be call'd by Royal Patrons in old Times: Thus JOSEPH was call'd ABRECH, or the King's Father; and this same HIRAM the Architect is called SOLOMON's Father, 2 *Chron.* iv. 6.

𝕲𝖓𝖆𝖘𝖆𝖍 𝕮𝖍𝖚𝖗𝖆𝖒 𝕬𝖇𝖇𝖎𝖋 𝖑𝖆 𝕸𝖊𝖑𝖊𝖈𝖍 𝕾𝖍𝖊𝖑𝖔𝖒𝖔𝖍

Did HIRAM *his Father make to King* SOLOMON.

But the Difficulty is over at once by allowing the Word ABBIF to be the Surname of HIRAM the *Artist*, call'd above *Hiram Abbi*, and here call'd *Huram Abbif*, as in the *Lodge* he is called HIRAM ABBIF, to distinguish him from King HIRAM: For this Reading makes the Sense plain and compleat, *viz.* that HIRAM King of *Tyre*, sent to King SOLOMON the cunning Workman call'd HIRAM ABBIF.

He is described in two Places, 1 *Kings* vii. 13, 14, 15. and 2 *Chron* ii. 13, 14. In the first he is call'd *a Widow's Son of the Tribe of* Naphtali, and in the other he is called *the Son of a Woman of the Daughters of* Dan; but in both, that his Father was *a Man of* Tyre: That is, she was of the Daughters of the City *Dan*, in the Tribe of *Naphtali*, and is call'd *a Widow of* Naphtali, as her Husband was a *Naphtalite*; for he is not call'd a *Tyrian* by Descent, but a Man of *Tyre* by Habitation, as *Obed Edom* the *Levite* is call'd a *Gittite*, and the Apostle *Paul a Man of* Tarsus.

But

SOLOMON partition'd the *Fellow Crafts* into certain *Lodges*, with a *Master* and *Wardens* in each; that they might receive Commands in a regular Manner, might take Care of their Tools and Jewels, might be regularly paid every Week, and be duly fed and clothed, &c. and the *Fellow Crafts* took Care of their Succession by educating 𝕰𝖓𝖙𝖊𝖗'𝖉 𝕻𝖟𝖊𝖓𝖙𝖎𝖈𝖊𝖘. According to the *Traditions* of old Masons, who talk much of these Things.

Thus a solid Foundation was laid of perfect *Harmony* among the Brotherhood, the *Lodge* was strongly cemented with Love and Friendship, every Brother was duly taught Secrecy and Prudence, Morality and good Fellowship, each knew his peculiar Business, and the *Grand Design* was vigorously pursued at a prodigious Expence.

For besides King DAVID's vast Preparations, his richer Son SOLOMON, and all the wealthy *Israelites*, nay even the Princes of the neighbouring *Gentiles*, largely contributed towards It, in Gold, Silver and rich Jewels, that amounted to a Sum almost incredible: but was all needful;

For the *Wall* round It was in Compass 7700 Foot, the Materials were the best that the Earth produced, and no Structure was ever like it for exactly proportion'd and beautiful Dimensions, from the most magnificent PORTICO on the *East*, to the glorious and reverend 𝕾𝖆𝖓𝖈𝖙𝖚𝖒 𝕾𝖆𝖓𝖈𝖙𝖔𝖗𝖚𝖒 on the *West*, with numerous Apartments, pleasant and convenient Chambers and Lodgings for the Kings and Princes, the *Sanhedrin*, the Priests and Levites
of

But tho' HIRAM ABBIF had been a *Tyrian* by Blood, that derogates not from his vast Capacity; for the *Tyrians* now were the best Artificers, by the Encouragement of King HIRAM: and those *Texts* testify that God had endued this HIRAM ABBIF with Wisdom, Understanding, and mechanical Cunning to perform every Thing that SOLOMON required, not only in building the TEMPLE with all its costly Magnificence; but also in founding, fashioning and framing all the holy *Utensils* thereof, according to *Geometry*, and to *find out every Device that shall be put to him!* and the Scripture assures us that He fully maintain'd his Character in far larger Works than those of *Aholiab* and *Bezaleel*, for which he will be honoured in the *Lodges* till the End of Time.

of *Israel*, and the outer *Court* of the *Gentiles* too, It being an *House of Prayer for all Nations*, and capable of receiving in all its Courts and Apartments together about 300000 People.

It was adorned with 1453 *Columns* of *Parian Marble* twisted, or sculptured or fluted, with twice as many *Pillasters*, both having exquisite *Capitels* or Chapiters of several different noble *Orders*, and about 2246 Windows, besides those in the curious Pavement; and it was lined with massy Gold, set with innumerable Diamonds and other precious Stones, in the most harmonious, beautiful and costly *Decoration*: tho' much more might be said, if it had not been so often delineated, particularly by *Villalpandus*.

So that its Prospect highly transcended all that we are now capable to imagine, and has been ever esteemed the finest Piece of *Masonry* upon Earth, before or since, the 2d and *Chief* of the 7 *Wonders of Art*, since the general *Migration* from *Shinar*.

It was finish'd in the short Space of 7 Years and 6 Months, to the Amazement of all the World; when the *Cape-Stone* was celebrated by the *Fraternity* with great Joy. But their Joy was soon inter- $\left. \begin{array}{l} A.\ M.\ 3000. \\ B.\ C.\ 1004. \end{array} \right\}$ rupted by the sudden Death of their dear Master H<small>IRAM</small> A<small>BBIF</small>, whom they decently interr'd in the *Lodge* near the *Temple* according to antient Usage.

After H<small>IRAM</small> A<small>BBIF</small> was mourn'd for, the 𝕿abernacle of M<small>OSES</small> and its holy Reliques being lodged in the 𝕿emple, S<small>OLOMON</small> in a General Assembly dedicated or consecrated It by solemn Prayer and costly Sacrifices past Number, with the finest Music, vocal and instrumental, praising J<small>EHOVAH</small>, upon fixing the *Holy* A<small>RK</small> in its proper Place between the *Cherubims*; when J<small>EHOVAH</small> fill'd his own 𝕿emple with a *Cloud of Glory*!

But leaving what must not, and indeed what cannot be committed to Writing, we may certainly affirm, that however ambitious and emulous the *Gentiles* were in improving the *Royal Art*, it was never perfected till the building of this 𝖌𝖔𝖗𝖌𝖊𝖔𝖚𝖘 *House* of G<small>OD</small> fit for the special Refulgence of his Glory upon Earth, where he

dwelt

dwelt between the *Cherubims* on the *Mercy Seat* above the *Ark*, and from thence gave his People frequent oraculous Responses. This glorious Edifice attracted soon the inquisitive Connoisseurs of all Nations to travel, and spend some Time at *Jerusalem*, to survey its peculiar Excellencies, as much as was allow'd to the *Gentiles*; and they soon discover'd that all the World, with their joint Skill, came far short of the *Israelites* in the *Wisdom, Strength* and *Beauty* of Architecture; when the *wise* King SOLOMON was 𝕲𝖗𝖆𝖓𝖉 𝕸𝖆𝖘𝖙𝖊𝖗 of all *Masons* at *Jerusalem*, and the *learned* King HIRAM * was Grand *Master* at *Tyre*, and inspired HIRAM ABBIF, had been *Master* of *Work*; when true compleat *Masonry* was under the immediate Care and Direction of Heaven; when the NOBLE and the *Wise* thought it their Honour to be the Associates of the ingenious Craftsmen in their well form'd *Lodges*; and so the 𝕿𝖊𝖒𝖕𝖑𝖊 of JEHOVAH, the one true God, became the just Wonder of all *Travellers*, by which, as by the most perfect Pattern, they resolved to correct the *Architecture* of their own Countries upon their Return.

* The *Tradition* is, that King HIRAM had been Grand *Master* of all *Masons*; but when the TEMPLE was finish'd, HIRAM came to survey It before its Consecration, and to commune with SOLOMON about *Wisdom* and *Art*; and finding the Great *Architect* of the Universe, had inspired SOLOMON above all mortal Men, HIRAM very readily yeelded the Pre-eminence to SOLOMON JEDIDIAH, the *Beloved of God.*

SOLOMON next employ'd the *Fraternity* in carrying on his other Works, viz. — His two PALACES at *Jerusalem* for himself and his Queen.—— The stately HALL of Judicature with his *Ivory Throne* and *Golden Lyons*.--- MILLO, or the *Royal Exchange*, made by filling up the Great Gulph, between Mount *Moriah* and Mount *Zion*, with strong Arches, upon which many beautiful *Piazzas* were erected with lofty *Collonading* on each Side, and between the Columns a spacious *Walk* from *Zion Castle* to the *Temple*, where Men of Business met.——— The HOUSE of the *Forrest* of *Lebanon* built upon 4 Rows of *Cedar-Pillars*, his Summer-House to retire from the Heat or Business, with a *Watch-Tower* that looked to the Road to *Damascus*. Several *Cities* on the Road between *Jerusalem* and *Lebanon*. Many Store-houses *West* of
the

the *Jordan* and several Store Cities *East* of that River well fortify'd,—— and the City 𝕷𝖆𝖇𝖒𝖔𝖗 (call'd afterwards by the *Greeks Palmyra*) with a splendid Palace in it, the glorious Ruins of which are seen by Travellers to this Day.

All these and many more costly Buildings were finish'd in the short Space of 13 Years after the *Temple*, by the Care of 550 𝕳𝖆𝖗𝖔𝖇𝖎𝖒 and 𝕸𝖊𝖓𝖆𝖙𝖟𝖈𝖍𝖎𝖒: for *Masonry* was carried on throughout all his Dominions, and many particular *Lodges* were constituted under *Grand Master* Solomon, who annually assembled the 𝕲𝖗𝖆𝖓𝖉 𝕷𝖔𝖉𝖌𝖊 at *Jerusalem* for transmitting their Affairs to Posterity: tho' still the Loss of good Hiram Abbif was lamented.

Indeed this wise *Grand Master* Solomon shew'd the Imperfection of *human* Nature, even at its Hight of Excellency, by loving too much many *strange Women*, who turn'd him from the true Religion: But our Business with him is only as a Mason; for even during his Idolatry he built some curious *Temples* to 𝕮𝖍𝖊𝖒𝖔𝖘𝖍, 𝕸𝖔𝖑𝖊𝖈𝖍 and 𝕬𝖘𝖍𝖙𝖆𝖗𝖔𝖙𝖍, the Gods of his Concubines, till about 3 Years before he died, when he composed his penitential Song, the *Ecclesiastes*; and fixed the true Motto on all earthly Glory, *viz.* Vanity of Vanities, all *is* Vanity *without the* Fear *of* God *and the keeping of his Commands, which is the whole Duty of Man!* and died aged 58 Years.

Many of Solomon's *Masons* before he died began to travel, and carry'd with 'em the *High Taste* of Architecture, with the Secrets of the Fraternity, into *Syria, Lesser Asia, Mesopotamia, Scythia, Assyria, Chaldæa, Media, Bactria, India, Persia, Arabia, Egypt*, and other Parts of great Asia and Africa; also into Europe, no doubt, tho' we have no History to assure us yet of the Transactions of *Greece* and *Italy*: But the Tradition is that they travell'd to Hercules Pillars on the *West*, and to China on the *East*: And the old *Constitutions* affirm, that one call'd Ninus, who had been at the building of *Solomon's Temple*, brought the refined Knowledge of the *Science* and the *Art* into *Germany* and *Gaul*.

A. M. —— 3029.
A. C. —— 975.

In

In many Places being highly esteem'd, they obtain'd special Privileges ; and because they taught their *liberal Art* only to the *Freeborn*, They were call'd FREE MASONS ; constituting *Lodges* in the Places where they built stately Piles, by the Encouragement of the Great and Wealthy, who soon requested to be accepted as Members of the *Lodge* and *Brothers* of the *Craft* ; till by Merit those *Free* and *accepted Masons* came to be *Masters* and *Wardens*.

Nay Kings, Princes and Potentates became 𝕲𝖗𝖆𝖓𝖉 𝕸𝖆𝖘𝖙𝖊𝖗𝖘, each in his own Dominion, in Imitation of King *Solomon*, whose Memory, *as a Mason*, has been duly worshipp'd, and will be, till *Architecture* shall be consumed in the general Conflagration ; for he never can be rivall'd but by one equally inspired from above.

After SOLOMON's Death, the Partition of his Empire into the Kingdoms of *Israel* and *Judah*, did not demolish the *Lodges* : For in *Israel*, King JEROBOAM erected the curious *Statues* of the two 𝕲𝖔𝖑𝖉𝖊𝖓 𝕮𝖆𝖑𝖛𝖊𝖘 at *Dan* and *Bethel*, with 𝕿𝖊𝖒𝖕𝖑𝖊𝖘 for their Worship ; King *Baasha* built *Tirzah* for his Palace, and King *Omri* built *Samaria* for his Capital ; where his Son King ACHAB built a large and sumptuous 𝕿𝖊𝖒𝖕𝖑𝖊 for his *Idol* 𝕭𝖆𝖆𝖑 (afterwards destroy'd by King *Jehu*) and a *Palace of Ivory*, besides many Castles and fenced Cities.

But SOLOMON's Royal Race, the Kings of *Judah*, succeeded him also in the GRAND MASTER's *Chair*, or deputed the High Priest to preserve the *Royal Art*. Their Care of the Temple with the many Buildings they raised, and strong Forts, are mention'd in holy Writ down to JOSIAH the last good King of *Judah*.

SOLOMON's 𝕿𝖗𝖆𝖛𝖊𝖑𝖑𝖊𝖗𝖘 improved the *Gentiles* beyond Expression. Thus the *Syrians* adorned their *Damascus* with a lofty *Temple* and a Royal *Palace*. Those of *Lesser Asia* became excellent *Masons*, particularly at *Sardis* in *Lydia*, and along the Sea Coasts in the mercantil Cities, as at 𝕰𝖕𝖍𝖊𝖘𝖚𝖘.

There the old *Temple* of 𝕯𝖎𝖆𝖓𝖆, built by some *Japhetites* about the Days of *Moses*, being burnt down about 34 Years after *Solomon*'s Death, the Kings of *Lesser Asia* refounded and adorn'd it with 127 *Columns* of the best Marble, each 60 Foot
D   high,

high, and 36 of them were of the moſt noble *Sculpture*, by the Direction of 𝔇𝔢𝔰𝔦𝔭𝔥𝔬𝔫 and 𝔄𝔯𝔠𝔥𝔦𝔭𝔥𝔯𝔬𝔫, the Diſciples of *Solomon's* Travellers; but it was not finiſhed till after 220 Years in the 7th Year of *Hezekiah* King of *Judah*. *A. M.* 3283.

This Temple was in Length 425. Foot, and in Breadth 220 Foot with a duly proportion'd Height, ſo magnificent, ſo admirable a Fabrick, that it became the 3d of the 7 *Wonders of Art*, the charming Miſtreſs of *Leſſer Aſia*, which even *Xerxes*, the avowed Enemy of *Image Worſhip*, left ſtanding, while he burnt all the other *Temples* in his Way to *Greece*.

But at laſt, it was burnt down by a vile Fellow, only for the Luſt of being talkt of in after Ages (whoſe Name therefore ſhall not be mention'd here) on the Birth Day of *Alexander* the *Great*, after it had ſtood 365 Years, about *A. M.* 3680. when jocoſe People ſaid, *The Goddeſs was ſo deeply engaged at the Birth of her Hero in* Pella *of* Macedonia *that ſhe had no Leiſure to ſave her* Temple *at* EPHESUS. It was rebuilt by the Architect *Denocrates* at the Expence of the neighbouring Princes and States.

The ASSYRIANS, ever ſince NIMROD and NINUS, had cultivated the Royal *Art*, eſpecially at their *Great* NINIVEH, down to King PUL (to whom *Jonah* preached) and his Son *Sardan Pul* or SARDANAPALUS, call'd alſo *Tonos Concoleros*, who was beſieged by his Brother *Tiglath Pul Eſer* and his General *Nabonaſſar*, till he burnt himſelf with his Concubines and Treaſure in old *Nimrod*'s Palace in the 12th Year of *Jotham* King of *Judah*, *A. M.* ----3257. when the Empire was partition'd between TIGLATH PUL ESER who ſucceeded at *NINIVEH*, and NABONASSAR who got *CHALDÆA*. *See the Margin of next Page.*

NABONASSAR, called alſo *Beleſis* or *Baladan*, an excellent Aſtronomer and Architect, built his new Metropolis upon the Ruins of a Part of old *Nimrod*'s Works near the Great *old Tower* of *Babel* then ſtanding, and call'd It BABYLON, founded in the firſt Year of the *Nabonaſſarian Era*. A. M. 3257.

For this City BABYLON is not mentioned by any Author before *Iſaiah*, who mentions both Its Riſe and Its Ruin *Ch.* XXIII. 13. See *Marſham's* Canon. Sec. 17

NABONASSAR reign'd 14 Years, ſucceeded by

4 Kings,

(19)

4 Kings, who reign'd 12 Years, till his Son was of Age, *viz.*

MERODACH BALADAN, or *Mardoch Empadus*, who reign'd 12 Years: and after him 5 more Kings, tho' not of his Issue, who reign'd 21 Years. Then follow'd an *Interregnum* of 8 Years, ending *An. Nabon.* 67.

The

* ASSYRIA *A. M.* 3257. *Sardanapalus* being dead 1. TIGLATH PUL ESER, called also *Arbaces* and NINUS *junior*, succeeded at *Niniveh*, and died *A. M.* 3275			MEDIA. The *Medes* revolting from *Senacherib* King of *Assyria* A.M. 3296 chose for their King
2 SALMAN ESER died 3289, and his Son 3 SENACHERIB died 3297			1 DEJOCES, who inlarged and adorned his Capital EKBATANA till slain in Battel by the *Assyrians* 3348
4 ESERHADDON succeeded his Father *Sennacherib*, and after he had reign'd at *Nineveh* 27 Years he took in BABYLON at the End of the *Interregnum An. Nabon.* 67. *A. M.* 3324 and so annexed *Chaldæa* again to *Assyria*. He died——— 3336			2 PHRAORTES died ——— 3370
5 SAOSDUCHINUS, call'd in *Judith*, NABUCHODONOSOR, died 3635			3 CYAXARES I. was the Patron of the Learned in the *East* and died 3410
6 CHINILADANUS slain by his General *Nabopolassar* 3378			
7 *Saracus* slain by *Nabopolassar* 3392	NABOPOLASSAR sometimes called NEBUCHADNEZZAR, I. then seized *Chaldæa* and reign'd in the Throne of old NABONASSAR at *Babylon*, years —————— 14 till he destroy'd *Saracus*, A. M. 3392		4 ASTYAGES married ARIENA Sister of *Croesus* King of *Lydia*. He died 3445, leaving a Son and two Daughters *viz.*
1. NABOPOLASSAR willing to please his Allies the *Medes*, demolish'd the Great NINIVEH. Thus BABYLON was now the *Capital* of the *Assyrian* Empire. He died —————— 3399			
2. NEBUCHADNEZZAR who captivated the *Jews* and adorned *Babylon*, died 3442.	AMYTIS the other Daughter of *Astyages* King of *Media*.	5 CYAXARES II. K. of *Media*, call'd in Scripture DARIUS *the Mede*, join'd his Nephew and Son-in-Law CYRUS in his Wars, reign'd at *Babylon* after *Belshazzar* 2 Years, died 3467	MANDANE the eldest Daughter, Wife of CAMBYSES a *Persian* Prince, call'd by some King of *Persia*, the Father and Mother of
3 EVILMERODACH slain A. M. ——— 3444	N. N. Wife of 4 NERIGLISSAR who slew *Evil-Merodach*, and reigned 3 Years.		
6 BELSHAZZAR succeeded *Laborosoarchod*, and was slain by CYRUS A. M. 3465		CASSENDANA the Heiress of *Media* and Wife of CYRUS.	CYRUS the *Great*, began the *Persian* Monarchy 3468
	5 LABOROSOARCHOD 1 Year.	CAMBYSES King of *Persia*, see Chapter IV	

The *Science* and the *Art* long flourish'd in Eastern *Asia* to the farthest *East Indies*. But also before the Days of *Nebuchadnezzar the Great*, we find that old *Masonry* took a Western Course: For the Disciples of *Solomon*'s Travellers, by the Encouragement of Princes and States *West* of the *Assyrian* Bounds, built, enlarged and adorn'd Cities past Number, as appears from the History of their Foundations in many Books of *Chronology*. *

After godly JOSIAH King of *Judah* fighting for his superior *Nabopolassar*, was slain in the Battel of *Hadad Rimmon* by *Pharoah Necho*, A. M. 3394. } all Things went wrong in *Judah*.
B. C.   610.

For the Grand Monarch NEBUCHADNEZZAR, first his Father's Partner having defeated *Necho*, made *Josiah*'s Son *Jehoiakim* his Vassal, and for his revolting He ruin'd him, and at length captivated all the remaining *Royal* Family of *Judah* with the Flower of the *Nobles*, especially of the more ingenious *Craftsmen*, laid waste the whole Land of *Israel*, burnt and demolisht all the fine Edifices, and also the *glorious* and *Inimitable* 𝕿emple of SOLOMON, after It was finisht and consecrated 416 Years,

A. M. 3416. } oh lamentable!
B. C.---588.

Mean while, *Nebuchadnezzar* was carrying on his Grand Design of inlarging and beautifying BABYLON, and employ'd the more Skillful Artists of *Judah*, and of his other captivated Nations, to join his *Chaldees* in raising the *Walls*, the *Palaces*, the *Hanging Gardens*, the amazing *Bridge*, the *Temples*, the long and broad Streets, the Squares, &c. of that proud *Metropolis*, accounted the 4th of the 7 *Wonders of Art*, described at large in many Books, and therefore needless to be rehearsed particularly here.

---

* Such as *Boristhenes* and *Sinope* in PONTUS: *Nicomedia*, *Prusias* and *Chalcedon* in BITHYNIA: *Bizantium* (now *Constantinople*) *Cyzicus* also and *Lampsacus* in the HELLESPONT: *Abdera* in THRACE: Many Cities in GREECE: *Tarentum*, *Regium*, *Rome*, *Ravenna*, *Crotona*, *Florence*, and many more in ITALY: *Granada*, *Malaga*, *Gades*, &c. in SPAIN: *Massilia* and others on the Coast of GAUL: while BRITAIN was unknown.

But

(21)

But for all his unspeakable Advantages of Wealth and Power, and for all his vast Ambition, he could not arrive at the *sublime* of the *Solomonian Stile*. 'Tis true, after his Wars, He was a mighty Encourager of Architecture, a sumptuous 𝕲𝖗𝖆𝖓𝖉 𝕸𝖆𝖘𝖙𝖊𝖗; and his Artists discover'd great Knowledge in raising his *Golden Image* in the Vale of *Dura* 60 Cubits high and 6 broad, and also in all the beautiful Parts of his *Great* BABYLON: Yet It was never fully peopled; for his Pride provoked God to afflict him with Brutal Madness for 7 Years, and when restored, He liv'd about one Year only and died *A. M.* 3442, but 23 Years after, his Grandson *Belshazzar* was slain by CYRUS, who conquer'd that Empire and soon removed the Throne to SUSIANA in *Persia*.

The MEDES and PERSIANS had much improved in the *Royal Art*, and had rivall'd the *Assyrians* and *Chaldeans* in *Masonry* at 𝕰𝖐𝖇𝖆𝖙𝖆𝖓𝖆, 𝕾𝖚𝖘𝖎𝖆𝖓𝖆, 𝕻𝖊𝖗𝖘𝖊𝖕𝖔𝖑𝖎𝖘, and many more fine Cities, before They conquer'd 'em in War; tho' They had nothing so large as 𝕹𝖎𝖓𝖎𝖛𝖊𝖍 and 𝕭𝖆𝖇𝖞𝖑𝖔𝖓, nor so accurate as the 𝕿𝖊𝖒𝖕𝖑𝖊 and the other Structures of SOLOMON.

The *Jewish* Captives, after *Nebuchadnezzar*'s Death, kept themselves at Work in regular *Lodges*, till the set Time of their Deliverance; and were thus the more capable, at the *Reduction*, of Rebuilding the *Holy Temple* and *City* of *Salem* upon the old Foundations; which was ordered by the *Decree* of CYRUS, according to God's Word that had foretold his Exaltation and that Decree, publisht *A. M.*————3468.⎫
    B. C. ————— 536.⎭

CHAP.

CHAP IV

From CYRUS to Grand Master SELEUCUS Nicator.

1. CYRUS now King of Kings, having founded the *Persian* Monarchy made his famous *Decree* to rebuild the *Temple* of *Jerusalem* and constituted, for { *A. M.* —— 3468. } { *B. C.* —— 536. }
his *Provincial* Grand Master in *Judah*, ZERUBBABEL the lineal Heir of DAVID's Royal Race and Prince of the *Reduction*, with the High Priest Jeshuah his *Deputy*; who next Year founded the *second* TEMPLE. CYRUS built a great Palace near *Saras* in *Persia*, but before *Zerubbabel* had half finish'd, the good CYRUS died *A. M.* 3474.

2. CAMBYSES neglected the *Temple*, being wholly Intent upon the Conquest of *Egypt*, that had revolted under AMASYS, the last of *Mitzraim*'s Race, a learned *Grand Master*; for whom the *Fellow Crafts* cut out of a Rock an House all of *one Stone* 21 Cubits long, 12 broad and 8 deep, the Labour of 2000 *Masons* for 3 Years, and brought it safe to *Memphis*.

He had built many costly Structures, and contributed largely to the Rebuilding of Apollo's famous *Temple* at *Delphi* in *Greece*, and died much lamented just as *Cambyses* had reached to *Egypt*, *A. M.* 3478.

Cambyses conquer'd the Land, and destroy'd many *Temples, Palaces, Obelisks* and other glorious Monuments of the antient *Egyptian Masonry*, and died on his Way home, *A. M.* 3482.

3. The false *Smerdis*, the *Magian*, usurped during Part of this Year, call'd by *Ezrah* Artaxerxes, who stopt the building of the *Temple*.

4. DARIUS HYSTASPES, one of the 7 Princes that cut off *Smerdis*, succeeded, married *Artistona* the Daughter of CYRUS, and confirmed his *Decree*.

(23)

So that in his 6th Year, just 20 Years after the Founding of the *Temple*, ZERUBBABEL finish'd it * and celebrated the *Cape-Stone* ; and next Year Its Confecration or Dedication was folemnized. $\{$ * *A. M.* — 3489. $B C.$ — 515. $\}$

And tho' It came far fhort of SOLOMON's *Temple* in Extent and Decorations, nor had in it the *Cloud of Glory* or Divine Shechinah, and the holy Reliques of *Mofes* ; yet being rear'd in the *Solomonian Stile*, It was the fineft Building upon Earth.

In his Reign Zoroaftres flourifh'd, the *Archimagus* or *Grand Mafter* of the *Magians* (who worfhipped the *Sun* and the *Fire* made by his Rays) who became famous every where, call'd by the *Greeks, the Teacher of all human and divine Knowledge* ; and his Difciples were great Improvers of *Geometry* in the liberal Arts, erecting many *Palaces* and *Fire Temples* throughout the Empire, and long flourifh'd in Eaftern *Afia*, even till the *Mahometans* prevail'd. Yet a Remnant of 'em are fcatter'd in thofe Parts to this Day, who retain many of the old Ufages of the *Free Mafons*, for which They are here mention'd, and not for their Religious Rites that are not the Subject of this Book : For we leave every Brother to Liberty of Confcience ; but ftrictly charge him carefully to maintain the *Cement of the Lodge*, and the 3 Articles of NOAH.

Zoroaftres was flain by *Argafp* the *Scythian*, *A. M.* 3517. and *Hyftofpes* died 3518.

5. XERXES his Son fucceeded, who encouraged the *Magian Mafons*, and deftroy'd all the *Image-Temples* (except That of *Diana* at *Ephefus*) in his Way to *Greece*, with an Army of 5 Millions, and Ships paft Number : But the confederated *Greeks* fhamefully beat this common Enemy both at Sea and Land. *A. M.* 3525, at laft *Xerxes* was murder'd, *A. M.* 3539.

6. ARTAXERXES *Longimanus* his Son fucceeded, call'd *Abafhuerus* ; and he married the handfome *Jewefs* Queen *Hefter*. In his 3d Year he made a Feaft during 6 Months, for all his Princes and Servants, at his Palace of *Sufa* or *Sufiana* ; and the *Drinking was*

was according to the Law; None was compell'd, for so the King had appointed to all the Officers of his House, that they should do according to every Man's Pleasure, Est. I. 5. &c.

He sent EZRAH the learned Scribe to succeed *Zerubbabel*, who built *Synagogues* in every City: And next NEHEMIAH who rebuilt the Walls of *Jerusalem*, and obliged the richer People to fill that City with fine Houses; whereby it recover'd its antient Splendor. When *Ahasuerus* died A. M. 3580.

7. XERXES his Son by Queen HESTER succeeded, but reign'd only 45 Days, being murder'd by

8. SOGDIANUS the Bastard of *Ahasuerus* who reign'd 6 Months till destroy'd by

9. DARIUS NOTHUS, another Bastard of that King who reign'd 19 Years

In his 15th Year *Nehemiah* made his last Reformation; and *Malachi* being dead, we read no more of the Prophets.   A. M. —— 3595.
B. C. —— 409.

This Year NOTHUS gave Leave to Sanballat to build the *Samaritan Temple* on Mount *Gerizzim*, like That of *Jerusalem*, and made his Son-in-Law *Manasseh* the High Priest of it; and It stood splendid till JOHN HYRCANUS, the *Asmonæan* King and *High Priest* demolisht it: when also he made the *Idumeans* or *Edomites* conform to the Law of *Moses*.

{ from the said A. M. 3595.
  during Years —— 279.

  till —— A. M. 3874.
  B. C. —— 130. }

After *Nehemiah*, the High Priest of *Jerusalem* for the Time being, was the *Provincial Grand Master* of *Judæa*, first under the Kings of *Persia*, and afterwards under the *Grecian* Kings of *Egypt* and *Syria*. *Darius Nothus* died A. M. 3599.

10. ARTAXERXES *Mnemon* his Son succeeded 46 Years. He was a great Encourager of the *Craft*, especially after the Ascent of his Brother *Cyrus*, and the Retreat of *Xenophon* A. M. 3603.

In

In his 12th Year the brave Conon rebuilt the Walls of *Athens*, The King died, *A. M.* 3645.

11. DARIUS OCHUS his Son succeeded 21 Years.

In his 6th Year, *A. M.* 3651. Mausolus King of *Caria*, in *Lesser Asia* died, and next Year his mournful Widow Artemisia (also his Sister) founded for him a most splendid Sepulchral Monument at *Halicarnassus*, of the best Marble, (Hence all great Tombs are call'd Mausoleums) in Length from North to South 63 Cubits in Circuit, 411 Foot, and in Height 140 Foot, surrounded with 136 *Columns* of most *accurate Sculpture*, and the Fronts East and West had Arches 73 Foot wide, with a Pyramid on the side Wall, ending in a pointed Broch, on which was a Coach with 4 Horses of *one* Marble *Stone*. All was perform'd by the 4 best *Masons* of the Age, viz. *Scopas, Leochares, Timotheus* and *Briax*. It is reckoned the 5th of the 7 *Wonders of Art*.

Ochus was murder'd by his favourite Eunuch *Bagoas*, who set up,

12. ARSES his youngest Son, (the rest being murder'd) 3667. But *Bagoas* fearing Arses, murder'd him in two Years, and set up one of the Royal Family, viz.

13. DARIUS CODOMANNUS, who began to reign 3669. *Bagoas* prepared a Dose of Poison for him, but *Darius* made him drink it himself. He reign'd 6 Years, till conquer'd by *Alexander the Great*.

At length the Royal Art flourish'd in *Greece*. Indeed we read of the old *Dedalus* and his Sons, the Imitators of the *Egyptians* and *Phenicians*, of the little Labyrinth in *Crete*, and the larger at *Lemnos*, of the Arts and Sciences early at *Athenes* and *Sicyon, Candia* and *Sicily* before the *Trojan War* ; of the *Temples* of 𝔍𝔲𝔭𝔦𝔱𝔢𝔯 *Olympius*, 𝔈𝔰𝔠𝔲𝔩𝔞𝔭𝔦𝔲𝔰, &c. of the *Trojan Horse*, and other Things : But we are all in Darkness, Fable and Uncertainty till the *Olympiads*.

Now

Now the 35th Year of *Uzziah* King of *Judah* is the firſt Year of the firſt OLYMPIAD ⎰ *A. M.* 3228. ⎱ before the Founding when ſome of their bright ⎱ *B. C.* 776. ⎰ of *Rome* 28 Years. Men began to travel.

So that their moſt antient famous Buildings, as the Cittadel of *Athenes*, the Court of *Areopagus*, the *Parthenion* or *Temple* of 𝕸𝖎𝖓𝖊𝖗𝖛𝖆, the *Temples* of *Theſeus* and 𝕬𝖕𝖔𝖑𝖑𝖔, their *Porticos* and *Forums, Theatres* and *Gymnaſiums*, ſtately publick *Halls*, curious *Bridges*, regular *Fortifications*, ſtout *Ships* of War, and magnificent *Palaces*, with their beſt *Statues* and *Sculpture*, were All of 'em, either at firſt erected, or elſe rebuilt fine, even after the *Temple* of ZERUBBABEL; for

THALES MILESIUS, their firſt Philoſopher, died eleven Years only before the *Decree* of *Cyrus*; and the ſame Year 3457, PYTHAGORAS, his Scholar, travell'd into *Egypt*; while PISISTRATUS, the Tyrant of *Athenes*, began to collect the *firſt Library* in *Greece*.

PYTHAGORAS liv'd 22 Years among the *Egyptian* Prieſts till ſent by *Cambyſes* to *Babylon* and *Perſia*, *A. M.* 3480, where he pickt up great Knowledge among the *Chaldæan Magians* and *Babyloniſh Jews*; and return'd to *Greece* the Year that *Zerubbabel*'s 𝕿𝖊𝖒𝖕𝖑𝖊 was finiſh'd *A. M.* 3489.

He became, not only the Head of a new Religion of Patch Work, but likewiſe of an *Academy* or *Lodge* of good *Geometricians*, to whom he communicated a Secret * viz. *That amazing Propoſition which   * *Euclid. lib.* 1. *Prop.* *is the Foundation of all Maſonry, of what-*   XLVII. *ever Materials or Dimenſions*, call'd by *Maſons* his *HEUREKA*; becauſe They think It was his own Invention.

But after *Pythagoras*, GEOMETRY was the darling Study of the *Greeks*, and their learned Men reduced the noble *Science* to the Uſe of the ingenious *Mechanicks* of all Sorts, that perform by *Geometry* as well as the Operators in *Stone* or *Brick*.

And

And as MASONRY kept pace with *Geometry*, so many *Lodges* appear'd, especially in the *Grecian* Republicks, where *Liberty*, *Trade* and *Learning* flourish'd; as at *Sicyon*, *Athenes*, *Corinth* and the Cities of *Ionia*, till They arrived at their beautiful DORIC, IONIC and CORINTHIAN *Orders*: And their Improvements were soon discover'd to the *Persians* with a Vengeance, when They defeated *Xerxes*, *A. M.* 3525.

GREECE now abounded with the best *Architects*, *Sculptors*, *Statuaries*, *Painters* and other fine *Designers*, most of 'em educated at the Academies of *Athenes* and *Sicyon*, who Instructed many Artists and *Fellow Crafts* to be the best Operators upon Earth: So that the Nations of *Asia* and *Africa*, who had taught the *Greeks*, were now taught by 'em.

The learned *Greeks* rightly judging, that the Rules of the beautiful Proportions in *Architecture* should be taken from the Proportions of the *Human Body*, their fine *Painters* and *Statuaries* were esteem'd *Architects*, and were then actually so (even as afterwards true *old Masonry* was revived in *Italy* by the *Painters* *) nor could They have been   * See Chap. VII. fine *Painters* without being *Architects*.

Therefore several of those in the *Margin below*, excellent *Painters* and *Philosophers*, are in the List of *antient Architects*: Nay They all openly taught *Geometry*, and many of 'em practis'd *Masonry*; and being Gentlemen of good Repute, They were generally at the *Head* of the *Craft*, highly useful to the *Fellow Crafts*, by their Designs and fine Drawings, and bred them up

---

* No Country but *Greece* could now boast of such Men as *Mycon*, *Phidias*, *Demon*, *Androcides*, *Metor*, *Anaxagoras*, *Dipænus* and *Scyllis*, *Glycon*, *Alcamenes*, *Praxitiles*, *Polycletus*, *Lysippus*, *Peneus*, *Euphranor*, *Perseus*, *Philostratus*, *Zeuxis*, *Appollodorus*, *Parhasius*, *Timanthes*, *Eupompus*, *Pamphilus*, *Apelles*, *Artemones*, *Socrates*, *Eudoxus*, *Metrodorus* (who wrote of *Masonry*) and the excellent *Theodorus Cyrenæus*, who amplify'd *Geometry*, and publisht the *Art Analytic*, thn Master of the divine PLATO *, from whose School came *Xenocrates* and *Aristotle* the Preceptor of ALEXANDER *the Great*.   * *Plato* died *A.M.* 3656. *B.C.* --.348.

(28)

clever Artifts: Only by a Law in *Greece*, no *Slave* was allowed to learn the 7 liberal Sciences, or thofe of the *Freeborn* *; fo that in *Greece* alfo They were call'd FREE MASONS, and in their many *Lodges*, the Noble and Learned were accepted as Brothers, down to the Days of ALEXANDER *the Great* and afterwards for many Ages.

* According to the old *Conftitutions* Thefe are, 1. *Grammar*. 2 *Rhetoric*. 3. *Logic*. 4. *Arithmetic*. 5. GEOMETRY. 6. *Mufic*. 7. *Aftronomy*.

That warlike Prince began to reign in *Macedonia* a little before DARIUS *Codomannus* began in *Perfia*, and next Year ALEXANDER entering *Afia*, won the Battel of *Granicus*; and next Year the Battel of *Iffus*, and next Year took in *Tyre* and *Gaza*, and overran *Egypt*; and next Year won the Battel of *Arbela*, after which poor DARIUS, flying into *Bactria*, was murder'd by his General *Beffus*, after he had reign'd 6 Years. After *Cyrus* began 207 Years.

A. M. 3669. *B. C.* 335.

A. M. 3674. *B. C.*--- 330.

when the *Perfian* Monarchy ended, and the *Grecian* commenced.

But tho' from Ambition ALEXANDER order'd 𝔇𝔢𝔫𝔬𝔠𝔯𝔞𝔱𝔢𝔰 the *Architect* to found *Alexandria* in *Egypt*, yet he is not reckon'd a MASON; becaufe at the Inftigation of a drunken Whore, in his Revels, he burnt the rich and fplendid 𝔓𝔢𝔯𝔰𝔢𝔭𝔬𝔩𝔦𝔰, a City of *Palaces* in the beft Stile, *which no true Mafon would do, was he ever fo drunk.*

He found the Lofs of that fine City when He returned from *India*, but did not retrieve it: Nor did he encourage the noble Propofal of *Denocrates* to difpofe Mount *Athos* in the Form of the *King's Statue*, with a *City* in one Hand, and in the other Hand a large *Lake* to water the City: Only He deftroy'd no more Monuments of Art. Indeed he lov'd *Apelles* who drew his Picture, and *Lyfippus* who formed his Statue, and intended to encourage Arts and Sciences throughout the World; but he was prevented by dying drunk at *Babylon*, 6 Years after CODOMANNUS. *A. M.* 3680. *B. C.*---324.

ALEXANDER

ALEXANDER left his new *Grecian* Monarchy to be partition'd among his Generals, which may be said to commence 12 Years after his Death, when SELEUCUS *Nicator* took in BABYLON and began the *Seleucian Era*.

A. M. 3692.
B. C.----312.

CHAP. V.

From SELEUCUS *to Grand Master* AUGUSTUS CÆSAR.

SELEUCUS *Nicator* prov'd an excellent *Grand Master*, founded the Great *Seleucia* on the *Euphrates* for his *Deputy* in the *East*; and in the *West* He built his stately Capital City the famous ANTIOCH in old *Syria*, with the Great Grove of *Daphne*, a sacred *Asylum*, in the Middle of which He rear'd the *Temple* of APOLLO and DIANA (tho' It prov'd afterwards the *Temple* of 𝕍enus and 𝔅acchus) and also the lesser Cities of old *Syria*, as *Apamia, Berræa, Seleucia, Laodicea, Edessa, Pella*, &c. and having reigned 33 Years He died *A. M.* 3725.

ANTIOCHUS *Soter* succeeded his Father, and died *A. M.* 3744.

ANTIOCHUS *Treos* succeeded his Father, and died *A. M.* 3759. the Progenitor of a long *Royal* Race that were all set aside by POMPEY. But in the 4th Year of *Theos*

ARSACES, a noble *Parthian*, revolted from the *Syro Grecian* Kings, and founded the famous Kingdom
of *Parthia*, *Anno Eræ Seleuci* 57. in *A. M.*———3748.
Eastern *Asia*, that in Time set Bounds to *B. C.*———256.
the *Romans*.

Yet the *Arsacidæ*, and also the *Seleucidæ*, being chiefly conversant in War, we must travel into *Egypt*, to find the best *Free-Masons*,

(30)

Masons, where the *Grecian* Architecture flourish'd under the *Ptolemaidæ*. For

PTOLEMY SOTER had set up his Throne at *Alexandria*, which he much inlarged and beautify'd.   *A. M.* ——— 3700.
A. C. ——— 304.

EUCLID the *Tyrian* came to *Ptolemy* in this first Year, who had collected in his Travels the scatter'd *Elements of Geometry*, and digested them into a Method that was never yet mended; for which his Memory will be fragrant in the *Lodges* to the End of Time.

PTOLEMY, *Grand-Master*, * with EUCLID the *Geometrician* and STRATON the *Philosopher*, as *Grand-Wardens*, built his Palace at *Alexandria*, and the curious *Musæum* or College of the Learned, with the Library of *Brucheum* near the Palace, that was fill'd with 400000 Books, or valuable Manuscripts, before It was burnt in the Wars of JULIUS CÆSAR. Soter died ——— *A. M.* 3719.

* According to the Traditions and the old Constitutions.

PTOLEMY PHILADELPHUS succeeded his Father in the Throne and *Solomon*'s Chair too: And in his 2d Year he carried on the Great *Tower* of Pharo, founded by his Father, * the 6th of the 7 *Wonders* of *Art*, built on an Island, as the Light House for the Harbour of *Alexandria*, (whence *Light Houses* in the *Mediterranean* are call'd *Faros*) a Piece of amazing Architecture, by the Care of his *Grand-Wardens* Deriphanes and his Son Sostratus, the Father built the *Heptastadium* for joining the Island to the Continent, while the Son rear'd the *Tower*.

---

* Some prefer to This the great *Obelisk* of Queen SEMIRAMIS 150 Foot high and 24 Foot square at Bottom, all of one intire Stone like a *Pyramid*, that was brought from *Armenia* to *Babylon*; also an huge Rock cut into the Figure of *Semiramis*, with the smaller Rocks by it in the Shape of tributary Kings: If we may believe *Ctesias* against the Advice of *Berosus* and *Aristotle*: For she is not so antient as is generally thought, and seems to be only the Queen of NABONASSAR.

PHILADELPHUS founded the City *Myos Hormus* on the *Red Sea* for the *East India* Trade, built the *Temple* of the *Zephyrian* 𝕍𝕖𝕟𝕦𝕤 in *Crete*, *Ptolemais* in *Palestine*, and rebuilt old *Rabbah* of the *Ammonites*, calling it *Philadelphia*. Nay he was so accurate an Architect that for a long Time all fine *Masonry* was call'd 𝕻𝖍𝖎𝖑𝖆𝖉𝖊𝖑𝖕𝖍𝖎𝖆𝖓, or after the *Stile* of *Philadelphus*. He died *A. M.* 3757.

PTOLEMY EUERGETES his Son succeeded the great Encourager of the *Craft*, with his *Grand-Wardens* his two learned Librarians, *viz.* 𝔈𝔯𝔞𝔱𝔬𝔰𝔱𝔥𝔢𝔫𝔢𝔰 of *Cyrene*, and 𝔄𝔭𝔬𝔩𝔩𝔬𝔫𝔦𝔲𝔰 of *Perga*. The Library of *Brucheum* being near full, He erected That of *Serapium*, which in Time contain'd 300000 *Manuscripts*, to which CLEOPATRA added 200000 more from the Library of *Pergamus* given to her by *Mark Antony*; but all were burnt in Ovens by the ignorant *Saracens* to bake Bread for their Army *, to the lasting and irreparable Da-   * *A. D.* 642. mage of the Learned.

EUERGETES was the last good *Grand Master* of *Egypt*; and therefore we shall sail over to the *Hellespont* to view the glorious *Temple* of *Cyzicus*, with Threads of beaten Gold in the Joints of the Insides of the Marble Stones, that cast a fine Lustre on all the *Statues* and *Images*: Besides the curious *Eccho* of the 7 *Towers* at the *Thracian* Gate of *Cyzicus*, and a large *Bouleutorion* or *Town-House*, without one Pin or Nail in the Carpenter's Work; so that the Beams and Rafters could be taken off, and again put on, without Laces or Keys to bind 'em.

The RHODIANS also employ'd CARES (the Scholar of *Lysippus*) the *Architect*, to erect the *great* COLOSSUS of *Rhodes*, the last of the 7 *Wonders of Art*, made of *Metal*, the greatest *human Statue* under the SUN, to whom It was dedicated.

It was 70 Cubits high and duly proportion'd in every Part and Limb, striding in the Harbour's Mouth, wide enough to receive between his Legs the largest Ship under sail, and appearing at a Distance like an high Tower.

It began in the 4th Year of
Ptolemy Soter   A.M. 3704 ⎫
and finish'd in Years   12 ⎭

                A. M. 3716 ⎫
It stood firm, Years —— 66 ⎭

and fell by an Earthquake 3782 ⎫
                 B. C.   222 ⎭
the last Year of PTOLEMY
Euergetes.
The great COLOSSUS lay in
Ruins, Years   ——   894
even till A D. ——   672
when Mahowias the 6. Caliph of
the Saracens carried It off to
Egypt, the Load of 900 Camels.

Tho' some prefer to It the Statue of *Jupiter* *Olympius* fitting on a fine Throne in his old *Doric* *Temple* of *Achaia*, made of innumerable Pieces of *Porphyre*, Gold and *Ivory*, exceeding Grand and exactly proportion'd ; for tho' the *Temple* was in Height 68 Foot clear, *Jupiter* could not stand upright. It was perform'd by the great *Phidias*, as was That of *Nemesis* at *Rhamnus*, 10 Cubits high, and That of *Minerva* at *Athens* 26 Cubits high.

While the *Greeks* were propagating the *Science* and the *Art* in the very best Manner, founding new Cities, repairing old ones, and erecting *Statues* past Numbers, the other *Africans* imitated the *Egyptians*, Southward in *Ethiopia* down to the *Cape of Good Hope* ; and also Westward to the *Atlantic Shore* : tho' History fails, and no *Travellers* have yet discover'd the valuable Remains of those many powerful Nations. Only we know that

The CARTHAGINIANS had formed a magnificent Republick long before the *Romans* ; had built some Thousands of stately *Cities* and strong *Castles*, and made their great Capital CARTHAGE the Terror of *Rome*, and her Rival for universal Empire. Great was their Skill in *Geometry* and *Masonry* of all Sorts, in Marble *Temples*, golden *Statues*, stately *Palaces*, regular *Forts*, and stout *Ships* that sail'd in all the known Seas, and carried on the Chief Trade of the known World : Therefore the *Emulous Romans* long design'd its Destruction, having a prophetical Proverb, *Delenda est Carthago* ! *Carthage must be demolish'd* ; which They accomplish'd, as in the Sequel.

Thus

Thus HANNIBAL the Warlike, in his Retreat from *Carthage* to *Armenia*, shew'd his great Skill in drawing for King *Artaxes* the Plan of the City *Artaxata*, and survey'd the *Palace, Temples* and *Citadel* thereof.

The learned SICILIANS, descended from the *Greeks*, follow'd their Instructions in Architecture throughout the Island very early, at *Agrigentum, Messana, Gela, &c.* especially at *Syracusa*; for when It was besieged by the *Romans* It was 22 Miles round, and *Marcellus* could not storm it, because of the amazing Devices of the learned Geometrician, Architect, Mechanic and Ingenier, the Noble * ARCHIMEDES, till by mastering an ill-guarded Tower, the City was taken by Surprize on a Festival Day. But tho' *Marcellus* gave a strict Charge to save ARCHIMEDES, a common Soldier slew him, while, not minding the Uproar, the noble and learned Man was deeply engaged in mechanical Speculations and Schemes to repulse the *Romans* and save *Syracuse*. MARCELLUS shed Tears for him as a publick Loss to the Learned, and gave him an honourable Burial in the Year of *Rome* 537. —— A. M. 3792. ⎫ while *Hannibal* distress'd B. C.--- 212. ⎭ *Italy*.

* Call'd by the old Masons the Noble and Excellent *Grand Master* of *Syracuse*.

Many of the *Grecian, Carthaginian* and *Sicilian* MASONS had travell'd into the *North* and *West* of Europe, and propagated their useful Skill, particularly in *Italy, Spain*, the *Belearic* Islands, and the Coast of *Gaul*; but History fails, till the *Roman* Armies came there. Nor have we certain Accounts of the *Chinese* and other *East Indians*, till the *Europeans* navigated thither in these later Times; only the Wall of *China* makes a Figure in the *Map*, tho' we know not yet when It was built: Also their Great Cities and most splendid Palaces, as described by Travellers, evidently discover that those antient Nations had long cultivated Arts and Sciences, especially *Geometry* and *Masonry*.

Thus hitherto the MASONS, above all other *Artists*, have been the Favourites of the Eminent, who wisely join'd the *Lodges* for the better conducting of their various Undertakings in old Architecture:

Architecture: And still great Men continued at the Head of the Craft; as will appear in the Sequel.

From *Sicily* we soon pass into ITALY, to view the first Improvements of the ROMANS, who for many Ages affected nothing but War, till by Degrees They learned the *Science* and the *Art* from their Neighbours. But

The HETRURIANS, or *Tuscans*, very early used their own natural TUSCAN ORDER, never used by the *Greeks*, and were the first in *Italy* that learned from the *Greeks* the DORIC, IONIC and CORINTHIAN *Orders*; till the *Royal Art* was there conspicuous under their King PORSENNA, who built a stately *Labyrinth*, not inferior to That of *Lemnos*, and the highest *Mausoleum* on Record.

PORSENNA died in the Year of *Rome* 303. *A. M.* 3558 the 19th Year of *Artaxerxes Longimanus*, while *B. C.* 446 the *Romans* were only engaged in subduing their Neighbours in *Italy*, and their *Taste* was yet but *low*; till

TURRENUS, the last King of the *Tuscans*, bequeathed his Kingdom to the *Romans*; in the 6th Year of *Philadelphus*, while *Pyrrhus* destress'd *Italy*. TURRENUS died *A. M.* —— 3725 The *Tuscans* had built many fine strong Places; and now their Disciples were invited to *Rome*, and taught the *Romans* the Royal *Art*, tho' still their Improvements were not considerable, till

MARCELLUS triumphed in the splendid Spoils of *Syracuse*, upon the Death of the *Great* ARCHIMEDES, as above.

MARCELLUS, the Patron of Arts and Sciences, employ'd his *Fellow-Crafts* to build at *Rome* his famous Theatre, with a *Temple* to Virtue, and another to Honour; yet the *High Taste* of the *Romans* was not general till

SCIPIO *Asiaticus* led 'em against *Antiochus Magnus* King of *Syria*, and took from him all the Country *West* of Mount *Taurus* —— *A. M.* 3814 In the Year of *Rome* 559 In the 15th Year of *Ptol. Epiphanes* B.C. 190 For then, with Astonishment, They beheld the unspeakable Beauties of the *Grecian* and *Asiatick* Architecture, standing in full Splendor, which They resolved to Imitate.

And

And so They went on Improving, till

Scipio *Africanus* (who had always a set of the Learned attending him as their *Patron*) took in the great Rival of *Rome* the glorious Carthage, which he demolish'd against his own Inclination by Command of the Senate; for

Delenda est Carthago A.M. 3858 } Year of *Rome* 603
The Account of its Destruction B.C. 146 }
is lamentable ———

while *Consul* Mummius the same Year sack'd *Corinth*, the wealthy Queen of *Greece*, who discover'd his Ignorance, when he threatned those that carried home, from *Corinth*, the Inimitable Pictures of Hercules and Bacchus, that if they lost 'em, They must make 'em good with new ones.

Both these Generals triumphed at *Rome* in the portable Monuments of Art, brought from those Cities, that had been the most opulent and glorious upon Earth. But now the Romans were so wise as to bring home too the ablest Professors of *Science*, and Practitioners of *Art*. After which we read of several stately Edifices at *Rome*, built in the finest *Grecian Stile*: as the famous Palace of Paulus Emilius of the best *Phrygian* Marble; the *Triumphal* Arch of Marius at *Orange* in *Gaul*, the Three surprizing *Theatres* of *Scaurus at *Rome*, &c.

The mighty Sylla brought the *Columns* of the *Temple* of Jupiter *Olympius* from *Greece*, to adorn the *Temple* of Jupiter *Capitolinus* at *Rome*, after the old one, built by *Tarquinius Superbus* was burnt; in whose Time *Jupiter* was only of *Clay*, but now of pure *Gold*.

Lucullus, the learned and brave, erected a fine *Library*, and a splendid House with Gardens, in the *Asiatick* Stile.

---

† The one held 80000 People at the Shows or Plays. It had 3 Scenes or Lofts one above another, with 360 Columns: the first Row of *Marble*, each 38 Foot high, the 2d Row was of *Chrystal*, and the 3d of *Gilded Wood*: between the Columns were 3000 *Statues* of Brass.

The other two *Theatres* were of *Wood*, sustained on great *Axles*, whereby They could be turn'd round, and joined in one great *Amphi-Theatre*.   Plin Pompey

Pompey the Great, built a *Theatre* that held 40000 People at the Shows, near his fine Palace, and his *Temple* of 𝔙𝔦𝔠𝔱𝔬𝔯𝔶.

These and other great Men, during the *Roman* Republick, much encouraged *Architects* and *Masons* as their *Patrons*; and in their Absence, the *Consul Resident*, or the *High Priest* of *Rome*, or the *Arch Flamin*, or some other Great Man on the Spot, thought it his honour to be the *Patron* of Arts and Sciences (what we now call *Grand Master*) attended duly by the most ingenious of the Fraternity; till the *Republic* was near its Exit by the Competition of *Pompey* and *Cæsar* for Pre-eminence.

But Pompey being routed at *Pharsalia*, and murder'd by the *Egyptians* in his Flight, the 𝔎epublic expired, and
Julius Cæsar obtain'd the Pre-eminence ——— A. M. 3956 ⎫
Cæsar now perpetual *Dictator* ⎧ Year of *Rome* 701 B.C. 48 ⎭
and *Imperator*, a learned Geome- ⎩ Before the Birth of Christ 44
trician, Architect, Ingenier and Astronomer, being *High Priest*, reformed the *Roman* Calendar B.C. or before the Christian Era 45.

He and his Legions had built much in *Gaul*, and at *Rome* he rais'd his Great *Circus* or Square, a true *Oblong*, 3 Furlongs in Length, and one in Breadth, that held 260,000 People at the Shows: also his stately Palace, and lovely *Temple* of 𝔙enus, and ordered *Carthage* and *Corinth* to be rebuilt, about 100 Years after They were demolish'd.

See *Pliny*, who gives a full Account of these Things.

But Cæsar, intending first to quell the *Parthians*; and then, as *Grand Master* of the *Roman Republic*, to encourage the *Science* and the *Art* beyond all before him in universal Peace, was basely murder'd by his ungrateful *Brutus* under *Pompey*'s Statue; upon which the Civil Wars ended, and the Preeminence was in Suspence during 14 Years,   A. M. ——— 3960 ⎫
   B. C.   44 ⎭

till first *Brutus* and *Cassius* were lost at *Philippi*, and next *Mark Antony* was defeated at *Actium* by Octavianus, who then conquer'd *Egypt*, and finish'd the Civil Wars: and so the *Grecian* Monarchy being fully ended, the Roman *Empire* began
In the Year of *Rome* 719 ——— A. M. 3974 ⎫
         Before the Christian Era ——— 30 ⎭

CHAP.

CHAP. VI.

From AUGUSTUS *till the* Havock *of the* Goths.

ROME, now the Mistress of the known World, became the Center of Learning a of Imperial Power, and arrived at her *Zenith* under

OCTAVIANUS, now called *Sebastos*, or AUGUSTUS CÆSAR, who patroniz'd the Fraternity as their Illustrious *Grand Master*, (so call'd always by the *old* MASONS) with his Deputy AGRIPPA, who adorned the *Campus Martius*, and built the Grand *Portico* of the ROUTNDA *Pantheon*, with many more charming Piles mention'd in History.

VITRUVIUS the Learned, the Principal *Warden*, by his Writings has justly acquir'd the Character of the Father or Teacher of all accurate Architects, and clever Connoisseurs to this Day.

AUGUSTUS first employ'd his *Fellow Crafts* in repairing all the publick Edifices (a most needful Work after the Wars) and in rebuilding some of 'em. But also he built the Bridge of *Ariminum*; and at *Rome* the *Temple* of MARS the *Avenger*, the *Temple* of Apollo, the *Rotunda* call'd *Galucio*, the great and sumptuous *Forum*, the principal and magnificent *Palace* of AUGUSTUS, with some lesser Palaces, the fine *Mausoleum*, the accurate *Statue* in the *Capitol*, the curious *Library*, the *Portico*, and the *Park* for People to walk in, &c. Nay, He fill'd the *Temples of Rome* with the most costly *Statues*, and wittily set up *That* of CLEOPATRA (of massy Gold brought from *Egypt*) in the *Temple* of VENUS.

In those Golden Days of AUGUSTUS, the Eminent following his Example, built above 100 *Marble Palaces* at *Rome*, fit for the

greatest

(38)

greateſt Kings; and every ſubſtantial Citizen rebuilt their Houſes too in *Marble*, all joining in the ſame Diſpoſition of adorning *Rome*: whereby many *Lodges* appear'd, in City and Suburbs, of the *Free* and *Accepted Maſons*: ſo that Augustus, when a dying, juſtly ſaid, *I found* Rome *built of* Brick, *but I leave it built of* Marble!

Therefore the preſent Remains of *antient Rome* in his Time, and of ſome following Emperors, are ſo accurate, that They are the beſt Patterns of *true Maſonry* extant, the Epitome of all the old *Grecian Architecture*, commonly expreſſed by the Augustan Stile: and we now wiſh to arrive at its glorious Perfection in *Wiſdom, Strength* and *Beauty*.

But before the Death of Augustus, we muſt travel into *Judæa*. The *High Prieſts* of *Jeruſalem* had been *Provincial Grand Maſters* there, under the Kings of *Egypt* then Sovereigns of the *Jews*, till Seleucus *Philopater* King of *Syria* ſeiz'd *Judæa*, or *Paleſtin*. His Son viz.
A. M. 3824
B. C. 180

Antiochus *Epiphanes* cruelly perſecuted the *Jews* till reſcued by the valiant *Aſmonæan* Prieſt *Judas Maccabæus*: for long after *Zerubbabel* and *Jeſhua* the High Prieſt, an ordinary Prieſt, call'd *Aſmonæus*, appear'd, not of the Houſe of *Jeſhua*, but only of the Courſe of *Joarib*, the Great Grand Father of *Mattathias*, the brave Prieſt of *Modin* and Father of Maccabæus.

For the lineal Succeſſor of *Jeſhua* was Onias IV. (Son of *Onias* III. the laſt good *High Prieſt*) who being depriv'd of his Right by the *Syrian* Kings, went to *Egypt*, where He got leave to build a Temple at *Heliopolis*, like That of *Jeruſalem*, for the *Jews* in *Egypt* and *Cyrene*, then more numerous and opulent than thoſe in *Judæa*. This *Temple* was founded *A. M.* 3855
But the *Aſmonæans* or *Maccabees* fought their *B. C.* 149
Way to Pre-eminence, It ſtood ſplendid till *A. D.* 73
againſt the *Syrian* Kings, during Years 222
and alſo obtain'd it as Till deſtroy'd by *Veſpaſion* the Emperor. *High Prieſts* and Princes of the *Jews*, during about 130 Years, till *Mark Antony* and *Octavicnus* got the *Senate* of *Rome* to create

Herod

(39)

HEROD the *Edomite*, or *Idumean Jew*, King of *Judæa* in the *Capitol A. M.* 3964, and by the Help of the *Romans*, HEROD conquer'd ANTIGONUS, and mounted the Throne at *Jerusalem*

See the ⎫   *A. M.* —— 3367 ⎫
Margin ⎬   Before the Christian Era   37 ⎬
Below. ⎭   Before the Birth of Christ   33 ⎭

* MATTATHIAS the *Asmonæan* Priest died *A. M* 3837. B. C. 167. And three of his Sons ruled the *Jews*, viz.

| 1 JUDAS MACCABÆUS died 3843 acted as High Priest and Ruler | 2 JONATHAN owned a Free Prince and High Priest. Murder'd 3860 | 3 SIMON the King and High Priest, erected over *Jonathan's* Grave a lofty Monument of *white Marble* |

ruled independent of the *Gentiles*, till murder'd *A. M.* 3868

4 JOHN HYRCANUS succeeded Father *Simon*, till he died 3897

5 ARISTOBULUS I. reign'd one year, viz. *A. M.* 3898 | 6 ALEXANDER JANNÆUS reign'd 27 years, and died *A. M.* 3925. leaving the Crown to
7 ALEXANDRA his Widow, and *Hyrcanus* wore the Mitre, till she died *A. M.* 3934

| 8 HYRCANUS, after his Mother died, was *King* and *High-Priest* 3 Months, till deprived by his Brother. He was restored by POMPEY only to the *Mitre*, till captivated by the *Parthians*, who set up ANTIGONUS 3964. *Hyrcanus* was beheaded by *Herod*, *A. M.* 3974 | 9 ARISTOBOLUS II. usurped 6 Years till deposed by POMPEY 3940 and poisoned —— 3955 |

| ALEXANDRA Wife of her first Cousin, viz. | ALEXANDER beheaded 3995 | 10 ANTIGONUS set up by the *Parthians* 3964. reign'd 3 Years, till conquer'd by *Herod* and crucify'd by the *Romans* —— 3967 |

| HEROD I. an *Idumæan Jew*, created at *Rome* K. of *Judæa* 3964 conquer'd *Antigonus* and began to reign 3967 and in the last Year of his Reign —— 33 | MARIAMNE *Herod's* Queen, was by him beheaded 3975. and by his Order her two Sons were strangled, but they left a Royal Race | ARISTOBULUS III. made *High Priest* by *Herod*, till drown'd in a Bath without Issue 3969 |

Christ *A. M.* —— 4000 was born but the *first* Year of our A. D. or *Christian Era*, is A. M. 4004. See Page 2.

He got rid of all the *Afmonæans*, made the *Sanhedrim* ufelefs, and fet up *High Priefts* at his Pleafure. But for all his great Faults,

HEROD became the greateft Builder of his Day, the Patron or *Grand Mafter* of many *Lodges*, and fent for the moft expert *Fellow Crafts* of *Greece* to affift his own *Jews*: For after the Battle of *Actium* B. C. 30. Before *Chrift*'s Birth 26.

HEROD, being reconciled to *Auguftus*, began to fhew his mighty Skill in *Mafonry*, by erecting a fplendid *Grecian* THEATRE at *Jerufalem*, and next built the ftately City *Sebafte*, (fo called from *Sebaftos* or *Auguftus*) formerly *Samaria*, with a curious little *Temple* in It like That of *Jerufalem*. He made the City *Cæfarea* the beft Harbour in *Paleftine*, and built a *Temple* of white Marble at *Paneas*——the Cities *Antipatris*, *Phafaelis* and *Cypron*, and the *Tower* of *Phafael* at *Jerufalem*, not Inferior to the *Pharo* of *Alexandria*, &c.

But his moft amazing Work was his Rebuilding of the **Temple** of ZERUBBABEL; for having prepared Materials (which with thofe of the old Temple were enough) and proper Inftruments, HEROD employ'd 10000 *Mafons* (befides Labourers) and marfhall'd 'em in *Lodges* under 1000 Priefts and Levites that were fkilful Architects, as *Mafters* and *Wardens* of the *Lodges*, and acted as GRAND MASTER himfelf with his Wardens HILLEL and SHAMMAI, two learned *Rabbins* of great Reputation.

He began to pull down the *Temple* of *Zerubbabel*, not all at once, but Piece by Piece, and levelled the Foot-ftone of this *Temple* of *Jerufalem*, viz.

After the founding of the *fecond Temple* 518 Years

In the 21ft Year of *Herod* and 13 Year of *Auguftus* and 29th *Julian* Year.

In the 4th Year of *Olympiad* CXC. and of *Rome* 732.

A. M. ———— 3987

Before the *Chr. Æra* 17

Before *Chrift*'s Birth 14

Juft 46 Years before the fecond Paffover of *Chrift*'s Miniftry for the *Jews* faid 46 *Years was this Temple in Building*, John xi. 20.

The *Holy Place*, and the *Holy of Holiest* in the West, and the great *Portico* in the East, were finish'd at a wondrous Cost, and in the short Space of 1 Year and 6 Months } 9 Y. and 6 M. and the Rest design'd by *Herod* in 8 Years more.

When the *Fraternity* celebrated the *Cape Stone* with great Joy and in due Form, and the King solemniz'd Its *Dedication* by Prayer and Sacrifice, on his Coronation Day, of the 31st Year of his Reign, } * *A. M.* ———— 3997 } and 23d of *Augustus* *. Before the Christian Era 7 } Before *Christ's Birth*

Josephus describes It †, as he † *Antiq.* lib. xv. cap xi. view'd It, with the Additions built after *Herod* died, a number of the most curious and magnificent Marble Edifices that had been rais'd since the Days of SOLOMON; yet more after the *Grecian Stile*, and much Inferior to *Solomon's* TEMPLE in Extent and Decoration, tho' larger than That of *Zerubbabel*, and was by the *Romans* esteemed the same: for *Tacitus* calls It the same that *Pompey* walk'd thro'.

But It was not fully finish'd, in all Its Appartments, till about 6 Years before It was destroy'd, viz. A. D. 64.

At length

AUGUSTUS having shut up the *Temple* of *JANUS*; for that all the World was at Peace, In the 26th Year of his Empire, after the Conquest of *Egypt*,

The WORD was made FLESH, or the LORD JESUS CHRIST IMMANUEL was born, tne Great Architect or *Grand Master* of the *Christian* Church.

After *Solomon's* Death 971 } In the Year of the *Julian Period* 4710
In the Year of *Rome* 745 } In the Year of *Masonry* or *A.M.* 4000
In the Year of *Herod* 34 } B. C. or Before the *Christ. Æra* 4

King HEROD died a few Months after the *Birth* of CHRIST, and, notwithstanding his vast Expence in *Masonry*, He died rich.

After the Birth of *Christ* 4 Years, or when CHRIST was going in his 4th Year, The CHRISTIAN Era begins *A. M.* 4004.

Commonly call'd ANNO DOMINI, ——— 1.
See the Margin of Page 2.

G

And when *Christ* was aged near 18 Years, the *Great* Augustus died at *Nola* in *Campania*, Aug. 19. ——— A. D. 14
In the Year of *Rome* 761 ⎫ In the *Vulgar* Year of *Masonry* 4014
After he had reign'd 44 ⎬ tho' the accurate Year is 4018
Years: when TIBERIUS I. his Collegue began to reign alone, who also encouraged the *Craft*.

In his 20th Year after *Augustus*, or the *Vulgar A*. D. 34.
The LORD JESUS CHRIST, aged 36 Years, and about 6 Months, was Crucified, without the Walls of *Jerusalem*, by *Pontius Pilat* the *Roman* Governor of *Judæa*, and rose again from the Dead on the 3d Day, for the Justification of all that believe in him.

Tiberius banish'd *Pontius Pilat* for his Injustice to Christ; and next Year That Emperor died *A*. D. 35

The Augustan Stile was well cultivated, and the clever *Craftsmen* were much encouraged by some following Emperors. Thus even

NERO, for all his gross Faults, rais'd his brazen *Statue* in *Via Sacra* 110 Foot high; and built his guilded Palace, a Nonsuch.

VESPASIAN, who commenced *A*. D. 68. sent his brave Son Titus to subdue the *Jews*. Titus took in *Jerusalem*, when a Soldier, without Orders, set fire to the Temple ⎫ *A*. D. ——— 70
Vespasian shut the *Temple* of Janus, and built ⎬ after Christ's ⎫
the *Temple* of Peace. He rais'd his famous ⎭ Crucifixion ⎬ 36
Amphi-Theatre, when the rich Composite ⎭
Order was first used. He order'd the *Jewish Temple* in *Egypt* to be demolish'd, *A*. D. 73. and died *A*. D. 77.

TITUS reign'd but 2 Years. He had built his *Triumphal* Arch with fine Ingravings; and a stately Palace with the famous Statue of *Laocoon* of one Stone, and died *A*. D. 79.	DOMITIAN succeeded Brother *Titus*, and rebuilt the *Temple* of Jupiter *Capitolinus*, most magnificent, overlaid It with Plates of Gold, and had all the *Columns* cut at *Athenes*.

Domitian built also the *Temple* of *MINERVA*, and That of the *Flavians*; and rais'd a *Palace* more Grand and Rich than
That

That of *Auguſtus*, with ſtately Galleries in the Portico, beſides Halls, Baths and beautiful Apartments for his Women. He died *A. D.* 93. ſucceeded by NERVA, who died — 95. after he had adopted

TRAJAN, whoſe Warden was *Apollodorus*, the Architect, He laid his wonderful Bridge over the *Danube*, built his noble *Circus* and *Palace*, his two *Triumphal* Arches, the one at *Ancona* ſtill ſtanding, and the other at *Rome*, afterwards pull'd to Pieces to adorn the *Arch* of CONSTANTIN: beſides *Trajan* erected his famous COLUMN, a Pattern of the Kind, well known to all Connoiſſeurs. He died *A. D.* 114.

ADRIAN ſucceeded, a learned Deſigner, and even a dexterous Operator, repair'd the publick Edifices, like a Wiſe *Grand Maſter*, built *Adrian*'s Wall in *Britain*, his commodious Bridge at *Rome*, and his famous *Mauſoleum* or MOLES ADRIANI, with accurate *Collonading*, and died *A. D.* 135.

ANTONINUS PIUS rais'd his curious Column, and died *A. D.* 159.

MARCUS AURELIUS countenanced the Artiſts till he died *A. D.* 178.

COMMODUS, tho' educated a *Deſigner*, turn'd vicious; and, in his Time, *Painting* and *Sculpture* began to decline at *Rome*, tho' not yet *Architecture*. He died *A. D.* 191.

SEVERUS built his *Corinthian Epizone* at *Rome*, and *Murſever* in *Britain*. He died at *York* A. D. 209.

CORACALLA erected his ſplendid *Circus*, and died *A. D.* 215. Nor find we much more till

CONSTANTIN the *Great*, who commenced in *Britain* Emperor of *Rome*, A. D. 306. He repair'd and beautify'd *Jeruſalem*, *Drepanum*, *Troy*, *Chalcedon*, *Theſſalonica*, &c. and rear'd at *Rome* the laſt *Triumphal* Arch in the *Auguſtan Stile*.

For He removed his Throne from *Rome* to *Bizantium*, which he call'd now *Conſtantinople*, and alſo carried off all the portable Monuments of Art from *Italy*, and the beſt Artiſts to embelliſh his new Metropolis, where He built at a vaft Rate, many artful Piles, *Forums, Hippodroms, Temples* or *Churches, Porticos, Fountains*, a *ftately Imperial Palace* and *Senate Houfe*, a *Pillar* of *Porphyre* of 8 Stones, about 87 Foot high above the Pedeftal, and the amazing *Serpentin Pillar* with his own *Equeftrian Statue*, &c. He died *A. D.* 336.

See *Petrus Gyllius* his Antiquities of *Conftantinople*, tranflated into *Englifh* by Mr *Ball*, A. D 1729.

CONSTANS brought with him to *Rome* the famous Architect HORMISDAS the King of *Perfia*'s Son, who was juftly aftonifh'd at the antient Structures and Statues, and declared them inimitable: for now all the *Arts of Defigning* dwindled at *Rome*, as They flourifh'd at *Conftantinople*. Nay the *Chriftians*, in Zeal againft Heathen Idolatry, demolifh'd many curious Things; till

The *Roman Empire* was partition'd between two Brothers, *viz.*

VALENTINIAN 1. Emperor of the *Weft* at *Rome*. Now the *Chriftians* at *Rome* adorn'd their old Church of St. *Peter's* with the Columns of *Adrian's Mole*, but could not follow the Juft Proportions of the Antients. He died *A. D.* 374. and this Empire was foon ingroffed by the *Eaftern*;

and VALENS Emperor of the *Eaft* at *Conftantinople*, who was diftrefs'd by the 𝔊𝔬𝔱𝔥𝔰, and died without Iffue, *A. D.* —— 378

THEODOSIUS *the Great* fucceeded, who built a fine *Column* like That of *Trajan*, with his brazen *Statue* on the Top of It, and a great *Circus*.

THEODOSIUS gloried in being the *Potron* of all the *Defigners* and *Operators* (the fame as *Grand Mafter*) and loved them fo well, that by a Law, he exempted *all the Craft* from Taxation.

The Northern Nations of *Europe*, the *Goths, Vandals, Huns. Allemans, Herules, Sweves, Dacians, Alans, Franks, Gepidans, Saxons, Angles, Longobards*, and many more, had gradually grown powerful as the *Roman Empire* decay'd, and invaded *Greece, Afia, Gaul, Spain* and *Africa*, nay *Italy* Itfelf, over-running the polite World like a Deluge, with warlike Rage and grofs Ignorance, the Enemies of *Arts* and *Sciences*.

But THEODOSIUS ftopt their Carrier, became fole Emperor of the *Eaft* and *Weft*, and died A. D 395.

THEODOSIUS divided the Empire between his two Sons, *viz.*

HONORIUS, Emperor of the *West* at *Rome*, in whose Reign *Alaricus* the warlike *Visogoth* took in *Rome* A.D. 409.

    HONORIUS died A. D. 423.

    VALENTINIAN III. succeeded, in whose Reign ATTILA the *Hun* laid *Italy* waste, and would have destroy'd *Rome* but for the Prudence of the Bishop. When he died *A. D.* ——— 455.
Ten *nominal* Emperors succeeded. Mean while GENSERICUS the *Vandal* came from *Carthage*, and plunder'd *Rome* 456
    At last
AUGUSTULUS, the Tenth of those *Nominal* Emperors, fairly abdicated for fear of *Odoacer* King of the *Herules* 475
So ended the *Western* Empire,
    when
The GOTHIC Kings of *Italy* succeeded, *viz.* ODOACER King of *Italy* reign'd 17 Years, till slain by

    THEODORIC the *Goth*. A. D. 492
He and his Race reign'd Kings of *Italy* during 48 Years, till *A. D.* 540. when

    TOTILA was elected King of *Italy*. But maliciously designing to extinguish the Name and Memorial of old *Rome*, TOTILA set it on fire during 13 Days, and had demolish'd about two Thirds of that lofty Metropolis of the World, before he was beat off by *Bellisarius*, A. D. 547
    O *Gothic* Ignorance!
And here we may date the *Total Departure* of the AUGUSTAN STILE in *Italy* and the *West*.
    See Its *Revival* in the next Chapter.

ARCADIUS Emperor of the *East* at *Constantinople*, who inriched that City with many fine Structures, and his lofty *Pillar*, with a Stair in the Heart of It, 147 Foot high. He died *A. D.* 408.

THEODOSIUS, *Jun.* erected there *Statues, Columns* and *Obelisks*, the Spoils of *Greece, Egypt* and *Asia*; repair'd the great Church of *St. Sophia*, and died 449

    The following Emperors of the *East* supported the *Lodges* or Academies of the Artists or *Craftsmen*, down to

    JUSTINIAN I. who began A. D. ——— 526.
He restor'd the whole *Roman* Empire almost to its Pristin Glory.
Nay, in laudable Zeal for the AUGUSTAN STILE, He sent his General, the brave BELLISARIUS, with an Army against TOTILA the *Goth*, whom he forced to run away; and so *Bellisarius* saved as much of old *Rome* as he could
    A.D. 547
    JUSTINIAN

JUSTINIAN I. by his General *Narses*, destroy'd TOTILA 551
He collected the *Roman* Laws in his *Codex Justinianus*; and expended 34 Millions of Gold in rebuilding the Church of St. *Sophia*, which he intended to be equal, in Decoration, to SOLOMON's Temple, tho' in vain.

When this learned *Grand Master* died A. D. 565

JUSTIN II. succeeded, who upon the Death of *Teyas* the last *Gothic* King of *Italy* A.D. 568. appointed the EXARCHS of *Ravenna* to succeed the *Roman Cousuls*, to rule *Italy* by the *Roman* Laws, and to stop the Incursions of the *LONGOBARDS*; which They did, till the last *Exarch* was expell'd by *Luitprandus* King of *Lombardy*, A. D. 741.

The *LONGOBARDS* began to reign in the North of *Italy* (from them called *Lombardy*) the same time with the *Exarchs* of *Ravenna*, till conquer'd by CHARLE MAIN, who captivated *Desiderius* the last King of *Lombardy*, A. D. 771. But to return,

JUSTIN II. died *A. D.* 582. succeeded by TIBERIUS II. and he by MAURICUS murder'd PHOCAS, and he was murder'd by

HERACLIUS, who commenced *A. D.* 610. Father of CONSTANTIN III. Father of CONSTANS II. Father of CONSTANTIN IV. Father of JUSTINIAN II. murder'd *A. D.* 710. When the *Eastern* Emperors called the *Iconoclastes*, or Destroyers of Images, began. So that here we may date the Departure of the AUGUSTAN STILE from the *East*; after the *Havock* of *TOTILA* 163 Years.

Thus the AUGUSTAN STILE was quite lost, and the Loss was publick.

Now the 12th Year of HERACLIUS *A.D.* 622. is the first Year of the *Mahometan* HEGIRA. And so if from this *A. D.* 1737
We substract Years 621

The present *Anno Hegiræ* is 1116 But the *Grand Design* of the MAHOMETANS was not to cultivate *Arts* and *Sciences*, but to convert the World by *Fire* and *Sword*: So that Architecture in *Asia* and *Africa* suffer'd by them as in *Europe* by the *GOTHS*.

For

For when the *Gothic Nations*, and those conquer'd by them, began to affect stately Structures, They wanted both Heads and Hands to imitate the Antients, nor could They do it for many Ages (as in the next Chapter) yet not wanting Wealth and Ambition, They did their best: and so the more Ingenious gradually coalesced in Societies or *Lodges*, in Imitation of the Antients, according to the remaining Traditions that were not quite obliterated, and hammer'd out a *New Stile* of their own, call'd the GOTHIC.

But tho' This is more expensive than the *old Stile*, and discovers now to us the Ignorance of the *Architect*, and the Improprieties of the *Edifice* ; yet the Inventions of the *Artists* to supply the Want of good old Skill, and their costly Decorations, have manifested their great Esteem of the *Royal Art*, and have render'd their *Gothic* Structures *Venerable* and *Magnificent* ; tho' not Imitable by Those that have the true *High Taste* of the *Grecian* or Augustan Stile.

CHAP. VII.

The Revival *of* Old Architecture, *or the* Augustan *Stile.*

THE *Royal Art* lies dead and buried still in the *East*, by the wilful Ignorance of the *Mahometan* Nations. But first in *Italy* It began to peep from under Its Rubbish in *Tuscany* : for the *Pisans* brought from *Greece* a few Marble *Columns* and other Fragments of *old Masonry* for their new Cathedral carried on by Buschetto the *Greek*, who first began to imitate the Antients.

After Totila's *Havock*, A. D. 547
Years —— 466
——
A. D. 1013

He join'd with Others to form a *New Lodge*, for that laudable Imitation, built St. *John*'s at *Pisa*, and educated many Artists that long'd for the *Revival*, till Il Buono flourish'd at *Ravenna*, and built at *Venice* the Steeple of St. *Mark*. A. D. 1152.

Oltro-

(48)

OLTROMONTANO and BONNANO built the Steeple of *Pisa* . 174
MARCHIONE of *Arezzo* rais'd the Marble Chappel of *Presepio* at St. *Mary Majore* ———— 1216
JAMES the *German* built the first fine Edifices of *Florence*, whose Son JACOPO ARNOLPHO LAPO, with the Painter CIMABOIUS, design'd the Cathedral of St. *Mary Delfiore* 1298

 CHARLES of *Anjou*, King of *Naples*, was the *first Prince* that publickly encouraged the *Revival* of the *Arts* of *Designing*, by employing the said *Cimaboius* and *Nicholas Pisan* to build an Abby in the Plain of *Taglia Cotzo*, where CHARLES had defeated the Pretender *Conradin*. JOHN PISAN, son of *Nicholas*, built for the King his new Castle of *Naples*. This Royal Patron, (the same as *Grand Master*) of the *Revivers*, died *A. D.* 1285. And his Successors inriched the Kingdom of *Naples* with learned Architects, and splendid Edifices.

 CIMABOIUS and the *Pisans*, educated many fine *Masters* and *Fellow Crafts*; particularly,

 GIOTTO the Architect; till the *Florentines* arrived at a pretty good Imitation of the Antients, which was discover'd in all the Parts of the Church in St. *Miniate*.

 After TOTILA's *Havoke* 547
 Years ———— 753
 A. D. 1300

 GIOTTO and his Pupils formed an Academy of *Designers*, or a learned *Lodge* at *Florence*, who, like those of old at *Athenes* and *Sicyon*, inlightened *all Italy*, by sending forth excellent Connoisseurs and dexterous Operators in all the Arts of *Designing*.

 ANDREW PISAN, one of them, was made a Magistrate of *Florence*; and many of 'em afterwards flourish'd Wealthy at *Pisa*, *Ravenna*, *Venice*, *Urbino*, *Rome*, and *Naples*.

 LAURENTIO GHIBERTO, educated there, conducted for some Time the Raising of the said St. *Mary Delfiore*, and framed the *Two Brazen Gates* of St. *John*'s, of which, long afterwards, *Michael Angelo* said in Rapture, that they were worthy of being the *Gates* of *Paradise*.

Do-

DONATELLO next appear'd with *Andrea Verrochio*, the Master of *Piedro Perrugino* and *Leonardo da Vinci*, prodigious Men! Also *Dominigo Ghirlandaio* the Master of *Michael Angelo* and *Maiano*, and other sublime and profound Architects.

Yet the *Gothic* Stile was not quite left off at *Florence*; till

BRUNELESCHI, having studied at *Rome* the Beauty and Accuracy of the old *Roman* Buildings there standing or prostrate, return'd full fraught to *Florence*, where He establish'd the ample and compleat Use of the *Doric, Ionic, Corinthian* and *Composite* ORDERS; and so the GOTHIC STILE was wholly laid aside there, and the AUGUSTAN STILE was entirely Reviv'd.

This *happy* REVIVAL was also much owing to the Countenance and Encouragement given to the Learned, by the *Princes* of the House of MEDICIS. Thus

After TOTILAH's *Havock* 547
——— Years just ——— 853
A. D. 1400

1. JOHN *de Medicis* Duke of *Florence*, became the learned *Patron* of the *Revivers*, or their *Grand Master*, and carefully supported the said *Lodge*, or Academy of Masters and Connoisseurs, at *Florence*, till he died A. D. 1428.

2. COSMO I. *de Medicis*, educated in that same Academy, succeeded his Father as Duke of *Florence*, and *Grand Master* of the *Revivers*. He erected a fine *Library* of the best Manuscripts brought from *Greece* and *Asia*, and a curious *Cabinet* of the rarest and most valuable Things that could be gather'd. He establish'd very great Commerce by Sea and Land, and justly acquir'd the Title of *Pater Patriæ*, the Father of his Country, and died A. D. 1464.

3 PETER I. *de Medicis* upheld the Lodge, and died Duke of *Florence* A. D. 1472. But he was not so Eminent as either his Father or his Son.   3. *Peter* I.

LAURENTIO *de Medicis*, a Lord in *Florence*, slain 1474.

JOHN JULIAN *de Medicis*, the most beautiful Youth and the most excellent Connoisseur in true old Architecture in all *Florence*.

This

3. Peter I.

4 LAURENTIO I. *de Medicis* Duke of *Florence*, ſtiled the *Magnificent*, was both *Horace* and *Mecenas*, and *Grand Maſter* of the *Revivers*. He inrich'd his Grandfather's *Library* and *Cabinet* at a vaſt Expence; and erected a great *Gallery* in his Garden, for educating the more promiſing Youth; among whom young *Michael Angelo*, as a Favourite, was admitted to the Duke's Table.

This kind Grand Maſter died 9 *April* 1492.

5 PETER II. *de Medicis* ſucceeded Duke of *Florence*, upheld his Father's curious Works, and countenanced the Academies and *Lodges*, till He died 1504.	JOHN *de Medicis* was elected POPE LEO X. 1513. a zealous Patron of the *Revivers* at *Rome*, eſpecially in Carrying on the *gorgeous Cathedral* of St. PETERS, till He died *A. D.* 1521.
By his Wife Duke *Peter* had	By his Miſtreſs Duke *Peter* had
6 LAURENTIO II. *de Medicis* ſucceeded his Father 1504, Duke of *Florence*, and *Patron* of the *Revivers*, till he died without Iſſue. 1519	7 ALEXANDER *de Medicis*, who ſucceeded *Laurentio* as Duke of *Florence* 1519, and by the Emperor *Charles* V. was made the firſt abſolute Duke *A.D.* 1531. He patroniz'd the *Deſigners* and *Operators*, till He died without Iſſue, *A. D.* 1537.

JULIAN *de Medicis* ſlain 1478 whoſe natural Son

JULIUS *de Medicis* was elected POPE Clement 7. 1523. He was beſieged by *Ch.* v. and forced the *Florentines* to ſubmit to his Kinſman Duke *Alexander* 1531. He was a moſt Ingenious Architect and carried on St. *Peter's* at *Rome*, till he died, 1534.

This Jo. JULIAN was alſo a dexterous operator, to the great Honour of the *Fellow Crafts*. He died 1498.

LEWIS, call'd JOHN *de Medicis*, was educated at *Florence* in Mathematical Learning: but his Genius was for War, and ſo affected the *military Architecture* He died 1526.

LEWIS

LEWIS, or JOHN *de Medicis.*

8 COSMO II. *de Medicis,* fucceeded Duke *Alexander* 1537. as abfolute Duke of *Florence.* He Inftituted the *Knights* of the Order of St. *Stephen* 1561. POPE PIUS V. and the Emperor *Ferdinand* I. gave him the Title of GREAT DUKE of *Tufcany* A. D. 1569.

He was the chief Patron, or *Grand Mafter,* of all the *Italian* Defigners and Craftfmen in *Architecture, Painting, Sculpture, Statuary, Carving* and *Plaftering.* He Inftituted the famous Academy or *Lodge* at *Pifa* for the Improvement of Difciples and *Enter'd Prentices.* He made fuch beautiful Alterations in the Buildings of *Florence,* that, like *Auguftus,* when a dying, He faid, *I found the City built of Brick and courfe Stone, but I leave It built of Polifh'd Marble.* He died aged only 55 Years, A. D. 1574. So much for the *Revivers* of the *Art,* in the Houfe of *Medicis.* But to return.

After the *Revival* of the AUGUSTAN STILE in *Italy,* A. D. 1400.

LEON BAPTISTA ALBERTI was the firft Modern that wrote of *Architecture,* and many excellent *Mafons* flourifh'd in this 15th Century; but more were born and educated, that prov'd the Wonders of the World in the next Century, and will be ever mention'd in the *Lodges* with the greateft Honour, for Improving the *Revival,* as if the *Auguftan Age* It felf had revived, under the generous Encouragement of the *Popes,* the *Princes* and *States* of *Italy,* the Patrons of the many Lodges then conftituted. Thus

BRAMANTE, the learned Monk of *Urbino,* ftudied *Mafonry* at *Milan* under CÆSARIANO; and after having narrowly examin'd all the Remains of the Antients throughout *Italy,* He was employ'd by 3 fucceffive *Popes* to build at *Rome* the *Cloifter* of the Church of *Peace,* the Palace of the *Chancery,* and St. *Laurence* in *Damafo.* He adorn'd many old Churches with *Frontifpieces* of his own Defigning, built the pretty little St. *Peters* in *Mont Orio,* rais'd fome Buildings in the *Vatican* and in the Palace of *Belvidere.*

Pope JULIUS II. the learned Patron or *Grand Mafter* of *Rome,* retain'd *BRAMANTE* as his Architect and Grand *Warden,* 1503 and order'd him as Mafter of Work, to draw the Grand Defign of St. PETERS new CATHEDRAL in *Rome*, the largeft and moft accurate *Temple* now in all the Earth: and the faid POPE with BRAMANTE led a folemn Affembly of *Cardinals*, *Clergymen* and *Craftsmen*, to level the *Foot-Stone* of Great St. PETER's in due Form, A. D. 1507.

BRAMANTE conducted that Work 7 Years, till he died, and was buried in It by POPE LEO X. duly attended by his *Craftsmen*, A. D. 1514.

RAPHAEL of *Urbino*, the *Prince* of *Painters*, had learn'd *Mafonry* of his unkle *Bramante*, and fucceeded him in furveying St. *Peter's*, till he died, aged only 37 Years, on his own Birth-Day, 6 *April* 1520. when he was to be made a *Cardinal* by POPE LEO X. and with a univerfal Mourning was buried in the *Rotunda Pantheon*.

JOCUNDE of *Verona*, and ANTONY SAN GALLO fucceeded *Raphael* at St. *Peter's*, till They died A. D. 1535. when POPE PAUL III. preferr'd to that Office

MICHAEL ANGELO, the greateft *Defigner* of his Time, and in his laft Years the greateft *Architect*, who finding fault with *San Gallo's* Draughts, made a new Model of St. *Peter's*, according to which that *lofty Temple* was finifh'd.

This *Grand Mafter* leaving his Warden PIRRO LIGORIO at St. *Peter's*, erected the new *Capitolium*, the Palace of *Farnefe*, and other accurate Structures. He had before built the *Maufoleum* in St. *Peter's ad Vincula*, with the curious Statue of *Mofes*, the fine Front of St. *Laurence* at *Florence*, by order of *Pope* LEO X, the *Sepulchre* of the *Houfe* of *Medicis* by order of Duke *Alexander*, and the *Apoftolical* Chamber at *Rome*.

MICHAEL ANGELO certainly carried on *Mafonry* to Its higheft Perfection, till he died at *Rome* aged 90 Years, on 17 *Feb.* 1564. highly efteem'd by all the Princes of *Europe*; and COSMO, the Great Duke of *Tufcany*, ftole his Corps from *Rome*, refolving that fince he could not have ANGELO alive, He would have him dead, and folemnly buried him in St. *Crofs* at *Florence*, attended by the *Fraternity*, and order'd *Vafario* to defign his Tomb inrich'd with the three great Marble Statues of *Architecture*, *Painting* and *Sculpture*.

James

James Barotzi da VIGNOLA succeeded *Michael Angelo* at St. *Peters*, by order of *Pope* PAUL V. but *Ligorio* the Grand *Warden*, for altering *Angelo*'s Design, was turn'd out by *Pope* GREGORY XIII. VIGNOLA, besides his accurate Edifices at *Rome* and elsewhere, design'd for *Philip* II. King of *Spain*, the famous ESCURIAL, and St. *Laurence*, Masterpieces of Art. He publish'd a Book of the *Orders*, and the Beauty of his *Profiles* is much admired. He designd' the Church of *Jesus* at *Rome*, the Castle of *Caprarola* and the side of the Palace of *Farnese* that is next the *Tiber*, and died at *Rome*, aged 66. *A.D.* 1573.

MADERNI succeeded *Vignola* at St. *Peters*, and built the stately *Frontispiece* of that vast *Temple*, about the Time that *Pope* GREGORY XIII. made a *New Calendar*, or began the NEW STILE call'd, from him, the *Gregorian*, the first Year of which is *A.D.* 1582. *Gregory* dying 1585. was succeeded by *Pope* SEXTUS QUINTUS, who employ'd

DOMINICO FONTANA in many curious Buildings, and to move the *Egyptian Obelisks* into publick Places erect. After which *Fontana* was chief Ingeneer of *Naples*, and built the magnificent Palace of the *Vice Roy*.

Tis endless to mention the ingenious Contemporaries of those *great Masters*, the other accurate *Revivers* and Improvers of the Royal *Art*, such as

BALDASSARE PERUZZI, who design'd and made the Model of the Palace of *Chighi*, and his Disciple *Sebastian Serglio*. ——*Julio Romano*, the chief Disciple of *Raphael*, built for the Duke of *Mantua* his Palace of △ Delta, ——Lombard of *Milan*— *James Sansovino*, recommended by Pope *Leo* X. to the *Venetians* ——— *Jerom Genga* built for Duke *Guido Baldo* his Palaces at *Urbino* and *Pesaro*. —*Pellegrino Tibaldi* built the great Church of *Milan*, and its Dome was made by *John James de la Porta*—Sir *Baccio Bandinelli*, who was knighted by Pope *Clement* VII. for being a most excellent *Sculptor.* ——*Benvenuto Cellini* ——*Daniel da Volterra* built pretty St. *Helens* in the great Church of *Trinity dell Monte* at Rome.—— *Perrin del Vaga* built at *Genua* the Grand Palace of Prince *Doria*, and was an inimitable *Plasterer*, a fine Art then much in Request.

At

(54)

At *Venice* also the *Revival* was carried on; for *Jocunde* of *Verona*, above-mention'd, built the *Stone Bridge*, and erected the stately *Gates* of *Verona*.

When *CHARLES* V. besieged *Rome* 1525, MICHAEL ANGELO retir'd to *Venice*, when the *Doge* got him to design the famous *Bridge* of *Realto*.

JAMES SANSOVINO constituted a *Lodge* of *Architects* (or *Masters*) at *Venice*, artfully supported the *Dome* of St. *Mark* then in Danger *, embellish'd the *Palace* and *Treasury*, and fortify'd the whole Republick as 𝕲𝖗𝖆𝖓𝖉 𝕸𝖆𝖘𝖙𝖊𝖗 of *Masons*. * 1527

But at *Venice* the *Augustan Stile* was also well improv'd by the learned VINCENT SCAMOTZI, DANIEL BARBARO, and the great
ANDREA PALLADIO.

PALLADIO's excellent Genius was highly discover'd by the sacred Edifices, the Palaces and Seats of Pleasure, and the other charming Buildings of his, throughout the State of *Venice*. He wrote also with great Judgment of the ORDERS of *Old Architecture*, and of the *Temples* of the *Antients*; which is a noble Monument of his Merit, useful to all Ages. He died renowned A. D. 1580.

Thus *Italy* was again the *Mistress* of the *World*, not for Imperial Power, but for the *Arts* of *Designing* revived from *Gothic Rubbish*.

But from the *first Revival*, the *Masons* began to form *New Lodges* (called by the Painters *Academies* or *Schools*, as all *true Lodges* ought to be) far more elegant than the former *Gothic Lodges*; for instructing Disciples or *Enter'd Prentices*, for preserving the *Secrets* of the *Fraternity* from Strangers and *Cowans*, and for Improving the *Royal Art*, under the Patronage of the *Popes* and the *Italian* Princes and *States*, as could be more amply prov'd.

After shewing in *Part* II. how the *Romans* brought the *Augustan Stile* into *Britain*, and carried it off with 'em; and how the *Gothic Stile* prevailed there, till the *Union* of the *Crowns*. I shall shew how the *Augustan Stile* was revived in this Island by INIGO JONES, in *Part* III.

(55)

PART II.

The History of MASONRY *in* BRITAIN, *from* JULIUS CÆSAR, *till the* Union *of the* Crowns, 1603.

CHAP. I.

From JULIUS CÆSAR *to the First Arrival of the* SAXONS *in* Britain.

HISTORY fails to tell, how long the *Europeans* in the *North* and *West* had lost their original Skill brought from *Shinar* before the *Roman* Conquest: but leaving our Brother *Masons* of other Nations to deduce their History of the *Royal* Art in their own Manner, we shall carry on our Deduction in the *Britannic* Isles.

CÆSAR in his Commentaries gives us the first certain Account of *Britain*. He landed at *Dover* on the 20*th* of August, and next Year He reached *London*; but pursued not his Conquests, because of his Design to be the GRAND MASTER of the *Roman* Republick. {A. M. — 3949? B.C. *or Christ.* Era 55 *Before Christ's Birth* 51} Yet the *Romans* did not follow his Tract during about 97 Years, even till

AULUS PLAUTIUS came from the Emperor *Claudius*, A. D. 42 Next Year CLAUDIUS came himself, and afterwards he sent OSTORIUS SCAPULA, who was succeded by several *Roman* Lieutenants, that soon formed *Lodges* for building Castles and other Forts to secure

their

their Conquests: till the Emperor VESPASIAN sent his brave Lieutenant, about A. D. 77. viz.

JULIUS AGRICOLA, who conquer'd as far as the *Isthmus*, between the Firths of *Clyde* and *Forth*, which he fortifi'd by a Wall of Earth against the *Northerns*. But after he was recall'd, the *Northerns* got over the *Wall*, and made bold Incursions into the *South*, till

ADRIAN the Emperor came himself, [A. D. 120] and finding the War tedious and hazardous, rather chose to fence the *Roman* Provnice by a Rampart from *Tine Mouth* to *Solway Firth*. Bu afterwards *Antoninus Pius* sent

LOLLIUS URBICUS, who subdued the *Brigantes*, and repuls'd the *Northerns*, even beyond *Agricola*'s Wall, which he fortify'd with Castles ——— A. D. 131.

After this we read of *Lud*, or LUCIUS, a *British* King under the *Romans*, who became Christian, and built Churches: while the War was carried on in the *North* with various Success, till the *Northerns* forced VIRIUS LUPUS to purchase Peace with a great Sum of Money. This inraged the Emperor, viz.

SEPTIMIUS SEVERUS, who came with a great Army [A. D. 207] vowing to extirpate them, but could not, even tho' he penetrated to the *Northern Sea*; and having lost 50000 Men in the Expedition, he was forced to imitate ADRIAN, and rais'd his old Rampart into a *Stone Wall*, call'd of old MUR SEVER, or Wall of *Severus*, also *Greme's Dyke*, or *Pict's Wall*.

When NONNIUS PHILIPPUS [A. D. 238] came from the Emperor *Gordian*, EMILIUS CRISPINUS, his Master of Horse, a fine Architect, built a pretty *Temple* at *Caerlisle*, the *Altar* Stone of which was lately found there, near old *Mur Sever*.

The *South Brittons* had been long softned in their Manners by the *Romans*, and affected their Politeness, wearing the *Roman* Dress, and speaking *Latin*; and abounding also in *Commerce*, they improv'd in Arts and Sciences, and found the *Roman* Conquest was a great Blessing to the Conquer'd, beholding with Pleasure their Country, formerly all grotesque and wild, now adorn'd with venerable *Temples*, solemn *Courts* of Justice, stately *Palaces* and
Mansions,

Manſions, large and beautiful *Cities*, regular *Forts* and *Caſtles*, convenient *Bridges*, &c.

The joint Emperors *Dioclefian* and *Maximian* employ'd Carausius as their Admiral againſt the *Saxon* Pirates, who being at Peace with the *Picts*, and gaining the Army, put on the *Purple* and was own'd by the other Two. A. D. 287.

CARAUSIUS encouraged the *Craft*, particularly at *Verulam*, (now St. *Albans, Hertfordſhire*) by the worthy Knight, ALBANUS, who afterwards turn'd Chriſtian, and was call'd St. *Alban*, (the Proto Martyr in *Britain* under the *Dioclefian* Perſecution) whom CARAUSIUS employ'd (as the old *Conſti-* | This is aſſerted by all the old Copies of the *Conſtitutions*, and the old *Engliſh Maſons* firmly believ'd it.

" *tutions* affirm) to inviron that City with a StoneWall, and to build
" him a fine *Palace*; for which that *Britiſh* King made St. ALBAN
" the Steward of his Houſhold and chief Ruler of the Realm.

" St. ALBAN loved *Maſons* well, and cheriſhed them much,
" and he made their Pay right good, *viz. Two Shillings per Week,*
" *and Three Pence to their Cheer;* whereas before that Time,
" through all the Land, *a Maſon had but a Penny a Day, and his*
" *Meat*, until St. *Alban* amended it. He alſo obtained of the
" King a Charter for the *Free Maſons*, for to hold a general
" Council, and gave it the Name of *Aſſembly*, and was thereat
" himſelf as *Grand Maſter*, and helped to make *Maſons*, and
" gave them good Charges, *&c.*

When *Dioclefian* and *Maximian* abdicated, A. D. 303.

CONSTANTIUS CHLORUS ſucceeded Emperor of the *Weſt*, a Lover of Arts and Sciences, and much encouraged the *Craft*, till he died at *York*, A. D. 306. the ſame Year that his *Britiſh* Empreſs HELENA girt *London* with a Stone Wall.

CONSTANTIN the *Great*, their Son, born in *Britain*, ſucceeded, who partition d *South Britain* into four Provinces. During his Reign the *Chriſtian* Religion flouriſh'd, the *Britons* enjoy'd Peace and Plenty, and old *Roman Maſonry* appear'd in many ſtately and curious Piles, till he died, A. D. 336.

I   After

After which, the *Northerns* joining the *Saxon* Pirates, invaded the *South*, till A. D. 367. when

THEODOSIUS (Father of the Emperor *Theodosius* the *Great*) came from the Emperor *Valentinian* I. and bravely beat them back, even over *Agricola*'s Wall, which he fortified with new *Castles* and *Forts*; and recovering the Land of the *old Meats* between the two Walls, he made it a fifth Province, calling it *Valentia*. He also beautified *London*, repair'd all the Cities and Forts, and left *Britain*, A. D. 374.

MAXIMUS (call'd the Tyrant) came next from the Emperor *Gratian*, who put on the *Purple*, sail'd into *Gaul* but was defeated in *Italy* by *Theodosius Magnus*, and beheaded A. D. 388.

CONSTANTIN, a common Soldier, for the Sake of his fortunate Name, was chosen by the *Southerns* to be their Leader, who also put on the *Purple*, sail'd into *Gaul*, and was there defeated and beheaded by the Emperor *Honorius*. And now

HONORIUS, not being able to protect the *Southerns* against the *Northerns*, fairly renounced his Sovereignty over *Britain*, the next Year after ALARIC had took in *Rome*, *viz*. A. D. 410. Yet

ÆTIUS, the General of *Valentinian* III, being victorious in *Gaul*, from Pity sent the *Britons* one Legion under GALLIO, who repell'd the *Northerns* beyond *Mur Sever*, which he rebuilt of Stone Work 8 Foot broad, and 12 Foot high: and being recall'd, he left the *South Britons* to defend themselves against the *Northerns*, and carried off his *Legion*, A. D. 426.

tho' the *Roman* Soldiers did not at All depart till   A. D. 430.

In the Vulgar Year of *Masonry*, 4430.

After *Cæsar*'s Invasion,   486 Years.

After *Aulus Plautius* came,   389

During which Time, the *Romans* had propagated *Masonry* in every Garrison, and had built fine Places past Number, even to the *North Border*, or the Wall of AGRICOLA, near which, at the *Forth*, they rais'd the little *Temple* of their God TERMINUS, that stands to this Day, now call'd by the Vulgar, *Arthur's Oven*, a curious *Rotunda* in Shape of the *Pantheon* at *Rome*, 20 Foot

high

high, and near 20 Foot in Diameter. Nay, in Times of Peace the *Northerns* might learn of the *Romans* to extend the *Art* to the fartheſt *North* and *Weſt*, or the ULTIMA THULE.

But true *old Maſonry* departed alſo from *Britain*, with the *Roman Legions*: for tho' many *Roman* Families had ſettled in the *South*, and were blended with the *Britons*, who had been well educated in the *Science* and the *Art*, yet the ſubſequent Wars, Confuſions and Revolutions in this Iſland, rnin'd ancient Learning, till all the fine Artiſts were dead without Succeſſion.

For the *Northerns* hearing that the *Roman Legions* were never to return, broke through *Mur Sever*, ſeiz'd all the Land *North* of the *Humber*, and ravaged the *South* the more eaſily, that the *Southerns* were divided by petty Kings, till they choſe a *General Monarch*, viz. A. D. 445

VORTIGERN, who being unable to retrieve Affairs, got the Conſent of his Nobles to invite the SAXONS in Lower *Germany* to come over and help him: and ſo *Prince* HENGIST, with 2000 *Saxons* landed in *Thanet* upon *Kent*, A. D. 449.

CHAP. II.

From the Firſt Arrival of the SAXONS, *To* WILLIAM *the Conqueror.*

THE SAXONS having aſſiſted *Vortigern* to repulſe the *Scots* and *Picts* beyond the *Humber*, built THONG CASTLE in *Lincolnſhire*; and being daily recruited from lower *Germany*, and the River *Elb*, they reſolved to ſettle here; and after much Bloodſhed in many Battles between the *Britons* and *Saxons*, they founded and eſtabliſh'd their HEPTARCHY, or *Seven Kingdoms*, viz.

 1. Kingdom of KENT, founded by HENGIST, A. D. 455.
 2. Kingdom of SUSSEX, by ELLA, ——— 491.
 3. Kingdom of WESSEX, by CHERDICK, ——— 519.
 4. Kingdom of ESSEX, by ERCHENWYNE, ——— 527.
 5. Kingdom of NORTHUMBRIA, by IDA the *Angle* 547.
 6. Kingdom of EAST ANGLES, by UFFA, ——— 571.
 7. Kingdom of MIDLE ANGLES or MERCIA, by CRIDA. 584.

And as the *Anglo Saxons* encreas'd, the *Britons* loſt Ground; till after the Death of AMBROSIUS *Aurelius*, and his brave Son King ARTHUR, the *Britons* had no *Grand Monarch*, but only a few petty Kings: but after CRIDA landed, many of them ſubmitted to him (as to other *Saxon* Kings) many fled to *Cornwal*, and by Sea to *Armorica*, (call'd ſtill *Bretagne* in *France*) and many went to *North Britain* among the *Scoto Walenſes*; tho' the greater Part fled beyond the *Severn*, where they were coop'd in between the Mountains and the *Iriſh* Sea, A. D. 589.

The *Anglo Saxons*, who had always call'd the *Britons* GUALISH or *Waliſhmen*, now call'd their Settlement beyond the *Severn* WALISHLAND or WALES, call'd ſtill by the *French* GALLES from the GAULS their Progenitors. And here they elected the noble CADWAN their King, the Progenitor of the *Chriſtian* Kings and *Princes* of WALES.

During the horrid Wars, ſince the Departure of the *Roman Legions*, about 160 Years, Maſonry was extinguiſh'd: nor have we any Veſtige of it, unleſs we reckon that of STONE HENG, and allow, with ſome, that AMBROSIUS, King of the *Britons*, rais'd that famous Monument on *Salisbury Plain*, by the Art of *Marvellous* MERLIN (whom the Populace counted a *Conjurer* and *Prophet*) in Remembrance of the *bloody Congreſs*, when HENGIST murder'd 300 *Britiſh* Nobles. Others think it an old *Celtic Temple* built by the *Britons* long before the *Romans* came here: and ſome have counted it only a *Daniſh* Monument. But the great INIGO JONES, and his Kinſman Mr. JOHN WEB, have learnedly prov'd it to be a *Roman Temple*, the largeſt Piece of Antiquity in the Iſland. | See STONE HENG reſtored.

The ANGLO SAXONS came over all rough, ignorant Heathens, deſpiſing every Thing but War; nay, in Hatred to the *Britons* and *Romans*, they demoliſh'd all acurate Structures, and all the glorious Remains of antient Learning, affecting only their own barbarous Manner of Life, till they became *Chriſtians*; as appears from *Bede*, the *Saxon* Annals, and other good Vouchers: therefore we have no Account of *Maſonry* in their firſt Settlements.

But

But where the WELCH dwelt, we find the earliest Accounts, at least, of *Sacred* Architecture; as at GLASTONBURY in *Devonshire*; *Padstow* in *Cornwal*; *Caerleon* or *Chester*, afterwards translated to St. *Asaph's* in *Flintshire*; *Llan Twit*, or Church of *Iltutus*; *Llan Badarn Vawr*, or Church of *Great St. Patern*; the Monastry of *Llan Carvan*; *Bangor* in *Caernarvonshire*; *Holyhead* in *Anglesey*; *Llandaff* in *Glamorganshire*; *Menevia*, or St. *David's* in *Pembrokeshire*; and many more Churches, Monastries, and Schools of Learning.

Some pious *Teachers* came from *Wales* and *Scotland*, and converted many of the *Anglo Saxons* to Christianity; but none of their Kings till A. D. 597. when AUSTIN, and forty more *Monks*, came from *Pope* GREGORY I. and baptized ETHELBERT King of *Kent*; and in about 60 Years, *all* the *Kings* of the HEPTARCHY were baptized.

Then affecting to build Churches and Monastries, Palaces and fine Mansions, they too late lamented the ignorant and destructive Conduct of their Fathers, but knew not how to repair the publick Loss of *old Architecture*: yet being zealous, they follow'd the *Gothic Stile*, then only used, and rear'd soon

They also built many *Palaces* and *Castles*, and fortified their *Cities*, especially on the Borders of each Kingdom. This requir'd many *Masons*, who soon form'd themselves into Societies, or *Lodges*, by Direction of Forreigners that came over to help them.	The Cathedral of *Canterbury*, A. D. 600 That of *Rochester*, 602 St. *Paul's London*, 604 St. *Peter's Westminster*, 605 And a great many more describ'd in the *Monasticon Anglicanum*.

These many *Saxon Lodges* gradually improved, till

ETHELBERT King of *Mercia* and *general* Monarch sent to CHARLES MARTEL, the Right Worshipful *Grand Master* of *France* (Father of *King Pippin*) who had been educated by Brother *Mimus Græcus*: He sent over from *France* [about A.D. 710] some expert *Masons* to teach the SAXONS those *Laws* and *Usages* of the antient Fraternity that had been happily preserv'd from the *Havock* of *the Goths*; tho' not the *Augustan Stile* that had been long lost in

the

the *West*, and now also in the *East*. This is strongly asserted in all the *old Constitutions*, and was firmly believ'd by the old *English* Masons.

The CLERGY now found it convenient to study *Geometry*, and *Architecture*, such as it was; because the noble and wealthy, nay *Kings* and *Queens*, thought it meritorious·to build *Churches*, and other *pious* Houses, where some of them ended their Days in sweet Retirement: for those *holy Houses* were all under the Direction of the Clergy; and the *Lodges* were held in Monastries before the Inundation of the *Danes*. Yet at first they built mostly of *Timber* only, till

BENNET, the Abbot of *Wirral*, introduced the Use of *Brick* and *Stone*, about A. D. 680: so that even the *Gothic Stile* was but in its Infancy during the *Heptarchy*, which lasted from *Hengist*'s Arrival. —— A. D. 449

At last during Years 381

EGBERT, King of *Wessex*, by Policy and Conquest, became Sovereign of the other six Kingdoms, *A.D.* 830. and the *Angles* being most numerous, he call'd his united Kingdom ENGLAND, and all the People ENGLISHMEN: tho' the *Welch*, the *Irish*, and *Scots* Highlanders, call them still SAXONS, after those that first came with *Hengist*. Thus

1. EGBERT, the *first* King of *All England*, A. D. 830. fortified his Sea Ports, and died A. D. 836.

2. ETHELWOLPH employ'd St. *Swithin* to repair the pious Houses, and died, A. D. 857.

3. ETHELBALD. died 860.	4. ETHELBERT. died 866.	5. ETHELRED I. died 872.	6. ALFRED the *Great*, the 4*th* Son, who commenc'd A.D. 872 subdu'd the *Danes*, tho' not expell'd them; he increased his Navy Royal, fortify'd and rebuilt many Towns, and founded the University of *Oxford*.
in whose Reigns the *Danes* settled in *East Anglia* and *Northumbria*, pillaging and demolishing the pious Houses.			

King

King ALFRED had about him the beſt *Architects*, and employ'd the *Fellow-Crafts* wholly in *Brick* or *Stone*. The *beſt* KING of *England*, and died illuſtrious, A. D. 900.

7. EDWARD *Senior*, left *Maſonry* to the Care, firſt of *ETHRED*, the Deputy King of *Mercia*, the Husband of *Edward*'s Siſter ELFREDA, the glorious Heroin, who by her Valour expell'd the *Danes* out of *Mercia*, and fortified many Towns and Caſtles to prevent their Incurſions. Next the King put his learned Brother *ETHELWARD* at the Head of the *Fraternity*, and founded the Univerſity of *Cambridge* that had been long a Nurſery of the Learned. The King died 924. leaving 3 Kings and a Queen.

8. ATHELSTAN the eldeſt Son ſucceeded, tho' only the Son of a *Concubine*, and at firſt left the *Craft* to the Care of his Brother *Edwin*, call'd in ſome Copies his *Son*: for in all the *old Conſtitutions* It is written to this Purpoſe, *viz.*

" That tho' the antient Records of the Brotherhood in *England*, " were moſt of them deſtroy'd or loſt in the Wars with the *Danes*, " who burnt the *Monaſtries* where the Records were kept; yet " King *Athelſtan* (the Grandſon of King *Alfred*) the firſt anointed " King of *England*, who tranſlated the *Holy Bible* into the SAXON " Language, when he had brought the Land into Reſt and Peace, " built many great Works, and encouraged many *Maſons* " from *France* and elſewhere, whom He appointed Overſeers " thereof: they brought with them the *Charges* and *Regulations* " of the foreign *Lodges*, and prevail'd with the King to increaſe " the Wages.

" That *Prince* EDWIN, the King's Brother, being taught " *Geometry* and *Maſonry*, for the Love he had to the ſaid Craft, " and to the honourable Principles whereon it is grounded, pur-" chaſed a *Free Charter* of King *Athelſtan* his Brother, for the " *Free Maſons* having among themſelves a CORRECTION, " or a Power and Freedom to regulate themſelves, to amend
" what

" what might happen amifs, and to hold an yearly *Communication*
" in a General *Aſſembly*.

" That accordingly *Prince* EDWIN ſummon'd all the *Free* and
" *Accepted Maſons* in the Realm, to meet him in a *Congregation*
" at YORK, who came and form'd the *Grand Lodge* under him
" as their *Grand Maſter*, A. D. 926.

" That they brought with them many old Writings and Re-
" cords of the *Craft*, ſome in *Greek*, ſome in *Latin*, ſome in
" *French*, and other Languages; and from the Contents thereof,
" they fram'd the CONSTITUTIONS of the *Engliſh Lodges*,
" and made a Law for Themſelves, to preſerve and obſerve the
" ſame in all Time coming, *&c. &c. &c.* "

But good *Prince* EDWIN died before the King [A. D. 938] without Iſſue, to the great Grief of the *Fraternity*; though his Memory is fragrant in the *Lodges*, and honourably mention'd in all the *old Conſtitutions*.

Some *Engliſh* Hiſtorians ſay that EDWIN being accuſed of a Plot, the King ſet him adrift in a Boat without Sail and Oars; that EDWIN proteſting his Innocence, went aboard and jumpt into the Sea; and that his Eſquire was drove into *Picardy*.

But the Hiſtorian *Malmsbury* disbelieves the whole Story as grounded only on ſome *old Ballad*, and becauſe of *Athelſtan*'s known Kindneſs and Love to all his Brothers and Siſters: and *Huntingdon* writes of the Loſs of EDWIN by Sea, as a very ſad Accident, and a great Misfortune to *Athelſtan*, who was very fond of him.

King ATHELSTAN built many Caſtles in *Northumbria* to bridle the *Danes* (whom he had ſubdu'd) and the famous *Abby of* St. *John* at *Beverley* (lately repair'd for Divine Service) and *Melton Abby* in *Dorſetſhire*; He rebuilt the City of *Exeter*, and repair'd the old Church of the CULDEES at *York*. He died without Iſſue, 940.

9. EDMUND I.

𝖘𝖆𝖝𝖔𝖓 Kings of *England*.

9 EDMUND I. succeeded Brother *Athelstan*, repaired the Cities and Churches, and leaving two Sons, died, *A. D.* 946.

10 EDRED succeeded his Brother *Edmund*, rebuilt *Glastonbury*, and died without Issue 955.

11 EDWI succeeded his Uncle *Edred*, and died without Issue, 959.

12 EDGAR built and rebuilt about 48 pious Houses, by the Direction of St. *Dunstan*, 𝕲𝖗𝖆𝖓𝖉 𝕸𝖆𝖘𝖙𝖊𝖗, and several more expert Masters. He also rigg'd out a good Navy, which prevented the Invasions of the *Danes*, and died 975.

13 EDWARD *Junior*, call'd the *Martyr*, died without Issue 979.

14 ETHELRED II. was always distressed by the *Danes*, and contrived their Massacre, *A. D.* 1002.

ETHELRED, upon the Death of *Swen Otto*, returned, but died inglorious 1016.

By his first Wife he had

16 EDMUND II. *Ironsides* reigned in the *West* till murder'd, *A. D.* 1017. Father of Prince

By his 2d Wife *Ethelred* had

20. EDWARD the

𝕯𝖆𝖓𝖎𝖘𝖍 Kings of *England*.

THYRA, Daughter of *Edward Senior* (according to the *Danish* Historians) was married to GORMO III. King of *Denmark*, and bore to him,

HAROLD VIII. King of *Denmark*.

SWEN OTTO, King of *Denmark*, who finding that *Ethelred* neglected his Fleet, allowed his *Danes* to invade *England* every Year, and they left many 𝕷𝖔𝖗𝖉 𝕯𝖆𝖓𝖊𝖘, to oppress the poor *English*. But hearing of the Massacre, SWEN OTTO sail'd over with great Force, and drove *Ethelred* into *Normandy*. And so,

15 SWEN OTTO was King of *England* -------- 1013 but died suddenly — 1014

17 CANUTUS or *Knut Magnus*, after the Death of King EDMUND *Ironsides*, was crown'd King of *all England, A. D.* 1017.

He built the Abby of St. *Edmund's-Bury*, and died———1036. Father of

18 HA-

K

Saxon Kings of *England*.

Prince *Edward* who died at *London* 1057.

Prince *Edgar Atheling* died without Issue.

Margaret, Wife of Malcolm *Keanmore*, King of *Scotland*.

the *Confessor*, who succeeded King *Hardy-Knut* in the Throne of *England*, 1041. He collected the *Saxon* Laws in a Body. In his Reign Arts and Sciences flourish'd.

Danish Kings of *England*.

18. Harold I. *Harefoot*, King of *England*, died without Issue. A.D. 1039.

19. Hardy-Knut, King of *England*, the last of the *Danish* race, died without Issue, A. D. 1041.

Leofrick the Wealthy Earl of *Coventry*, at the Head of the *Free Masons*, built the Abby of *Coventry*, and Others built 12 more pious Houses. The King rebuilt *Westminster-Abby*, tho' not as it now stands, and died without Issue on 5 *Jan.* 106$\frac{5}{6}$, when the Nobles and People chose,

21. Harold II. Son of Earl *Goodwin*, who reign'd nine Months, even till William the *Bastard*, the Duke of *Normandy*, slew *Harold* bravely fighting in the Battle of *Hastings* in *Sussex*, where the *English* were totally routed by the *Normans*, on the 14th of *October*, A. D. —————————— 1066.

In the vulgar Year of *Masonry* 5066.
After *Hengist*'s Arrival ——— 617.
After the End of the *Heptarchy*, 236.

As for the Danes, having no Princely Head, They had submitted to the *Saxon* Kings, and daily losing their Genealogy, They were gradually blended with the *Anglo-Saxons*, having much the same Language.

CHAP.

CHAP. III.

MASONRY *in* England *from* WILLIAM *the* Conqueror *to* King HENRY IV.

1. **WILLIAM I.** the *Conqueror*, having settled *England*, appointed 𝕲𝖚𝖓𝖉𝖚𝖑𝖕𝖍 Bishop of *Rochester*, 𝕽𝖔𝖌𝖊𝖗 de *Montgomery* Earl of *Shrewsbury* and *Arundel*, and other good Architects, to be at the Head of the *Fellow Crafts*, first in civil and military Architecture, building for the King the *Tower* of *London*, and the Castles of *Dover*, *Exeter*, *Winchester*, *Warwick*, *Hereford*, *Stafford*, *York*, *Durham*, and *New-Castle* upon *Tine*; whereby the proud *Normans* bridled the *English*.

Next in *sacred* Architecture, building *Battle-Abby* near *Hastings*, in memory of his Conquest, St. *Saviour's Southwark*, and 9 more pious Houses; while Others built 42 such, and 5 Cathedrals. The King brought many expert *Masons* from *France*, and died in *Normandy*, A. D. 1087.

---

2. WILLIAM II. *Rufus*, succeeded his Father, and employ'd his Architects and Craftsmen in building a new Wall round the *Tower*, and in rebuilding *London-Bridge*; and by Advice of his *Grand Lodge* of *Masters*, He built the Great Palace of *Westminster*, with large *Westminster-Hall*. 270 Foot long, and 74 Foot broad, the largest one Room upon Earth; and 4 pious Houses, while Others built 28 such. He died without Issue, A. D. 1100.

3. HENRY I. *Beau Clerc*, born at *Selby* in *Yorkshire*, succeeded Brother *William*, tho' the eldest Brother *Robert* Duke of *Normandy*, was alive.

Now the *Norman* 𝕭𝖆𝖗𝖔𝖓𝖘, perceiving their great Possessions in *England* depended only on Royal Pleasure; and finding the Laws of the *Anglo-Saxons* to be better for securing Property than the Laws of *Normandy*;

Normandy; the 𝔑𝔬𝔯𝔪𝔞𝔫𝔰 began to call themselves ENGLISHMEN, to assert the *Saxon-Rights*, and prevail'd with this King to grant them the first 𝔐𝔞𝔤𝔫𝔞 𝔈𝔥𝔞𝔯𝔱𝔞, or larger *Paper* and Deed of *Rights* in this first Year of his Reign, *A. D.* 1100.

This King built the great Palace of *Woodstock*, and a little one at *Oxford* to converse with the Learned, and 14 pious Houses, while Others built about 100 such, besides many fine Mansions. He died *A. D.* 1135. succeeded by his Nephew, *viz.*

King HENRY I. by his Wife MAUD (Daughter of MALCOLM *Keanmore* King of *Scotland* by his Wife MARGARET the *Saxon* Heiress of *England*) left only a Daughter *viz.*

MAUD the *Empress*, who next married 𝔊𝔢𝔬𝔣𝔣𝔯𝔢𝔶 *Plantagenet* Count of *Anjou*, *A.D.* 1127.

She came over, tho' too late, to assert her Claim (to which her Father had sworn the whole Kingdom, even *Stephen* also) and fought like a brave Heroine; but refusing to confirm *Magna Charta*, she was deserted: And her best Friends dying, she was forced to return to *Anjou*, A. D. 1147. But her Son HENRY came over and asserted his Claim, till King *Stephen* agreed that *Henry* should succeed him,

4. STEPHEN, Count of *Boulloign*, Son of ADELA Daughter of *William* the *Conqueror*, by the Power of the Clergy. During the Civil Wars between him and MAUD the *Empress*, the Nobles and Gentry, being courted by both, laid hold of the Occasion to build about 1100 Castles, that proved afterwards very convenient for them in the *Barons Wars*; so that the *Masons* were as much employ'd as the Soldiers, under their 𝔊𝔯𝔞𝔫𝔡 𝔐𝔞𝔰𝔱𝔢𝔯 *Gilbert de Clare* Marquis of *Pembroke*, by whom the King built 4 Abbies and 2 Nunneries, with St. *Stephen*'s Chapel in the Palace of *Westminster*: While Others built about 90 pious Houses. King *Stephen* died without Issue Male, the last of the Royal *Normans*. } *A. D.* ———— 1154. After the *Conquest* 88 Years.

Accordingly, when *Stephen* died,

The

The *PLANTAGENETS* of *Anjou* commenced, *viz.*

1. HENRY II. *Plantagenet*, Count of *Anjou* became King of *England*, A. D. 1154, who fortify'd some Castles against the *Welch* and *Scots*, built some little Palaces, and 10 pious Houses, while Others built about 100 such. The *Grand Master* of the *Knights Templars* erected their Society and built their **Temple** in *Fleetstreet*, *London*. The King died A. D. 1189.

2. RICHARD I. much abroad, died without Issue 1199; yet in this Reign about 20 pious Houses were built.

3. King JOHN succeeded Brother *Richard*, and first made his Chaplain **Peter** *de Cole-Church* **Grand Master** of the *Masons* in rebuilding *London-Bridge* of Stone, which was finish'd by the next Master *William Almain*, A. D. 1209. Next **Peter** de *Rupibus* Bishop of *Winchester* was **Grand Master**, and under him *Geoffrey Fitz Peter* was chief Surveyor or *Deputy* Grand Master, who built much for the King; while Others built about 40 pious Houses. The King died A. D. 1216, succeeded by his Son,

4. HENRY III. a Minor of nine Years. When **Peter** de *Rupibus*, the old *Grand Master*, came to be the King's Guardian, he levell'd the *Footstone* of *Westminster* Abby, in that Part call'd *Solomon's Porch*, A. D. 1220.

PETER Count of *Savoy* (Brother of the Queen's Mother) built the Palace of *Savoy* in the *Strand London*: And *John Balliol*, Lord of *Bernard* Castle in *Durham*, (Father of JOHN King of *Scotland*) founded *Balliol College* in *Oxford*. The *Templars* built their *Domus Dei* at *Dover*, and Others built 32 pious Houses. The King died A. D. 1272.

5. EDWARD I. being deeply engaged in Wars, left the *Craft* to the Care of several successive *Grand Masters*, as **Walter Giffard** Archbishop of *York*, **Gilbert** de *Clare* Earl of *Glocester*, and **Ralph** Lord of *Mount Hermer*, the Progenitor of the *Montagues*; and by these the King fortify'd many Castles, especially against

the

the *Welch*, till they submitted to him, *A. D.* 1284, when *Edward* the King's Son and Heir was born at *Caermarthen*, the first *English* Prince of *Wales*.

The King celebrated the *Cape-stone* of *Westminster* Abby, *A. D.* 1285, just 65 Years after it was founded. But that *Abby* and the *Palace* being burnt down, 1299, the King order'd the Palace to be repair'd, but was diverted from repairing the *Abby* by his Wars in *Scotland*. In this Reign *Merton* College *Oxford*, the Cathedral of *Norwich*, and about 20 more pious Houses were founded. The King died in his Camp on *Solway Sands*, 7th of *July*, 1307.

6. EDWARD II. made **Walter Stapleton** Bishop of *Exeter* Grand *Master*, who built *Exeter* and *Oriel* Colleges in *Oxford*; while Others built *Clare-Hall Cambridge*, and 8 pious Houses. The King died *A. D.* 1327.

7. EDWARD III. became the Patron of Arts and Sciences. He set up a Table at *Windsor*, 600 Feet round, for feasting the gallant *Knights* of all Nations, and rebuilt the Castle and Palace of *Windsor*, as a *Royal* **Grand Master**, by his several Deputies or Masters of Work, *viz.*

1. **John** de *Spoulee*, call'd *Master* of the *Ghiblim*, who rebuilt St. *George*'s Chapel; where the King constituted the *Order* of the *Garter*, *A. D.* 1350.

2. **William a Wickham**, at the Head of 400 *Free Masons*, rebuilt the Castle strong and stately, *A. D.* 1357, and when he was made Bishop of *Winchester*, A. D.——1367. then next

3. **Robert** *a Barnham* succeeded at the Head of 250 *Free Masons*, and finish'd St. *George*'s great Hall, with other Works in the Castle, *A. D.* 1375.

4. **Henry Yevele** (call'd at first, in the old Records, the King's *Free Mason*) built for the King the *London Charter-house*, *King's-Hall Cambridge*, *Queenborough Castle*, and rebuilt St. *Stephen*'s Chapel, now the House of Commons in Parliament.

5. **Simon Langham**, Abbot of *Westminster*, who repair'd the Body of that Cathedral as it now stands.

The

The King also founded the Abby of *Eaſtminſter* near the *Tower*; and his laudable Example was well follow'd; for the Queen endow'd *Queen's College Oxford*, while Others built many ſtately Manſions, and about 30 pious Houſes, for all the expenſive Wars of this Reign.

The CONSTITUTIONS were now meliorated; for an old Record imports, " *that in the glorious Reign of* King EDWARD III. *when Lodges were many and frequent, the* Grand Maſter *with his* Wardens, *at the Head of the* Grand Lodge, *with Conſent of the* Lords *of the Realm, then generally* Free Maſons, *ordain'd,*

That for the future, at the Making or Admiſſion of a Brother, the Conſtitutions *ſhall be read, and the* Charges *hereunto annexed.*

That Maſter Maſons, *or* Maſters of Work, *ſhall be examined whether they be* able of Cunning *to ſerve their reſpective* Lords, *as well the Higheſt as the Loweſt, to the Honour and Worſhip of the foreſaid Art, and to the Profit of their Lords; for they be their* Lords *that employ and pay them for their Travel.*

That when the Maſter *and* Wardens *preſide in a Lodge, the* Sheriff, *if need be, or the* Mayor, *or the* Alderman *(if a Brother) where the Chapter is held, ſhall be* ſociate *to the* Maſter, *in help of him againſt Rebels, and for upholding the Rights of the Realm.*

That Enter'd Prentices *at their Making ſhall be charged not to be* Thieves, *nor* Thieves Maintainers. *That the* Fellow Crafts *ſhall travel honeſtly for their Pay, and love their Fellows as themſelves; and, That all ſhall be true to the* King, *to the* Realm, *and to the* Lodge.

That if any of the Fraternity ſhould be fractious, mutinous, or diſobedient to the Grand Maſter's *Orders, and after proper Admonitions, ſhould perſiſt in his Rebellion, He ſhall forfeit all his Claim to the Rights, Benefits, and Privileges of a true and faithful Brother, &c. Concluding with,* AMEN, So mote it be.

(72)

King EDWARD III. died 21 *June* 1377.

| EDWARD the 𝔅lack Prince of *Wales* died before his Father, A. D. 1376. | See the other Sons, with respect to the *Succeſſion*, in the *Margin* below. * |

8. RICHARD II. ſucceeded his Grandfather, *A. D.* 1377. He employ'd 𝔚illiam a *Wickham*, Biſhop of *Wincheſter*, Grand Maſter, to rebuild *Weſtminſter-Hall* as it now ſtands; and 𝔚illiam, at his own Coſt, built *New College Oxford*, and founded *Wincheſter College*, while Others built about 15 pious Houſes.

At laſt, while King *Richard* was in *Ireland*, his Couſin *Henry* Duke of *Lancaſter* landed in *Yorkſhire*, rais'd a great Army ſeiz'd King *Richard* upon his Return, got the Parliament to depoſe him, and ſucceeded in the Throne, *A. D.* 1399; and next Year *Richard* was murder'd without Iſſue.

---

* The other Sons of King EDWARD III. with reſpect to the Succeſſion.

LIONEL Duke of *Clarence*, the ſecond Son, left only	EDMUND Duke of *York*, the fourth Son, Patriarch of the 𝔚hite 𝔅oſe, by his Wife *Iſabella*, ſecond Daughter of *Piedro Crudelis*, King of *Caſtile*.	JOHN *a Gaunt* Duke of *Lancaſter*, the third Son, Patriarch of the 𝔅ed 𝔅oſe. Wives. 1. *Blanche* of *Lancaſter*, Mother of King *Henry* IV. 2. *Conſtantia*, eldeſt Daughter of *Piedro Crudelis* King of *Caſtile*, Mother of *Katharine* married to *Henry* III. King of *Caſtile*. 3. *Katharine Roet*, his Concubine, whom at laſt he married, and her Children were legitimated by Act of Parliament, but not to inherit the Crown. Mother of
PHILIPPA of *Clarence*, Wife of *Edmund Mortimer*, Earl of *March*, Mother of		
Roger Mortimer, Earl of *March*, left only		
Ann Mortimer, the Heireſs of *Clarence* and *March*.	*Richard* Earl of *Cambridge*, beheaded 1415.	
Richard Duke of *York*, ſlain, 1460.		*John Beaufort*, (not *Plantagenet*) Earl of *Somerſet*.
King EDWARD IV.	King RICHARD III.		*John Beaufort* Duke of *Somerſet*.
		Margaret Beaufort, Mother of King HENRY VII.

CHAP.

CHAP. IV.

MASONRY in *England* from HENRY IV. to the *Royal* TEWDORS.

KING EDWARD III.

JOHN *a Gaunt*, Duke of *Lancaster*, Patriarch of the 𝕽𝖊𝖉 𝕽𝖔𝖘𝖊, or the Royal *Lancastrians*, by his first Wife, *Blanche* of *Lancaster*, had

9. HENRY IV. Duke of *Lancaster*, who supplanted and succeeded King *Richard* II. *A. D.* 1399. He appointed 𝕿𝖍𝖔𝖒𝖆𝖘 *Fitz-Allen* Earl of *Surrey*, to be *Grand Master*; and after his famous Victory of *Shrewsbury*, the King founded *Battle-Abbey* there, and afterwards that of *Fotheringay*. Others built 6 pious Houses, and the *Londoners* founded their present *Guild-Hall*, a large and magnificent Fabrick. The King died 1413.

10. HENRY V. while triumphing in *France*, order'd the Palace and Abbey of *Sheen* (now call'd *Richmond* upon *Thames*) to be rebuilt by the Direction of the *Grand Master* 𝕳𝖊𝖓𝖗𝖞 𝕮𝖍𝖎𝖈𝖍𝖊𝖑𝖊𝖞 Archbishop of *Canterbury*; while Others built 8 pious Houses. The King died *A. D.* 1422.

By his Queen, *Katherine* of *France* (afterwards the Wife of 𝕺𝖜𝖊𝖓 𝕿𝖊𝖜𝖉𝖔𝖗 below.) He had

11. HENRY VI. a Minor of nine Months, in whose third Year an ignorant Parliament endeavour'd to disturb the *Lodges*, tho' in vain, by the following Act, *viz.*

3 *Hen.* VI. Cap. I. *A. D.* 1425.

Title. MASONS *shall not confederate in Chapters and Congregations.*

WHEREAS *by yearly Congregations and Confederacies made by the* Masons *in their General Assemblies, the good Course and Effect of the Statutes of Labourers be openly violated and broken, in Subversion of the Law, and to the great Damage of all the Commons* ; Our Sovereign Lord the King *willing in this Case to provide a Remedy, by the Advice and Consent aforesaid, and at the special Request of the Commons*, Hath Ordain'd and Establish'd,

That such Chapters *and* Congregations *shall not be hereafter holden: And if any such be made, They that cause such* Chapters *and* Congregations *to be assembled and holden, if they thereof be convict, shall be judged for* Felons: *And that other* Masons *who come to such Chapters and Congregations be punished by Prisonment of their Bodies, and make Fine and Ransom at the King's Will.*

But this Act is explain'd in Judge COKE's Institutes, Part III. fol. 19. where we find that the Cause why this Offence was made *Felony*, is for that the good Course and Effect of the Statutes of Labourers was thereby violated and broken. Now says my Lord *Coke*,

All the Statutes concerning Labourers before this Act, and whereunto this Act doth refer, are repealed by the 5 ELIZ. Cap. 4. *about* A. D. 1562. *whereby the Cause and End of making this Act is taken away, and consequently the Act is become of no Force*; *for* cessante ratione legis cessat ipsa lex! *and the Inditement of* Felony *upon this Statute must contain, That those* Chapters and Congregations *are to the violating and breaking of the good Course and Effect of the Statutes of Labourers! which now cannot be so alledged, because those Statutes be repeal'd. Therefore this would be put out of the Charge of Justices of the Peace.*

But this Act was never executed, nor ever frightned the *Free Masons* from holding their *Chapters* and *Congregations*, lesser or larger ; nor did ever the *Working Masons* desire their Noble and Eminent Brothers to get it repeal'd, but always laugh'd at it: For they ever had, and ever will have their own Wages, while they coalesce in due Form, and carefully preserve the Cement under their own 𝕲𝖗𝖆𝖓𝖉 𝕸𝖆𝖘𝖙𝖊𝖗 ; let *Cowans* do as they please.

Nay even during this King's Minority, there was a good *Lodge* under *Grand Master* 𝕮𝖍𝖎𝖈𝖍𝖊𝖑𝖊𝖞 held at *Canterbury*, as appears from the Latin Regifter of *William Mo-lart* * Prior of *Canterbury* in Manufcript, pap. 88. in which are named *Thomas Sta-pylton* the Mafter, and *John Morris* Cuftos de la Lodge Lathomorum or *Warden* of *the Lodge of Mafons*, with fifteen *Fellow-Crafts*, and three *Enter'd Prentices* all named there. And a Record in the Reign of EDW. IV. fays, *the Company of* Mafons, *being otherwife termed* Free Mafons, *of auntient Staunding and good Reckoning, by Means of affable and kind Meetings dyverfe Tymes, and as a loving Brotherhood ufe to do, did frequent this mutual Affembly in the Tyme of* Henry VI. *in the Twelfth Year of his Moft Gracious Reign viz. A. D.* 1434. when HENRY was aged thirteen Years.

* Intituled *Liveratu generalis Domini Gulielmi Prioris Ecclefiæ Chrifti Cantuarienfis erga Feftum Natalis Domini* 1429.

Grand Mafter CHICHELEY held alfo a *Lodge* at *Oxford*, where he built *All-Soul's-College*, and *Bernard*, now St. *John's* College, &c. till he died 1445. when the King appointed,

𝖂𝖎𝖑𝖑𝖎𝖆𝖒 𝖂𝖆𝖎𝖓𝖊𝖋𝖑𝖊𝖊𝖙, Bifhop of *Winchefter*, to be *Grand Mafter* in building *Eaton* College near *Windfor*, and *King's* College *Cambridge*, tho' before the Civil Wars in this Reign, the *Chapel* of it was only finifh'd, a Mafter-Piece of the richeft *Gothic* that can hardly be matched. The King alfo founded *Chrift's* College *Cambridge* (afterwards finifh'd by *Margaret Beaufort* Countefs of *Richmond*) and his Queen MARGARET of *Anjou* founded *Queen's* College *Cambridge*. While Ingenious 𝖂𝖆𝖎𝖓𝖊𝖋𝖑𝖊𝖊𝖙 at his own Coft built *Magdalene* College *Oxford*; and Others about 12 pious Houfes.

So that before the King's Troubles, the *Mafons* were much employ'd, and in great Efteem; for the forefaid Record fays farther, *That the* Charges *and* Laws *of the* Free Mafons *have been feeen and perufed by our late Soverain King* Henry VI. *and by the Lords of his moft honourable Council, who have allow'd them, and declared, that They be right good and reafonable to be holden, as They have been drawn out and collected from the Records of auntient Tymes*, &c. &c.

At laft *Mafonry* was neglected during the feventeen Years of the bloody Civil Wars between the two *Royal* Houfes of *Lancafter* and *York*, or the 𝕽𝖊𝖉 and 𝖂𝖍𝖎𝖙𝖊 *Rofes*: For

𝕽𝖎𝖈𝖍𝖆𝖗𝖉

(76)

Richard Plantagenet, Duke of *York*, Son of *Richard* Earl of *Cambridge*, and *Anne Mortimer* the Heiress of *Clarence* (as in the *Margin* Page 72.) claim'd the Crown in Right of his Mother, *A. D.* 1455. and after twelve sore Battles the **Red** *Rose* lost the Crown, poor King *Henry* VI. was murder'd, and *all* the *Males* of every Branch of *Lancaster* were cut off; after *John a Gaunt's* Offspring had reigned 72 Years, *A. D.* 1471.

White Rose, see Page 72.
Thus *Richard* Duke of *York* slain in the Battle of *Wakefield*, 1460.

12 Edward IV. crown'd 1561. sometimes a King, and sometimes not a King, till *A. D.* 1471. when Edward reigned without a Rival, and employ'd the *Grand Master* **Richard Beauchamp**, Bishop of *Sarum*, to repair the Royal Castles and Palaces after the Wars, and to make the Castle and Chapel of *Windsor* more magnificent; for which the Bishop was made *Chancellor* of the *Garter*.

Great Men also repair'd and built apace; and now the *Londoners* rebuilt their Walls and Gates; while Others rais'd 7 pious Houses. The King died 9 *April* 1483.

13 Edward V. a Minor, proclaim'd, but not crown'd.

Richard, Duke of *York*.

Elizabeth Plantagenet, Wife of King *Henry* VII. below.

These two Sons were said to be murder'd in the *Tower* by Order of their Uncle and Guardian *Richard* III. on 23 *May*, 1483.

14 Richard III. kill'd and took Possession, and was crown'd on 6 *July*, 1483. and reign'd a wise and valiant Prince, till he was slain, bravely contending for the Crown with his Rival Henry *Tewdor* Earl of *Richmond*, in the Battle of *Bosworth Leicestershire*, on the 22 *Aug.* 1485. without legal Issue.

So ended the **White Rose**, or House of *York*: And also the 14 *Kings* call'd *Plantagenets*, of the House of *Anjou*, who had reign'd from King *Stephen's* Death, *A. D.* —— 1154 } during Years —— 331 } till *A. Dom.* —— 1485

For

For connecting the History.
The GENEALOGY of the Royal TEWDORS

They are clearly descended (tho' not in Male Issue) from CADWAN the First, King of *Wales*, (Page 60.) down to RODERIC *Mawr*, who partition'd his Kingdom into 3 Principalities among his 3 Sons, and died A. D. 876.

1. AMARAWDD, Prince of *North Wales*, whose *Male* Issue fail'd in LLEWELIN *ap Daffyd*, the last Soveraign Prince of *all Wales*, slain in Battle, A. D. 1283. when the *Welch* began to submit to the Crown of *England*.

2 CADELH, Prince of *South Wales*, whose lineal *Male* Issue ended in GRUFFYD *ap Rhyse*, the last Prince of *South Wales*, who died, A. D. 1202. But his Sister, viz.
 GWENLIAN, was the Wife of Ednyfed Fychan, Lord of *Brynseingle*.

3. MERFYN, Prince of *Powis Land*, soon fail'd.

EDWARD III. King of *England*.

JOHN a *Gaunt*, by his third Wife, *Katharine Roet*, Page 72.

JOHN BEAUFORT, Earl of *Somerset*

JOHN BEAUFORT, Duke of *Somerset*, After all the *Males* of *John a Gaunt* were extinct, left his only Child. viz.

CHARLES VI. King of *France*.

Queen KATHARINE, Widow of King *Henry* V.

Gronw *ap Ednyfed*
Theodore, or *Tewdor ap Gronw*.
Gronw *ap Tewdor*.
Tewdor *ap Gronw*, married MARGARET, Grand Daughter of LEWELIN *ap Daffyd*, the last Soveraign Prince of *Wales*.
Meredith *ap Tewdor*.
OWEN TEWDOR, slain in the Battle of *Mortimer*'s Cross, 1461.

Margaret Beaufort.

Edmund Tewdor, Earl of *Richmond*.

Jasper Tewdor, Duke of *Bedford*, without legal Issue.

Owen Tewdor, a Monk.

HENRY VII. *Tewdor*, King of *England*.

CHAP.

(78)

CHAP. V.

Masonry in *England* from King Henry VII. till the Union of the *Crowns*, A. D. 1603.

WHEN King *Richard* III. was slain at *Bosworth*, his Crown was forthwith put upon the Head of the Conqueror, Henry Tewdor Earl of *Richmond*, in the Field of Battle, and the Army proclaim'd him

1. Henry VII. King of *England*, on 22 *Aug.* 1485. nor did he ever affect another Title and Claim.

But his Wife Elizabeth Plantagenet, Daughter of King *Edward* IV. was truly the Heiress of all the *Royal* Plantagenets, and conveyed hereditary Right to her Offspring.

New Worlds are now discovered,
  The *Cape of Good Hope*, A. D. 1487.
  and *America*, ——————— 1493.

In this Reign the Gothic *Stile* was brought to it's highest Perfection in *England*, while it had been wholly laid aside in *Italy* by the Revivers of the old *Augustan Stile*; as in Part I. Chap. VII.

John Islip, Abbot of *Westminster*, finished the Repairs of that Abby, *A. D.* 1493. so as it stood till the late Reparations in our Time.

The Grand Master and Fellows of the Order of St. John at *Rhodes* (now at *Malta*) assembled at their *Grand Lodge*, chose King Henry their Protector, *A. D.* 1500.

This *Royal* Grand Master chose for his Wardens of *England*, the foresaid John Islip, Abbot of *Westminster*, and

Sir Reginald Bray, Knight of the *Garter*,

} or *Deputies*, by whom the King summon'd a *Lodge* of *Masters* in the Palace, with whom he walked in ample Form to the *East* End of *Westminster* Abby, and

and levell'd the *Footstone* of his famous Chapel on 24 *June*, 1502. tho' it well deserves to stand clean alone, being justly call'd by our Antiquary *Leland* the eighth *Wonder of Art*, the finest Piece of *Gothic* upon Earth, and the Glory of this Reign. It's *Capestone* was celebrated *A. D.* 1507.

The King employ'd *Grand Warden* 𝕭𝖗𝖆𝖞 to raise the middle Chapel of *Windsor*, and to rebuild the Palace of *Sheen* upon *Thames*, which the King call'd 𝕽𝖎𝖈𝖍𝖒𝖔𝖓𝖉; and to enlarge the old Palace of *Greenwich*, calling it 𝕻𝖑𝖆𝖈𝖊𝖓𝖙𝖎𝖆, where he built the pretty Box call'd the *Queen's-House.*

He rebuilt *Baynard* Castle, *London*, founded six Monasteries, and turn'd the old Palace of *Savoy* into an *Hospital*: while Others built *Brasen-Nose* College *Oxford*, *Jesus*'s and St. *John*'s Colleges *Cambridge*, and about 6 pious Houses; till the King, aged only 54 Years, died at *New Richmond*, on 22 *April*, 1509. leaving three Children, viz.

2. HENRY VIII. *Tewdor*, Prince of *Wales*, aged 18 Years, succeeded his Father, *A. D.* 1509. Cardinal 𝖂𝖔𝖔𝖑𝖘𝖊𝖞 was chosen *Grand Master*, who built *Hampton-*	MARGARET *Tewdor*, first the Wife of *James* IV. King of *Scotland*, next of *Archibald Dowglass*, Earl of *Angus*; next of *Henry Stewart*, Lord *Methuen*.	MARY *Tewdor*, first the Wife of *Lewis* XII. King of *France*; and next of *Charles Brandon*, Duke *Suffolk*.

Court; and next rear'd *White-Hall*, the College of *Christ*'s Church *Oxford*, and several more good Edifices, which upon his Disgrace were forfeited to the Crown, *A. D.* 1530.

𝕿𝖍𝖔𝖒𝖆𝖘 𝕮𝖗𝖔𝖒𝖜𝖊𝖑𝖑 Earl of *Essex* was the next Patron of the *Craft* under the King, for whom he built St. *James*'s Palace, *Christ*'s Hospital *London* and *Greenwich* Castle. Mean while

The King and Parliament threw off the old Yoke of the *Pope*'s Supremacy, and the King was declared the Supreme Head of the Church *A. D.* 1534. and *Wales* was united to *England*, A. D. 1536.

(80)

The *pious Houses*, in number about 926. were suppress'd, *A.D.* 1539. *Cromwell*, Earl of *Essex*, being unjustly beheaded, *A.D.* 1540.

John Touchet, Lord *Audley*, became *Grand Master*.

But the Suppression of the religious Houses did not hurt *Masonry*; nay Architecture of a finer Stile gain'd Ground: for those *pious* Houses and their Lands being sold by the King at easy Rates to the Nobility and Gentry, they built of those Ruins many stately Mansions: Thus Grand Master *Audley* built *Magdalen* College *Cambridge*, and his great House of *Audley End*.

King *Henry* VIII. aged near 56 Years, died on 28 *Jan.* 154$\frac{6}{7}$. and left three Children.

---

3. EDWARD VI. *Tewdor*, born by Queen *Jane Seymour*, a Minor of 9 Years, under the Regency of his Mother's Brother, EDWARD Duke of *Somerset*, who establisht the *Protestant* Religion; and as **Grand Master** built his Palace in the *Strand*, call'd still *Somerset-House*, tho' forfeited to the Crown, *A.D.* 1552. and when the *Regent* was beheaded, JOHN POYNET, Bishop of *Winchester*, was the Patron of the *Free-Masons* till the King died without Issue, *A.D.* 1553.

4. MARY *Tewdor*, Daughter of Queen *Katharine* of *Aragon*, aged 38 Years, succeeded her Brother *Edward*, as Queen Sovereign.

She restored the *Romish* Religion, and persecuted the *Protestants*; married *Philip* II. King of *Spain*, and died without Issue, 17 *Nov.* 1558.

5. ELIZABETH *Tewdor*, Daugh. of Queen *Anne Bollen*, aged 25 Years, succeded Sister *Mary* as Queen Sovereign. She restored the *Protestant* Religion, and was declared Supreme Head of the Church. Now Learning of all Sorts revived, and the good old AUGUSTAN STILE in *England* began to peep from under it's Rubbish: And it would have soon made great Progress, if the Queen had affected Architecture: But hearing the *Masons* had certain *Secrets* that could not be reveal'd to her (for that she could not be *Grand Master*) and being jealous of all secret Assemblies,

she

she sent an armed Force to break up their annual *Grand Lodge* at *York*, on St. *John*'s Day, 27 *Dec.* 1561.

But Sir **Thomas Sackville**, *Grand Master*, took Care to make some of the chief Men sent *Free-Masons*, who then joining in that *Communication*, made a very honourable Report to the Queen; and she never more attempted to dislodge or disturb them, but esteem'd them as a peculiar sort of Men that cultivated Peace and Friendship, Arts and Sciences, without meddling in the Affairs of Church or State.

<small>This Tradition was firmly believ'd by all the old *English* Masons.</small>

In this Reign some Colleges were built, and many stately Mansions, particularly famous *Burleigh-House*: For Travellers had brought home some good Hints of the happy *Revival* of the Augustan *Stile* in *Italy*, with some of the fine Drawings and Designs of the best Architects; whereby the *English* began apace to slight the **Gothic** *Stile*, and would have entirely left it off, if the Queen had frankly encouraged the *Craft*.

Here it is proper to signify the Sentiment and Practice of the *Old Masons*, viz. That *Kings* and other *Male* Sovereigns, when made *Masons*, are *Grand Masters by Prerogative* during Life, and appoint a *Deputy*, or approve of his Election, to preside over the Fraternity with the Title and Honours of *Grand Master*; but if the Sovereign is a *Female*, or not a Brother, or a *Minor* under a *Regent*, not a Brother; or if the *Male* Soveraign or the *Regent*, tho' a Brother, is negligent of the *Craft*, then the *old* Grand Officers may assemble the *Grand Lodge* in due Form to elect a *Grand Master*, tho' not during Life, only he may be annually rechosen while he and they think fit.

Accordingly, when *Grand Master* Sackville demitted, *A. D.* 1567. Francis Russel, Earl of *Bedford* was chosen in the *North*; and in the *South* Sir Thomas Gresham, who built the first *Royal Exchange* at *London*, A. D. 1570. Next

<small>This is the Tradition of the *Old Masons*.</small>

Charles Howard Lord of *Effingham*, was *Grand Master* in the *South* till 1588. then George Hastings Earl of Huntington,

Huntington, till the Queen died unmarried, on 24 *March*, 160¾. when

The Crowns of *England* and *Scotland* (tho' not yet the Kingdoms) were united in her Succeffor, viz.

JAMES VI. *Stewart*, King of *Scotland*, Son of MARY *Stewart* Queen Soveraign, Daughter of King JAMES V. Son of King JAMES IV. by his Queen MARGARET TEWDOR eldeft Daughter of HENRY VII. King of *England*, by his Queen ELIZABETH *Plantagenet* the Heirefs of *England*. And he was proclaim'd at *London*, JAMES I. King of *England*, *France* and *Ireland*, on 25 *March*, 1603. See Part III.

CHAP. VI.

MASONRY *in* Scotland *till the* UNION *of the* Crowns.

THE Hiftory of the *firft* Kings of the *Scots* in *Albin*, or the *Weftern* Parts beyond the *Clyde* and the middle *Grampian* Hills ; and alfo that of the *Picts* in *Caledonia* along the *German* Sea Coaft and towards *England*, not containing much to our Purpofe, we may begin with the Reftoration of the Kingdom of *Albin* (according to the *Scottifh* Chronicle) made by

King FERGUS II. Mac Erch, A. D. 403.

And even after that Period, the Hiftory of both thefe Nations confifts moftly of War ; only we learn that the *Picts* were a more mechanical and mercantil People than the *Scots*, had built many Cities, and firft founded all the old ftrong Caftles in their Dominion ; while the *Scots* affected rather to be a Nation of Soldiers, till

KENNETH II. *Mac Alpin*, King of *Scots*, demolifh'd the Kingdom of the *Picts*, and fo became the *firft* King of all *Scotland*, A. D. ———— 842. [* See his Race in the Margin of next Page.]

He repair'd the publick Edifices after the Wars, and died, 858.

But both the Branches of his *Royal* Race were moftly engaged in War till King MALCOLM II. *Mac Kenneth*, fucceeded his Coufin King *Grimus*, A. D. 1008. as on the next Page.

For

(83)

For King *Malcolm* II. firſt compil'd the Laws in the famous Book of *Scotland* call'd Regiam Majestatem, partition'd the Land into *Baronies*, founded the Biſhoprick of *Aberdeen* (in Memory of his routing the *Norwegians*) A. D. 1017. cultivated *Arts* and *Sciences*, and fortified his Towns and Caſtles till he died, leaving only two Daughters, *viz.*

Beatrix the Eldeſt, Wife of 𝔄𝔩𝔟𝔞𝔫𝔞𝔠𝔥 Thane of the *Iſles*.	Docha the Younger, Wife of 𝔅𝔢𝔱𝔥𝔣𝔦𝔫𝔩𝔢𝔤 Thane of *Angus*.
1. Duncan I ſucceeded his Grandfather, *A. D.* 1033. murder'd by *Mackbeth*--1040. but King Duncan I. was the *Patriarch* of the following Kings on the next Page.	2. Mackbeth kill'd and took Poſſeſſion, 1040. built the Caſtle of *Dunſinnan* and *Lumfannan*, &c. and much encouraged the *Craft*, till cut off by *Macduff*, A. D. 1057.

* 1. Keneth II. *Mac Alpin* died 858. Father of

3. Constantin II ſucceeded *Donald V.*	Ethus ſucceeded *Conſtantin* II.	2. Donald V. ſucceeded his Brother *Kenneth* II.
6. Donald VI. ſucceeded *Gregory*.	Constantin III. ſucceeded *Donald* VI.	
8. Malcolm I. ſucceeded *Conſtantin* III He received *Cumberland* and *Weſtmoreland* from Edmund I. King of *England*, Father of	9 Indulphus ſucceeded *Malcolm* I	5. Gregory, Son of King *Congallus*, (who had reign'd before *Kenneth* II.) ſucceeded Ethus. He built *Aberdeen*.
	11. Culenus ſucceeded *Duffus*.	
	13. Constantin IV. ſucceeded *Kenneth* III.	

10 Duffus, who ſucceeded *Indulphus*.	12. Kenneth III. ſucceeded *Culenus*, A. D. 976. the Year after *Edgar* King of *Eng*-*land* died. Kenneth enacted the Crown *hereditary* in his Family, and died, *A. D.* 994.	𝔐𝔬𝔤𝔞𝔩𝔩𝔲𝔰 the Prince,
		14. Grimus ſucceeded *Conſtantin* IV. and died 1008.
		𝔉𝔞𝔫𝔠𝔥𝔬 murder'd by *Mackbeth*. Below

15. Malcolm II. ſucceeded *Grimus*, A. Dom. 1008.

King

King *Duncan* I.

3. MALCOLM III. *Keanmore*, or *Head Great*, was restor'd when *Macbeth* was slain, 1057. He built the old Church of *Dunfermling*, a Royal Sepulchre, and levell'd the *Footstone* of the old Cathedral of *Durham*, which he richly endow'd. He fortified his Borders, Castles and Seaports, as the Royal 𝕲𝖗𝖆𝖓𝖉 𝕸𝖆𝖘𝖙𝖊𝖗 and Patron of Arts and Sciences, till he died, *A. D.* 1093.

4. DONALD *Bane*, or *White* DONALD, *Malcolm's* younger Brother mounted the Throne, *A D.* 1093. and after the Usurper *Duncan* was slain 1095. *Donald* reign'd till his Nephew King *Edgar* imprison'd him for Life. *A. D.* 1098.

5. DUNCAN II. a Bastard of King *Malcolm*, usurped, *A D.* 1094.

By his Queen MARGARET, Sister of Prince *Edgar Atheling*, and Grand-Daughter of King EDMUND *Ironsides*, the *Saxon* Heiress of *England* (by the *Scots* call'd St. *Margaret*.) He had

6. EDGAR succeeded *Donald*, and died without Issue. 1107.

7. ALEXANDER I. succeeded Brother *Edgar*, built the Abbies of *Dunfermlin*, and St. *Colms's Inch*, St. *Michael's* at *Scone*, &c. and patroniz'd the *Craft* till he died, *A. D.* 1124. without Issue.

8. DAVID I. succeeded Brother *Alexander*, built the Abby of *Holy-Rood House*, and the Cathedrals of four Bishopricks that he establish'd. The Clergy call'd him St. *David* for his great Endowments to the Church; and the *Masons* worshipped him as their beneficent 𝕲𝖗𝖆𝖓𝖉 MASTER, till he died, *A. D.* 1153.

MAUD, Wife of *Henry* I. King of *England.*

MAUD, the Empress.

MARY, Wife of *Eustace*, Count of *Boulogne.*

MAUD, Wife of King *Stephen.*

By his Q. MAUD, the Heiress of *Huntington*, King DAVID I. had

𝕳𝖊𝖓𝖗𝖞, Prince of *Scotland*, died before his Father, 1152. leaving three Sons, *viz*.

9. MALCOLM IV. call'd the *Maiden*, succeeded Grand-father *David*, and died without Issue. *A. D.* 1165.

10. WILLIAM the *Lion*. See next Page.

DAVID, Earl of *Huntington.* See next Page.

10. WILLIAM

(85)

10. WILLIAM the *Lion* succeeded Brother *Malcolm*, built a Palace at *Aberdeen*, rebuilt the whole Town of *Perth* after a Fire, and was an excellent 𝕲𝖗𝖆𝖓𝖉 𝕸𝖆𝖘𝖙𝖊𝖗, by the Assistance of the Nobility and Clergy, till he died A. D. 1214. See the next *Page*.

𝕯𝖆𝖛𝖎𝖉 Earl of *Huntington* died in *England*, A. D. 1219. But all King WILLIAM's Race failing in the *Maiden* of *Norway*, as on the next Page, the Right of *Succession* was in the Heirs of this 𝕯𝖆𝖛𝖎𝖉; and they made the *Competition* for the Crown, as in the Margin below. 10. WIL-

---

Competition of BRUCE and BALLIOL.
Prince DAVID Earl of *Huntingdon* had 3 Daughters, *viz.*

1. MARGARET, Wife of 𝕬𝖑𝖆𝖓 Lord of *Galloway*.

DORNAGILLA, Wife of John 𝕭𝖆𝖑𝖑𝖎𝖔𝖑 Lord of *Bernard* Castle in *Durham*.

1. JOHN BALLIOL, the *Competitor*, as descended from *David*'s Eldest Daughter, was declar'd King of *Scotland*, by the Umpire of the Competition King EDW. I. of *England*, A. D. 1292. for *John*'s owning him his Superior.

But JOHN revolting, Edward depós'd him, 1296. banish'd him into *Normandy*, and garrison'd *Scotland* for himself. But the *English* were expell'd first by Sir 𝖂𝖎𝖑𝖑𝖎𝖆𝖒 𝖂𝖆𝖑𝖑𝖆𝖈𝖊, and next by King ROBERT BRUCE. See the next *Margin*.

2. ISABELLE, Wife of ROBERT BRUCE, an *English* Lord, made Lord of *Anandale* in *Scotland*.

ROBERT BRUCE, the *Competitor*, as the *first Male* from Prince *David*: But his Claim was over-ruled by the Umpire; and *Robert* soon died.

𝕽𝖔𝖇𝖊𝖗𝖙 𝕭𝖗𝖚𝖈𝖊, Lord of *Anandale*, and by Marriage, Earl of *Carrick*, was by King EDWARD I. made Earl of *Huntington* to make him easy: And after *John Balliol* was banish'd, King EDWARD promis'd to make BRUCE King of *Scotland*, in order to engage him against 𝖂𝖆𝖑𝖑𝖆𝖈𝖊. But next Day after the Battle of *Falkirk*, A. D. 1298. at a Conference or Interveiw.

𝖂𝖆𝖑𝖑𝖆𝖈𝖊.
See the next Margin.

3. ADA, Wife of Lord *Hastings*.

𝕯𝖊𝖘𝖈𝖊𝖓𝖙 of the ROYAL STEWARTS from GRIMUS King of *Scotland* who died 1008.

𝕭𝖆𝖓𝖈𝖍𝖔, Thane of *Loch-Abyr*, murder'd by *Macbeth*, 1040. Page 83.

𝕱𝖑𝖊𝖆𝖓𝖈𝖊 fled to *Wales*, and married *Nersta*, Daughter of GRUFFYD *ap Llewelin*, Prince of *Wales*, and died there.

𝖂𝖆𝖑𝖙𝖊𝖗 I. the young *Welchman* came to *Scotland* upon the Restoration of King *Malcolm Keanmore*, who made him heritable Lord 𝕳𝖎𝖌𝖍 𝕾𝖙𝖊𝖜𝖆𝖗𝖙.

WALTER I

(86)

10. WILLIAM the *Lion*.

11. ALEXANDER II. rebuilt *Coldingham*, and died, *A. D.* 1249

12. ALEXANDER III. the laſt *Male* from *Duncan* I. died *A.D.* 1285.

MARGARET, Queen of *Ericus* King of *Norway*.

MARGARET, *the Maiden* of *Norway*, died coming over 1290. But from the Diſſolution of the *Pictiſh* Kingdom, *A. D.* 842. the 𝔊𝔬𝔱𝔥𝔦𝔠 𝔖𝔱𝔦𝔩𝔢 was well improv'd in *Scotland* during Years 448. till the *Maiden* of *Norway* died, and the *Competition* began.

This

King JOHN *Balliol*.	Houſe of BRUCE.	Houſe of STEWART.
3. EDWARD *Balliol*, was by King EDW. III of *England*, ſent to *Scotl and*, join'd his Party, expell'd young King *David Bruce*, and wa crown'd *A. D.* 1332 but expell'd ——— 1341. Some ſay his Race are ſtill in *France*.	𝔚allace convinced 𝔅ruce of his Error, who never ſought more againſt the *Scots*, and died 1303.	WALTER I. the *Stewart*.
		ALAN the *Stewart*.
		ALEXANDER I. the *Stewart*.
	2. ROBERT I. 𝔅ruce fled to *Scotland*, and was crown'd 1306 And after many ſore Conflicts, he totally routed King EDWARD II. of	WALTER II. the *Stewart*.
		ALEXANDER II. the *Stewart*. JOHN the *Stewart*.	Sir 𝔑obert *Stewart*, Lord *Darnley*, Patriarch of the STEWARTS of 𝔏ennot, from whom deſcended HENRY Lord *Darnley*, Father of K. *James* VI. below.
England at *Bannockburn*, *A. D.* 1314. obtain'd an honourable Peace, and died illuſtrious, *A. D.* 1329.		
4. DAVID II. *Bruce* ſucceeded, a Minor of 8. Years born of King *Robert's* ſecond Wife, was ſent to *France* till *Edward Balliol* was expell'd, He was afterwards captivated in *England* till ranſom'd, and died without Iſſue, 1370.	MARJORY BRUCE born of King *Robert's* *firſt* Wife, *Iſabella*, Daughter of *Donald*, Earl of *Mar*, a noble *Pict*.	WALTER III. the *Stewart*, the lineal *Male* of the *Old Royal Race*, and Patriarch of the *Royal Stewarts*, by his Wife *Marjory Bruce*.
	King ROBERT II. *Stewart*. See the next Margin.	

(87)

This had been more amply and accurately discover'd, if the *Learn'd* of *Scotland* had publish'd a *Monasticon Scoticanum*, with an Account of the old Palaces and Castles (as fine as any in *Europe*) before the *Competition* of BRUCE and BALLIOL, in a Chronological Deduction: *A Work long and much desiderated!*

During the *Competition*, MASONRY was neglected; but after the Wars, King ROBERT I. *Bruce*, having settled his Kingdom, forthwith employ'd the *Craft* in repairing the Castles, Palaces and pious Houses; and the *Nobility* and *Clergy* follow'd his Example till he died, A. D. 1329.

King DAVID II. *Bruce*, after his Restoration, much affected *Masonry*, and built *David's Tower* in *Edinborough* Castle, till he died without Issue, A. D. 1370. leaving the Crown to his Sister's Son, *viz.*

Royal Stewards. See the last Margin.

1. ROBERT II. *Stewart*, who left the Care of *Masonry* to the Eminent Clergy, then very active in raising fine religious Houses, till he died A. D. 1390.

2. ROBERT III. *Stewart*, being sickly, left the Government to the Care of his Brother **Robert** Duke of *Albany*, a great Patron of the *Craft*, till the King died A. D. 1406.

2. ROBERT

ROYAL STEWARDS. See the last *Margin*.

1. ROBERT II. *Stewart*, so call'd from his hereditary Office that now reverted to the *Crown*: and hence the King's Eldest Son is stiled the *Prince* and STEWART of *Scotland*. This King was first the *Earl of Strathern*, till his Uncle King *David* died, A. D. 1370. and King *Robert* II. died 1390.

His first Wife ELIZABETH MUIR, was only *Countess* of *Strathern*, for she died before he was King: Yet her Son, *viz.*	His 2d Wife EUPHEMIA ROSS, was Queen of *Scotland*.
2. ROBERT III. *Stewart* (call'd JOHN *formerly*) succeeded his Father, A D 1390. Upon hearing that his only Son JAMES, in his Voyage to *France*, was captivated by King *Henry* IV. of *England*, tho' in Time of Peace, King *Robert* broke his Heart, 1406.	Walter *Stewart*, Earl of *Athol* who murder'd King *James* I. at *Perth*.

3. JAMES I. *Stewart*, after 18 Years was ransom'd and crown'd, 1424.

2. *Robert* III.

3. JAMES I. *Stewart*, tho' unjuſtly captivated, ruled by his *Regent* the ſaid *Robert* Duke of *Albany*.

𝕳𝖊𝖓𝖗𝖞 𝖂𝖆𝖗𝖉𝖑𝖆𝖜, Biſhop of St. *Andrews*, was now *Grand Maſter*, and founded the *Univerſity* there, A. D. 1411. tho' it was long before a Place of Education.

Robert Duke of *Albany* died A. D. 1420. and his Son *Duke* 𝕸𝖚𝖗𝖉𝖔𝖈𝖍 was *Regent* till the King was ranſom'd, reſtor'd and crown'd, A. D. 1424.

King JAMES I. prov'd the *beſt* King of *Scotland*, the Patron of the Learned, and countenanced the *Lodges* with his Preſence as the 𝕽𝖔𝖞𝖆𝖑 *Grand* 𝕸𝖆𝖘𝖙𝖊𝖗 ; till he ſettled an Yearly Revenue of 4 Pounds *Scots* (an *Engliſh Noble*) to be paid by every *Maſter Maſon* in Scotland, to a 𝕲𝖗𝖆𝖓𝖉 𝕸𝖆𝖘𝖙𝖊𝖗 <u>This is the *Tradition* of the *Old Scottiſh Maſons*, and found in their Records.</u> choſen by the *Grand Lodge*, and approv'd by the Crown, one *nobly* born, or an eminent *Clergyman*, who had his Deputies in Cities and Counties: and every *new* Brother at Entrance paid him alſo a Fee. His Office impower'd him to regulate in the *Fraternity* what ſhould not come under the Cognizance of Law-Courts: to him appeal'd both *Maſon* and *Lord*, or the Builder and Founder, when at Variance; in order to prevent *Law-Pleas*; and in his Abſence, they appeal'd to his *Deputy* or *Grand Warden* that reſided next to the Premiſſes.

This Office remain'd till the *Civil Wars*, A. D. 1640. but is now obſolete; nor can it be reviv'd but by a ROAYL *Grand* MASTER. And now the *Maſons* joyfully toaſted

TO THE KING AND THE CRAFT.

This excellent King repair'd *Falkland* and his other Palaces, fortified all his Caſtles and Sea-Ports, and influenc'd the *Nobility* to follow his Example in much employing the *Craft*, till he was baſely murder'd in the *Dominicans* Abby at *Perth*, by his Uncle *Walter Stewart* Earl of *Atholl*, A. D. 1437. and being juſtly lamented by All, his Murderers were ſeverely puniſh'd.

By

By his Wife JOAN BEAUFORT, eldeſt Daughter of *John Beaufort* Earl of *Somerſet*, eldeſt Son of *John a Gaunt*, by his 3d Wife *Katharine Roet*, he had

4. JAMES II. *Stewart*, a Minor of 7 Years, under the Regency of Lord *Calendar*.

In this Reign 𝖂illiam 𝖘inclair the great *Earl of Orkney* and *Caitneſs* was *Grand Maſter*, and built *Roſlin Chapel* near *Edinborough*, a Maſter Piece of the beſt *Gothic*, A. D. 1441. next Biſhop 𝖙urnbull of *Glaſgow*, who founded the Univerſity there, A. D. 1454

And the King, when of Age, encouraged the *Craft* till he died, ⎬1460

By his Wife MARY, Daughter of *Arnold* Duke of *Guelders*,

5. JAMES III. *Stewart*, a Minor of 7 Years ſucceeded, and when of Age, he employ'd the *Craft* in more curious Architecture than any King before him, particularly at *Sterling*, where he erected a ſpacious *Hall*, and a ſplendid *Chapel Royal* in the Caſtle, by the Direction firſt of Sir 𝕽obert 𝕮ockeran *Grand Maſter*, and next of 𝕬lexander Lord *Forbes*, who continued in Office till the King died, A. D. 1488.

By his Wife MARGARET Daughter of *Chriſtiern* I. K. of *Denmark*.

6. JAMES IV. *Stewart* aged 16 Years ſucceeded, and by the *Grand Maſter* 𝖂illiam 𝕰lphinſton Biſhop of *Aberdeen*, the King founded the *Univerſity* there A. D. 1494. *Elphinſton* at his own Coſt founded the curious *Bridge of Dee* near *Aberdeen*, finiſh'd by his Succeſſor Biſhop 𝕲avin 𝕯unbar an excellent *Grand Maſter*, who built many other fine Structures.

The King delighted moſt in *Ship Building*, and encreas'd his *Navy* Royal, a very Warlike Prince: till aſſiſting the *French* in a Diverſion of War, he was loſt in *Flowden-Field*, A. D. 1513.

By his Wife MARGARET TEWDOR, eldeſt Daughter of *Henry* VII. King of *England*, He had

7. JAMES V. *Stewart*, a Minor of 17 Months; and when of Age he became the ingenious Patron of the Learned, especially of the *Muses*.

In this Reign the noble **Gavin Dowglas**, Bishop of *Dunkeld*, was *Grand Master* till he died, *A. D.* 1522. Next

George Creighton *Abbot* of *Holyrood-House*, till *A. D.* 1527. and then

PATRICK, Earl of *Lindsay* (the Progenitor of our late *Grand Master* CRAWFURD) who was succeeded in that Office by Sir **David Lindsay**, *Lion* King at *Arms*, still mention'd among *Scottish Masons* by the Name of DAVY LINDSAY the *learned Grand Master*; till the King died, 13 *Dec.* 1542.

By his Wife MARY, Daughter of *Claud* of *Lorrain* Duke of *Guise*, He left only

8. MARY *Stewart*, Queen *Soveraign* of *Scotland*, a Minor of 7 Days, who became Queen *Consort* of *France*; and after the Death of her first Husband King *Francis* II. without Issue, she return'd to *Scotland* A. D. 1561. and brought with her some fine Connoisseurs in the AUGUSTAN Stile.

She next married, *A. D.* 1565. HENRY STEWART, Lord *Darnley*, eldest Son of **Matthew** Earl of *Lennox*, the lineal *Male* descended from Sir *Robert Stewart* Lord *Darnley* of the *Old Royal Race*, as in the Margin of Page 86.

She fell out with her Nobles, who dethroned her; and being defeated in Battle, she fled for Shelter into *England* 1568. where Queen ELIZABETH detain'd her a Prisoner, and at last, for Reasons of State, beheaded her on 8 *Feb.* 158$\frac{6}{7}$.

9. JAMES VI. *Stewart*, born 19 *June*, 1566. Upon his Mother's Abdication he was crown'd King of *Scotland*, aged 13 Months, under 4 successive *Regents*; and when aged near 12 Years he assum'd the Government *A. D.* 1578.

He founded the *University* of *Edinburg* A. D. 1580. He sail'd to *Denmark*, and married ANN Princess *Royal*, A. D. 1589. when he visited the noble **Tycho Brahe**, the Prince of *Astronomers*, in his *Scarlet Island*.

The

The Nobility and Gentry having divided the Spoil of the Church's Revenues, built many stately Mansions of the Ruins of the pious Houses, as was done in *England*; and the *Masons* began to imitate the *Augustan Stile*, under the Direction of several successive *Grand Masters*.

For after the Death of *Davy Lindsay*, **Andrew Stewart** Lord *Ochiltree* was *Grand Master*; next Sir **James Sandilands** Knight of *Malta*: Then **Claud Hamilton** Lord *Paisley* (Progenitor of our late *Grand Master* ABERCORN) who made King JAMES a *Brother Mason* and continued in Office till the *Union* of the *Crowns*, A. D. 1603.

Before this Period, not only the Crown was possess'd of many fine Palaces and strong Castles, but also the Nobles and Chiefs of Clans had fortify'd themselves; because of their frequent Feuds or Civil Wars; and the *Clergy* had built many Abbies, Churches, Monastries and other pious Houses, of as fine *Gothic* as any in *Europe*, most venerable, sumptuous, and magnificent.

The *Fraternity* of old met in *Monasteries* in foul Weather; but in fair Weather they met early in the Morning on the Tops of Hills, especially on St. JOHN *Evangelist*'s *Day*, and from thence walk'd in due Form to the Place of Dinner, according to the Tradition of the old *Scots Masons*, particularly of those in the antient Lodges of *Killwinning*, *Sterling*, *Aberdeen*, &c.

CHAP. VII.

MASONRY in *Ireland* till *Grand Master* KINGSTON, A. D. 1730.

THE antient *Romans* having never invaded *Ireland*, we have no good Vouchers of what happened there before St. **Patrick** in the Days of King LEOGHAIR, |See Sir *James Ware's* about *A. D.* 430. He founded St. *Patricks* at |Antiq. Hibern.

Ardmagh,

Ardmagh, and the Priory of St. *Avog* at *Loch-Derg*, near the Cave call'd St. *Patrick*'s *Purgatory*: But afterwards many pious Houses appear'd throughout *Ireland*.

Nor did the *Anglo-Saxons* invade *Ireland*: But 𝔅𝔢𝔡𝔢 and Others, in the 8th Century affirm, that then many *Britons*, *Saxons* and *Franks* reforted to the Schools of *Ireland* for Education.

But the *Norwegians* and *Danes* conquer'd the moft Part of the Ifland; and tho' at firft they deftroy'd the pious Houfes, they built many Caftles and Forts with lofty Beacons, to alarm the whole Country in an Hour; till they were converted to Chriftianity by the *Irish*, when the *Danes* built many religious Houfes; as at *Dublin* St. 𝔐𝔞𝔯𝔶's Abbey and *Chrift Church*, about *A. D.* 984.

At length, BRIEN BOROM, the Grand Monarch of *all Ireland* of *Heber*'s Race, after defeating the *Danes* in many Battels, totally routed 'em, *A. D.* 1039.

From whom our late *Grand Mafter* INCHIQUIN is defcended in a lineal Male Race.

So the far greater Part of the *Danes* were forced to fail home, and carried with 'em (as the *Irish* affirm) the beft old *Records* of *Ireland*, an irreparable Damage! But the Learned of Other Nations long to fee the remaining Manufcripts of *Ireland* publifh'd with good Tranflations, and alfo a better *Monafticon Hibernicum*; that among other Antiquities, the Veftiges of their old *Celtic* Architecture might be trac'd, if poffible; for the *Auguftan Stile* had never been there, and the *Gothic* was only introduc'd by St. *Patrick*.

After the Expulfion of the *Danes*, the *Milefian* Kings of *Ireland* order'd the Palaces, Caftles and pious Houfes to be repair'd, and much employ'd the *Craft* down to RODERIC O CONNOR, the laft Monarch of *all Ireland*, who built the wonderful Caftle of *Tuam* (now demolifh'd) *A. D.* 1168.

But the *Royal* Branches having made themfelves *Petty Soveraigns*, were imbroil'd in frequent Civil Wars: One of them, *viz.*

DERMOT King of *Leinfter*, being defeated by the Others, came to HENRY II. King of *England*, and got Leave to contract

tract with Adventurers, *viz.* 𝕽𝖎𝖈𝖍𝖆𝖗𝖉 𝕾𝖙𝖗𝖔𝖓𝖌𝖇𝖔𝖜 Earl of *Pembroke*, 𝕽𝖔𝖇𝖊𝖗𝖙 *Fitz-Stephen* of *Cardigan*, and 𝕸𝖆𝖚𝖗𝖎𝖈𝖊 *Fitz-Gerald*; who brought over an Army of *Welch* and *English* to DERMOT's Assistance, took in *Dublin*, *Waterford* and many other Places, which they fortify'd and surrender'd into the Hands of their King HENRY II. as soon as he had follow'd 'em into *Ireland*, A. D. 1172.

Kings of ENGLAND now *Lords* of IRELAND.

The *Irish*, not without Reason, say, that King HENRY II. did not conquer *Ireland*; only some of their *Petty* Kings and Princes, rather than be farther imbroil'd in *Civil* Wars, chose to come under his Protection, and of their own Accord receiv'd the *Laws* of *England*, with the *Freedom* of a Parliament at *Dublin*. But where the *English* prevail'd, *Masonry* and other Arts were most encouraged.

Thus the said STRONGBOW Lord *Warden* of *Ireland* Built the Priory of *Kill Mainham*; while St. *Bar* founded the | A. D. 1174 | Aboy of *Finbar*.

𝕵𝖔𝖍𝖓 𝕯𝖊 𝕮𝖔𝖚𝖈𝖞, Earl of *Kingsail*, rebuilt the Abby | A. D. 1183 | of St. *Patrick* in *Down*, the Priories of *Nedrum* and St. *John's*, with St. *Mary's* Abby of *Innys*, &c.

In the Reign of RICHARD I. 𝕬𝖑𝖚𝖗𝖊𝖉, a noble *Dane*, built St. *John's* in *Dublin*; and Archbishop *Comin* rebuilt | A. D. 1190 | St. *Patrick's* there, all of Stone, which before was only of Timber and *Waties*.

King JOHN was King of *Ireland* (as the *Irish* affirm) till his Brother *Richard* died, 1199. and afterwards went into *Ireland*, and employ'd 𝕳𝖊𝖓𝖗𝖞 𝕷𝖆𝖚𝖓𝖉𝖊𝖗𝖘 Archbishop of *Dublin* and Lord *Justice*, as *Grand Master*, in building the Castle | A. D. 1210 | of *Dublin*; while 𝖂𝖎𝖑𝖑𝖎𝖆𝖒 Earl of *Pembroke* built the Priory of *Killkenny*.

King HENRY III. granted *Ireland* a 𝕸𝖆𝖌𝖓𝖆 | A. D. 1216 | 𝕮𝖍𝖆𝖗𝖙𝖆 the same with that of *England*. 𝕱𝖊𝖑𝖎𝖝 𝕺 𝕯𝖚𝖆𝖉𝖆𝖒, Archbishop of *Tuam*, rebuilt St. *Mary's Dublin*, and cover'd it with Lead; while 𝕳𝖚𝖌𝖍 𝕯𝖊 𝕷𝖆𝖈𝖞, Earl of *Ulster*, | about A. D. 1210 | founded

(94)

founded *Carrick-Fergus*, a Friary in *Down*, the Priory of *Ards*, and famous *Trim Castle*, &c. as 𝕲𝖗𝖆𝖓𝖉 𝕸𝖆𝖘𝖙𝖊𝖗, or Patron of the *Craft*.

The *Native* Princes liv'd pretty well with the *English*, till the Reign of King EDWARD II. when Prince EDWARD BRUCE (Brother of *Robert Bruce* King of *Scotland*) headed the confederated *Irish*, conquer'd the Island, was crown'd *King* of | A. D. 1315 | all *Ireland*, and reign'd three Years, till Sir *Roger Mortimer* Earl of *March* landed with a strong *English* Army and slew King *Edward Bruce* in Battle.

After this, *Masonry* in the *English* Settlements revived; and in the *North* of *Ireland* too, where the *Scots* had gradually settled, and brought with them good *Gothic Masonry*. At last,

The *Natives* regarded the *Kings* of *England* as the lawful *Soveraign* Lords of *Ireland* down to King HENRY VIII. who in Defiance of the *Pope*, proclaim'd himself King of *Ireland*, which was confirm'd in the Parliament at *Dublin*, A. D. 1542.

Kings of ENGLAND now *Kings* of IRELAND.

HENRY King of *Ireland* was succeeded by his Son King EDWARD, and he by his Sister Queen MARY *Tewdor*, who got *Pope* PAUL IV. to make her Queen of *Ireland*; succeeded by her Sister Queen ELIZABETH *Tewdor*, who founded the famous *University* of *Dublin*, A. D. 1591.

Masonry made some Progress in *Ireland* in the Reigns of JAMES I. and CHARLES I. till the *Civil* Wars, when all the Fabrick was out of Joint till the *Restoration* A. D. 1660. After which it was revived by some of the Disciples of *Inigo Jones* in the Reign of CHARLES II. and till the Wars of King JAMES II. But after King WILLIAM had settled the Country, Arts and Sciences were again well cultivated in the Reigns of Queen ANNE and King GEORGE I.

Many are the beautiful Remains of the best *Gothic* Architecture in this fine Island, of which the Learned of *Ireland* can best give a Chronological Deduction. But since the *Revolution* the AUGUSTAN STILE has been much encouraged there, both by the Government and the Nobility and Gentry: So that the Metropolis *Dublin* is now adorned with a stately *Tollsell* or *Town-house*,

an

an excellent *Custom-house*, a curious *Armory* in the Castle, a fine *Library* in the *University*, neat and convenient *Barracks* for the Garrison, a Royal *Hospital* for old Soldiers, *Stephen's Green-Square*, the largest in *Europe*, being an *English* Mile round, or 1760 Yards, *Stephens's* Hospital, besides Churches and other Edifices rais'd by good Architects, particularly by **Thomas Burgh** Esq; late *Surveyor* General of *Ireland*, and his Successor Sir **Edward Lovet Pearce**, the Architect of the new magnificent *Parliament-House* (far beyond *that of England*) founded on the 3d *Feb.* 172$\frac{8}{9}$, when Lord *Carteret*, then Lord *Lieutenant*, the Lords *Justices*, several *Peers* and Members of *Parliament*, some eminent *Clergy*, with many *Free Masons*, attended by the King's *Yeomen* of Guard, and a Detachment of *Horse* and *Foot*, made a solemn Procession thither; and the Lord *Lieutenant*, having in the King's Name levell'd the *Footstone* at the *South-side*, by giving it 3 Knocks with a Mallet, the Trumpets sounded, the solemn Croud made joyful Acclamations, a Purse of Gold was laid on the Stone for the Masons, who drank *to the King and the Craft*, &c. And in the Stone were placed Two *Silver Medals* of King GEORGE II. and Queen CAROLINE, over which a Copper Plate was laid with the following Inscription.

SERENISSIMUS ET POTENTISSIMUS
REX GEORGIUS SECUNDUS
PER EXCELLENT. DOMINUM
JOANNEM DOMINUM ET BARON. DE HAWNES
LOCUM-TENENTEM,
ET PER EXCELLENT. DOMINOS
HUGONEM ARCHIEP: ARMACHAN:
THOMAM WINDHAM CANCELL.
GULIEL: CONOLLY DOM: COM: PROLOCUT.
JUSTICIARIOS GENERALES,
PRIMUM HUJUSCE DOMUS PARLIAMENT: LAPIDEM
POSUIT
TERTIO DIE FEBRUARII MDCCXXVIII.

At last the antient *Fraternity* of the *Free* and accepted Masons in *Ireland*, being duly assembled in their *Grand Lodge* at *Dublin*, chose a *Noble* 𝕲𝖗𝖆𝖓𝖉 𝕸𝖆𝖘𝖙𝖊𝖗, in Imitation of their Brethren of *England*, in the 3d Year of his present Majesty King George II. *A. D.* 1730. even our *noble Brother*

James King Lord Viscount *Kingston*, the very next Year after his Lordship, had, with great Reputation, been the 𝕲𝖗𝖆𝖓𝖉 𝕸𝖆𝖘𝖙𝖊𝖗 of *England*; and he has introduced the same *Constitutions* and antient *Usages*.

He has been annually succeeded by noble Brothers in *Solomon*'s Chair, and the *Grand Lodge* of *Ireland* are firmly resolved to persevere in propagating the Knowledge of the *Noble Science* of Geometry and the *Royal Art* of Masonry.

PART

(97)

PART III.

The History of MASONRY in *Britain*, from the UNION of the *Crowns* to thefe Times.

CHAP. I.

The AUGUSTAN STILE in *Britain*, from the *Union* of the CROWNS 1603. till the RESTORATION 1660.

BEFORE this *Period*, fome Gentlemen of fine Tafte returning from their Travels full of laudable Emulation, refolved, if not to excel the *Italian Revivers*, at leaft to imitate them in old *Roman* and *Grecian* MASONRY. But no Remains being here, no Veftiges of the good old AUGUSTAN Stile, thofe ingenious Travellers brought home fome Pieces of *old Columns*, fome curious Drawings of the *Italian Revivers*, and their Books of *Architecture*; efpecially

INIGO JONES, born near St. *Paul's London*, A. D. 1572. (Son of Mr. *Ignatius* or *Inigo Jones*, a Citizen of *London*) bred up at *Cambridge*, who naturally took to the *Arts* of *Defigning*, and was firft known by his Skill in *Landskip-Painting*; for which he was patroniz'd by the noble and learned WILLIAM HERBERT (afterwards Earl of *Pembroke*) at whofe Expence *Jones* made the Tour of *Italy*, where he was inftructed in the *Royal Art* by fome of the beft Difciples of the famous
ANDREA PALLADIO.

O INIGO

INIGO JONES, upon his Return, laid aside his *Pencil*, and took up the *Square*, *Level* and *Plumb*, and became the 𝕍𝕚𝕥𝕣𝕦𝕧𝕚𝕦𝕤 𝔅𝔯𝔦𝔱𝔞𝔫𝔫𝔦𝔠𝔲𝔰, the Rival of *Palladio* and of all the *Italian* Revivers; as it soon appear'd after

The UNION of the CROWNS, *A. D.* 1603.
When the ROYAL TEWDORS expired, and the ROYAL STEWARTS succeeded.

SCOTTISH Kings of all *Britain*.

1. JAMES I. *Stewart*, now the *first* King of *all Britain*, a *Royal* Brother *Mason*, and *Royal Grand Master* by Prerogative, wishing for proper Heads and Hands for establishing the *Augustan Stile* here, was glad to find such a Subject as 𝕴𝖓𝖎𝖌𝖔 𝕵𝖔𝖓𝖊𝖘; whom he appointed his General *Surveyor*, and approv'd of his being chosen *Grand Master* of *England*, to preside over the *Lodges*.

The King order'd him to draw the Plan of a *new* Palace at *Whitehall*, and so when the old *Banquetting-House* was pull'd down, the KING with *Grand Master* 𝕵𝖔𝖓𝖊𝖘 and his *Grand Wardens*, (the foresaid WILLIAM HERBERT Earl of *Pembroke*, and *Nicholas Stone* the Sculptor,) attended by many Brothers in due Form, and many eminent Persons, walk'd to *Whitehall* Gate, and levell'd the *Footstone* of the *New Banquetting-House* with 3 great Knocks, loud Huzza's, Sound of Trumpets, and a Purse of broad Pieces of Gold laid upon the Stone for the *Masons* to drink

𝕿𝖔 𝖙𝖍𝖊 𝕶𝖎𝖓𝖌 𝖆𝖓𝖉 𝖙𝖍𝖊 𝕮𝖗𝖆𝖋𝖙!
A. D. 1607.

Tho' for want of a Parliamentary Fund, no more was built but the said glorious BANQUETTING-HOUSE, the finest single Room of that large Extent since the Days of *Augustus*, and the Glory of this Reign. Afterwards the lofty Ceiling was adorned by the fine Pencil of *Peter Paul* RUBENS.

The best *Craftsmen* from all Parts resorted to *Grand Master* JONES, who always allow'd good Wages and seasonable Times for Instruction in the Lodges, which he constituted with excellent By-Laws, and made 'em like the *Schools* or *Academies* of the

Designers

Defigners in *Italy*. He alfo held the Quarterly *Communication* * of the Grand Lodge of *Mafters* and *Wardens*, and the Annual General Affembly and *Feaft* on St. *John's* Day, when he was annually rechofen, till *A. D.* 1618. when the forefaid

So faid Brother Nicholas Stone his Warden, in a Manufcript burnt 1720.

WILLIAM Earl of *Pembroke* was chofen *Grand Mafter*; and being approved by the King, he appointed Inigo Jones his *Deputy* Grand Mafter.

Mafonry thus flourifhing, many eminent, wealthy and learned Men, at their own Requeft, were accepted as *Brothers*, to the Honour of the *Craft*, till the King died 27 *March* 1625. leaving two Children, *viz.*

2. CHARLES I. *Stewart*, aged 25 Years fucceeded; alfo a Royal Brother and *Grand Mafter* by Prerogative: Being well fkill'd in all the Arts	*Elizabeth Stewart* Queen of *Bohemia*.
	Princefs *Sophia*, Electrefs of *Brunfwig*.
	George I. King of Great *Britain*. Below.

of Defigning, he encouraged the beft foreign *Painters, Sculptors, Statuaries, Plaifterers,* &c. but wanted no Foreigners for Architecture, becaufe none of 'em equall'd his own *Inigo Jones* and his excellent Difciples. When *Grand Mafter* PEMBROKE demitted, *A. D.* 1630.

HENRY DANVERS Earl of *Danby* fucceeded in *Solomon's* Chair by the King's Approbation; and at his own Coft erected a fmall, but moft accurate Piece of the old Architecture, by the Defign of his *Deputy* Jones, even the famous beautiful *Gate* of the *Phyfic Garden* at *Oxford*, with this Infcription.

GLORIÆ DEI OPTIMI MAXIMI HONORI CAROLI REGIS,
IN USUM ACADEMIÆ ET REIPUBLICÆ, *A. D.* 1632.
HENRICUS COMES DANBY.

THOMAS HOWARD Earl of *Arundel* (the Progenitor of our late *Grand Mafter* NORFOLK) then fucceeded *Danby* at the Head of the Fraternity, a moſt excellent Connoiſſeur in all the *Arts* of *Deſigning*, and the great Reviver of learned Antiquities, who will be ever famous for his *Marmora Arundeliana*! But *Deputy* **Jones** was never out of Office; and join'd *Grand Maſter* Arundel, in perſuading **Francis Ruſſel** Earl of *Bedford*, to lay out his Grounds of *Covent-Garden* in an Oblong-Square *Eaſt* and *Weſt*, where he built the regular Temple of St. *Paul* with its admirable *Portico*, made Parochial *A. D.* 1635. when

Grand *Maſter* Bedford ſucceeded, and employ'd his *Deputy* **Jones** to build the *North* and *Eaſt* Sides of that Square with large and lofty *Arkades* (commonly call'd *Piazzas*) which, with the ſaid Church on the *Weſt* End, make a moſt beautiful Proſpect after the *Italian* or antient Manner.

Inigo Jones ſucceeded *Bedford* in *Solomon*'s *Chair* again; and before the Wars the King employ'd him to build the ſtately great *Gallery* of *Somerſet-Houſe* fronting the *Thames*: And the King intended to carry on *Whitehall* according to *Jones*'s Plan, but was unhappily prevented by the *Civil* Wars: For the *Parliament*'s Army conquer'd the *King* and *Parliament* too, and murder'd him at his own Gate on 30 *January* 164$\frac{8}{9}$.

Yet even during the Wars, the *Maſons* met occaſionally at ſeveral Places: Thus **Elias Aſhmole** in his Diary Page 15. ſays, *I was made a Free Maſon at* Warrington, Lancaſhire, *with Colonel* Henry Manwaring, *by Mr.* Richard Penket *the Warden, and the Fellow Crafts* (there mention'd) *on* 16 Oct. 1646.

The *Great* Inigo Jones aged 80 Years died at *London*, and was buried in St. *Bennet*'s Church at *Paul*'s Wharf on 26 *June* 1652. the **Grand Maſter** of *Architects*, who brought the *Auguſtan* Stile into *England*.

He ſhew'd his great Skill alſo in deſigning the magnificent *Rowe* of great *Queen-ſtreet*, and the *Weſt* Side of *Lincoln's-Inn-Fields*, with beautiful *Lindſey-Houſe*, the *Chirurgeons Hall* and *Theatre*, *Shaftſbury-Houſe* in *Alderſgate-ſtreet*, *Southampton-Houſe Bloomſbury* (now the Duke of *Bedford*'s) *Berkeley-Houſe Piccadilly* (now the Duke of *Devonſhire*'s) lately burnt and rebuilt; accurate *York-Stairs* at the *Thames*, &c. And in the Country,

Gunnersbury-Houſe

Gunnersbury-House near *Brentford, Wilton-House Wiltshire, Castle-Abby Northamptonshire, Stoke-Park*, &c.

Some of his *best Disciples* met privately for their mutual Improvement till the *Restoration*, who preserved his clean Drawings and accurate Designs (still preserved by the skilful *Architect*, the noble RICHARD BOYLE the present Earl of *Burlington*) and after the *Restoration* they propagated his *lofty Stile*.

CHAP. II.

From the RESTORATION 1660. till the REVOLUTION 1688.

3. CHARLES II. *Stewart*, succeeded his Father, and was magnificently restor'd, aged 30 Years, on his own Birth-Day, 29 *May* 1660. In his Travels he had been made a *Free Mason*, and having observed the exact Structures of foreign Countries, he resolved to encourage the *Augustan* Stile by reviving the *Lodges*, and approv'd their Choice of

HENRY JERMYN Earl of St. *Albans* as their 𝕲𝖗𝖆𝖓𝖉 𝕸𝖆𝖘𝖙𝖊𝖗, who appointed Sir JOHN DENHAM his *Deputy Grand Master*, Sir 𝕮𝖍𝖗𝖎𝖘𝖙𝖔𝖕𝖍𝖊𝖗 𝖂𝖗𝖊𝖓, } *Grand* { According to a Copy of the Mr. 𝕵𝖔𝖍𝖓 𝖂𝖊𝖇, } *Wardens.* { old *Constitutions*, this *Grand Master* held a *General* Assembly and *Feast* on St. JOHN's Day 27 *Dec.* 1663. when the following *Regulations* were made.

1. *That no Person of what Degree soever, be made or accepted a* Free Mason *unless in a regular Lodge, whereof one to be a* Master *or a* Warden *in that Limit or Division where such Lodge is kept, and another to be a* Craftsman *in the Trade of* Free Masonry.

2. *That no Person hereafter shall be accepted a* Free Mason, *but such as are of able Body, honest Parentage, good Reputation, and an Observer of the Laws of the Land.*

3. *That no Person hereafter who shall be accepted a* Free Mason, *shall be admitted into any* Lodge *or* Assembly, *until he has brought a Certificate of the Time and Place of his Acceptation from the Lodge*

Lodge that accepted him unto the Master of that Limit or Division where such Lodge is kept: And the said Master shall enrol the same in a Roll of Parchment to be kept for that Purpose, and shall give an Account of all such Acceptations at every General Assembly.

4. That every Person who is now a Free Mason, shall bring to the Master a Note of the Time of his Acceptation, to the End the same may be enroll'd in such Priority of Place as the Brother deserves; and that the whole Company and Fellows may the better know each other.

5. That for the Future the said Fraternity of Free Masons shall be regulated and govern'd by One GRAND MASTER, and as many Wardens as the said Society shall think fit to appoint at every Annual General Assembly.

6. That no Person shall be accepted unless he be 21 Years old or more.

THOMAS SAVAGE Earl of *Rivers* succeeded St. *Albans* as Grand Master, 24 *June* 1666. who appointed Sir Christopher Wren his *Deputy*; { Mr. *John Web*, Mr. *Grinlin Gibbons*, } Grand Wardens. but the *Deputy* and *Wardens* manag'd all Things.

This Year on 2 *Sept*. the Great Burning of *London* happen'd, and the *Free Masons* became necessary to rebuild it.

Accordingly,

The *King* and *Grand Master* order'd the *Deputy* Wren to draw up a fine Plan of the new City, with long, broad and regular Streets; but tho' private Properties hinder'd it's taking Effect, yet that noble City was soon rebuilt in a far better *Stile* than before.

The *King* levell'd the *Footstone* of the *New Royal-Exchange* in solemn Form, on 23 *Oct*. 1667. and it was open'd, the finest in *Europe*, by the Mayor and Aldermen on 28 *Sept*. 1669. Upon the Insides of the *Square* above the *Arkades*, and between the Windows, are the *Statues* of the Soveraigns of *England*. Afterwards the *Merchant* Adventurers employ'd *Grand Warden* Gibbons, to erect in the Middle of the Square the KING's *Statue*

to

to the Life, in *Cæsarian* Habit, of white Marble, with an elegant Inscription, * below.

GILBERT SHELDON Archbishop of *Canterbury*, an excellent Architect, shew'd his great Skill in designing his famous *Theatrum Sheldonianum* at *Oxford*, and at his Cost it was conducted and finish'd by *Deputy* Wren and *Grand Warden* Web; and the *Craftsmen* having celebrated the *Cape-Stone*, it was open'd with an elegant Oration by Dr. *South*, on 9 *July* 1669. D. G. M. Wren built also that other *Master Piece*, the pretty *Musæum* near the *Theatre*, at the Charge of the *University*. Mean while

LONDON was rebuilding apace; and the Fire having ruin'd St. *Paul*'s Cathedral, the KING with *Grand Master* RIVERS, his Architects and Craftsmen, Nobility and Gentry, Lord Mayor and Aldermen, Bishops and Clergy, &c. in due Form levell'd the *Footstone* of New St. *Paul*'s, design'd by D. G. *Master* Wren A. D. 1673. and by him conducted as *Master of Work* and Surveyor, with his Wardens Mr. *Edward Strong* Senior and Junior, upon a Parliamentary Fund.

The City rear'd beautiful *Moor-Gate*, and rebuilt *Bedlam-Hospital* in the best *Old Stile*, A. D. 1675. and where the Fire

---

* CAROLO SECUNDO CÆSARI BRITANNICO
PATRIÆ PATRI
REGUM OPTIMO CLEMENTISSIMO AUGUSTISSIMO
GENERIS HUMANI DELICIIS
UTRIUSQUE FORTUNÆ VICTORI
MARIUM DOMINO AC VINDICI
SOCIETAS MERCATORUM ADVENTUR. ANGLIÆ
QUÆ PER CCCC JAM PROPE ANNOS
REGIA MAJESTATE FLORET
FIDEI INTEMERATÆ ET GRATITUDINIS ÆTERNÆ
HOC TESTIMONIUM
VENERABUNDA POSUIT
ANNO SALUTIS HUMANÆ MDCLXXXIV.

began

began, the City rais'd the famous *Monument* of White Stone, a fine fluted *Column* of the *Doric* Order, 202 Foot high from the Ground, and the *Shaft* is 15 Foot in Diameter, with an eafy *Stair* of black Marble within the Shaft leading up to an *Iron Balcony*, guilded at the Top, the higheft *Column* upon Earth. It's *Pedeftal.* is 21 Foot Square and 40 Foot high, with moft ingenious *Emblems* in Baffo Relievo, wrought by the forefaid *Gabriel Cibber*, with *Latin Infcriptions*. It was finifh'd *A. D.* 1677.

So where the Fire ftopt at *Temple-Bar*, the City built a fine *Roman* Gate, with the Statues of Queen ELIZABETH and King JAMES I. on the *Eaft* Side, and thofe of King CHARLES I. and CHARLES II. on the *Weft* Side.

The 𝕻𝖍𝖞𝖋𝖎𝖈𝖎𝖆𝖓𝖘 difcover'd alfo their fine Tafte by their accurate *College*, a *Mafter-Piece*; and the 𝕷𝖆𝖜𝖞𝖊𝖗𝖘 by the Front of *Middle Temple-Lane*.

And after the Fire, the *Parifh* Churches were many of 'em elegantly rebuilt, efpecially St. *Mary-le-Bow* with it's Steeple of feveral Orders, and St. *Mary Wool-Church* with it's admirable *Cupola*, &c.

The KING alfo founded *Chelfea-Hofpital* for old Soldiers, and a moft curious New *Palace* at *Greenwich* from a Defign of *Inigo Jones*, conducted by *Grand Warden* 𝖂𝖊𝖇 as *Mafter* of Work; and another *Palace* at *Winchefter*, defign'd by *Grand Mafter* WREN, an excellent Pile of the richeft *Corinthian* Order, cover'd in before the King's Death, but never finifh'd, and now in Ruins.

The King order'd Sir WILLIAM BRUCE, *Baronet, Grand Mafter* of *Scotland*, to rebuild his Palace of *Holyrood-Houfe* at *Edinburg* in the beft *Auguftan* Stile, and the *Scottifh* Secretary-Office at *Whitehall*. G. *Mafter* BRUCE built alfo his own pretty Seat at *Kinrofs*.

So

(105)

So that the *Fellow Crafts* were never more employ'd than in this Reign, nor in a more lofty *Stile*; and many *Lodges* were constituted throughout the Islands by Leave of the several noble G. Masters: For after G. *Master Rivers* demitted, *A. D.* 1674.

For besides many other fine *Structures* in and about *London*, many noble *Mansions* in the Country were built or founded; as—*Wing-House Bedfordshire*—*Chevening* in Kent—*Ambrosebury* in *Wiltshire*—*Hotham-House* and *Stainborough Yorkshire*—Palace of *Hamilton* in *Clydesdale*—*Sterling-House* near the Castle—*Drumlanrig* in *Nidsdale*, and many more.

GEORGE VILLARS Duke of *Bucks*, an old *Mason*, succeeded as G. *Master* of *England*; but being indolent, he left all Business to his *Deputy* Wren and his *Wardens*; and when he demitted *A. D.* 1679.

HENRY BENNET Earl of *Arlington* succeeded, who was too deeply engag'd in Affairs of *State* to mind the *Lodges*: Yet in his *Mastership* the Fraternity was considerable still, and many Gentlemen requested to be admitted. Thus the foresaid Brother *Ashmole* (in his *Diary* Page 66.) says,

On the 10 March 1682. *I received a Summons to appear next Day at a Lodge in* Masons-Hall London, *when we admitted into the Fellowship of Free Masons Sir* William Wilson, *Capt.* Richard Borthwick, *and four more. I was the senior Fellow, it being* 35 *Years since I was admitted; and with me were Mr.* Thomas Wife *(Master of the* London Company *of Masons) and eight more old Free Masons. We all dined at the* Half-Moon Tavern *in* Cheapside, *a noble Dinner, prepared at the Charge of the new accepted Masons.*

But many of the Fraternity's *Records* of this and former Reigns were lost in the next and at the *Revolution*; and many of 'em were too hastily burnt in our Time from a Fear of making Discoveries: So that we have not so ample an Account as could be wish'd of the *Grand Lodge*, &c.

King *Charles* II. dying on 6 *February* 168¼. his Brother succeeded, *viz.*

4. JAMES II. *Stewart*, aged 51 Years. A most excellent Statue of him still stands in *Whitehall*. But not being a *Brother Mason*, the *Art* was much neglected, and People of all sorts were

P otherwise

otherwise engag'd in this Reign: Only upon the Death of Grand Master *Arlington* 1685 the *Lodges* met and elected

Sir CHRISTOPHER WREN 𝕲𝖗𝖆𝖓𝖉 𝔐𝖆𝖘𝖙𝖊𝖗, who appointed Mr. *Gabriel Cibber*, } *Grand Wardens.* { and while carrying on Mr. *Edward Strong*, } { St. *Paul*'s, he annually met those Brethren that could attend him, to keep up good old *Usages*, till the Revolution, when

𝔚𝔦𝔩𝔩𝔦𝔞𝔪 of *Nassau* Prince of *Orange*, landed on 5 *Nov.* 1688. and King JAMES sail'd to *France* on 23 *Dec.* following, and died there on 6 *Sept.* 1701.

CHAP. III.

From the REVOLUTION to *Grand Master* MONTAGU, 1721.

UPON King *James*'s going off, the *Convention* of *States* entail'd the Crown of *England* upon King *James*'s two Daughters and their Issue, *viz.* MARY Princess of *Orange*, and ANN Princess of *Denmark*: And failing them on WILLIAM Prince of *Orange*; for his Mother *Mary Stewart* was King *James*'s eldest Sister: But ORANGE was to reign during Life. Accordingly on 13 Feb. 168$\frac{8}{9}$.

5. King WILLIAM III. aged 38 Years, } were proclaim'd *King* and his Wife } and *Queen*, Joint So-
6. Queen MARY II. *Stewart,* aged 26 } *vereigns* of *England*; Years, } and *Scotland* soon
She died at *Kensington* without Issue on } proclaim'd them. 28 *Dec.* 1694.

Particular *Lodges* were not so frequent and mostly *occasional* in the *South*, except in or near the Places where great Works were carried on. Thus Sir *Robert Claytor* got an *Occasional* Lodge of his Brother *Masters* to meet at St. *Thomas*'s *Hospital Southwark*, A. D. 1693. and to advise the Governours about the best Design of rebuilding that Hospital as it now stands moſt beautiful; near which a *ſtated* Lodge continued long afterwards.

Beſides that and the *old* Lodge of St. *Paul*'s, there was another in *Piccadilly* over againſt St. *James*'s Church, one near *Weſtminſter* Abby, another near *Covent-Garden*, one in *Holborn*, one on *Tower-Hill*, and ſome more that aſſembled ſtatedly.

The *King* was privately made a *Free Maſon*, approved of their Choice of *G. Maſter* WREN, and encourag'd him in rearing St. *Paul*'s *Cathedral*, and the great *New* Part of 𝔥𝔞𝔪𝔭𝔱𝔬𝔫-𝔈𝔬𝔲𝔯𝔱 in the *Auguſtan Stile*, by far the fineſt *Royal* Houſe in *England*, after an old Deſign of *Inigo Jones*, where a bright *Lodge* was held during the Building. The King alſo built his *little* Palace of *Kenſington*, and finiſh'd *Chelſea Hoſpital*; but appointed the fine *new* Palace of *Greenwich* (begun by King *Charles* II.) to be an *Hoſpital* for old *Seamen*, A. D. 1695. and order'd it to be finiſh'd as begun after *Jones*'s old *Deſign*.

This Year our moſt noble Brother CHARLES LENNOS Duke of *Richmond* and *Lennox* (Father of the preſent Duke) *Maſter* of a Lodge at *Chicheſter*, coming to the annual Aſſembly and Feaſt at *London*, was choſen *Grand Maſter* and approv'd by the King. Sir 𝔈𝔥𝔯𝔦𝔰𝔱𝔬𝔭𝔥𝔢𝔯 𝔚𝔯𝔢𝔫 was his *D. G. Maſter*, who acted as before at the Head of the *Craft*, { *Edward Strong*, ſen. *Edward Strong*, jun. } *Grand Wardens*. and was again choſen *Grand Maſter*, A. D. 1698.

In this Reign *Naval* Architecture was wonderfully improv'd, and the *King* diſcover'd his High Taſte in building his elegant Palace at *Loo* in *Holland*, till he died at *Kenſington* 8 *March* 170½. when

7. ANN *Stewart*, the other Daughter of King *James* II. aged 38 Years, ſucceeded as Queen *Soveraign*, Wife of GEORGE Prince of *Denmark*: He was the Patron of *Aſtronomers* and *Navigators*, and died at *Kenſington* 28 *Oct.* 1708.

Queen ANN enlarg'd St. *James*'s Palace, and after the famous Battle of *Blenheim*, A. D. 1704. demoliſh'd the *old* Royal Caſtle of *Woodſtock* in *Oxfordſhire*, and built in its ſtead the Caſtle of *Blenheim* for her General *John Churchill* Duke of *Marleborough*.

The Queen, in her 5th Year, united the *two* Kingdoms of *England* and *Scotland* into the *one* Kingdom of *Great-Britain* which commenced on 1 *May* 1707.

After the *Union* of the *Crowns* 104 Years.

The *Queen* and *Parliament* enacted the building of 50 new *Churches* in the Suburbs of *London*; and the Surveyors shew'd their Skill in *Buckingham* House and *Marleborough* House in St. *James*'s Park, *Powis* House in *Ormond-street*, the *Opera* House in *Haymarket*, and many more about Town: As in the Country the Duke of *Devonshire*'s fine *Chatsworth* in *Derbyshire*, *Stourton Wiltshire*, the Earl of *Carlisle*'s Castle *Howard* near *York*, *Helmsley* House or *Duncomb-Park*, *Mereworth* House in *Kent*, *Wilbury* House in *Wiltshire*, &c. Nay after the Peace of *Utrecht* many rich old Officers in the Army, returning home good Connoisseurs in Architecture, delighted in raising stately Mansions.

But the *Augustan* Stile was mostly richly display'd at *Oxford* in the *New* Chapel of *Trinity* College by Dr. **Bathurst**, in *Peek-Water-Square* of *Christ's-Church* College by Dr. **Aldrige**, in *Queen's-College* by Dr. **Lancaster** elegantly rebuilt, in *Allhallow*'s Church, the new *Printing* House, &c.

Yet still in the *South* the Lodges were more and more disused, partly by the Neglect of the *Masters* and *Wardens*, and partly by not having a *Noble Grand Master* at *London*, and the annual Assembly was not duly attended.

G. M. WREN, who had design'd St. *Paul*'s *London*, A.D. 1673. and as *Master* of *Work* had conducted it from the *Footstone*, had the Honour to finish that noble *Cathedral*, the finest and largest *Temple* of the *Augustan* Stile except St. *Peter*'s at *Rome*; and celebrated the *Capestone* when he erected the Cross on the Top of the Cupola, in *July* A. D. 1708.

Some few Years after this Sir *Christopher Wren* neglected the Office of *Grand Master*; yet the *Old Lodge* near St. *Paul*'s and a few more continued their stated Meetings till

Queen *Ann* died at *Kensington* without Issue on 1 *Aug*. 1714. She was the last of the Race of King *Charles* I. upon the Throne of *Britain*; for the Others, being *Romans*, are excluded by the

Act

Act of Parliament for settling the *Crown* upon the *Protestant* Heirs of his Sister Elizabeth *Stewart* Queen of *Bohemia* above, *viz.* on her Daughter the Princess Sophia Electress Dowager of *Brunswig-Luneburg*; and she dying a little before Queen Ann, her Son the *Elector* succeeded on the said 1 *Aug.* 1714.

𝕾𝖆𝖝𝖔𝖓 *Kings of Great-Britain.*

1. King George I. enter'd *London* most magnificently on 20 *Sept.* 1714. and after the Rebellion was over *A. D.* 1716. the few *Lodges* at *London* finding themselves neglected by Sir *Christopher Wren*, thought fit to cement under a *Grand Master* as the Center of Union and Harmony, *viz.* the *Lodges* that met,

1. At the *Goose* and *Gridiron* Ale-house in St. *Paul*'s *Church-Yard.*
2. At the *Crown* Ale-house in *Parker*'s-*Lane* near *Drury-Lane.*
3. At the *Apple-Tree* Tavern in *Charles-street, Covent-Garden.*
4. At the *Rummer* and *Grapes* Tavern in *Channel-Row, Westminster.*

They and some old Brothers met at the said *Apple-Tree*, and having put into the Chair the *oldest Master* Mason (now the *Master* of a *Lodge*) they constituted themselves a Grand Lodge pro Tempore in *Due Form*, and forthwith revived the Quarterly *Communication* of the *Officers* of Lodges (call'd the 𝕲𝖗𝖆𝖓𝖉 𝕷𝖔𝖉𝖌𝖊) resolv'd to hold the *Annual* Assembly *and Feast*, and then to chuse a Grand Master from among themselves, till they should have the Honour of a *Noble Brother* at their Head.

Accordingly

On St. *John Baptist*'s Day, in the 3d Year of King George I. *A. D.* 1717. the ASSEMBLY and *Feast* of the *Free and accepted Masons* was held at the foresaid *Goose and Gridiron* Alehouse.

Before Dinner, the *oldest Master* Mason (now the *Master* of a *Lodge*) in the Chair, proposed a List of proper Candidates; and the Brethren by a Majority of Hands elected

Mr.

Mr. ANTONY SAYER Gentleman, *Grand Master of Masons*, who being forthwith in- ⎧ Capt. *Joseph Elliot*. ⎫ *Grand* vested with the Badges ⎩ Mr. *Jacob Lamball*, Carpenter, ⎭ *Wardens*. of Office and Power by the said *oldest Master*, and install'd, was duly congratulated by the Assembly who pay'd him the *Homage*.

SAYER *Grand Master* commanded the *Masters* and *Wardens* of Lodges to meet the *Grand* Officers every *Quarter* in *Communication*, * at the Place that he should appoint in his Summons sent by the *Tyler*.

* N. B. It is call'd the *Quarterly Communication*, because it should meet *Quarterly* according to antient Usage. And
When the *Grand Master* is present it is a Lodge in *Ample Form*; otherwise, only in *Due Form*, yet having the same Authority with *Ample Form*.

ASSEMBLY and *Feast* at the said Place 24 *June* 1718.

Brother *Sayer* having gather'd the Votes, after Dinner proclaim'd aloud our Brother

GEORGE PAYNE Esq; *Grand Master* of *Masons* who being duly invested, ⎧ Mr. *John Cordwell*, City Carpenter, ⎫ *Grand* install'd, congra- ⎩ Mr. *Thomas Morrice*, Stone Cutter, ⎭ *Wardens*. tulated and homaged, recommended the strict Observance of the Quarterly Communication; and desired any Brethren to bring to the Grand Lodge any old *Writings* and *Records* concerning *Masons* and *Masonry* in order to shew the Usages of antient Times: And this Year several old Copies of the *Gothic Constitutions* were produced and collated.

ASSEMBLY and *Feast* at the said Place, 24 *June* 1719.

Brother *Payne* having gather'd the Votes, after Dinner proclaim'd aloud our Reverend Brother

JOHN THEOPHILUS DESAGULIERS, L.L.D. and F.R.S. *Grand Master* of *Masons*, and be- ⎧ Mr. *Antony Sayer* foresaid, ⎫ *Grand* ing duly invested, install'd, ⎩ Mr. *Tho. Morrice* foresaid, ⎭ *Wardens*. congratulated and homaged, forthwith reviv'd the old regular and peculiar Toasts or Healths of the *Free Masons*.

Now several *old* Brothers, that had neglected the *Craft*, visited the *Lodges*; some *Noblemen* were also made Brothers, and more *new* Lodges were constituted.

ASSEMBLY and *Feast* at the foresaid Place 24 *June* 1720.

Brother *Desaguliers* having gather'd the Votes, after Dinner proclaim'd aloud

GEORGE PAYNE Esq; again *Grand Master of Masons*; who being duly invested, install'd, congratulated and homag'd, { Mr. *Thomas Hobby*, Stone-Cutter, Mr. *Rich. Ware*, Mathematician, } *Grand Wardens*. began the usual Demonstrations of Joy, Love and Harmony.

This Year, at some *private* Lodges, several very valuable *Manuscripts* (for they had nothing yet in Print) concerning the Fraternity, their Lodges, Regulations, Charges, Secrets, and Usages (particularly one writ by Mr. *Nicholas Stone* the Warden of *Inigo Jones*) were too hastily burnt by some scrupulous Brothers, that those Papers might not fall into strange Hands.

At the *Quarterly* Communication or *Grand Lodge*, in *ample* Form, on St. *John Evangelist*'s Day 1720. at the said Place

It was agreed, in order to avoid Disputes on the *Annual* Feast-Day, that the *new Grand Master* for the future shall be named and proposed to the *Grand Lodge* some time before the Feast, by the present or *old Grand Master*; and if approv'd, that the Brother proposed, if present, shall be kindly saluted; or even if absent, his Health shall be toasted as *Grand Master Elect*.

Also agreed, that for the future the *New Grand Master*, as soon as he is install'd, shall have the sole Power of appointing both his *Grand Wardens* and a *Deputy* Grand Master (now found as necessary as formerly) according to antient Custom, when *Noble* Brothers were *Grand* Masters.

Accordingly,

At the 𝕲𝖗𝖆𝖓𝖉 𝕷𝖔𝖉𝖌𝖊 in *ample* Form on *Lady-Day* 1721. at the said Place *Grand Master* PAYNE proposed for his Successor our most Noble Brother

JOHN Duke of MONTAGU, *Master* of a Lodge; who being present, was forthwith saluted *Grand Master Elect*, and his Health drank in *due* Form; when they all express'd great Joy at the happy Prospect of being again patronized by *noble Grand Masters*, as in the prosperous Times of *Free Masonry*.

PAYNE

PAYNE *Grand Master* observing the *Number* of Lodges to encrease, and that the General *Assembly* requir'd more Room, proposed the next *Assembly* and *Feast* to be held at *Stationers-Hall Ludgate-street*; which was agreed to.

Then the *Grand Wardens* were order'd, as usual, to prepare the Feast, and to take some *Stewards* to their Assistance, Brothers of Ability and Capacity, and to appoint some Brethren to attend the Tables; for that no Strangers must be there. But the *Grand* Officers not finding a proper Number of *Stewards*, our Brother Mr. Josiah Villeneau, Upholder in the *Burrough Southwark*, generously undertook the whole himself, attended by some Waiters, *Thomas Morrice, Francis Bailey*, &c.

CHAP. IV.

From *Grand Master* the Duke of MONTAGU to *Grand Master* RICHMOND.

ASSEMBLY and *Feast* at *Stationers-Hall*, 24 *June* 1721. In the 7th Year of King GEORGE I.

PAYNE *Grand Master* with his *Wardens*, the former *Grand* Officers, and the *Masters* and *Wardens* of 12 Lodges, met the *Grand Master Elect* in a *Grand Lodge* at the *King's-Arms* Tavern *St. Paul's Church-yard*, in the Morning; and having forthwith recognized their Choice of Brother MONTAGU, they made some new Brothers, particularly the noble PHILIP Lord *Stanhope*, now Earl of *Chesterfield*: And from thence they marched on Foot to the *Hall* in proper Clothing and due Form; where they were joyfully receiv'd by about 150 *true* and *faithful*, all clothed.

After Grace said, they sat down in the antient Manner of *Masons* to a very elegant Feast, and dined with Joy and Gladness. After Dinner and Grace said,

Brother

Brother PAYNE the old *Grand Master* made the *first Procession* round the *Hall*, and when return'd, he proclaim'd aloud the most noble Prince and our Brother. [See the Form of it at *Richmond*, Page 117.]

1. JOHN MONTAGU Duke of Montagu GRAND MASTER of *Masons*! and Brother *Payne* having invested his *Grace's* WORSHIP with the Ensigns and Badges of his Office and Authority, install'd him in *Solomon*'s Chair and sat down on his Right Hand; while the Assembly own'd the Duke's Authority with due Homage and joyful Congratulations, upon this Revival of the *Prosperity* of *Masonry*.

MONTAGU *G. Master*, immediately call'd forth (without naming him before) as it were carelesly, John Beal, M. D. as his *Deputy Grand Master*, whom Brother *Payne* invested, and install'd him in *Hiram Abbiff*'s Chair on the *Grand Master's Left Hand*.

In like Manner his *Worship* call'd forth and appointed, Mr. *Josiah Villeneau* Mr. *Thomas Morrice* Grand Wardens. who were invested and install'd by the last *Grand* Wardens.

Upon which the *Deputy* and *Wardens* were saluted and congratulated as usual.

Then MONTAGU *G. Master*, with his *Officers* and the *old Officers*, having made the 2d *Procession* round the *Hall*, Brother Desaguliers made an eloquent Oration about *Masons* and *Masonry*: And after Great Harmony, the Effect of brotherly Love, the *Grand Master* thank'd Brother *Villeneau* for his Care of the *Feast*, and order'd him as *Warden* to close the *Lodge* in good Time.

—The Grand Lodge in *ample* Form on 29 *Sept.* 1721. at *King's-Arms* foresaid, with the former *Grand* Officers and those of 16 *Lodges*.

His Grace's *Worship* and the *Lodge* finding Fault with all the Copies of the *old Gothic Constitutions*, order'd Brother *James Anderson*, A. M. to digest the same in a new and better Method.

—The Grand Lodge in *ample* Form on St. JOHN's Day 27 *Dec.* 1721. at the said *King's Arms*, with former *Grand* Officers and those of 20 *Lodges*.

MONTAGU *Grand Master*, at the Desire of the *Lodge*, appointed 14 learned Brothers to examine Brother *Anderson*'s Manuscript, and to make Report. This *Communication* was made very entertaining by the Lectures of some *old Masons*.

—𝕲𝖗𝖆𝖓𝖉 𝕷𝖔𝖉𝖌𝖊 at the *Fountain Strand*, in ample Form 25 *March* 1722. with former *Grand* Officers and those of 24 *Lodges*.

The said *Committee* of 14 reported that they had perused Brother *Anderson*'s Manuscript, *viz.* the *History, Charges, Regulations and Master's Song*, and after some Amendments had approv'd of it: Upon which the *Lodge* desir'd the *Grand Master* to order it to be printed. Mean while

Ingenious Men of all Faculties and Stations being convinced that the *Cement* of the *Lodge* was Love and Friendship, earnestly requested to be made *Masons*, affecting this amicable Fraternity more than other Societies then often disturbed by warm Disputes.

Grand Master MONTAGU's good Government inclin'd the better Sort to continue him in the Chair another Year; and therefore they delay'd to prepare the *Feast*.

But *Philip* Duke of *Wharton* lately made a Brother, tho' not the *Master* of a *Lodge*, being ambitious of the Chair, got a Number of Others to meet him at *Stationers-Hall* 24 *June* 1722. and having no *Grand* Officers, they put in the Chair the *oldest Master Mason* (who was not the *present* Master of a *Lodge*, also irregular) and without the usual decent Ceremonials, the said *old Mason* proclaim'd aloud

Philip Wharton Duke of *Wharton* Grand Master of *Masons*, and Mr. *Joshua Timson*, Blacksmith, Mr. *William Hawkins*, Mason, *Grand Wardens*, but his Grace appointed no *Deputy*, nor was the *Lodge* opened and closed in due Form.

Therefore the *noble* Brothers and all those that would not countenance Irregularities, disown'd *Wharton*'s Authority, till worthy Brother MONTAGU heal'd the Breach of Harmony, by summoning

— The 𝕲𝖗𝖆𝖓𝖉 𝕷𝖔𝖉𝖌𝖊 to meet 17 *January* 172¾. at the *King's-Arms* foresaid, where the *Duke* of *Wharton* promising to be *True* and *Faithful*, *Deputy Grand* Master *Beal* proclaim'd aloud the most noble Prince and our Brother.

II. PHILIP

(115)

II. PHILIP WHARTON Duke of *Wharton* GRAND MASTER of *Masons*, who appointed Dr. Desaguliers the *Deputy Grand* Master,

{ *Joshua Timson*, foresaid, } *Grand* { for *Hawkins* demitted as al-
{ *James Anderson*, A. M. } *Wardens*. { ways out of Town.

When former *Grand* Officers, with those of 25 *Lodges* paid their Homage.

G. Warden *Anderson* produced the *new* Book of *Constitutions* now in Print, which was again approv'd, with the Addition of the *antient Manner of Constituting a Lodge.*

Now *Masonry* flourish'd in Harmony, Reputation and Numbers; many Noblemen and Gentlemen of the first Rank desir'd to be admitted into the *Fraternity*, besides other Learned Men, Merchants, Clergymen and Tradesmen, who found a *Lodge* to be a safe and pleasant Relaxation from Intense Study or the Hurry of Business, without Politicks or Party. Therefore the *Grand Master* was obliged to constitute more *new Lodges*, and was very assiduous in *visiting* the *Lodges* every Week with his *Deputy* and *Wardens*; and his *Worship* was well pleas'd with their kind and respectful Manner of receiving him, as they were with his affable and clever Conversation.

— Grand Lodge in *ample* Form, 25 *April* 1723. at the *White-Lion Cornhill*, with former *Grand* Officers and those of 30 *Lodges* call'd over by G. Warden *Anderson*, for no *Secretary* was yet appointed. When

WHARTON *Grand Master* proposed for his Successor the Earl of *Dalkeith* (now *Duke of Buckleugh*) *Master* of a *Lodge*, who was unanimously approv'd and duly saluted as *Grand Master Elect*.

The *Tickets* for the next *Feast* were order'd to be Ten Shillings each, impress'd from a curious *Copper Plate*, and seal'd with the G. *Master's Seal* of Office, to be disposed of by the *Grand Wardens* and the *Stewards*.

ASSEMBLY and *Feast* on Monday 24 *June* 1723. at *Merchant-Taylors-Hall*.

The *Committee* appointed to keep out *Cowans* came early, and the *Stewards* to receive the *Tickets* and direct the Servants.

(116)

WHARTON *Grand Master* came attended by some eminent Brothers in their Coaches; and forthwith walking with his *Deputy* and *Wardens* into the *Lodge-Room*, he sent for the *Masters* and *Wardens* of *Lodges*, who came from the *Hall* and form'd the *Grand Lodge* call'd over by Brother *William Cowper*, Esq; now appointed *Secretary*.

Some observing that Brother *Dalkeith* was now in *Scotland*, proposed to the *G. Master* to name another for Successor; but 𝔇alkeith's *Wardens* declar'd that his Lordship would soon return. Adjourn'd to Dinner.

About 400 Free Masons, all duly clothed, dined elegantly in due Form.

See its Description at *Richmond*, G. M. After Dinner, Brother WHARTON made the *first Procession* round the Tables, and when return'd, proclaim'd aloud our noble Brother.

III. FRANCIS SCOT Earl of *Dalkeith* 𝔊rand 𝔐aster of *Masons*. He had left with the *Wardens* of his *Lodge* a Power to appoint in his Name

Dr. 𝔇esaguliers his ⎰ *Francis Sorrell*, Esq; ⎱ *Grand- Deputy Grand Master*, ⎱ *John Senex* Bookseller, ⎰ *Wardens*. who fill'd the Chair; and having thank'd the *Stewards*, order'd *Grand* Warden *Sorell* to close the Lodge in good Time. *

— 𝔊rand 𝔏odge at the *Crown* in *Threadneedle-street* 25 *Nov.* 1723. in *ample* Form, with former *Grand* Officers and Those of 30 *Lodges*. They agreed on several Things for the Good of *Masonry*, which, with other Things afterwards determin'd at *Grand* Lodges, are dispers'd in the *New Regulations, Committee of Charity*, &c. below: and special Care was taken to prevent Disturbance and preserve Harmony on *Feast-Days*.

— 𝔊rand 𝔏odge in *ample* Form at the foresaid *Crown* 19 *Feb.* 1723/4. with former G. *Officers* and Those of 26 *Lodges*.

— 𝔊rand 𝔏odge in *ample* Form at the *Crown* foresaid 28 *April* 1724. with former G. *Officers* and Those of 31 *Lodges*.

---

* Stewards that acted at the Feast on 24 *June* 1723. and were publickly thank'd

Mr. *Henry Prude*,	Capt. *Benjamin Hodges*,
Mr. *Giles Clutterbuck*,	Mr. *Edward Lambert*,
Mr. *John Shepherd*,	Mr. *Charles Kent*.

𝔇alkeith

Dalkeith *G. Master* proposed for his Successor the Duke of *Richmond* and *Lennox* (now also Duke *d'Aubigny*) Master of a *Lodge*, who was joyfully saluted *Grand Master Elect*.

CHAP. V.
From *Grand Master* RICHMOND to *Grand Master* NORFOLK.

ASSEMBLY and *Feast* at *Merchant-Taylors-Hall* on 24 *June* 1724.

DALKEITH *Grand Master* with his *Deputy* and *Wardens* waited on Brother *Richmond* in the Morning at *Whitehall*, who with many Brothers duly clothed, proceeded in Coaches from the *West* to the *East*, and were handsomely received at the *Hall* by a vast *Assembly*. The *Grand Lodge* met, and having confirm'd their Choice of Brother *Richmond*, adjourn'd to Dinner. After Dinner G. Master DALKEITH made the *first* Procession round the Tables, *viz*.

Brother *Clinch* to clear the Way.
The *Stewards* 2 and 2 a Breast with *white* Rods. | This, as a Specimen, to avoid Repetitions.
Secretary COWPER with the *Bag*, and on his Left
the *Master* of a *Lodge* with *One* Great *Light*.
Two other *Great Lights* born by two *Masters* of *Lodges*.
Former *Grand Wardens* proceeding one by one, according to *Juniority*.
Former *Grand Masters* proceeding, according to *Juniority*.
SOREL and SENEX the two *Grand Wardens*.
DESAGULIERS D. G. *Master* alone.

On the *Left* Hand.	On the *Right* Hand.
The *Sword* carried by the *Master* of the *Lodge* to which the *Sword* belong'd.	The Book of *Constitutions* on a Cushion carried by the *Master* of the *Senior Lodge*.
RICHMOND *Grand Master Elect*.	DALKEITH *Grand Master*.

During the *Procession*, 3 Times round the *Tables*, the Brethren stood up and fac'd about with the *regular* Salutations; and when return'd

Brother

(118)

Brother *Dalkeith* ſtood up, and bowing to the *Aſſembly*, thank'd 'em for the Honour he had of being their *Grand Maſter*, and then proclaim'd aloud the moſt noble Prince and our Brother

IV. CHARLES LENNOS Duke of *Richmond* and *Lennox* 𝕲𝖗𝖆𝖓𝖉 𝕸𝖆𝖘𝖙𝖊𝖗 of *Maſons*!

The *Duke* having bow'd to the *Aſſembly*, Brother DALKEITH inveſted him with the proper *Enſigns* and *Badges* of his Office and Authority, inſtall'd him in *Solomon*'s Chair, and wiſhing him all Proſperity, ſat down on his Right Hand. Upon which the Aſſembly join'd in due Homage, affectionate Congratulations and other Signs of Joy.

RICHMOND *Grand Maſter* ſtanding up, call'd forth (as it were by Accident) and appointed

𝕸𝖆𝖗𝖙𝖎𝖓 𝕱𝖔𝖑𝖐𝖊𝖘, Eſq; his D. G. *Maſter*, { *George Payne* Eſq; formerly G.M. *Francis Sorell* late G. Warden, } Grand Wardens. inveſted and inſtall'd by the laſt Deputy in the Chair of *Hiram Abbif*.

William Cowper Eſq; was continued *Secretary* by the G. Maſter's returning him the Books, and all of 'em were formally congratulated by the *Aſſembly*.*

RICHMOND *Grand Maſter* made the 2d *Proceſſion* round the Tables like the *Firſt*, except that Brother DALKEITH walked firſt as the youngeſt late *Grand Maſter*, cloſe after the former *Grand Wardens*; and RICHMOND walk'd *alone* laſt of all, with his *Deputy* immediately before him, and his *two G. Wardens* before the *Deputy*, and before them the *Sword* and *Conſtitutions*.

When return'd,

The G. *Maſter* began to toaſt the regular *Healths*, and due Reſpects to our noble Brothers preſent and abſent, particularly to our laſt good *Grand Maſter* DALKEITH.

After which, the uſual Expreſſions of Joy, Love and Friendſhip

---
*Stewards that acted at the Feaſt on 24 *June* 1723. and were publickly thank'd.

Theſe firſt 6 acted at the laſt Feaſt.
{ Mr. *Henry Prude*.
Capt. *Benjamin Hodges*.
Mr. *Giles Clutterbuck*.
Mr. *John Shepherd*.
Mr. *Edward Lambert*.
Mr. *Charles Kent*. }

Capt. *Samuel Tuffnell*.
Mr. *Giles Taylor*.
Capt. *Nathaniel Smith*.
Mr. *Richard Crofts*.
Mr. *Peter Paul Kemp*.
Mr. *North Stainer*.

went

went round; and the *Assembly* was most agreeably entertain'd with Orations, Musick and Mason Songs, till the *G. Master* order'd his Warden *Payne* to close the *Lodge* in good Time.

Now MASONRY was illustrious at home and abroad, and *Lodges* multiplied.

— **Grand Lodge** in *ample* Form at the *Crown* foresaid, 21 *Nov.* 1724. with former *Grand* Officers and Those of 40 *Lodges*. When Our noble Brother DALKEITH, in Pursuance of *Regulation* XIII. proposed a *Fund* of Gene- | See the Committee of *Charity*. ral Charity for poor Brothers, which was agreed to by all.

— **Grand Lodge** in *ample* Form at the *Bell Westminster* 17 *March* 172⅘. with former G. Officers and Those of 36 *Lodges*.

— **Grand Lodge** in *due* Form at the *Devil Temple-Bar* 20 *May* 1725, with former *G. Officers* and those of 38 *Lodges*. D. G. *Master* FOLKES in the Chair prompted a most agreeable *Communication*.

Grand Lodge in *Due* Form at the *Crown* foresaid on 24 *June* 1725. when the *Grand* Officers were continued Six Months longer.

— **Grand Lodge** in *ample* Form at the *Bell* foresaid 27 *Nov.* 1725. with former *G. Officers* and Those of 49 *Lodges*. When RICHMOND G. *Master* proposed for his Successor the Lord *Paisley* (now Earl of *Abercorn*) *Master* of a *Lodge*, who was gladly saluted as *Grand Master Elect*. And no *Stewards* being appointed, G. M. RICHMOND desired our Brother *John James Heidegger* to prepare the *Feast* in the best Manner.

ASSEMBLY and *Feast* at *Merchant-Taylor's-Hall* on St. JOHN's Day 27 *Dec.* 1725.

Lord PAISLEY being in the Country, had by Letter made the *Duke* of RICHMOND his *Proxy*, and all Things being regularly transacted as above, Brother *Richmond* proclaim'd aloud our noble Brother

V. JAMES HAMILTON Lord *Paisley* **Grand Master** of *Masons*. Brother RICHMOND as *Proxy* continued in the Chair, and in G. *Master* PAISLEY's Name appointed

Dr. **Desaguliers** a- Colonel *Daniel Houghton*;   } Grand gain D. G. *Master*,   Sir *Thomas Prendergast*, Bart. } Wardens. The *Secretary* was continued, and in both Processions the DUKE walk'd *alone*. Brother

Brother *Heidegger* was thank'd for the elegant and sumptuous Feast, and the G. *Master* order'd his Warden *Houghton* to close the *Lodge* in good Time.

— **Grand Lodge** in ample Form at the *Bell* foresaid on *Monday* 28 Feb. 1725/6 with former G. *Officers* and Those of 36 *Lodges*.

— **Grand Lodge** in *ample* Form at the *Crown* foresaid, on *Monday* 12 *Dec.* 1726. with former G. *Officers* and those of 30 *Lodges*.

In this long Interval the D. G. *Master* duly visited the *Lodges* till the *Principal* came to Town, who now proposed for his Successor the *Earl* of *Inchiquin* Master of a *Lodge* and he was gladly saluted as *Grand Master Elect*.

No *Stewards*; but Brother *Edward Lambert* undertook to prepare the *Feast*.

ASSEMBLY and *Feast* at *Mercer's-Hall* on *Monday* 27 Feb. 1726/7. All Things being regularly transacted as above, Brother *Pailey* proclaim'd aloud our noble Brother

VI. WILLIAM O BRIEN Earl of *Inchiquin* **Grand Master** of *Masons*, who appointed

William Cowper Esq; *(formerly Secretary)* his D. G. *Master*.
{ *Alexander Choke* Esq; } Grand { Mr. *Edw. Wilson*, was made
{ *William Burdon* Esq; } *Wardens*. { *Secretary*, and Brother *Lambert* was thank'd for his Care of the *Feast*.

— **Grand Lodge** in *ample* Form at the *Crown* foresaid on *Wednesday* 10 *May* 1727. with former G. *Officers* and Those of 40 *Lodges*, in great Harmony.

During the *Mastership* of INCHIQUIN

King GEORGE I. having reign'd near 13 Years, died at *Osnabruck* where he was born, in his Way to *Hannover*, where he was buried, aged 67 Years, on 11 *June* 1727. when his Son succeeded, *viz.*

---

2. King GEORGE II. aged 44 Years, who with his Queen CAROLINE were Crown'd at *Westminster* on 11 *Oct.* 1727.

In the last Reign sundry of the 50 *new Churches* in the Suburbs of *London* were built in a fine *Stile* upon the Parliamentary Fund, particularly the beautiful St. *Mary le Strand*. But
St.

St. *Martin*'s *in Campis* was at the Charge of the Parishioners rebuilt strong and regular: And it being a *Royal* Parish *Church*, King GEORGE I. sent his Lord *Almoner* and *Surveyor* General, attended by Brother *Gib*, (the Architect of that grand Pile) with many *Free Masons*, in a solemn Procession from the Palace, to level the *Footstone* of the *South East* Corner, by giving it 3 Great Knocks with a Mallet in the King's Name, and laying upon it a Purse of 100 *Guineas*: when the Trumpets sounded, all join'd in joyful Acclamations, and the *Craftsmen* went to the Tavern to drink 𝕿𝖔 𝖙𝖍𝖊 𝕶𝖎𝖓𝖌 𝖆𝖓𝖉 𝖙𝖍𝖊 𝕮𝖗𝖆𝖋𝖙.

The *Inscription* below was cut in the Stone and Lead put upon it. *

In this Reign also the *Art* was display'd in the *New Buildings* in and about *Hanover-Square*, as in the net Houses of the Dukes of *Bolton*, *Montrose*, and *Roxborough*, of Sir *Robert Sutton* and General *Wade*, of the Earl of *Burlington* in *Picadilly*, of the Duke of *Chandois* at *Canons* near *Edger*, the Court of the *Rolls*, *Wanstead-House* in *Epping-Forest* by the Earl of *Tilney*, *Houghton-Hall* in

---

D. S.
SERENISSIMUS REX GEORGIUS
PER DEPUTATUM SUUM
REVERENDUM ADMODUM IN CHRISTO PATREM
RICHARDUM EPISCOPUM SARISBURIENSEM
SUMMUM SUUM ELEEMOSINARIUM
ADSISTENTE (REGIS JUSSU)
DOMINO THOMA HEWET EQUITE AURATO
ÆDIFICIORUM REGIORUM CURATORI PRINCIPALI
PRIMUM HUJUS ECCLESIÆ LAPIDEM
POSUIT
MARTII 19. ANNO DOMINI 1721.
ANNOQUE REGNI SUI OCTAVO.

(122)

Norfolk by Sir *Robert Walpole* Knight of the Garter, Sir *Gregory Page*'s House on *Blackheath*, and many more either finish'd or founded before the King's Death that shew a fine Improvement in the *Royal Art*.

In the *First* Year of King George II.

— INCHIQUIN *Grand Master* assembled the *Grand* Lodge in *Quarterly* Communication, with former *G. Officers* and Those of 40 *Lodges* at the *Devil Temple-Bar* on *Saturday* 24 *June* 1727.

— 𝕲𝖗𝖆𝖓𝖉 𝕷𝖔𝖉𝖌𝖊 in *Due* Form at the *Bell* foresaid on *Saturday* 28 *Oct.* 1727. with former *G. Officers* and Those of 35 *Lodges*. D. G. *Master* COWPER in the Chair.

— 𝕲𝖗𝖆𝖓𝖉 𝕷𝖔𝖉𝖌𝖊 in *Due* Form at the *Devil* foresaid on *Tuesday* 19 *Dec.* 1727. with former *G. Officers* and those of only 18 *Lodges*. D. G. *Master* COWPER in the Chair, eloquently excused the *Grand Master*'s Absence in *Ireland*, and his sudden Calling them together; for that the *Feast* drew nigh, and that the *Grand Master* had, by Letter, impower'd him to propose, for his Successor, the Lord *Colerane* Master of a *Lodge*, who was forthwith saluted as *Grand Master Elect*.

No *Stewards* being appointed, Brother *Lambert* again undertook to prepare the Feast.

ASSEMBLY and *Feast* at *Mercer's-Hall* on St. JOHN's Day *Wednesday* 27 *Dec.* 1727. All Things being regularly transacted as above, D. *Grand Master* COWPER proclaim'd aloud our noble Brother

VII. HENRY HARE Lord *Colerane* 𝕲𝖗𝖆𝖓𝖉 𝕸𝖆𝖘𝖙𝖊𝖗 of *Masons*! who appointed 𝕬𝖑𝖊𝖝𝖆𝖓𝖉𝖊𝖗 𝕮𝖍𝖔𝖐𝖊 Esq; *Deputy Grand Master*,
{ *Nathaniel Blakerby*, Esq; } *Grand*
{ Mr. *Joseph Highmore* Painter, } *Wardens*.

Mr. *William Reid* was made *Secretary*, and Brother *Lambert* was thank'd for his Care.

𝕲𝖗𝖆𝖓𝖉 𝕷𝖔𝖉𝖌𝖊 in *Ample* Form at the *Crown* foresaid on *Wednesday* 17 *April* 1728. with former *G. Officers* and Those of 27 *Lodges*. — 𝕲𝖗𝖆𝖓𝖉

— **Grand Lodge** in *Ample* Form at the *King's-Arms* foresaid on *Tuesday* 25 *June* 1728. with former G. *Officers* and Those of 28 *Lodges*.

— **Grand Lodge** in *Due* Form at the *Queen's-Head* in *Great Queen-street* on *Tuesday* 26 *Nov.* 1728. with the Earl of INCHIQUIN and other former G. *Officers* and Those of 30 *Lodges*. D. G. *Master* **Choke** in the Chair excused the *Grand Master's* Absence, and in his Name proposed for Successor the Lord Viscount *Kingston* Master of a *Lodge*, who was well recommended also by Brother INCHIQUIN, and was forthwith saluted as *Grand Master Elect*.

Brother *Desaguliers* moved to revive the *Office* of *Stewards* to assist the *Grand Wardens* in preparing the *Feast*, and that their Number be 12, which was readily agreed to. See their Names in the Margin below. *

A S E M B L Y and *Feast* at *Mercer's-Hall* on St. JOHN's Day *Friday* 27 *Dec.* 1728. D. *Grand Master* CHOKE with his *Wardens*, several *noble* Brothers, former *Grand* Officers, and many Brethren, duly clothed, attended the *Grand Master Elect* in Coaches from his Lordship's House in *Leicester-Square* to the Hall *Eastward*: And all Things being regularly transacted as above, D.G. M. *Choke* proclaim'd aloud our noble Brother

VIII. JAMES KING Lord Viscount *Kingston* **Grand Master** of *Masons!* who appointed **Nathaniel Blakerby** Esq; D. G. *Master*, {Sir *James Thornhill*,} *Grand* {and the *Secretary* was continued. Mr *Martin O Connor*,} *Wardens*,

— **Grand Lodge** in *Ample* Form at the 3 Tons *Swithin's-Alley* near the *Royal-Exchange* 27 March 1729. with former G. *Officers* and Those of 31 *Lodges*.

---

* **Stewards** that acted on 27 *Dec.* 1728. and were publickly thank'd.

1. Mr. *John Revis*.
2. Mr. *Edwin Ward*.
3. Mr. *Samuel Stead*.
4. Mr. *Theodore Cheriholm*.
5. Mr. *William Benn*.
6. Mr. *Gerard Hatley*.
7. Mr. *William Wilson*.
8. Mr. *William Tew*.
9. Mr. *William Hopkins*.
10. Mr. *Thomas Reason*.
11. Mr. *Thomas Alford*.
12. Mr. *H. Smart*.

(124)

—Grand Lodge in *Due* Form at the *King's-Arms* foresaid on *Friday* 11 *July* 1729. with former *G. Officers* and Those of 26 *Lodges*. D. G. M. BLAKERBY was in the Chair.

Grand Lodge in *Ample* Form at the *Devil* foresaid on *Tuesday* 25 *Nov*. 1729. with former *G. Officers* and Those of 27 *Lodges*.

KINGSTON *Grand Master* at his own Cost provided a curious *Pedestal*, and a rich *Cushion* with golden *Knops* and *Fringes* for the *Top* of the *Pedestal*; a fine *Velvet Bag* for the *Secretary*, and a Badge of *Two golden Pens a-cross* on his Breast: For which very handsome Presents the *Lodge* return'd hearty Thanks in solemn Manner.

Grand Lodge in *Due* Form at the *Devil* foresaid on St. JOHN's Day, *Saturday* 27 *Dec*. 1729. with our noble Brother INCHIQUIN and other former *G. Officers*, and Those of 32 *Lodges*: when **Blakerby** D. G. Master in the Chair, in the Grand Master's Name and by his Letter, proposed for Successor the Duke of *Norfolk* Master of a *Lodge*, who was joyfully saluted *Grand Master Elect*.

CHAP. VI.

From *Grand Master* NORFOLK to *Grand Master* CRAUFURD.

ASSEMBLY and *Feast* at *Merchant-Taylor's-Hall* on *Thursday*, 29 *Jan*. 17$\frac{19}{30}$. in the 3d Year of King GEORGE II.

KINGSTON *Grand Master* with his *Deputy* and *Wardens*, attended the *Grand Master Elect* in the Morning, at his Grace's House in St. *James's-Square*; where he was met by a vast Number of Brothers duly clothed, and from thence they went to the Hall *Eastward* in the following *Procession* of March, viz.

<small>This is a Specimen to avoid Repetitions.</small>

Brother

(125)
Brother *Johnson* to clear the Way.
* *Six* of the *Stewards* clothed proper with their *Badges* and *White Rods*, Two in each Chariot.
Brothers without Distinction duly clothed, in Gentlemen's Coaches.
The *noble* and *eminent* Brethren duly clothed, in their own Chariots.
Former *Grand Officers* not noble, clothed proper, in Gentlemens Coaches.
Former *noble Grand Masters* clothed proper, in their own Chariots.
The *Secretary alone* with his *Badge* and *Bag*, clothed, in a Chariot.
The Two *GrandWardens* clothed proper with their Badges, in one Chariot.
The D. G. *Master alone* clothed proper with his Badge in a Chariot.
KINGSTON **Grand** *Master* clothed proper with his Badge. ⎫
NORFOLK G. M. *Elect* clothed only as a *Mason*. ⎭ in one Coach.
The Duke of *Norfolk*'s Coach of State empty.
The *Stewards* halted at *Charing-Cross* till the Messenger brought Orders to move on slowly, and till the Rest follow'd: And when the *Grand Master* moved from the Square, Brother *John Pyne* the Marshal made haste to the *Hall* to conduct the
Procession of **Entry** at the *Hall-Gate*, viz.
The 12 *Stewards* standing, 6 on each Side of the Passage, with their *White Rods*, made a Lane.
Brother *Johnson* to clear the Way.
Former *Grand Wardens* walk'd one by one according to *Juniority*.
Former *D. Grand Masters* walk'd one by one according to *Juniority*.
Former *Grand Masters* by *Juniority*, viz.

---

* **Stewards** that acted on 29 *January* 17$\frac{29}{30}$.

1. Mr. *John Revis*.	7. Mr. *Gerard Hatley*.	⎫ The *first Eight* acted at the *last Feast*, and they were all publickly thank'd for their Care.
2. Mr. *Samuel Stead*.	8. Mr. *William Tew*.	
3. Mr. *Edwin Ward*.	9. Mr. —— *Pread*	
4. Mr. *William Wilson*	10. Mr. ——*Bardo*, Senior.	
5. Mr. *William Hopkins*	11. Mr. ——*Bardo*, Junior.	
6. Mr. *Thomas Reason*.	12. Mr. *Charles Hoar*.	⎭

Lord

(126)

Lord COLERANE, *Earl* of INCHIQUIN, *Lord* PAISLEY, *Duke* of RICHMOND, *Earl* of DALKEITH, *Duke* of MONTAGU, Dr. DESAGULIERS, GEORGE PAYNE Efq; and Mr. ANTONY SAYER.

Then the *Stewards* clofed, walking Two and Two.
The *Secretary* alone.
The Two *Grand Wardens* together.
The *D. Grand Mafter* alone.

On the *Left* Hand.	On the *Right* Hand.
The 𝕾𝖜𝖔𝖗𝖉 born by the *Mafter* of the *Lodge* to which it be-long'd.	The *Book* of CONSTITUTIONS on the fine *Cufhion* carried by the *Mafter* of the *Senior Lodge*.
NORFOLK *Grand Mafter Elect*.	KINGSTON *Grand Mafter*.

Marfhal Pyne with his *Truncheon Blew*, tipt with *Gold*.

In this Order they decently walk'd into the *Lodge Room* (while the Others walk'd into the *Hall*) and there the *Mafters* and *Wardens* of Lodges received their G. MASTER with Joy and Reverence in due Form. He fat down in his Chair before the *Pedeftal*, cover'd with the rich *Cufhion*, upon which were laid the *Conftitutions* and the *Sword*; and the G. M. *Elect* on his Right Hand.

After opening the *Lodge*, the laft Minutes were read by the *Secretary*, and the Election of Brother *Norfolk* was folemnly recogniz'd.

Adjourn'd to Dinner, a *Grand Feaft* indeed!

As at *Richmond*, Page 117. After Dinner and the *firft* Proceffion round the *Tables*, Brother *Kingfton* proclaim'd aloud the moft noble *Prince*, the *firft* Duke, Marquis and Earl of *Great Britain*, and our Brother

IX. THOMAS HOWARD Duke of *Norfolk* 𝕲𝖗𝖆𝖓𝖉 𝕸𝖆𝖘𝖙𝖊𝖗 of *Mafons!* and having invefted him and inftall'd him in *Solomon*'s Chair, fat down on his Right Hand. Upon which the *Affembly* join'd in their Homage and Congratulations.

NORFOLK *Grand Mafter* forthwith appointed

𝕹𝖆𝖙𝖍𝖆𝖓𝖎𝖊𝖑 𝕭𝖑𝖆𝖐𝖊𝖗𝖇𝖞 Efq; to continue D. G. M.
The *Secretary* was continued.

Col. *Geo. Carpenter*, now Lord *Carpenter*,
Tho. Batfon Efq; Counfellor at Law,

} Grand *Wardens*. And

And having made the 2d *Proceffion* round the Tables (as at *Richmond)* great Harmony abounded, till the G. Mafter order'd G. Warden *Carpenter* to clofe the Lodge in good Time.

— 𝕲𝖗𝖆𝖓𝖉 𝕷𝖔𝖉𝖌𝖊 in *Ample* Form at the *Devil* forefaid on *Tuefday* 21 *April* 1730. with the noble Brothers *Richmond, Inchiquin, Kingfton, Colerane,* and other former *G. Officers,* with thofe of 31 *Lodges.* Much Time was fpent in receiving and beftowing Charity.

𝕲𝖗𝖆𝖓𝖉 𝕷𝖔𝖉𝖌𝖊 in *Due* Form at the *Devil* forefaid on *Friday* 28 *Aug.* 1730. with former *G. Officers* and Thofe of 34 *Lodges.* D. G. *Mafter* BLAKERBY in the Chair.

— 𝕲𝖗𝖆𝖓𝖉 𝕷𝖔𝖉𝖌𝖊 in *Due* Form at the *King's-Arms* forefaid on *Tuefday* 15 *Dec.* 1730. with our noble Brother *Colerane* and other former *G. Officers* and Thofe of 41 *Lodges.* D. G. *Mafter* BLAKERBY in the Chair, moved to poftpone the *Feaft,* the 𝕲𝖗𝖆𝖓𝖉 *Mafter* being at *Venice,* which was agreed to.

— 𝕲𝖗𝖆𝖓𝖉 𝕷𝖔𝖉𝖌𝖊 in *Due* Form at the *Devil* forefaid 29 *Jan.* 173⁰⁄₁. with former *G. Officers* and Thofe of 31 *Lodges.* D. G. *Mafter* BLAKERBY acquainted the *Lodge,* that tho' our Right Worfhipful G. MASTER was now at *Venice,* he was not unmindful of us, but had fent us 3 kind Prefents, *viz.*

1. TWENTY POUNDS to the Fund of *Mafons Charity,* See the *Conftitution* of it, below.

2. A Large *Folio* Book of the fineft Writing Paper for the Records of the *Grand Lodge,* moft richly bound in *Turkey* and guilded, and on the Frontifpiece in Vellum, the *Arms* of *Norfolk* amply difplay'd with a *Latin* Infcription of his noble *Titles.*

3. The *Old Trufty Sword* of GUSTAVUS ADOLPHUS King of *Sweden,* that was wore next by his Succeffor in War the brave 𝕭𝖊𝖗𝖓𝖆𝖗𝖉 Duke of *Sax-Weimar,* with both their Names on the Blade; which the *Grand Mafter* had order'd Brother *George Moody* (the King's Sword-Cutler) to adorn richly with the *Arms* of *Norfolk* in Silver on the Scabbard; in order to be the *Grand Mafter's* 𝕾𝖜𝖔𝖗𝖉 of *State* for the future.

The *Lodge* exprefs'd their grateful Acceptance in their own agreeable Manner. The Feaft was again poftponed.

𝕲𝖗𝖆𝖓𝖉

— 𝕲𝖗𝖆𝖓𝖉 𝕷𝖔𝖉𝖌𝖊 in *Due* Form at the *Devil* foresaid on *Wednesday* 17 *March* 173⁰/₁. with our Brothers RICHMOND and COLERANE and other former *G. Officers*, Lord LOVELL and the Officers of 29 *Lodges*, when D. G. M. BLAKERBY in the Chair proposed (in the *Grand Master's* Name) for Successor, the *Lord Lovel* Master of a *Lodge*, who was saluted *Grand Master Elect*.

ASSEMBLY and *Feast* at *Mercer's-Hall* 27 *March* 1731. The *Procession* of *March* was from Lord *Lovell's* House in *Great Russel-street Bloomsbury Eastward* to the *Hall*: But Lord LOVEL being ill of an Ague, return'd home, and left Lord COLERANE his Proxy for the Day. All Things being regularly transacted as above,

D. G. Master *Blakerby* proclaim'd aloud our noble Brother

X. THOMAS COOK Lord *Lovel* 𝕲𝖗𝖆𝖓𝖉 𝕸𝖆𝖘𝖙𝖊𝖗 of *Masons*: and Lord *Colerane* being invested in his Name, appointed

𝕿𝖍𝖔𝖒𝖆𝖘 𝕭𝖆𝖙𝖘𝖔𝖓 foresaid ⎰ *George Dowglas*, M. D. ⎱ Grand
Deputy Grand Master,   ⎱ *James Chambers*, Esq; ⎰ Wardens.

The *Secretary* was continued, and Brother *George Moody* was appointed *Sword-Bearer*. * See the *Stewards* in the Margin below.

— 𝕲𝖗𝖆𝖓𝖉 𝕷𝖔𝖉𝖌𝖊 in *Ample* Form at the *Rose* in *Mary-la-Bonne* on *Friday* 14 *May* 1731. with the noble Brothers NORFOLK, INCHIQUIN, COLERANE, and other former *G. Officers*, and Those of 37 *Lodges*. When LOVEL *Grand Master* moved that the *Lodge* should now return Thanks to kind Brother *Norfolk* for his *noble* Presents to the *Fraternity*; which was forthwith done in solemn Form, and receiv'd by the *Duke* with Brotherly Affection.

---

* 𝕾𝖙𝖊𝖜𝖆𝖗𝖉𝖘 that acted on 27 *March* 1731. who were all publickly thank'd.
  1. *George Dowglas*, M. D. | 7. Mr. *John Haines*.
  2. *James Chambers*, | 8. Mr. *William Millward*.
  3. *Thomas Moor*,   Esqs;   9. Mr. *Roger Lacy*
  4. *John Atwood*,   10. Mr. *Charles Trinquand*.
  5. *Thomas Durant*, | 11. Mr. *John Calcot*,
  6. Mr. *George Page*, | 12. Mr. *John King*.

His *Royal Highness* FRANCIS Duke of *Lorrain* (now *Grand Duke* of TUSCANY) at the *Hague* was made an *Enter'd Prentice* and *Fellow Craft*, by Virtue of a *Deputation* for a *Lodge* there, consisting of Rev. Dr. DESAGULIERS *Master*, { *John Stanhope*, Esq; *Jn. Holtzendorf*, Esq; } *Grand Wardens*. and the other Brethren, *viz.* PHILIP STANHOPE Earl of *Chesterfield* Lord Ambassador,— *Strickland* Esq; Nephew to the Bishop of *Namur*, Mr. *Benjamin Hadley* and an *Hollandish* Brother.

Our said *Royal* Brother LORRAIN coming to *England* this Year, *Grand Master* LOVEL formed an Occasional Lodge at Sir *Robert Walpole*'s House of *Houghton-Hall* in *Norfolk*, and made Brother LORRAIN and Brother THOMAS PELHAM Duke of *Newcastle* 𝕸𝖆𝖘𝖙𝖊𝖗-𝕸𝖆𝖘𝖔𝖓𝖘. And ever since, both in the *G. Lodge* and in particular *Lodges*, the Fraternity joyfully remember His ROYAL HIGHNESS in the proper Manner.

— 𝕲𝖗𝖆𝖓𝖉 𝕷𝖔𝖉𝖌𝖊 in *Ample* Form at the *Half-Moon Cheapside*, on *Thursday* 24 *June* 1731. with former *G. Officers* and Those of 29 *Lodges*.

— 𝕲𝖗𝖆𝖓𝖉 𝕷𝖔𝖉𝖌𝖊 in *Due* Form at the *Devil* foresaid, on *Friday* 3 *Dec.* 1731. with Lord *Colerane* and other former *Grand Officers*, Capt. *Ralph Far Winter* the *Provincial* Grand Master of *East-India*, and the Officers of 46 *Lodges*.

— 𝕲𝖗𝖆𝖓𝖉 𝕷𝖔𝖉𝖌𝖊 in *Due* Form at the *Devil* foresaid on *Thursday* 2 *March* 173½. with the Duke of *Richmond*, and other former *G. Officers*, Viscount *Montagu*, and the Officers of 37 Lodges.

D. G. *Master* BATSON in the Chair proposed, in the *Grand Master's* Name, for Successor, the *Lord* Viscount *Montagu* Master of a *Lodge*, who was immediately saluted as *Grand Master Elect*.

— 𝕲𝖗𝖆𝖓𝖉 𝕷𝖔𝖉𝖌𝖊 in *Due* Form at the *Devil* foresaid, on *Thursday* 13 *April* 1732. with former *G. Officers* and Those of 27 *Lodges*.

ASSEMBLY and *Feast* at *Merchant-Taylor's-Hall* on *Wednesday* 19 *April* 1732. D. Grand *Master* BATSON with his *Wardens* attended the *G. Master Elect* at his House in *Bloomsbury-Square*; and with some noble Brothers, the Dukes of *Montagu* and *Richmond*, the Lord *Colerane*, the Lord *Carpenter*, the Earl of *Strathmore* and

Lord *Teynham*, and many Others, all duly clothed in Coaches, made the *Procession* of 𝕸𝖆𝖗𝖈𝖍 *Eastward* to the *Hall*, where all Things being regularly transacted as above, D. G. M. *Batson* proclaim'd aloud our noble Brother.

XI. ANTONY BROWN *Lord* Viscount *Montagu* 𝕲𝖗𝖆𝖓𝖉 𝕸𝖆𝖘𝖙𝖊𝖗 of *Masons*, who appointed 𝕿𝖍𝖔𝖒𝖆𝖘 𝕭𝖆𝖙𝖘𝖔𝖓 to continue D. G. *Master*.

{ *George Rook*, Esq; } *Grand* { The *Secretary* and *Sword*-
{ *James Moor-Smythe*, Esq; } *Wardens*. { *Bearer* were continued.

— 𝕲𝖗𝖆𝖓𝖉 𝕷𝖔𝖉𝖌𝖊 in *Due* Form at the *Castle* in *Drury-Lane*, on *Thursday* 8 *June* 1732. with the Earl of *Inchiquin* and other former G. *Officers* and Those of 39 *Lodges*.

— 𝕲𝖗𝖆𝖓𝖉 𝕷𝖔𝖉𝖌𝖊 in *Due* Form at the *Devil* foresaid, on *Tuesday* 21 *Nov.* 1732. with Lord *Colerane*, Lord *Southwell*, and other former G. *Officers* and Those of 49 *Lodges*.

— 𝕲𝖗𝖆𝖓𝖉 𝕷𝖔𝖉𝖌𝖊 in *Due* Form at the *Devil* foresaid, on *Tuesday* 29 *May* 1733. with Lord *Southwell*, former G. *Officers* and Those of 42 *Lodges*.

D. G. M. BATSON in the Chair, proposed, in the *Grand Master*'s Name, for Successor, the *Earl* of *Strathmore* Master of a *Lodge*; who being in *Scotland*, our *Noble* Brother THOMAS Lord SOUTHWELL undertook to be *Proxy* at the next Feast, and was saluted now as STRATHMORE *Grand Master Elect*.

ASSEMBLY and *Feast* at *Mercer*'s-*Hall*, on *Thursday* 7 *June* 1733. D. G. M. BATSON with his G. *Wardens* attended Lord *Southwell* at his House in *Grosvenor-street*, and with some *Noble* Brothers, and many Others, all duly clothed in Coaches, made the *Procession* of 𝕸𝖆𝖗𝖈𝖍 *Eastward* to the *Hall*. And all Things being regularly transacted as above, D. G. M. *Batson* proclaim'd aloud our Noble Brother

---

* 𝕾𝖙𝖊𝖜𝖆𝖗𝖉𝖘 that acted at the Feast 19 *April* 1732. who were all publickly thank'd.

George Rook,		Colonel *John Pitt*,
James Moor Smythe,		*Claud Crespigny*, } Esq;
John Bridges, } Esq;		*William Blunt*,
Wyrriot Ormond,		Mr. *Henry Tatam*,
Arthur Moor,		Mr. *Thomas Griffith*,
Vizial Taverner,		Mr. *Solomon Mendez*.

XII. JAMES

XII. JAMES LYON Earl of *Strathmore* 𝕲𝖗𝖆𝖓𝖉 𝕸𝖆𝖘𝖙𝖊𝖗 of *Masons!* His Proxy Lord SOUTHWELL being duly invested and install'd, appointed

𝕿𝖍𝖔𝖒𝖆𝖘 𝕭𝖆𝖙𝖘𝖔𝖓 to con- {*James Smythe*, Esq; } Grand
tinue D. G. *Master!*   {*John Ward*, Esq; } *Wardens.*
The *Secretary* and *Sword-bearer* were continued. See the *Stewards* below. *

— 𝕲𝖗𝖆𝖓𝖉 𝕷𝖔𝖉𝖌𝖊 in *Ample* Form at the *Devil* foresaid on *Tuesday* 13 Dec. 1733. with Sir *Edward Mansel*, Bart. Pro. G. Master of *South Wales*, former *G. Officers*, the Earl of *Crawfurd* and the Officers of 53 *Lodges.*

STRATHMORE *Grand Master* moved, that Business greatly encreasing, the *Grand Loage* do refer what they cannot overtake at one Time, to the *Committee of Charity*, who can make Report to the next *Grand Lodge*; which was unanimously agreed to. See the *Committee of Charity* below.

D. G. M. 𝕭𝖆𝖙𝖘𝖔𝖓 recommended the *New* Colony of *Georgia* in *North America* to the Benevolence of the particular *Lodges.* And

Brother *Thomas Edwards* Esq; *Warden* of the Duke of *Richmond's Lodge* at the *Horn Westminster*, acquainted this *Grand Lodge.* that our Brother Capt. *Ralph Farwinter*, 𝕻𝖗𝖔𝖛𝖎𝖓𝖈𝖎𝖆𝖑 GRAND MASTER of *East-India*, had sent from his *Lodge* at *Bengal* a Chest of the best *Arrack* for the Use of the *Grand Lodge*, and TEN GUINEAS for the *Masons-Charity*; which the *Lodge* gratefully receiv'd and order'd solemn Thanks to be return'd to the 𝕷𝖔𝖉𝖌𝖊 at *Bengal.*

— 𝕲𝖗𝖆𝖓𝖉 𝕷𝖔𝖉𝖌𝖊 in *Due* Form at the *Devil* foresaid on *Monday* 18 *March* 173¾. with former *G. Officers*, the Earl of *Craufurd*, Sir *George Mackenzy*, Bart. and the Officers of 47 *Lodges*: when D. G. M. BATSON in the Chair proposed, in the *Grand Master's* Name, for Successor, the *Earl of Craufurd*, Master of a *Lodge*, who was gladly saluted as *Grand Master Elect.*

---

* 𝕾𝖙𝖊𝖜𝖆𝖗𝖉𝖘 that acted at the Feast 7 *June* 1733. who were all publickly thank'd.

1. *John Ward.*
2. *John Po exfen,*
3. *Henry Butler Pauy,* } Esqs;
4. *John Read,*
5. *William Bushy,*
6. *Philip Barnes,*

7. *John Mizaubin*, M. D.
8. Mr. *John Dwight.*
9. Mr. *Richard Baugh.*
10. Mr. *Thomas Shank,* } Gent.
11. Mr. *James Cosens,*
12. Mr. *Charles Robinson.*

S 2   CHAP.

CHAP. VII.

From *Grand Master* CRAUFURD, To the *present* G. MASTER CAERMARTHEN.

ASSEMBLY and *Feast* at *Mercer's-Hall* on *Saturday* 30 *March* 1734. D. G. M. BATSON with his *G. Wardens* attended the *Grand Master Elect* at his House in *Great Marlborough-street*, with Noble Brothers, and many Others, all duly clothed in Coaches, and made the *Procession* of MARCH *Eastward* to the Hall with a Band of *Musick*, viz. *Trumpets, Hautboys, Kettle-Drums* and *French-Horns*, to lead the *Van* and play at the *Gate* till all arrive: and all Things being regularly transacted as above,

D. G. M. *Batson* proclaim'd aloud, the *first Earl* of *Scotland* and our Noble Brother

XIII. JOHN LINDSAY *Earl* of *Craufurd* 𝕲𝖗𝖆𝖓𝖉 𝕸𝖆𝖘𝖙𝖊𝖗 of *Masons*, who appointed Sir 𝕮𝖊𝖈𝖎𝖑 𝖂𝖗𝖆𝖞, *Baronet*, D. G. *Master*, { *John Ward*, Esq; } *Grand* { Brother *John Revis* was { Sir *Edward Mansel*, Bart. } *Wardens*. { made *Grand Secretary*, and Brother *Mody* was continued *Sword-bearer*. After the 2d *Procession* round the Tables, much Harmony abounded. *

— 𝕲𝖗𝖆𝖓𝖉 𝕷𝖔𝖉𝖌𝖊 in Ample Form at the *Devil* foresaid on *Monday* 24 *Feb.* 173⅘. the Dukes of *Richmond* and *Buccleugh*, and other former Grand Officers, the Earl of *Belcarras*, the Viscount *Weymouth*, and the Officers of 47 Lodges.

---

* 𝖘𝖙𝖊𝖜𝖆𝖗𝖉𝖘 that acted at the Feast 30 *March* 1734. who were all publickly thank'd.

1. Sir *Edward Mansell* Baronet.
2. *Charles Holtzendorf*,
3. *Isaac Mueve*,
4. *Prescot Pepper*
5. *Christopher Nevile*,
6. *Richard Matthews*, } Esqs;
7. *Richard Rawlinson*, L. L. D. and F. R. S.
8. *Fotherby Baker*,
9. *Samuel Berrington*,
10. *John Pitt*,
11. *William Varelst*
12. *Henry Hutchinson*. } Gentlemen.

(133)

CRAUFURD *Grand Master* made a very handsome Speech, excusing his not calling them together sooner, even because of the Elections for Parliament and other publick Business; and proposed for his Successor the *Lord* Viscount *Weymouth* Master of a *Lodge*, who was forthwith saluted as *G. Master Elect*.

Brother *Anderson*, Author of the *Book* of CONSTITUTIONS, representing that a *new Edition* was become necessary, and that he had prepared Materials for it, the GRAND MASTER and the *Lodge* order'd him to lay the same before the present and former *Grand Officers*; that they may report their Opinion to the G. Lodge. Also the Book call'd the *Free Mason's Vade Mecum* was condemn'd by the G. Lodge as a pyratical and silly Thing, done without Leave, and the Brethren were warned not to use it, nor encourage it to be sold.

— 𝕲𝖗𝖆𝖓𝖉 𝕷𝖔𝖉𝖌𝖊 in *Ample* Form at the *Devil* foresaid on *Monday* 31 *March* 1735. with former *Grand Officers* and Those of 41 *Lodges*.

CRAUFURD *Grand Master*, in a judicious Speech, proposed several Things for the Good of the *Fraternity*, which were approv'd, and the Substance of 'em are in the *New Regulations* and *Committee* of *Charity*, below.

Brother *Anderson* was order'd also to insert in the New Edition of the Constitutions, the PATRONS of *antient* 𝕸𝖆𝖘𝖔𝖓𝖗𝖞 that could be collected from the Beginning of Time, with the *Grand Masters* and *Wardens*, antient and modern, and the Names of the *Stewards* since G. M. *Montagu*. Never more Love and Harmony appear'd.

ASSEMBLY and *Feast* at *Mercer's-Hall* on *Thursday* 17 *April* 1735.

CRAUFURD *Grand Master* with his *Deputy* and *Wardens*, and the noble Brothers the Dukes of *Richmond* and *Atholl*, the Marquis of *Beaumont*, the Earls of *Winchelsea, Weems, Loudoun* and *Balcarras*, the Lord *Cathcart* and Lord *Vere Berty*, with many Other Brothers all duly clothed, attended the *Grand Master Elect*, and from his House in *Grovenor-Square* made the PROCESSION of 𝔐𝔞𝔯𝔠𝔥 with the band of *Musick* leading the Van *Eastward* to the *Hall*. And

All

(134)

All Things being regularly transacted as above, Brother *Craufurd* proclaim'd aloud our noble Brother *

XIV. THOMAS THYNNE, *Lord* Viscount *Weymouth* **Grand Master** of *Masons*; who appointed **John Ward** Esq; *D. G. Master.*
{ Sir *Edward Mansel*, Bart.   } *Grand* { The*Secretary*
{ *Martin Clare*, A. M. and F. R. S. } *Wardens.* { and *Swordbearer* continued.

— **Grand Lodge** in *Due* Form at the *Devil* foresaid on *Thursday* 24 *June* 1735. with former G. *Officers* and Those of 31 *Lodges*.

D. G. *Master* WARD in the Chair, in an excellent Speech recommended *Temper* and *Decency*. The Brothers that served the Office of *Stewards* ever since *Grand Master* the Duke of MONTAGU, address'd the *Grand Lodge* for certain *Privileges*, which were granted. See the *New Regulation* 23.

— **Grand Lodge** in *Due* Form at the *Devil* foresaid on *Thursday* 11 *Dec.* 1735. with former G. *Officers* and Those of 57 *Lodges*. GEORGE PAYNE, Esq; formerly *Grand Master*, in the Chair; *Martin Clare* the G. W. acted as *Dep. Gr. Master*, and
{ *James Anderson*, D. D. { *Grand*   { pro Tempore.
{ *Jacob Lamball*,   { *Wardens.*{

Brother *Rigby* from *Bengall*, who brought from thence 20 GUINEAS for the *Charity*.

Sir *Robert Lawley* Master of the *Stewards Lodge*, with his *Wardens* and 9 more, with their *new Badges*, appear'd full 12 the *first* Time.

The **Lodge** order'd a Letter of Thanks to be sent to the *Lodge* at *Bengal* for their very generous and kind *Presents*.

---

* **Stewards** that acted at the *Feast* on 17 *April* 1735. who were all publickly thanked.

1. Sir *Robert Lawley*, Baronet,
2. *William Græme*, M. D. and F. R. S.
3. *Martin Clare*, A. M. and F. R. S.
4. *John Theobald*, M. D.
5. *Charles Fleetwood*, Esq;
6. *Thomas Beech*, Esq.
7. Captain *Ralph Farwinter*,
8. *Meyer Shamberg*, M. D.
9. *Robert Wright*, Gentleman,
10. *Thomas Slaughter*, Laceman,
11. *James Nash*, Gentleman,
12. *William Hogarth*, Painter.

— **Grand Lodge** in Due Form at the *Devil* foresaid on *Tuesday* 6 *April* 1736. with the Duke of *Richmond*, the Earl of *Craufurd* and other former *G. Officers*, the Earl of *Loudoun*, the *Stewards* Lodge and 5 present *Stewards*, with the *Officers* of 61 Lodges.

D. G. *Master* WARD in the *Chair* proposed some *Rules of Communication* that were approved and now make the 40th GENERAL REGULATION. Below.

Then he proposed, in the *Grand Master's* Name, for Successor, the *Earl* of *Loudoun* Master of a *Lodge*, who was forthwith saluted as *Grand Master Elect*.

ASSEMBLY and **Feast** at *Fishmongers-Hall* on *Thursday* 15 *April* 1736. D. G. *Master* WARD with his *Wardens* and the noble Brothers, the Duke of *Richmond*, the Earls of *Craufurd* and *Albemarle*, Viscount *Harcourt*, Lord *Erskine*, Lord *Southwell*, Mr. *Anstis* **Garter** King at *Arms*, Mr. *Brody* **Lion** King at *Arms*, with many other Brothers all duly clothed, attended the *Grand Master Elect*; and from his House in *Whitehall* made the *Procession* of *March*, with the Band of Musick, *Eastward* to the *Hall*: Where all Things being regularly transacted as above, *

D. G. *Master Ward* proclaim'd aloud, our noble Brother
XV. JOHN CAMPBELL Earl of *Loudoun* **Grand Master** of *Masons*, who appointed **John Ward**, Esq; to continue *Deputy* ⎰Sir **Robert Lawley**, Baronet, ⎱ *Grand*
GrandMaster, ⎱**William Graeme**, M. D. and F. R. S. ⎰*Wardens*. and continued the *Secretary* and *Sword-bearer*.

---

* STEWARDS that acted at the *Feast* on 15 *April* 1736. who were publickly thank'd.

1. *Edward Hody*, M. D. and F. R. S
2. *James Ruck*, jun. Esq;
3. Mr. *Charles Champion*,
4. Mr. *John Gowland*,
5. *John Jesse*, Esq;
6. *Isaac Shamberg*, jun. M. D.
7. Mr. *Benjamin Gascoyne*,
8. *James Styles*, Esq;
9. Mr. *Walter Weldon*,
10. Mr. *Richard Sawle*,
11. Mr. *James Pringle*,
12. Mr. *Francis Blythe*.

— **Grand**

—— **Grand Lodge** in *Ample* Form at the *Devil* forefaid on *Thurfday* 17 *June* 1736. with the Earl of *Craufurd* and other former *G. Officers*, the *Stewards* Lodge, the *new* Stewards, and the *Officers* of 36 *Lodges*.

G. **Warden Graeme** acted ⎫ Lord **Ereskine,** ⎫ *GrandWardens* as D. G. *Mafter* pro tempore. ⎭ Capt.——*Young*, ⎭ pro tempore.

—— **Grand Lodge** in *Due* Form at the *Devil* forefaid on St. JOHN *Evangelift's* Day, *Monday* 27 *Dec.* 1736. with former *G. Officers*, the *Stewards* Lodge, the *prefent* Stewards, and the *Officers* of 52 Lodges.

Sir ROBERT LAWLEY Sen. G. W. was in the Chair as *Grand Mafter* pro tempore.

William Graeme J. G. W. was ⎫ *Martin Clare,* ⎫ G. *Wardens Deputy* G. *Mafter* pro tempore, ⎭ *Jacob Lamball,* ⎭ pro tempore.

The curious *By-Laws* of the *Lodge* at *Exeter* were publickly read and applauded, and a Letter of Thanks was order'd to be fent to them for their handfome Beneficence to the General *Charity*.

—— **Grand Lodge** in *Ample* Form at the *Devil* forefaid on *Thurfday* 13 *April* 1737. with the Earl of *Craufurd* and other former *G. Officers*, the Earls of *Weems, Hume* and *Darnley*, the *Stewards* Lodge, the *prefent* Stewards, and the *Officers* of 75 *Lodges*. After the Affair of *Charity* was over,

LOUDOUN *Grand Mafter* propofed for his Succeffor the Earl of *Darnley* Mafter of a *Lodge*, who was forthwith faluted as *Grand Mafter Elect*.

ASSEMBLY and **Feaft** at *Fifhmongers-Hall* on *Thurfday* 28 *April* 1737.

LOUDOUN G. *Mafter* with his *Deputy* and *Wardens*, the noble Brothers, the Duke of *Richmond*, the Earls of *Craufurd* and *Weemes*, Lord *Grey* of *Grooby*, the *Stewards* and many other Brothers all duly clothed, attended the *Grand Mafter Elect* at his Houfe in *Pall-Mall*, and made the *Proceffion* of *March Eaftward* to the *Hall* in a very folemn Manner, having 3 Bands of Mufick, Kettle-Drums, Trumpets and *French* Horns, properly

(137)

properly disposed in the *March*: Where all Things being regularly transacted as above, *

The Earl of *Loudoun* proclaim'd aloud our noble Brother

XVI. EDWARD BLYTHE Earl and Viscount *Darnley*, Lord *Clifton*, 𝕲𝖗𝖆𝖓𝖉 𝕸𝖆𝖘𝖙𝖊𝖗 of *Masons*, who continued

John Ward, Esq; D. Grand *Master*, } Sir *Robert Lawley*, Baronet, } Grand
William Græme, M. D. and F. R. S. } Wardens.

and continued the 𝕾𝖊𝖈𝖗𝖊𝖙𝖆𝖗𝖞 and *Sword-bearer*.

— 𝕲𝖗𝖆𝖓𝖉 𝕷𝖔𝖉𝖌𝖊 in *Ample* Form at the *Devil* foresaid on *Wednesday* 29 *June* 1737. with the Earl of *Loudoun* and other former G. Officers, the *Stewards Lodge*, the *New* Stewards and the Officers of 49 Lodges.

On 5th *Nov.* 1737. an Occasional *Lodge* was held at the *Prince* of *Wales*'s Palace of *Kew* near *Richmond*, viz.

The *Rev.* Dr. DESAGULIERS (formerly *Grand Master*) 𝕸𝖆𝖘𝖙𝖊𝖗 of this *Lodge*,

Mr. *William Gofton*, Attorney at Law, Senior } Grand }
Mr. *Erasmus King*, Mathematician, Junior } Warden. }

The Right Hon. *Charles Calvert Earl* of *Baltimore*, the Hon. Colonel *James Lumley*, the Hon. Major *Madden*, Mr. de *Noyer*, Mr. *Vraden*; and when formed and tiled,

His *Royal* Highness FRIDERIC Prince of WALES was in the usual Manner introduced, and made an *Enter'd Prentice* and *Fellow Craft*.

Our said *Royal* Brother FRIDERIC was made a 𝕸𝖆𝖘𝖙𝖊𝖗 𝕸𝖆𝖘𝖔𝖓 by the same *Lodge*, that assembled there again for that Purpose. And ever since, both in the *Grand Lodge* and in particular *Lodges*, the *Fraternity* joyfully remember his ROYAL HIGHNESS and his SON, in the proper Manner.

---

* STEWARDS that acted at the *Feast* on 28 *April* 1737. who were publickly thank'd

1. Sir *Bouchier Wray*, Baronet,
2. *George Bothomley*, } Esq;
3. *Charles Murray*, }
4. Capt. *John Lloyd*,
5. Capt. *Charles Scot*,
6. Mr. *Pet. Mac-Culloch*, Surgeon.
7. *Lewis Theobald* M. D.
8. Mr. *Thomas Jeffreys*, Merchant,
9. Mr. *Peter Leigh*,
10. Mr. *Thomas Boehm*,
11. Mr. *Benjamin Da Costa*,
12. Mr. *Nathaniel Adams*.

(138)

— **Grand Lodge** in *Ample* Form at the *Devil* foresaid on *Wednesday* 25 *January* 173⅞. with the Earl of *Loudoun*, Dr. *Desaguliers*, *George Payne*, *Nathaniel Blakerby*, *Thomas Batson*, Esq; Dr. *Anderson*, and other former Grand *Officers*, Lord *George Graham*, the *Stewards* Lodge, the *present* Stewards and the *Officers* of 66 Lodges. After the Affair of *Charity* was over,

The **Grand Lodge** approved of this *New* Book of *Constitutions*, and order'd the Author Brother *Anderson* to print the same, with the Addition of the *New Regulation* IX. See the *Approbation* below.

—**Grand Lodge** in *Ample* Form at the *Devil* foresaid on *Thursday* 6 *April* 1738.

DARNLEY G. *Master* in the Chair, **John Ward**, D. G. *Master*, *William Graeme*, fen. G. W. ⎱pro tem-⎰ The Earl of *Inchiquin*, Dr. *Desaguliers*, *James Anderson*, Jun. G. W. ⎱ pore. ⎰ *George Payne*, late G. *Masters*, *John Hammerton* Esq; Provincial G. M. of *Carolina*, *Thomas Batson* late D. G. M. *Nath. Blakerby* Treasurer, the Marquis of *Caernervon*, the *Stewarts* Lodge, the *present* Stewards and the *Officers* of 60 Lodges. After the Affair of *Charity* was over,

Nathaniel Blakerby, Esq; the *Treasurer*, having justly cleared his Accounts, demitted or laid down his *Office*. Upon which the *Grand* **Master** and the *Lodge* appointed the *Secretary* **Revis** to be *Treasurer*.

DARNLEY G. *Master* proposed for his Successor the Marquis of *Caernarvon* Master of a *Lodge*, who was forthwith saluted as Grand Master Elect.

ASSEMBLY and **Feast** at *Fishmongers-Hall* on *Thursday* 27 *April* 1738.

DARNLEY Grand *Master* with his *Deputy* and *Wardens*, the noble Brothers *Richmond*, *Inchiquin*, *Loudoun* and *Colerane*, late Gr. *Masters*, Earl of *Kintore*, Lord *Grey* of *Grooby*, the *Stewards* and a great many other Brothers all duly clothed, attended the Grand *Master Elect* at his House in *Grovenor-street*, and made the *Procession* of *March*, with the Band of Musick, *Eastward* to the *Hall*, where all Things being regularly transacted as above,

The

(139)

The Earl of *Darnley* proclaim'd aloud our noble Brother
XVII. HENRY BRIDGES Marquis of *Caernarvon*, Son and Heir apparent to the Duke of *Chandos*, Knight of the *Bath*, and one of the *Bed-Chamber* to our *Royal* Brother FRIDERIC Prince of *Wales*, 𝕲𝖗𝖆𝖓𝖉 𝕸𝖆𝖘𝖙𝖊𝖗 of *Masons*, who appointed 𝕵𝖔𝖍𝖓 𝖂𝖆𝖗𝖉, Esq; to continue Deputy Grand Master, Lord 𝕲𝖊𝖔𝖗𝖌𝖊 𝕲𝖗𝖆𝖍𝖆𝖒, ⎱ *Grand* ⎰ and continued the 𝕾𝖊𝖈𝖗𝖊𝖙𝖆𝖗𝖞
Capt. *Andrew Robinson*, ⎰ *Wardens*. ⎱ and *Sword-bearer*. *

Brother *Revis* the *Secretary* declin'd the Office of *Treasurer*; because, he said, that one Person should not take upon him both *Offices*, for that the One should be a *Check* upon the Other.

— 𝕲𝖗𝖆𝖓𝖉 𝕷𝖔𝖉𝖌𝖊 in *Due* Form at the *Devil* foresaid on *Wednesday* 28 *June* 1738.
Lord GEORGE GRAHAM, S. G. W. in the Chair, as *Grand Master*, 𝖂𝖎𝖑𝖑𝖎𝖆𝖒 𝕲𝖗𝖆𝖊𝖒𝖊, M. D. as D. G. *Master* pro tempore,
Capt. *Andrew Robinson* as sen. ⎱ *Grand* ⎰ with former *Grand*
Mr. *Benjamin Gascoyne* as jun. ⎰ *Warden*. ⎱ Officers, the *Stewards* Lodge, the *present* Stewards and the *Officers* of 61 Lodges.

The Minutes of the last *Quarterly* Communication and of the *Committe* of Charity were read and approved. Most of the Time was spent in receiving the *Charity* of the *Lodges*, and in relieving poor Brothers.

Brother *Revis* the *Secretary* having declin'd the Office of *Treasurer*, the *Lodge* desired him to act as such, till One to their Mind can be found.

* STEWARDS that acted at the *Feast* on 27 *April* 1738. and were publickly thank'd.

1. Capt. *Andrew Robinson*.
2. *Robert Foy*, Esq; ⎱
3. *James Colquhon*, ⎰ Esqs;
4. *William Chapman*, ⎱
5. Mr. *Moses Mendez*,
6. Mr. *George Monkman*,
7. *Stephen Beaumont*, M. D.
8. Mr. *Stephen Le Bas*,
9. Mr. *Henry Higden*,
10. Mr. *Christopher Taylor*,
11. Mr. *Simon de Charmes*.
12. Mr. *Harry Leigh*.

The old Stewards named their Successors for next Annual Feast, viz. Hon. *John* CHICHESTER, Esq; Capt. *Charles Fitzroy*, *John Ciff*, Esq; *Nathaniel Oldham*, Esq; Mr. *Alexander Pollock*, Surgeon, Mr. *Richard Robinson*, Confectioner, Mr. *Henry Robinson*, Mr. *Isaac Barrett*, Mr. *Samuel Lowman*, Mr. *Edward Masters*, Mr. *Thomas Adamson*, Mr. *Joseph Harris*.   A List

(140)

A *List* of the Grand Masters or *Patrons* of the Free Masons in *England*, from the Coming in of the *Anglo-Saxons* to these Times, who are mention'd in this Book.

— Austin the *Monk*, the first Archbishop of *Canterbury*, appear'd at the Head of the *Craft* in founding the *old Cathedral*, under *Ethelbert* King of *Kent*. Page 61
— Bennet Abbot of *Wirrall* under *Kenred* King of *Mercia* (call'd by Mistake in this Book *Ethelbert*) who wrote to *Charles Martel*. 62
— St. Swithin under the *Saxon* King *Ethelwolph*. *Ibid*
— King Alfred the Great. *Ibid*
— Ethred the Deputy King of *Mercia*,
— Prince Ethelward the Learned, both under King *Edward* Senior. } 63
— Prince Edwin under his Brother King *Athelstan*. *Ibid*.
— St. Dunstan Archbishop of *Canterbury* under King *Edgar*. 65
— King Edward the *Confessor*, and
— Leofrick Earl of *Coventry*. 66
— Roger de *Montgomery* Earl of *Arundel*, and
— Gundulph Bishop of *Rochester*, both under King *William* I. the Conqueror, and also under King *William* II. *Rufus*. } 67
— King Henry I. *Beauclerk*. 68
— Gilbert de Clare Marquis of *Pembroke* under King *Stephen*. *Ibid*.

— The Grand Masters of the Knights Templars under King *Henry* II. Page 69
— Peter de *Cole-Church*, and
— William Almain, under King *John*. } *Ibid*.
— Peter de *Rupibus*, and
— Geoffrey FitzPeter, under King *Henry* III. } *Ibid*.
— Walter Giffard Archbishop of *York*,
— Gilbert de Clare Earl of *Glocester*,
— Ralph Lord of *Mount-Hermer*, all under King *Edward* I. } *Ibid*.
— Walter Stapleton Bishop of *Exeter* under K. *Edward* II. 70
— King Edward III. and under him.
— John de Spoulee Master of the Chiblim,
— William a Wickham Bishop of *Winchester*,
— Robert a Barnham,
— Henry Yeuele the King's *Free-Mason*,
— Simon Langham Abbot of *Westminster*, also under King *Richard* II. } *Ibid*. 72
— Thomas Fitz-Allan Earl of *Surrey* under King *Henry* IV. 73

—Henry

(141)

—HENRY CHICHELEY Archbishop of *Canterbury* under King *Henry* V. and VI.   Page 73
—WILLIAM WANEFLEET Bishop of *Winchester* under King *Henry* VI.   75
—RICHARD BEAUCHAMP Bishop of *Sarum* under King *Edward* IV.   76
—King HENRY VII. and under him
—JOHN ISLIP Abbot of *Westminster*, and
—Sir REGINALD BRAY Knight of the *Garter*.   } 78
—Cardinal WOOLSEY.
—THOMAS CROMWELL Earl of *Essex*,
—JOHN TOUCHET Lord *Audley*, all under King *Henry* VIII.   } 79
—EDWARD SEYMOUR Duke of *Somerset*,
—JOHN POYNET Bishop of *Winchester*, both under King *Edward* VI.   } 80
—Sir THOMAS SACKVILLE,
—FRANCIS RUSSEL Earl of *Bedford*,
—Sir THOMAS GRESHAM,
—CHARLES HOWARD Earl of *Effingham*,
—GEORGE HASTINGS Earl of *Huntington*, all under Queen *Elizabeth*.   } 81
King JAMES I. and under him
—INIGO JONES,
—WILLIAM HERBERT Earl of *Pembroke*,   } 98

King CHARLES I. and under him
—HENRY DANVERS Earl of *Danby*.   Page
—THOMAS HOWARD Earl of *Arundel*.
—FRANCIS RUSSEL Earl of *Bedford*,   } 99 and 100.
—INIGO JONES again.
King CHARLES II. and under him
—HENRY JERMYN Earl of St. *Albans*,
—THOMAS SAVAGE Earl of *Rivers*,
—GEORGE VILLARS Duke of *Bucks*,
—HENRY BENNET Earl of *Arlington*.   } 101, 102, 105.
And under King *James* II.
—Sir CHRISTOPHER WREN.   106
King WILLIAM III. and under him
—Sir CHRISTOPHER WREN again,
—CHARLES LENNOS Duke of *Richmond*.   } 107
And under Queen ANNE,
—Sir CHRISTOPHER WREN again, till he finish'd St. *Paul*'s Cathedral *A. D.* 1708.   108
After which, no 𝕲𝖗𝖆𝖓𝖉 𝕸𝖆𝖘𝖙𝖊𝖗 till the *Lodges* met and chose one from among themselves, *viz*.
—ANTONY SAYER in the 3d Year of King *George* I. *A. D.* 1717.
—GEORGE PAYNE, Esq;   110
—Rev. Dr. JESAGULIERS.   *Ibid.*
GEORGE PAYNE again.   111
After whom, the *Fraternity* came to be govern'd by the following *Noble* 𝕲𝖗𝖆𝖓𝖉 𝕸𝖆𝖘𝖙𝖊𝖗𝖘, *viz*.

I. JOHN

(142)

1. John Montagu Duke of Montagu. 113
2. Philip Wharton Duke of Wharton. 115
3. Francis Scot Duke of Buccleugh. 116
4. Charles Lennos Duke of Richmond, Lennox and d'Aubigny. 118
5. James Hammilton Earl of Abercorn. 119

These were under King *George* I. And the following *Noble* 𝔊𝔯𝔞𝔫𝔡 𝔐𝔞𝔣𝔱𝔢𝔯𝔰 have acted under his present Majesty King *George* II. viz.

6. William O Brien Earl of Inchiquin. 120
7. Henry Hare Lord Colerane. 122
8. James King Lord Viscount Kingston. 123
9. Thomas Howard Duke of Norfolk. 126
10. Thomas Cooke Lord Lovel. 128
11. Antony Brown Lord Viscount *Montagu*. 130
12. James Lyon Earl of *Strathmore*. 131
13. John Lindsay Earl of *Craufurd*. 132
14. Thomas Thynne Lord Viscount *Weymouth*. 134
15. John Campbell Earl of *Loudoun*. 135
16. Edward Blythe Earl of *Darnley*. 137
17. Henry Bridges Marquis of *Caernarvon* the present 𝔊𝔯𝔞𝔫𝔡 𝔐𝔞𝔣𝔱𝔢𝔯. 139

THE

THE OLD
CHARGES
OF THE
Free and Accepted Masons,

Collected by the *Author* from their old *Records*, at the Command of the *Grand Master* the present Duke of Montagu.

Approved by the 𝕲𝖗𝖆𝖓𝖉 𝕷𝖔𝖉𝖌𝖊, and order'd to be printed in the first Edition of the *Book* of *Constitutions* on 25 *March* 1722.

I. Charge. *Concerning* God *and Religion*.

 A Mason is obliged by his Tenure to observe the Moral Law, as a true *Noachida*; and if he rightly understands the *Craft*, he will never be a Stupid Atheist, nor an Irreligious Libertin, nor act against Conscience.

In antient Times the *Christian Masons* were charged to comply with the *Christian* Usages of each Country where they travell'd or work'd: But *Masonry* being found in all Nations, even of divers Religions, they are now only charged to adhere to that Religion in which all Men agree (leaving each Brother to his

own

own particular Opinions) that is, to be Good Men and True, Men of Honour and Honesty, by whatever Names, Religions or Persuasions they may be distinguish'd: For they all agree in the 3 great *Articles* of NOAH, enough to preserve the Cement of the Lodge. Thus *Masonry* is the Center of their Union and the happy Means of conciliating Persons that otherwise must have remain'd at a perpetual Distance.

II. CHARGE. Of the *Civil* 𝔐𝔞𝔤𝔦𝔰𝔱𝔯𝔞𝔱𝔢, *Supreme* and *Subordinate*.

A *Mason* is a peaceable Subject, never to be concern'd in Plots against the State, nor disrespectful to *Inferior* Magistrates. Of old, Kings, Princes and States encourag'd the Fraternity for their *Loyalty*, who ever flourish'd most in Times of Peace. But tho' a *Brother* is not to be countenanced in his *Rebellion* against the State; yet if convicted of no other Crime, his Relation to the *Lodge* remains indefeasible.

III. CHARGE. Concerning 𝔏𝔬𝔡𝔤𝔢𝔰.

A LODGE is a Place where *Masons* meet to work in: Hence the *Assembly*, or duly organiz'd Body of *Masons*, is call'd a LODGE; just as the Word *Church* is expressive both of the *Congregation* and of the *Place* of Worship.

Every Brother should belong to some *particular Lodge*, and cannot be absent without incurring Censure, if not necessarily detain'd.

The Men made *Masons* must be *Freeborn* (or no Bondmen) of mature Age and of good Report, hail and sound, not deform'd or dismember'd at the Time of their making. But no *Woman*, no *Eunuch*.

When Men of *Quality*, Eminence, Wealth and Learning apply to be made, they are to be respectfully accepted, after due Examination: For such often prove Good *Lords* (or Founders) of Work, and will not employ *Cowans* when true *Masons* can be had; they also make the best *Officers* of *Lodges*, and the best

Designers,

Designers, to the Honour and Strength of the *Lodge*: Nay, from among them, the *Fraternity* can have a *Noble* 𝕲𝖗𝖆𝖓𝖉 𝕸𝖆𝖘𝖙𝖊𝖗. But those Brethren are equally subject to the *Charges* and *Regulations*, except in what more immediately concerns Operative *Masons*.

IV. CHARGE. Of 𝕸𝖆𝖘𝖙𝖊𝖗𝖘, 𝖂𝖆𝖗𝖉𝖊𝖓𝖘, *Fellows* and *Prentices*.

All Preferment among *Masons* is grounded upon real Worth and personal *Merit* only, not upon *Seniority*. No MASTER should take a *Prentice* that is not the Son of honest Parents, a perfect Youth without Maim or Defect in his Body, and capable of learning the *Mysteries* of the *Art*; that so the *Lords* (or Founders) may be well served, and the *Craft* not despised; and that, when of Age and Expert, he may become an *Enter'd Prentice*, or a *Free-Mason* of the lowest Degree, and upon his due Improvements a *Fellow-Craft* and a *Master-Mason*, capable to undertake a *Lord*'s Work.

The WARDENS are chosen from among the *Master-Masons*, and no Brother can be a *Master* of a *Lodge* till he has acted as *Warden* somewhere, except in extraordinary Cases; or when a *Lodge* is to be form'd where none such can be had: For then 3 *Master-Masons*, tho' never *Masters* or *Wardens* of Lodges before, may be constituted *Master* and *Wardens* of that *New Lodge*.

But no Number without 3 *Master-Masons* can form a *Lodge*; and none can be the GRAND MASTER or a GRAND WARDEN who has not acted as the *Master* of a *particular* Lodge.

V. CHARGE. Of the 𝕸𝖆𝖓𝖆𝖌𝖊𝖒𝖊𝖓𝖙 *of the* Craft *in Working*.

All *Masons* should work hard and honestly on Working-Days, that they may live reputably on Holy-Days; and the Working-Hours appointed by Law, or confirm'd by Custom, shall be observ'd.

A *Master-Mason* only must be the Surveyor or *Master of Work*, who shall undertake the *Lord*'s Work reasonably, shall truly dispend difpend his Goods as if they were his own, and fhall not give more Wages than juft to any *Fellow* or *Prentice*.

The *Wardens* fhall be true both to *Mafter* and *Fellows*, taking Care of all Things, both within and without the *Lodge*, efpecially in the *Mafter's* Abfence; and their Brethren fhall obey them.

The *Mafter* and the *Mafons* fhall faithfully finifh the *Lord's* Work, whether *Tafk* or *Journey*; nor fhall take the Work at *Tafk* which hath been accuftomed to *Journey*.

None fhall fhew Envy at a Brother's Profperity, nor fupplant him or put him out of his Work, if capable to finifh it.

All *Mafons* fhall meekly receive their Wages without Murmuring or Mutiny, and not defert the *Mafter* till the *Lord's* Work is finifh'd: They muft avoid ill Language, calling each Other *Brother* or *Fellow*, with much Courtefy, both within and without the *Lodge*. They fhall inftruct a younger Brother to become bright and expert, that the *Lord's* Materials may not be fpoiled.

But *Free* and Accepted *Mafons* fhall not allow *Cowans* to work with them; nor fhall they be employ'd by *Cowans* without an urgent Neceffity: And even in that Cafe they muft not teach *Cowans*, but muft have a *feparate* Communication.

No *Labourer* fhall be employ'd in the proper Work of *Free-Mafons*.

VI. CHARGE. Concerning *Mafons* 𝔅𝔢𝔥𝔞𝔳𝔦𝔬𝔲𝔯.

1. 𝔅𝔢𝔥𝔞𝔳𝔦𝔬𝔲𝔯 in the *Lodge* before *Clofing*.

You muft not hold private Committees or feparate Converfation without Leave from the *Mafter*; nor talk of any Thing impertinent; nor interrupt the *Mafter* or *Wardens*, or any Brother fpeaking to the *Chair*; nor act ludicroufly while the *Lodge* is engaged in what is ferious and folemn: But you are to pay due Reverence to the *Mafter*, *Wardens* and *Fellows*, and put them to worfhip.

Every Brother found guilty of a Fault fhall ftand to the *Award* of the *Lodge*, unlefs he appeals to the *Grand Lodge*; or unlefs a
Lord's

Lord's Work is retarded: For then a particular Reference may be made.

No private Piques, no Quarrels about Nations, Families, Religions or Politicks must be brought within the Door of the Lodge: For as *Masons*, we are of the oldest *Catholick Religion* above hinted, and of all Nations upon the *Square*, *Level* and *Plumb*; and like our Predecessors in all Ages, we are resolv'd against political Disputes, as contrary to the Peace and Welfare of the *Lodge*.

2. 𝔅𝔢𝔥𝔞𝔳𝔦𝔬𝔲𝔯 *after the* Lodge *is closed and the* Brethren *not gone*,

You may enjoy yourselves with innocent Mirth, treating one another according to Ability, but avoiding all Excess; not forcing any Brother to eat or drink beyond his own Inclination (according to the Old Regulation **-of King Aha-|* Page 24. Line 1. suerus) nor hindering him from going home when he pleases: For tho' after *Lodge Hours* you are like other Men, yet the Blame of your Excess may be thrown upon the *Fraternity*, tho' unjustly.

3. 𝔅𝔢𝔥𝔞𝔳𝔦𝔬𝔲𝔯 *at meeting without* Strangers, *but not in a* Formed *Lodge*.

You are to salute one another as you have been or shall be instructed, freely communicating Hints of Knowledge, but without disclosing *Secrets*, unless to those that have given long Proof of their Taciturnity and Honour; and without derogating from the Respect due to any Brother, were he not a Mason: For tho' all *Brothers* and *Fellows* are upon the *Level*, yet *Masonry* divests no Man of the Honour due to him before he was made a *Mason*, or that shall become his Due afterwards; nay rather, it adds to his Respect, teaching us *to give Honour to whom it is due*, especially to a *Noble* or Eminent *Brother*, whom we should distinguish from all of his Rank or Station, and serve him readily, according to our Ability.

4. **Behaviour** *in Presence of* Strangers *not* Masons.

You must be cautious in your Words, Carriage and Motions; that so the most penetrating Stranger may not be able to discover what is not proper to be intimated: and the impertinent or insnaring Questions, or ignorant Discourse of Strangers must be prudently manag'd by *Free-Masons*.

5. **Behaviour** *at* Home *and in your Neighbourhood*.

Masons ought to be Moral Men, as above charged; consequently good Husbands, good Parents, good Sons, and good Neighbours, not staying too long from Home and avoiding all Excess; yet wise Men too, for certain Reasons known to them.

6. **Behaviour** *towards a* foreign *Brother or* Stranger.

You are cautiously to examine him, as Prudence shall direct you; that you may not be imposed upon by a *Pretender*, whom you are to reject with Derision, and beware of giving him any Hints. But if you discover him to be true and faithful, you are to respect him as a *Brother*; and if in want, you are to relieve him, if you can; or else to direct him how he may be reliev'd: you must employ him, if you can; or else recommend him to be employ'd; but you are not charg'd to do beyond Ability.

7. **Behaviour** *behind a Brother's* Back *as well as before his* Face.

Free and Accepted *Masons* have been ever charged to avoid all Slandering and Backbiting of a true and faithful Brother, or talking disrespectfully of his Person or Performances; and all Malice or unjust Resentment: Nay you must not suffer any others to reproach an honest Brother, but shall defend his Character as far as is consistent with Honour, Safety and Prudence; tho' no farther.

VII. CHARGE.

VII. Charge. Concerning Law-Suits.

If a Brother do you Injury, apply first to your own or his *Lodge*; and if you are not satisfy'd, you may appeal to the *Grand Lodge*; but you must never take a legal Course till the Cause cannot be otherwise decided: For if the Affair is only between *Masons* and about *Masonry*, Law-Suits ought to be prevented by the good Advice of prudent Brethren, who are the best Referees of such Differences.

But if that Reference is either impracticable or unsuccessful, and the Affair must be brought into the Courts of *Law* or *Equity*; yet still you must avoid all Wrath, Malice and Rancour in carrying on the Suit, not saying nor doing any Thing that may hinder either the Continuance or the Renewal of Brotherly Love and Friendship, which is the *Glory* and *Cement* of this antient *Fraternity*; that we may shew to all the World the benign Influence of *Masonry*, as all wise, *true* and *faithful*, Brothers have done from the Beginning of Time, and will do till *Architecture* shall be dissolved in the general Conflagration.

Amen! So mote it be!

All these *Charges* you are to observe, and also Those that shall be communicated unto you in a Way that cannot be written.

The *Antient* Manner of Constituting a *Lodge*.

A New Lodge, for avoiding many Irregularities, should be solemnly *Constituted* by the *Grand Master* with his *Deputy* and *Wardens:* Or in the G. *Master's* Absence, the Deputy acts for his *Worship*, the *Senior* G. Warden as *Deputy*, the *Junior* G. Warden as the *Senior*, and a present *Master of a Lodge* as the *Junior*.

Or if the *Deputy* is also absent, the *Grand Master* may depute either of his G. Wardens, who can appoint Others to be G. *Officers* pro tempore.

The Lodge being open'd, and the *Candidates*, or the *New Master* and *Wardens* being yet among the *Fellow Crafts*, the G. 𝕸𝖆𝖘𝖙𝖊𝖗 shall ask his *Deputy*, if he has examin'd them, and finds the *Candidate Master* well skill'd in the Noble *Science* and the Royal *Art*, and duly instructed in our *Mysteries?* &c.

The 𝕯𝖊𝖕𝖚𝖙𝖞 answering in the Affirmative, shall (by the G. *Master's* Order) take the *Candidate* from among his *Fellows* and present him to the G. *Master*, saying, *Right Worshipful* GRAND MASTER, *the Brethren here desire to be form'd into a* Lodge; *and I present my worthy Brother* A. B. *to be their* Master, *whom I know to be of good Morals and great Skill, true and trusty, and a Lover of the whole* Fraternity *wheresoever dispers'd over the Face of the Earth.*

Then the 𝕲𝖗𝖆𝖓𝖉 𝕸𝖆𝖘𝖙𝖊𝖗 placing the Candidate on his Left Hand, having ask'd and obtain'd the unanimous Consent of the Brethren, shall say, *I constitute and form these good Brethren into a* New Lodge, *and appoint you Brother* A. B. *the* Master *of it, not doubting of your Capacity and Care to preserve the* Cement of the Lodge, *&c.* with some other Expressions that are proper and usual on that Occasion, but not proper to be written.

Upon this the *Deputy* shall rehearse the *Charges* of a *Master*; and the 𝕲𝖗𝖆𝖓𝖉 𝕸𝖆𝖘𝖙𝖊𝖗 shall ask the *Candidate*, saying, *Do you submit to these Charges, as Masters have done in all Ages?* And the *New* Master signifying his Cordial Submission thereunto,

The 𝕲𝖗𝖆𝖓𝖉 𝕸𝖆𝖘𝖙𝖊𝖗 shall by certain significant Ceremonies and antient Usages, instal him and present him with the *Book* of *Constitutions*, the *Lodge-Book* and the *Instruments* of his Office; not altogether, but one after another; and after each of 'em the G. *Master* or his *Deputy* shall rehearse the short and pithy Charge that is suitable to the Thing presented.

Next, the *Members* of this NEW LODGE, bowing all together to the G. *Master*, shall return his Worship their Thanks; and shall immediately do *Homage* to their *New Master*, and signify their Promise of Subjection and Obedience to him by the usual Congratulation.

The

The *Deputy* and *G. Wardens* and any other Brethren present that are not Members of this *New Lodge*, shall next congratulate the NEW MASTER, and he shall return his becoming Acknowledgments to the *G. Master* first, and to the Rest in their Order.

Then the 𝕲𝖗𝖆𝖓𝖉 𝕸𝖆𝖘𝖙𝖊𝖗 orders the *New Master* to enter immediately upon the Exercise of his Office, viz. in chusing his *Wardens*: And calling forth two *Fellow-Crafts* (*Master-Masons*) presents them to the *G. Master* for his Approbation, and to the *New Lodge* for their Consent. Upon which

The *Senior* or *Junior* G. 𝖂𝖆𝖗𝖉𝖊𝖓, or some Brother for him, shall rehearse the Charges of each *Warden* of a private Lodge: And they signifying their cordial Submission thereunto,

The NEW MASTER shall present them singly with the several *Instruments* of their Office, and in due Form instal them in their proper Places: And the Brethren of this *New Lodge* shall signify their Obedience to those NEW WARDENS by the usual Congratulation.

Then the *G. Master* gives all the Brethren Joy of their *New Master* and *Wardens*, and recommends Harmony; hoping their only Contention will be a laudable Emulation in cultivating the Royal *Art* and the Social *Virtues*.

Upon which all the *New Lodge* bow together in returning Thanks for the Honour of this CONSTITUTION.

The 𝕲𝖗𝖆𝖓𝖉 𝕸𝖆𝖘𝖙𝖊𝖗 also orders the *Secretary* to register this *New Lodge* in the *Grand Lodge Book*, and to notify the same to the other particular *Lodges*; and after the *Master's Song* he orders the *G. Warden* to close the *Lodge*.

This is the Sum, but not the whole *Ceremonial* by far; which the *Grand Officers* can extend or abridge at Pleasure, explaining Things that are not fit to be written: tho' none but Those that have acted as *Grand Officers* can accurately go through all the several Parts and Usages of a new Constitution in the just Solemnity.

The General REGULATIONS

OF THE

Free and *Accepted* MASONS.

Compiled firſt by Brother George Payne, Eſq; when *Grand Maſter*, A. D. 1720. and approv'd by the General *Aſſembly* at *Stationers-Hall* on 24 *June* 1721. Next by Order of the *Duke* of Montagu when *Grand Maſter*, the Author James Anderſon compared them with the antient Records of the *Fraternity*, and digeſted them into this Method with proper Additions and Explications from the ſaid *Records*; and the *Grand Lodge* having revis'd and approv'd them, order'd 'em to be printed in the *Book of Conſtitutions* on 25 *March* 1722.

To which are now added, in a diſtinct oppoſite Column.

The New Regulations, or the Alterations, Improvements and Explications of the Old, made by ſeveral *Grand Lodges*, ſince the *firſt* Edition.

Old Regulations.	New Regulations.
I. THE *G. Maſter* or *Deputy* has full Authority and Right, not only to be preſent, but alſo to preſide in every Lodge, with the *Maſter* of the Lodge on his Left Hand;	I. * THAT is, only when the G. Wardens are abſent: For the *G. Maſter* cannot deprive 'em of their Office, without ſhewing Cauſe fairly appearing to the *G. Lodge* according to the *Old Regulation* XVIII. ſo that if they are preſent in a *particular Lodge*

(153)

Old Regulations.

Hand; and to order his *Grand Wardens* to attend him, who are not to act as *Wardens* of *particular Lodges* but in his Presence and at his Command: For the *G. Master*, while in a *particular Lodge*, may command the *Wardens* of that *Lodge*, or any Other *Master-Masons*, to act there as his *Wardens* pro tempore. *

II. The Master of a *particular* Lodge has the Right and Authority of congregating the *Members* of his Lodge into a *Chapter* upon any Emergency or Occurrence; as well as to appoint the Time and Place of their usual *Forming*: And in Case of Death or Sickness, or necessary Absence of the *Master*, the Senior Warden shall act as *Master* pro tempore, if no Brother is present who has been *Master* of that *Lodge* before: For the *Absent Master's* Authority reverts to the *last Master present*, tho' he cannot act till the *Senior Warden* has congregated the *Lodge*.

New Regulations.

Lodge with the *Grand Master*, they must act as Wardens there.

On 17 *March* 1731.

The *Grand Lodge*, to cure some Irregularities, order'd, that None but the *G. Master*, his *Deputy* and *Wardens* (who are the only *Grand Officers*) shall wear their *Jewels* in *Gold* pendant to *Blue Ribbons* about their Necks, and *White Leather* Aprons with *Blue Silk*; which Sort of *Aprons* may be also worn by former *G. Officers*.

II. On 25 *Nov.* 1723.

It was agreed, that if a *Master* of a particular *Lodge* is deposed or demits, the *Senior Warden* shall forthwith fill the *Master's* Chair till the next Time of chusing; and ever since, in the *Master's* Absence, he fills the Chair, even tho' a former *Master* be present. [But was neglected to be recorded.]

On 17 *March* 1731.

Masters and *Wardens* of particular Lodges may line their *white* Leather *Aprons* with white Silk, and may hang their *Jewels* at *white* Ribbons about their Necks.

III. The   X   III. In

𝔒𝔩𝔡 Regulations.

III. The *Master* of each particular *Lodge*, or one of the *Wardens*, or some Other Brother by Appointment of the *Master*, shall keep a Book containing their *By-Laws*, the *Names* of their Members, and a List of all the *Lodges* in Town; with the usual Times and Places of their forming: And also all the Transactions of their own Lodge that are proper to be written.

IV. No *Lodge* shall make more than *Five New* Brothers at one and the same Time without an urgent Necessity; nor any Man under the Age of 25 Years (who must be also his own Master) unless by a *Dispensation* from the G. *Master*.

V. No Man can be accepted a *Member* of a *particular* Lodge without previous Notice one *Month* before given to the *Lodge*; in order to make due Enquiry into the Reputation and Capacity of the Candidate, unless by a *Dispensation*. VI. But

𝔑𝔢𝔴 Regulations.

III. In the Mastership of Dalkeith, a List of *all* the *Lodges* was engraven by Brother *John Pyne* in a very small Volume; which is usually reprinted on the Commencement of every *New Grand Master*, and dispersed among the Brethren.

On 21 *Nov*. 1724.

If a *particular* Lodge remove to a *New Place* for their stated Meeting, the *Officers* shall immediately signify the same to the Secretary.

On 27 *Dec*. 1727.

The *Precedency* of *Lodges* is grounded on the Seniority of their *Constitution*.

On 27 *Dec*. 1729.

Every *New Lodge*, for the Future, shall pay two *Guineas* for their *Constitution* to the General *Charity*.

IV. On 19 *Feb*. 172$\frac{3}{4}$. No Brother shall belong to more than *one Lodge* within the Bills of Mortality (tho' he may visit them all) except the Members of a *foreign* Lodge.

But this *Regulation* is neglected for several Reasons, and now obsolete.

V. The *Secretary* can direct the Petitioners in the *Form* for a *Dispensation*, if wanted. But if they know the Candidate, they don't require a Dispensation. VI. On

Old Regulations.

VI. But no Man can be enter'd a *Brother* in any *particular* Lodge, or admitted a *Member* thereof, without the *unanimous Consent* of *all* the Members of that *Lodge* then present when the *Candidate* is proposed, and when their Consent is formally asked by the *Master*. They are to give their Consent in their own prudent Way, either virtually or in Form, but with *Unanimity*. Nor is this inherent Privilege subject to a *Dispensation*; because the Members of a *particular* Lodge are the best Judges of it; and because if a *turbulent* Member should be imposed on them, it might spoil their Harmony or hinder the Freedom of their Communication, or even break and disperse the *Lodge*, which ought to be avoided by *all True* and *Faithful*.

VII. Every *New* Brother, at his *Entry*, is decently to *clothe the Lodge*, that is, all the Brethren present; and to deposite something for the Relief of indigent and decay'd Brethren, as the *Candidate* shall think fit to bestow, over and above the small Allowance that may be stated in the *By-Laws* of that *particular* Lodge: Which *Charity* shall be kept by the Cashier. *

Also the *Candidate* shall solemnly promise to submit to the *Constitutions* and other good Usages, that shall be intimated to him in Time and Place convenient.

New Regulations.

VI. On 19 *Feb.* 172$\frac{3}{4}$. No *Visitor*, however skill'd in Masonry, shall be admitted into a *Lodge*, unless he is personally known to, or well vouched and recommended by one of that Lodge present.

But it was found inconvenient to insist upon *Unanimity* in several Cases: And therefore the *Grand Masters* have allow'd the *Lodges* to admit a Member, if not above 3 *Ballots* are against him; though some *Lodges* desire no such *Allowance*.

VII. * See this explain'd in the Account of the *Constitution* of the General Charity below.

Only *particular* Lodges are not limited, but may take their own Method for *Charity*.

(156)

Old Regulations.

VIII. No Set or Number of Brethren shall withdraw or separate themselves from the *Lodge* in which they were made, or were afterwards admitted Members, unless the *Lodge* become too numerous; nor even then without a *Dispensation* from the G. Master or *Deputy*: And when thus separated, they must either immediately join themselves to such other *Lodges* that they shall like best, or else obtain the G. Master's *Warrant* to join in forming a *New Lodge* to be regularly constituted in good Time.

If any Set or Number of *Masons* shall take upon themselves to *form a Lodge*, without the G. Master's Warrant, the *regular* Lodges are not to countenance them, nor own them as *fair Brethren* duly formed, nor approve of their Acts and Deeds; but must treat them as *Rebels* until they humble themselves, as the G. Master shall in his Prudence direct

New Regulations.

VIII. On 25 *April* 1723.
Every Brother concern'd in making *Masons* clandestinely, shall not be allow'd to visit *any Lodge* till he has made due Submission, even tho' the Brothers so made may be allow'd.

On 19 *Feb*. 1724.
None who form a *Stated Lodge* without the G. *Master's* Leave shall be admitted into *regular* Lodges, till they make Submission and obtain Grace.

On 21 *Nov*. 1724.
If any Brethren *form a Lodge* without Leave, and shall irregularly make *New* Brothers, they shall not be admitted into any *regular* Lodge, no not as *Visitors*, till they render a good Reason or make due Submission.

On 24 *Feb*. 173$\frac{4}{5}$.
If any *Lodge* within the Bills of Mortality shall cease to meet regularly during 12 Months successive, its *Name* and *Place* shall be erazed or blotted out of the *Grand Lodge* Book and Engraven *List*: And if they petition to be again inserted and own'd as a *regular Lodge*, it must lose its former Place and Rank of *Precedency*, and submit to a *New* Constitution.

On 31 *March* 1735.
Seeing that some *extraneous* Brothers have been made lately in a clandestine Manner, that is, in no *regular* Lodge nor by any Authority or Dispensation from the G. *Master*, and upon

Old Regulations.	**New Regulations.**
direct, and until he approve of them by his *Warrant* signified to the *Other Lodges*; as the Custom is when a *New Lodge* is to be register'd in the *Grand Lodge Book*.	upon small and unworthy Considerations, to the Dishonour of the *Craft*; The *Grand Lodge* decreed, that no Person so made, nor any concern'd in making him, shall be a *Grand Officer*, nor an *Officer* of a *particular* Lodge, nor shall any such partake of the General *Charity*, if they should come to want it.
IX. But if any *Brother* so far misbehave himself as to render his *Lodge* uneasy, he shall be thrice duly admonish'd by the *Master* and *Wardens* in a *Lodge formed:* And if he will not refrain his Imprudence, nor obediently submit to the Advice of his Brethren, he shall be dealt with according to the *By-Laws* of that *particular* Lodge, or else in such a Manner as the *Quarterly*	IX. On 25 *Jan.* 173¾. The *Grand Lodge* made the following Regulation. Whereas Disputes have arisen about the *Removal* of *Lodges* from One House to Another, and it has been question'd in whom that Power is vested; it is hereby declar'd, That *no Lodge* shall be removed without the *Master's* Knowledge; that no Motion be made for removing in the *Master's* Absence; and that if the Motion be *seconded* or *thirded*, the *Master* shall order Summons to every individual Member, specifying the Business, and appointing a Day for Hearing and Determining the Affair, at least Ten Days before: and that the Determination shall be made by the *Majority*, provided the *Master* be one of *that* Majority: but if he be of the *Minority* against Removing, the *Lodge* shall not be removed unless the *Majority* consists of full *Two Thirds* of the Members present. But if the *Master* shall refuse to direct such Summons, either of the *Wardens* may do it: and if the *Master* neglects to attend on the Day fix'd, the *Warden* may preside in determining the Affair in the Manner prescribed; but they shall

Old Regulations.	New Regulations.
Quarterly Communication shall in their great Prudence think fit; for which a *New Regulation* may be afterwards made.	shall not in the *Master's* Absence, enter upon any other Cause but what is particularly mention'd in the *Summons*: and if the *Lodge* is thus regularly order'd to be removed, the *Master* or *Warden* shall send Notice thereof to the *Secretary* of the G. *Lodge* for publishing the same at the next *Quarterly* Communication.
X. The *Majority* of every *particular* Lodge, when congregated (not else) shall have the Privilege of giving Instructions to their *Master* and *Wardens* before the meeting of the *Grand Chapter* or Quarterly *Communication*; because the said *Officers* are their Representatives, and are supposed to speak the Sentiments of their Brethren at the said G. *Lodge*.	X. Upon a sudden Emergency the *Grand Lodge* has allow'd a private Brother to be present, and with Leave ask'd and given to signify his Mind, if it was about what concern'd *Masonry*.
XI. All *particular* Lodges are to observe the same *Usages* as much as possible: in order to which, and also for cultivating a good Understanding among *Free-Masons*, some Members of every Lodge shall be deputed to visit the other *Lodges* as often as shall be thought convenient.	XI. The same *Usages*, for Substance, are actually observed in every *Lodge*; which is much owing to *visiting* Brothers who compare the *Usages*.
XII. The GRAND LODGE consists of, and is formed by, the *Masters* and *Wardens* of all the *particular* Lodges upon Record, with the GRAND MASTER at their Head, the DEPUTY on his Left Hand, and the GRAND	XII. On 25 *Nov.* 1723. No *New* Lodge is own'd, nor their *Officers* admitted into the G. *Lodge*, unless it be regularly constituted and register'd. On 21 *Nov.* 1724. All who have been or shall be Grand *Masters*, shall be Members of and vote in all G. *Lodges*. On

(359)

Old Regulations.

Grand Wardens in their proper Places.

These must have 3 *Quarterly Communications*, before the *Grand Feast*, in some convenient Place, as the *Grand Master* shall appoint; where none are to be present but it's own proper Members, without Leave asked and given: And while such a Stranger (tho' a *Brother*) stays, he is not allow'd to vote, nor even to speak to any Question without Leave of the *Grand Lodge*; or unless he is desir'd to give his Opinion.

All Matters in the *Grand Lodge* are to be determin'd by a *Majority* of Votes, each Member having *one Vote*, and the Grand Master *two Votes*; unless the *Lodge* leave any particular Thing to the Determination of the *Grand Master* for the Sake of Expedition.

XIII. At the G. *Lodge* in *Quarterly* Communication, all Matters that concern the *Fraternity* in *general*, or *particular*,

New Regulations.

On 28 *Feb.* 172⅚.
All who have been or shall be *D.* Grand *Masters* shall be Members of and Vote in all *G. Lodges*.

On 10 *May* 1727.
All who have been or shall be Grand *Wardens* shall be Members of and Vote in all *G. Lodges*.

On 25 *June* 1728.
Masters and *Wardens* of *Lodges* shall never attend the *G. Lodge* without their *Jewels* and *Clothing*.

On 26 *Nov.* 1728.
One of the 3 *Officers* of a *Lodge* was admitted into the *G. Lodge* without his *Jewel*, because the *Jewels* were in the Custody of the *Officer* absent.

If any Officer cannot attend, he may send a *Brother* of that *Lodge* (but not a mere *Enter'd Prentice*) with his *Jewel*, to supply his Room and support the Honour of his *Lodge*.

On 24 *Feb.* 173¾.
Upon a Motion made by the former Grand Officers, it was resolv'd that the *Grand Officers* present and former, each of 'em who shall attend the Grand Lodge in Communication (except on the *Feast* Day) shall pay *Half a Crown* towards the Charge of such *Communication* when he attends.

XIII. On 13 *Dec.* 1733.
1. What Business cannot be transacted at *one Lodge*

Old Regulations.

particular Lodges, or *single* Brothers, are sedately and maturely to be discours'd of, 1.

Apprentices must be admitted *Fellow Crafts* and *Masters* only here, unless by a *Dispensation* from the *Grand Master*. 2.

Here also all Differences that cannot be made up or accommodated privately, nor by a *particular* Lodge, are to be seriously consider'd and decided: and if any Brother thinks himself aggrieved by the *Decision*, he may appeal to the *Annual Grand Lodge* next ensuing, and leave his *Appeal* in Writing with the *G. Master*, the *Deputy* or *G. Wardens*. 3.

Hither also all the *Officers* of *particular* Lodges shall bring a *List* of such Members as have been made, or even admitted by them since the last *Grand Lodge*.

There shall be a Book kept by the *G. Master* or *Deputy*, or rather by some Brother appointed *Secretary* of the *Grand Lodge*; wherein shall be recorded *all the Lodges*, with the usual Times and Places of their *Forming* and the *Names* of all the Members of Each *Lodge*: also all the Affairs of the *G. Lodge* that are proper to be written. 4.

The G. Lodge shall consider of the most prudent and effectual Method of collecting and disposing of what **Money** shall be lodged with them in *Charity*, towards the Relief only of any *true Brother* fallen into Poverty and Decay, but of none else.

But each *particular* Lodge may dispose of their *own Charity* for poor Brothers according

New Regulations.

Lodge, may be referr'd to the *Committee* of *Charity*, and by them reported to the *next Grand Lodge*.

2. On 22. *Nov.* 1725.

The *Master* of a Lodge with his *Wardens* and a competent *Number* of the Lodge assembled in due Form, can make *Masters* and *Fellows* at Discretion.

3. On 25 *Nov.* 1723.

It was agreed (tho' forgotten to be recorded in the *Grand Lodge Book*) that no Petitions and Appeals shall be heard on the *Feast-Day* or *Annual* Grand *Lodge*, nor shall any Business be transacted that tends to interrupt the *Harmony* of the *Assembly*, but shall be all referr'd to the next *G. Lodge*.

4. On 24 *June* 1723.

The *G. Lodge* chose *William Cowper*, Esq; to

Old Regulations.

according to their own *By-Laws*; until it be agreed by all the *Lodges* (in a NEW REGULATION) to carry in the *Charity* collected by them to the *G. Lodge* at the *Quarterly* or *Annual* Communication; in order to make a *Common Stock* for the more handsome Relief of poor Brethren.

They shall also appoint a **Treasurer**, a Brother of good Worldly Substance, who shall be a Member of the *G. Lodge* by Virtue of his Office, and shall be always present, and have a Power to move to the *G. Lodge* any Thing that concerns his *Office*.

To him shall be committed all Money rais'd for the General *Charity*, or for any other Use of the *G. Lodge*; which he shall write down in a *Book* with the respective Ends and Uses for which the several Sums are intended, and shall expend or disburse the same by such a certain *Order* sign'd, as the *G. Lodge* shall hereafter agree to in a *New Regulation*. 5.

But by Virtue of his Office as *Treasurer*, without any other Qualification, he shall not vote in chusing a *New G. Master* and *Wardens*; tho' in every other Transaction.

In like Manner the **Secretary** shall be a Member of the *G. Lodge* by Virtue of his *Office*, and shall vote in every Thing except in chusing *Grand Officers*.

The *Treasurer* and *Secretary* may have each a *Clerk* or Assistant, if they think fit, who must be a Brother and a *Master-Mason*; but must never be a *Member* of the *G. Lodge*, nor speak without being allow'd or commanded.

The GRAND MASTER or **Deputy** have Authority always to command the *Treasurer* and *Secretary* to attend him with their *Clerks* and *Books*; in order to see how Matters go on, and to know what is expedient to be done upon any Emergency.

Another Brother and *Master-Mason* should be appointed the *Tyler*, to look after the Door; but he must be no Member of the *G. Lodge*.

New Regulations.

to be their *Secretary*. But ever since then, the New *G. M.* upon his Commencement appoints the *Secretary*, or continues him by returning him the Books. His *Badge* is of *two Golden Pens* across on his *Left* Breast. And On 19 Feb. 172¾. The *Officers* of particular *Lodges* shall bring to the *G. Lodge* the *Lists* of all the Members of their respective *Lodges* to be inserted in the *G. Lodge Book*.

Y But 5. See

Old Regulations.

But these Offices may be farther explain'd by a *New Regulation*, when the Necessity or the Expediency of 'em may more appear, than at present, to the *Fraternity*.

XIV. If at any G. Lodge, stated or Occasional, Quarterly or Annual, the *Grand Master* and *Deputy* should both be absent; then the present *Master* of a *Lodge*, that has been longest a *Free-Mason*, shall take the Chair and preside as *Grand Master* pro tempore, and shall be vested with all his Honour and Power for the Time being; provided there is no Brother present that has been *Grand Master* or *Deputy* formerly; for the last former *Grand Master* or *Deputy* in Company takes place, of Right, in the Absence of the present *G. Master* or *Deputy*.

XV. In the *G. Lodge* none can act as *Wardens* but the *present* G. Wardens if in Com-

New Regulations.

5. See *This* at large in the *Constitution* of the *Committee* of *Charity*, Below.

XIV. In the *first* Edition, the Right of the G. Wardens was omitted in this *Regulation*; and it has been since found that the *Old Lodges* never put into the Chair the *Master* of a *particular Lodge*, but when there was no *Grand Warden* in Company, *present* nor *former*, and that in such a Case a *Grand Officer* always took place of any *Master* of a *Lodge* that has not been a *G. Officer*.

Therefore in Case of the Absence of all *G. Masters* and *Deputies*, the present *Sen.* G. Warden fills the Chair, and in his Absence the present *Jun.* G. Warden, and in his Absence the *oldest* former G. Warden in Company; and if no *former G. Officer* be found, then the *oldest Free-Mason* who is now the *Master* of a *Lodge*.

But to avoid Disputes, the *G. Master* usually gives a particular Commission under his Hand and Seal of Office, countersign'd by the *Secretary*, to the *Senior G. Warden*, or in his Absence, to the *Junior*, to act as *D. G. Master* when the *Deputy* is not in Town.

XV. Soon after the *first* Edition of the *Book* of *Constitutions*, the Grand Lodge finding it was always the antient Usage that the oldest *former* G Wardens

(163)

Old Regulations.

Company; and if absent, the *G. Master* shall order private *Wardens* to act as *G. Wardens* pro tempore; whose Places are to be supplied by two *Fellow-Crafts*, or *Master-Masons* of the same *Lodge*, call'd forth to act or sent thither by the *Master* thereof; or if by him omitted, the G. Master, or *He* that presides, shall call 'em forth to act; that so the G. *Lodge* may be always compleat.

XVI. The *Grand Wardens*, or any Others, are first to advise with the *Deputy* about the Affairs of the *Lodges* or of private single Brothers; and are not to apply to the *G. Master* without the Knowledge of the *Deputy*, unless he refuse his Concurrence. 1.

In which Case, or in Case of any Difference of Sentiment between the *Deputy* and *G. Wardens* or other Brothers, both Parties are to go to the *G. Master* by Consent; who, by Vertue of his great Authority and Power, can easily decide the Controversy and make up the Difference. 2.

The G. Master should not receive any private Intimations of Business concerning Masons and Masonry but from his *Deputy* first, except in such Cases as his *Worship* can easily judge of: And if the Application to the *G. Master* be *irregular*, his Worship can order the *G. Wardens*, or any Other so applying, to wait upon the *Deputy*,

New Regulations.

G. Wardens supplied the Places of those of the Year when absent, the *G. Master* ever since has order'd them to take place immediately and act as *G. Wardens* pro tempore; which they have always done in the Absence of the *G. Wardens* for the Year, except when they have waved their Privilege for that Time, to honour some Brother whom they thought more fit for the present Service.

But if no *former Grand Wardens* are in Company, the Grand Master, or *He* that *presides*, calls forth whom he pleases to act as *Grand Wardens* pro tempore.

XVI. 1. This was intended for the Ease of the *G. Master*, and for the Honour of the *Deputy*.

2. No such Case has happened in our Time; and all *Grand Masters* have govern'd more by Love than Power.

3. No irregular Applications have been made to the *G. Master*

Y 2 who

(164)

Old Regulations.

who is speedily to prepare the Business, and to lay it orderly before his *Worship*. 3.

XVII. No G. *Master*, D. G. *Master*, G. *Warden*, *Treasurer*, *Secretary*, or whoever acts for them or in their Stead *pro tempore*, can, at the same Time, act as the *Master* or *Warden* of a *particular Lodge*; but as soon as any of 'em has discharg'd his publick *Office*, he returns to that Post or Station in his particular *Lodge* from which he was call'd to officiate.

XVIII. If the Deputy be sick or necessarily absent, the G. *Master* can chuse any Brother he pleases to act as his *Deputy pro tempore*. 1.

But he that is chosen Deputy at the *Annual* Feast, and also the G. Wardens, cannot be discharg'd, unless the Cause fairly appear to the G. *Lodge*: For the G. Master, if he is uneasy, may call a G. *Lodge* on Purpose, to lay the Cause before 'em, for their Advice and Concurrence. 2.

And if the Members of the G. *Lodge* cannot reconcile the G. *Master* with his *Deputy* or *Wardens*, they are to allow the G. *Master* to discharge his *Deputy* or *Wardens*, and to chuse another *Deputy* immediately; and the same G. *Lodge*, in that Case, shall forthwith chuse other G. *Wardens*; that so Harmony and Peace may be preserved. 3.

XIX. If

New Regulations.

Master in our Time.

XVII. *Old* G. *Officers* are now, some of 'em, *Officers* of *particular Lodges*; but are not thereby deprived of their Privilege in the G. *Lodge* to sit and vote there as *old* G. *Officers*: Only he deputes one of his particular *Lodge* to act *pro tempore* as the *Officer* of *that Lodge* at the *Quarterly* Communication.

XVIII. 1. The *Senior* G. Warden now ever supplies the Deputy's Place, the *Junior* acts as the Senior, the *oldest* former G. *Warden* a the Junior, also the *oldest Mason* as above.

2. This was never done in our Time. See *New Regulation* I.

3. Should this Case ever happen, the G. Master appoints his G. *Officers*, as at first. See *Old Regulation* XXXV.

XIX. The

Old Regulations.	New Regulations.
XIX. If the G. MASTER should abuse his great Power, and render himself unworthy of the Obedience and Subjection of the *Lodges*, he shall be treated in a Way and Manner to be agreed upon in a *New Regulation*: Because hitherto the antient *Fraternity* have had no Occasion for it.	XIX. The *Free-Masons* firmly hope that there never will be any Occasion for such a *New Regulation*.
XX. The G. MASTER with his *Deputy*, G. *Wardens* and *Secretary*, shall, at least *once*, go round and visit *all the Lodges* about Town during his *Mastership*.	XX. Or else he shall send his G. *Officers* to visit the *Lodges*. This old and laudable Practice often renders a *Deputy* necessary: And when he visits them, the *Senior* G. WARDEN acts as *Deputy* the *Junior* as the SENIOR, as above: Or if both or any of 'em be absent, the DEPUTY, or *he* that *presides* for him, may appoint whom he pleases in their Stead *pro tempore*. For when both the G. *Masters* are absent, the *Senior* or the *Junior* G. *Warden* may preside as *Deputy* in visiting the *Lodges*, or in the *Constitution* of a *New Lodge*; neither of which can be done without, at least, *one* of the *present* G. *Officers*.
XXI. If the G. MASTER die during his *Mastership*, or by Sickness, or by being beyond'Sea, or any other Way should be render'd uncapable of discharging his Office, the *Deputy*, or in his Absence the *Senior* G. WARDEN, or in his Absence the *Junior* G. WARDEN, or in his Absence any 3 present *Masters* of *Lodges*, shall assemble the G. *Lodge* immediately; in order to advise together upon that Emergency, and to send two of their Number to invite the *last* G. MASTER to resume his Office, which now of Course reverts to him: And if he refuse to act, then the *next Last*, and so backward.	XXI. Upon such a Vacancy, if no *former* G. MASTER nor *former* DEPUTY be found, the present *Senior* G. WARDEN fills the Chair, or in his Absence the *Junior* till a *N. G. Master* is chosen: And if no present nor former *G. Warden* be found, then the *Oldest Free-Mason* who

Old Regulations. | **New Regulations.**

ward. But if no *former* G. MASTER be found, the *present* DEPUTY shall act as Principal till a *New* G. *Master* is chosen: Or if there be no *Deputy*, then the *oldest Mason* the present *Master* of a *Lodge*.	who is now the *Master* of a *Lodge*.
XXII. The *Brethren* of *all the Lodges* in and about *London* and *Westminster*, shall meet *annually* in some convenient Place or publick Hall. 1. They shall assemble either on St. JOHN *Evangelist's* Day or St. JOHN *Baptist's* Day, as the G. *Lodge* shall think fit by a *New Regulation*; having of late Years met on St. JOHN *Baptist's* Day. 2. Provided the *Majority* of the G. *Lodge*, about *Three* Months before, shall agree that there shall be a *Feast* and a general *Communication* of *all the Brethren*: For if they are against it, others must forbear it at that Time. But whether there shall be a *Feast* or not for all the Brethren, yet the G. *Lodge* must meet in some convenient Place on St. JOHN'S Day; or if it be a *Sunday*, then on the next Day, in order to chuse or recognize every Year a *New* G. *Master*, *Deputy* and *Wardens*.	XXII. 1. Or any *Brethren* round the Globe, who are *True* and *Faithful*, at the Place appointed, till they have built a Place of their own. 2. The *annual Feast* has been held on both the St. JOHN's Days, as the G. *Master* thought fit. And On 25 *Nov.* 1723. it was ordain'd that one of the *Quarterly Communications* shall be held on St. JOHN *Evangelist's* Day, and another on St. JOHN *Baptist's* Day every Year, whether there be a *Feast* or not, unless the G. *Master* find it inconvenient for the Good of the *Craft*, which is more to be regarded than Days. But of late Years, most of the *Eminent* Brethren being out of Town on both the St. JOHN'S Days, the G. *Master* has appointed the *Feast* on such a Day as appeared most convenient to the *Fraternity*. On 29 *January* 173$\frac{0}{1}$. It was ordain'd that no *particular Lodge* shall have a *separate Feast* on the Day of the General *Feast*.
XXIII. If.	XXIII. The

(167)

Old Regulations.

XXIII. If the G. Master and Lodge shall think it expedient to hold the *Annual General Assembly* and *Feast*, according to the antient and laudable Custom of *Masons*; then the G. Wardens shall have the Care of preparing *Tickets* seal'd with the *G. Master's Seal* of *Office*, of disposing the *Tickets*, of buying the Materials of the *Feast*, of finding out a proper and convenient Place to feast in, and of every other Thing that concerns the Entertainment.

But that the Work may not be too burdensome to the *Two Grand Wardens*, and that all Matters may be expeditiously and safely

New Regulations.

XXIII. The Grand Wardens were antiently assisted by a certain Number of *Stewards* at every Feast, or by some general Undertaker of the Whole.

On 28 *April* 1724. the G. Lodge ordain'd, that at the Feast, the *Stewards* shall open no Wine till Dinner be laid on the Tables; that the *Members* of *each Lodge* shall sit together as much as possible: That after *Eight a Clock* at Night, the *Stewards* shall not be oblig'd to furnish any Wine or other Liquors; and that either the *Money* or *Tickets* shall be return'd to the *Stewards*.

On 26 *November* 1728. The *Office* of Stewards, that had been disused at 3 preceding *Feasts*, was revived by the G. *Lodge*, and their Number to be always 12. who, together with the G. Wardens, shall prepare the *Feast*.

On 17 *March* 173$\frac{0}{1}$. The Stewards for the Year were allow'd to have *Jewels* of Silver (tho' not guilded) pendent to *Red* Ribbons about their Necks, to bear *White* Rods, and to line their *White* Leather *Aprons* with *Red* Silk.

Former Stewards were also allow'd to wear the same Sort of Aprons, *White* and *Red*.

On 2d *March* 173$\frac{1}{2}$. The G. Lodge allow'd each of the acting Stewards for the future, at the *Feast*, the Privilege of Naming his Successor in that Office for the Year ensuing.

On 24 *June* 1735. Upon an Address from Those that have been Stewards, the G. *Lodge*, in Consideration of their past Service and future Usefulness, ordain'd,

1. That

(168)

Old Regulations.	New Regulations.
safely managed, the *G. Master* or his *Deputy* shall have Power to nominate and appoint a certain Number of Stewards, as his *Worship* shall think fit, to act in Concert with the *two* G Wardens: And all Things relating to the *Feast* shall be decided amongst 'em by a *Majority* of Votes; except the *G. Master* or his *Deputy* interpose by a particular Direction or Appointment.	1. That they should be constituted a *Lodge* of *Masters*, to be call'd the Stewards Lodge, to be register'd as such in the *Grand Lodge Books* and printed *List*, with the Times and Place of their Meetings. 2. That the Stewards Lodge shall have the Privilege of sending a Deputation of 12 to every *G. Lodge*, viz. the *Master*, *Two Wardens* and *Nine* more, and *Each* of the 12 shall vote there, and *Each* of 'em that attends shall pay *Half a Crown*, towards the Expence of the *G. Lodge*. 3. That no Brother who has not been a *Steward* shall wear the same Sort of *Aprons* and *Ribbons*. 4. That each of the 12 *Deputies* from the *Stewards Lodge* shall, in the *G. Lodge*, wear a peculiar *Jewel* suspended in the *Red* Ribbon; the Pattern of which was then approved. 5. That the 12 Stewards of the current Year shall always attend the *G. Lodge* in their proper *Clothing* and *Jewels*, paying at the Rate of 4 *Lodges* towards the Expence of the *Communication:* But they are not to vote, nor even to speak, except when desired, or else of what relates to the ensuing *Feast* only.
XXIV. The G. Wardens and Stewards shall in due Time wait upon the G. *Master* or *Deputy* for Directions and Orders about the Premises: But if both their *Worships* are sick or necessarily absent, they may call together the *Masters* and *Wardens* of *Lodges*, on Purpose for their Advice and Orders: Or else they may take the whole Affair upon themselves and do the best they can.	XXIV. The Stewards now take the whole Affair upon themselves and do the best they can. Nor are their Accounts now audited

The

(169)

Old Regulations.   **New Regulations.**

The G. *Wardens* and *Stewards* are to account for all the Money they receive or expend, after Dinner, to the G. *Lodge*, or when the *Lodge* shall think fit to audite their Accounts.

| audited by the G. *Lodge*; for that generally the *Stewards* are out of Pocket.

XXV. The MASTERS of *Lodges* shall each appoint one experienced and discreet Brother of his *Lodge*, to compose a Committee consisting of One from *every Lodge*, who shall meet in a convenient Apartment to receive every Person that brings a *Ticket*; and shall have Power to discourse him, if they think fit, in order to admit or debar him, as they shall see Cause. Provided

They send no Man away before they have acquainted all the Brethren *within Doors* with the Reasons thereof; that so no *true* Brother may be debarr'd, nor a *false* Brother or a mere *Pretender* admitted. This *Committee* must meet very early on St. JOHN's Day at the Place, before any Persons come with Tickets.

| XXV. On 25 *Jan.* 1723. The G. *Lodge* order'd that the *Committee* of *Enquiry* and the *Stewards* with Others, shall be early at the Place of the *Feast* for those Purposes mention'd in this *Old Regulation*, and the *Order* was confirm'd by the G. *Lodge*, viz. on 17 *Nov.* 1725.

XXVI. The G. MASTER shall appoint *Two* or more true and trusty Brothers to be *Porters* and *Door-Keepers*, who are also to be early at the Place for some good Reasons; and who are to be at the Command of the said *Committee*.

| XXVI. The *Tylers* and other Servants, within or without Doors, are now appointed only by the *Stewards*.

XXVII. The G. WARDENS or the STEWARDS shall before-hand, appoint such a Number of Brethren to serve at *Table* as they think fit: and they may advise with the *Officers* of *Lodges* about the most proper Persons, if they please, or may
             Z   retain

| XXVII. Now only the STEWARDS appoint the *Attenders* at Table; who are

Old Regulations.

retain such by their Recommendation: For none are to serve that Day but *Free and Accepted Masons*; that the Communication may be free and harmonious.

XXVIII. All the Members of the G. LODGE must be at the *Place* of the *Feast* long before Dinner, with the G. MASTER or his DEPUTY at their Head; who shall retire and form themselves. And this in order,

1. To receive any *Appeals* duly lodged as above regulated; that the *Appellant* and *Respondent* may both be heard, and the Affair may be amicably decided before Dinner, if possible.

But if it cannot, it must be delay'd till after the *New G. Master* takes the Chair.

And if it cannot be decided after Dinner, the *G. Master* must refer it to a special *Committee*, that shall quickly adjust it and make Report to the next *G. Lodge*; that so brotherly Love may be preserved.

2. To prevent any Difference or Disgust which may be fear'd to arise that Day; that so no Interruption may be given to the Harmony and Pleasure of the *General Assembly* and *Grand Feast*.

3. To consult about whatever concerns the Decency and Decorum of

New Regulations.

are the more necessary if the *Cooks* and *Butlers* are not *Brothers*.

XXVIII. No *Petitions* or *Appeals* on the Day of the General *Assembly* and *Feast*. See *New Regulation* XIII. at 25 *Nov.* 1723.

In antient Times the *Master*, *Wardens* and *Fellows* on St. JOHN's Day met either in a *Monastery*, or on the *Top* of the highest *Hill* near them, by Peep of Day: And having there chosen their *New G. Officers*, they descended walking in due Form to the *Place* of the *Feast*, either a *Monastery*, or the House of an *Eminent Mason*, or some large House of Entertainment as they thought best tyled.

But of late they go in *Coaches*, as described in the *March* of NORFOLK, Part III. Pag. 125.

Sometimes the *Masters* and *Wardens* of particular *Lodges* have met the G. MASTER and his Retinue at the Door or Gate, and have attended him into the *Lodge-Room*: And sometimes he with his Retinue has gone in first, and sent his *Wardens* for the said *Masters* and *Wardens*. But

Old Regulations.	**New Regulations.**
of the *Grand Assembly*, and to prevent ill Manners; the Assembly being promiscuous, that is, of all Sorts of *Free-Masons*.	But it is equal: for the G. Lodge must be formed before *Dinner*.
XXIX. After these Things are discuss'd, the G. Master, the Deputy, the G. Wardens, the Stewards, the Treasurer, the Secretary, the *Clerks* and every other Person, shall withdraw and leave the *Masters* and *Wardens* of particular *Lodges* alone; in order to their amicable Consulting about the Election of a New G. Master, or the Continuing of the *Present* another Year; if the said *Masters* and *Wardens* have not met and done it the Day before.	XXIX. This old Regulation was found inconvenient: Therefore at the *Assembly* on 27 *Dec*. 1720. (Page 111.) it was agreed that the *New G. Master* should by the *Present* be propos'd to the *G. Lodge* at their Communication, some time before the Day of the *Annual Feast*; and that if he was approv'd then, or no Objection made, he was to be forthwith saluted G. Master *Elect*, if there; or if absent, his Health was to be toasted as such; and that as such he was to march to the *Feast* on the *present* G. Master's Left Hand.
And if they agree by a Majority to continue the *present* G. Master, his *Worship* shall be call'd in; and, after Thanks, shall be humbly desir'd to do the *Fraternity* the *Honour* of ruling them another Year. And after Dinner, it will be known whether he accepts of it or not; for it should not be discover'd till then.	Thus on *Lady-day* 1721. P. 111. Payne G. *Master* proposed the Duke of Montagu: and All have since been so proposed. Therefore Now, before Dinner, there is no *Election*, but only a *Recognizing* of the former Approbation of the *New G. Master*, which is soon done.
XXX. Then the *Masters* and *Wardens*, and all the Brethren may converse promiscuously, or as they please to sort together	XXX. The G. Master may say Grace himself, or employ some Brother who is a *Clergyman*, or else the *Secretary*,

(172)

Old Regulations.

ther until the *Dinner* is coming in, when every Brother takes his Seat at Table.

XXXI. Some Time after *Dinner* the G. Lodge is form'd, not in Retirement, but in Presence of all the Brethren, who yet are not Members of it; and none of those that are not, must speak, until they are desir'd and allow'd.

XXXII. If the G. Master of last Year has consented with the *Masters* and *Wardens* in private before Dinner to cont. nue for the Year ensuing, then *One* of the G. *Lodge*, deputed for that Purpose, shall represent to all the Brethren *his Worship's good Government*, &c. and turning to him, shall in the Name of the G. *Lodge*, humbly request him to do the *Fraternity* the *great Honour* (if nobly born, if not) the great *Kindness* of continuing to be their G. Master for the Year ensuing: And his *Worship* declaring his Consent by a Bow or a Speech, as he pleases, the said deputed Member of the G. Lodge shall proclaim him aloud

GRAND MASTER of Masons!

All the Members of the G. *Lodge* shall salute him in due Form; and all the Brethren shall, for a few Minutes, have leave to declare their Satisfaction, Pleasure and Congratulation.

XXXIII. But if either the *Masters* and *Wardens* have not in private this Day before Dinner,

New Regulations.

to say Grace, both before and after Dinner.

XXXI. This *old* Method was found inconvenient: Therefore as the whole *Assembly* sit together at Dinner in the Form of a *Grand Lodge*, there is no Alteration, but the *Members* of the G. *Lodge* continue promiscuous in their Seats.

XXXII. There has been no Occasion yet in our Time of putting this *Old Regulation* in Practice; because the *New* Grand Master is proposed by the *present* Grand Master, and approved by the G. *Lodge*, some Time before the Feast; as in the *New Regulation* XXIX. and because no G. *Master* has been yet requested to continue a 2d Year.

XXXIII. There has been no Occasion

(173)

Old Regulations.

Dinner, nor the Day before, desir'd the *last* G. *Master* to continue in his Mastership another Year; or if He, when desir'd, has not consented, Then;

The *present* G. Master shall nominate his Successor for the Year ensuing, who, if unanimously approv'd by the *Grand Lodge*, and there present, shall be proclaim'd, saluted and congratulated the *New* G. Master, as above hinted, and immediately install'd by the last G. *Master* according to Usage.*

XXXIV. But if that *Nomination* is not unanimously approv'd, the *New* G. Master shall be chosen immediately by *Ballot*; every *Master* and *Warden* writing his Man's Name, and the *last* G. *Master* writing his Man's Name too; and the Man whose Name the *last* G. *Master* shall first take out casually or by Chance, shall be

Grand Master *of* Masons

for the Year ensuing; and if present, he shall be proclaim'd, saluted and congratulated, as above hinted, and forthwith install'd by the *last* G. *Master* according to Usage.

XXXV. The *last* G. Master thus continued, or the *New* G. Master thus install'd, shall next nominate and appoint his *Deputy* G. Master, either the *Last* or a *New One*, who shall be also proclaim'd, saluted and congratulated in due Form.

The *New* G. Master shall also nominate

New Regulations.

casion yet for putting this *Old Regulation* in Practice; because no *Grand Master* has been requested in our Time to continue a 2d Year. * See the Manner of *Instalment* at Richmond, Part III. Page 117.

XXXIV. There has been no Occasion in our Time for this *old Regulation*, nor can be now; for that there must be no *Balloting* nor any *Controversy* on the *Feast-Day*, according to Agreement. See *New Regulation* XIII. at 25 *Nov.* 1723.

XXXV. A Deputy was always needful when the G. Master was *nobly born:* And in our Time, the G. Master *Elect* has not publickly signified before Hand the

Old Regulations.

nominate his *New* G. Wardens; and if unanimously approv'd by the G. *Lodge*, they shall be forthwith proclaim'd, saluted and congratulated in due Form.

But if not, they shall be chosen by *Ballot* in the same Way as the G. *Master* was chosen, and as *Wardens* of *private* Lodges are chosen when the Members do not approve of their *Master's* Nomination.

XXXVI. But if the Brother whom the *present* G. Master shall nominate for his Successor, or whom the G. *Lodge* shall chuse by *Ballot*, as above, is by Sickness, or other necessary Occasion, absent, he cannot be proclaim'd G. Master; unless the *old* G. *Master*, or some of the *Masters* and *Wardens* of *Lodges*, can vouch upon the *Honour* of a *Brother*, that the said Person, so nominated or chosen, will readily accept of the *Office*. In which Case the *old* G. *Master* shall act as *Proxy*, and in his Name shall nominate the *Deputy* and *Wardens*; and in his Name shall receive the usual Honours, Homage and Congratulations.

XXXVII. Then the G. Master shall allow any Brother, a *Fellow-Craft*, or *Enter'd Prentice*, to speak, directing his Discourse to his *Worship* in the Chair; or to make any Motion for the Good of the *Fraternity*, which shall

New Regulations.

the Names of his intended *Deputy* and *Wardens*, nor till he is first install'd in *Solomon's* Chair.

For then *first* he calls them forth by Name, and appoints them to officiate instantly, as soon as they are install'd.

XXXVI. The Proxy must be either the *last* or a *former* G. Master; as the Duke of *Richmond* was for Lord *Paisley*, Page 119, or else a very reputable Brother; as Lord *Southwell* was for the Earl of *Strathmore*, Page 130.

But the *New Deputy* and G. *Wardens* are not allow'd *Proxies* when appointed.

XXXVII. This is not allow'd till the *New* G. Master has made the 2d *Procession* round

Old Regulations.

shall be either immediately confider'd, or elfe referr'd to the Confideration of the *Grand Lodge* at their next *Communication* ftated or occafional. When that is over,

XXXVIII. The G. Master, or *Deputy*, or fome other appointed by him, fhall harangue all the Brethren and give them good Advice. And laftly,

After fome other *Tranfactions* that cannot be written in any Language, the Brethren may ftay longer or go away, as they pleafe, when the *Lodge* is clofed in good Time.

XXXIX. Every *Annual* G. Lodge has an inherent Power and Authority to make *New Regulations*, or to alter *Thefe* for the real Benefit of this antient *Fraternity*, provided always that the *Old Land Marks* be carefully preferved, and that fuch *New Regulations* and Alterations be propofed and agreed to at the 3d *Quarterly* Communication preceding the *Annual* Grand *Feaft*; and that they be offer'd to the Perufal of *all the Brethren* before Dinner in writing, even of the youngeft *Enter'd Prentice*; the Approbation and Confent of the *Majority* of *all the Brethren* prefent being abfolutely neceffary to make

New Regulations.

round the *Tables*; as at Richmond, Page 118.

XXXVIII. After the *Oration*, the 5 publick *Healths* may be toafted; and before or after each, a *Mafons Song* with the beft Inftruments of Mufick.

Other Things relating to the *Charges*, &c. of the G. Master, are beft known to the *Fraternity*.

XXXIX. On 24 *June* 1723. at the *Feaft*, the G. Lodge before Dinner made this Resolution, that *it is not in the Power of any Man or Body of Men to make any Alteration or Innovation in the Body of Mafonry, without the Confent firft obtain'd of the* G. Lodge. And on 25 *Nov.* 1723. the G. Lodge in *Ample Form* refolved, that *any G. Lodge duly met has a Power to amend or explain any of the printed Regulations in the Book of Conftitutions, while they break not in upon the antient Rules of the Fraternity.*

But that no *Alterations* fhall be made in this printed Book of Conftitutions

(176)

Old Regulations.	New Regulations.
make the same Binding and Obligatory; which must therefore after Dinner, and after the *New G. Master* is install'd, be solemnly desir'd; as it was desir'd and obtain'd for these *Old Regulations*, when proposed by the G. Lodge to about 150 Brethren at *Stationers-Hall* on St. John *Baptist's* Day 1721.	*Constitutions without Leave of the G. Lodge.* Accordingly, All the *Alterations* or New Regulations above written are only for amending or explaining the Old Regulations for the Good of *Masonry*, without breaking in upon the antient *Rules* of

The End of the Old Regulations.

the *Fraternity*, still preserving the *Old Land Marks*; and were made at several Times, as Occasion offer'd, by the Grand Lodge; who have an inherent Power of amending what may be thought inconvenient, and ample Authority of making New Regulations for the Good of *Masonry*, without the Consent of *All the Brethren* at the *Grand* Annual Feast; which has not been disputed since the said 24 *June* 1721. for the *Members* of the G. Lodge are truly the Representatives of *All the Fraternity*, according to Old Regulation X.

And so on 6 *April* 1736.

John Ward, Esq; *D. Grand Master* in the Chair, proposed a *New Regulation* of 10 Rules for explaining what concern'd the *Decency* of *Assemblies* and *Communications*; which was agreed to by that *Grand Lodge*, viz.

XL. 1. That no *Brothers* be admitted into the G. Lodge but those that are the known *Members* thereof; viz. The *four present* and all *former* G. Officers, the *Treasurer* and *Secretary*, the *Masters* and *Wardens* of all *regular Lodges*, the *Masters* and *Wardens* and *Nine* more of the *Stewards Lodge*: except a Brother who is a Petitioner or a Witness in some Case, or one call'd in by a Motion.

2. That at the 3d *Stroke* of the G. Master's Hammer (always to be repeated by the *Senior Grand Warden*) there shall be a general Silence; and that he who breaks Silence without Leave from the Chair shall be publickly reprimanded. 3. That

(177)

3. That under the same Penalty, every Brother shall take his Seat and keep strict Silence whenever the G. MASTER or *Deputy* shall think fit to rise from the Chair and call to order.

4. That in the G. LODGE every Member shall keep in his Seat, and not move about from Place to Place, during the *Communication*; except the G. WARDENS, as having more immediately the Care of the *Lodge*.

5. That according to the Order of the G. LODGE on 21 *April* 1730. (as in the *Lodge-Book*) no Brother is to speak but *once* to the same Affair; unless to explain himself, or when call'd by the *Chair* to speak.

6. Every one that speaks shall rise and keep standing, addressing himself to the *Chair*: Nor shall any presume to interrupt him, under the foresaid Penalty; unless the G. MASTER, finding him wandering from the Point in Hand, shall think fit to reduce him to Order; for then the said *Speaker* shall sit down: But after he has been set right, he may again proceed, if he pleases.

7. If in the G. LODGE any Member is twice call'd to *Order*, at one *Assembly*, for transgressing these Rules, and is guilty of a 3d *Offence* of the same Nature, the *Chair* shall peremptorily command him to quit the *Lodge-Room* for that Night.

8. That whoever shall be so rude as to *hiss at a Brother*, or at what another says or has said, he shall be forthwith solemnly excluded the *Communication*, and declared incapable of ever being a *Member of any Grand Lodge* for the Future, till another Time he publickly owns his Fault and his Grace be granted.

9. No Motion for a *New Regulation*, or for the Alteration of an *Old One*, shall be made, till it is first handed up in *writing* to the CHAIR: And after it has been perused by the G. MASTER at least about Ten Minutes, the Thing may be moved publickly; and then it shall be audibly read by the *Secretary*: And if *he* be seconded and thirded, it must be immediately committed to the Consideration of the *whole Assembly*, that their Sense may be fully heard about it: After which the G. MASTER shall put the Question *pro* and *con*.

10. The Opinions or *Votes* of the *Members* are always to be signified by each holding up *one of his Hands:* Which uplifted *Hands* the G. WARDENS are to count; unless the *Numbers* of *Hands* be so unequal as to render the Counting useless. Nor should any other Kind of *Division* be ever admitted among MASONS. The End of the 𝔑𝔢𝔴 REGULATIONS.

The CONSTITUTION of the COMMITTEE of *Masons* 𝔈𝔥𝔞𝔯𝔦𝔱𝔶 first proposed at the *Grand Lodge* on 21 *Nov.* 1724.

CHARLES LENNOS Duke of *Richmond* and *Lennox* (and now also Duke *d'Aubigny*) being *Grand Master*; 𝔐𝔞𝔯𝔱𝔦𝔫 𝔉𝔬𝔩𝔨𝔢𝔰, Esq; *Deputy* Grand ⎰ 𝔊𝔢𝔬𝔯𝔤𝔢 𝔓𝔞𝔶𝔫𝔢, Esq; ⎱ *Grand* ⎰ with several *Master*, ⎱ 𝔉𝔯𝔞𝔫𝔠𝔦𝔰 𝔖𝔬𝔯𝔢𝔩𝔩, Esq; ⎰ *Wardens.* ⎱ *noble*Brothers, and the Officers of 45 Lodges.

Brother FRANCIS SCOT Earl of *Dalkeith* (now Duke of *Buckleugh*) the last Grand *Master,* proposed, in Pursuance of the *Old Regulation* XIII. *That in Order to promote the charitable Disposition of* FREE-MASONS, *and to render it more extensively beneficial to the Society,* each Lodge *may make a certain Collection, according to Ability, to be put into a* Joint-Stock, *lodged in the Hands of a* Treasurer *at every* Quarterly Communication, *for the Relief of distress'd Brethren that shall be recommended by the* Contributing Lodges *to the* Grand Officers *from Time to Time.*

The Motion being readily agreed to,

RICHMOND *Grand Master* desir'd all present to come prepar'd to give their Opinion of it, at next 𝔊𝔯𝔞𝔫𝔡 𝔏𝔬𝔡𝔤𝔢; which was held in *Ample* Form on 17 *March* 172$\frac{4}{5}$. When

At the *Lodge's* Desire, G. M. RICHMOND named a *Committee* for considering of the best Methods to regulate the said *Masons*

General

(179)

General *Charity*: They met and chose for Chairman **William Cowper**, Esq; Clerk of the Parliament, who drew up the *Report*.

But the Affair requiring great Deliberation, the *Report* was not made till the **Grand Lodge** met in *Ample* Form on 27 *Nov.* 1725. when RICHMOND G. M. order'd the *Report* to be read. It was well approved and recorded in the Book of the *Grand Lodge*; for which that Committee receiv'd publick Thanks, and Copies of it were order'd to be sent to the particular *Lodges*.

Yet no **Treasurer** was found, till at the *Grand Lodge* in *Ample* Form on 24 *June* 1727, INCHIQUIN G. M. requested Brother **Nathaniel Blakerby**, Esq; to accept of that Officer, which he very kindly undertook.

Then also it was resolv'd, that the 4 *Grand Officers* for the Time being, together with Brother *Martin Folkes, Francis Sorell* and *George Payne*, Esqs; as a COMMITTEE of 7, should, upon due Recommendations, dispose of the intended Charity; and fresh Copies of the *Report* were sent to the *Lodges*.

At last this good Work of **Charity** was begun at the *Grand Lodge* on 25 *Nov.* 1729. KINGSTON being *Grand Master*, and in his Absence D. G. Master **Blakerby**, the *Treasurer*, in the Chair; who after a warm Exhortation, order'd the *Lodges* to be call'd over a second Time, when some *Officers* gave in the Benevolence of their respective *Lodges*; for which they were thank'd, and their *Charity* being forthwith recorded, was put into the Hands of the *Treasurer*, as an hopeful Beginning: and other *Lodges* following the good Example,

At the **Grand Lodge** in *Due* Form on 27 *Dec.* 1729. D. G. M. **Blakerby** the *Treasurer*, in the Chair, had the Honour to thank many *Officers* of *Lodges*, for bringing their liberal *Charity*: When by a Motion of Brother *Thomas Batson* Counsellor at Law, the *Grand Lodge* ordain'd *that every* new Lodge, *for their* Constitution, *shall pay two Guineas towards this General* Charity *of* Masons.

And ever since, the *Lodges*, according to their Ability, have, by their Officers, sent their Benevolence to every Grand Lodge, except on the Grand *Feast* Day: And several distress'd Brothers have been handsomely reliev'd.

But finding the foresaid *Committee* of *Seven* too few for the good Work, the **Grand Lodge** in *Due* Form on 28 *Aug.* 1730. Norfolk being *Grand Master*, and in his Absence D. G. M. **Blakerby**, the *Treasurer*, in the Chair, resolv'd, *That the* Committee *of Charity shall have added to 'em* 12 **Masters** *of contributing Lodges ; that the first* 12 *in the* printed List *shall be succeeded by the next* 12, *and so on : And that for Dispatch, any* 5 *of 'em shall be a Quorum, provided one of the* 5 *is a present* Grand *Officer.* Accordingly,

The Committee of *Charity* met the *Treasurer* **Blakerby** the first Time in the *Mastership* of Norfolk.

On 13 *Nov.* 1730. When

They consider'd the Petitions of some poor Brethren, whom they reliev'd, not exceeding 3 Pounds to each Petitioner: And ever since they have adjourn'd, from Time to Time, for supplying the Distress'd according to their Powers ; or else have recommended 'em to the greater Favour of the *Grand Lodge.*

Yet the Committee had not all their Powers at once : For at the **Grand Lodge** on 15 *Dec.* 1730. Norfolk being *Grand Master*, and in his Absence the *Deputy* **Blakerby** in the Chair, it was ordain'd, *That for Dispatch, all Complaints and Informations about* Charity, *shall be referred, for the future, to the* Committee *of Charity ; and that they shall appoint a Day for hearing the same, shall enter their Proceedings in their own Book, and shall report their Opinion to the* Grand Lodge.

And now hence forward, the *Minutes* of the Committee of *Charity* are read and consider'd at every *G. Lodge*, except on the *G. Feast* Day.

At the Committee of Charity 16 *March* 173$\frac{0}{1}$. it was agreed *that no Petition shall be read, if the Petitioner don't attend the Committee in Person ; except in the Cases of Sickness, Lameness or Imprisonment.*

At the **Grand Lodge** on 14 *May* 1731. upon the Motion of Lovel *Grand Master* it was resolv'd, 1. *That all former Grand* Masters *and* Deputies *shall be Members of the* Committee *of* Charity.

2. That

2. That the Committee shall have a Power to give 5 Pounds, as casual Charity, to a poor Brother, but no more, till the Grand Lodge assemble.

At the Committee of Charity on 18 June 1731. it was agreed, that no poor Brother, that has been once assisted, shall, a second Time, present a Petition, without some new Allegation well attested.

At the 𝕲𝖗𝖆𝖓𝖉 𝕷𝖔𝖉𝖌𝖊 on 8 June 1732. Viscount Montagu being G. Master, and in his Absence D. G. M. 𝕭𝖆𝖙𝖘𝖔𝖓 in the Chair, having signified, That notwithstanding the General Charity, some poor Brothers had molested Noblemen and Others (being Masons) with private Applications for Charity, to the Scandal of the Craft; it was resolv'd, that any Brother who makes such private Applications for the future, shall be for ever debarr'd from any Relief from the Committee of Charity, the Grand Lodge, or any Assemblies of Masons.

At the Committee of Charity on 5 July 1732. it was agreed that no Brother shall be reliev'd, unless his Petition be attested by 3 Brothers of the Lodge to which he does, or did once, belong.

At the 𝕲𝖗𝖆𝖓𝖉 𝕷𝖔𝖉𝖌𝖊 on 21 Nov. 1732. Viscount Montagu being G. Master, and in his Absence Deputy 𝕭𝖆𝖙𝖘𝖔𝖓 in the Chair, it was resolv'd, that all former and present Grand Officers, viz. G. Masters, Deputies and Wardens, with 20 𝕸𝖆𝖘𝖙𝖊𝖗𝖘 of contributing Lodges in a Rotation, according to the printed List, shall be Members of the Committee of Charity. And

At the 𝕲𝖗𝖆𝖓𝖉 𝕷𝖔𝖉𝖌𝖊 on 13 Dec. 1733. upon the Motion of Srathmore G. Master in the Chair, it was resolv'd,

1. That all Masters of regular Lodges, that have contributed to the Charity within 12 Months past, shall be Members of the Committee, together with all former and present Grand Officers.

2. That considering the usual Business of a Quarterly Communication was too much for one Time; whatever Business cannot be dispatched here, shall be referr'd to the Committee of Charity, and their Opinion reported to the next Grand Lodge.

3. *That all Questions debated at the said Committee shall be decided by a Majority of those present.*

4. *That all Petitions for* Charity *presented to the* Grand Lodge *shall be referred to the said Committee, who are to report their Opinion to the next* Grand Lodge, *viz. Whether or not the Case of any distress'd Brother deserves more Relief than is in the Power of the Committee to give?*

5. *That the said* Committee *shall twice give publick Notice, in some publick* News Paper, *of the Time and Place of their Meetings.*

At the **Grand Lodge** on 24 *Feb.* 1734/5. CRAUFURD *G. Master* in the Chair, it was recommended by the *Committee*, and now resolv'd here,

1. *That no* Master *of a* Lodge *shall be a* Member *of the said* Committee, *whose* Lodge *has not contributed to the* General Charity *during* 12 *Months past.*

2. *That one of the Brethren, signing and certifying a poor Brother's* Petition, *shall attend the* Committee *to attest it.*

At the **Grand Lodge** on 31 *March* 1735. Upon the Motion of CRAUFURD *Grand Master* in the Chair, it was resolv'd,

1. *That no extraneous Brothers, that is, not regularly made, but clandestinely, or only with a View to partake of the* Charity; *nor any assisting at such irregular Makings, shall be ever qualified to partake of the* Masons *general* Charity.

2. *That the* Brothers *attesting a* Petition *for* Charity *shall be able to certify, that the* Petitioner *has been formerly in reputable, at least, in tolerable Circumstances.*

3. *That every* Petition *receiv'd shall be sign'd or certified by the* Majority *of the* Lodge *to which the Petitioner does, or did, belong.*

4. *That the* Name *and* Calling *of the Petitioner be expresly mention'd.*

At the **Grand Lodge** on 6 *April* 1736. WEYMOUTH being *Grand Master*, and in his Absence, *D. G. Master* WARD in the Chair; upon the Motion of the COMMITTEE of *Charity*, it was resolv'd, *That no* Petition *for* Charity *shall be receiv'd which has*

has not been offer'd first to the Secretary *and laid in his Hands Ten Days, at least, before the Meeting of the* Committee *of Charity, that he may have Time to be inform'd of its Allegations, if they are dubious.*

Thus the COMMITTEE of *Charity* has been establish'd among the FREE and Accepted MASONS of *England*, who have very handsomely contributed to their *General* Fund, and do still persevere in the Good Work.

The COMMITTEE regularly meets and has reliev'd many distress'd Brothers with small Sums, not exceeding 5 *l.* to each: And the 𝕲𝖗𝖆𝖓𝖉 𝕷𝖔𝖉𝖌𝖊 have order'd the *Treasurer* to pay more to some Petitioners, according to Exigence; sometimes 10, or 15, or 20 Pounds, as they thought the Case requir'd: So that the *Distress'd* have found far greater Relief from this *General Charity*, than can be expected from particular *Lodges*; and the Contributions, being paid by the Lodges in *Parcels*, at various Times, have not been burdensome.

The 𝕿𝖗𝖊𝖆𝖘𝖚𝖗𝖊𝖗'𝖘 *Accounts* have been audited and ballanced at every *Grand Lodge*; whereby all know the Stock in Hand, and how every Parcel of the *Charity* has been dispos'd of; every Thing being duly recorded in the Grand *Lodge-Book*, and in *that* of the COMMITTEE, of which every *Master* of a *contributing Lodge* is a Member.

The *Treasurer* 𝕭𝖑𝖆𝖐𝖊𝖗𝖇𝖞 has not employ'd a Clerk or Assistant for saving Charges; being hitherto assisted only by the *Secretary* of the *Grand Lodge*: And when the *Treasurer* is call'd abroad, he leaves Money with the *Secretary* REVIS to pay what is drawn upon him; and for all his generous Cares and good Conduct, the 𝕿𝖗𝖊𝖆𝖘𝖚𝖗𝖊𝖗 is publickly and solemnly thank'd by every *Grand Lodge*.

At last on 6 *April* 1738. at the 𝕲𝖗𝖆𝖓𝖉 𝕷𝖔𝖉𝖌𝖊, the *Treasurer* 𝕭𝖑𝖆𝖐𝖊𝖗𝖇𝖞, having justly cleared his Accounts, and stated the Ballance, thought fit to demit or lay down his Office. Upon which the *Secretary* 𝕽𝖊𝖛𝖎𝖘 was appointed *Treasurer*. But

At

(184)

At the GENERAL ASSEMBLY on 27 *April* 1738. Mr *John Revis* the **Secretary** declin'd the Office of *Treasurer*; for that both those Offices should not be reposed in one Man, the One being a Check to the Other: Yet the *Grand Master* CAERNARVON and the Brethren, desir'd Brother *Revis* to act as *Treasurer* till one is appointed.

May this good Work of CHARITY abound, as one of the happy Effects of the Love and Friendship of *true Masons*, till Time and Architecture shall be no more!

A LIST of the LODGES in and about *London* and *Westminster*.

MANY *Lodges* have by Accidents broken up, or are partition'd, or else removed to new Places for their Conveniency, and so, if subsisting, they are called and known by those new Places or their *Signs*.

But the *subsisting Lodges*, whose *Officers* have attended the **Grand Lodge** or *Quarterly Communication*, and brought their Benevolence to the General *Charity* within 12 Months past, are here set down according to their Seniority of *Constitution*, as in the *Grand Lodge-Books* and the *Engraven List*.

Signs of the Houses.	Dates of Constitution.	Days of *Forming*.
Thus the LODGES at 1. KING'S-ARMS Tavern in St. *Paul*'s *Church-Yard*, removed from the GOOSE and GRIDIRON, meet in Form. This is the *Senior Lodge*, whose *Constitution* is immemorial.	- - - -	Every first *Tuesday* in the Month.

2. HORN

Signs of the Houses.	Dates of Constitution.	Days of Forming.
2. HORN Tavern in *New Palace-Yard, Westminster*, the Old Lodge removed from the RUMMER and GRAPES, *Channel Row*, whose Constitution is also immemorial, it being one of the *four Lodges* mention'd Page 109.	— — — —	2d *Thursday*.
3. SHAKESPEAR's-HEAD in *Marlborough-street*.	17 *Jan.* 172⁰⁄₁.	2d *Monday*.
4. BELL in *Nicholas-Lane* near *Lombard-street*.	11 *July* 1721.	2d *Wednesday*.
5. BRAUND's-HEAD Tavern in *New Bond-street*.	19 *Jan.* 172¹⁄₂.	2d and 4th *Tuesday*.
6. RUMMER Tavern in *Queen-street, Cheapside*.	28 *Jan.* 172¹⁄₂.	2d and 4th *Thursday*.
7. DANIEL's *Coffee-house* within *Temple-Bar*.	25 *April* 1722.	1st *Monday*.
8. RED-CROSS in *Barbican*.	*May* 1722.	1st *Wednesday*.
9. KING's-ARMS Tavern in *New Bond street*.	25 *Nov.* 1722.	Last *Thursday*.
10. QUEEN's-HEAD in *Knave's-Acre*. This was one of the *four Lodges* mention'd Page 109. viz. the APPLE-TREE Tavern in *Charles-street, Covent-Garden*, whose Constitution is immemorial: But after they removed to the QUEEN's Head, upon some Difference, the Members that met there came under a *new Constitution*, tho' they wanted it not, and it is therefore placed at this Number. N B. The CROWN in *Parker's-Lane*, the Other of the *four* old *Lodges*, is now extinct.	27 *Feb.* 172²⁄₃.	1st and 3d *Wednesday*.
11. CASTLE Tavern in *Drury-Lane*.	*March* 172²⁄₃.	1st and 3d *Wednesday*.
12. BURY's *Coffee-house* in *Bridges-street*, where there is also a *Masters-Lodge*.	28 *March* 1723.	2d and 4th *Tuesday*.
13. QUEEN's-HEAD Tavern in *Great Queen-street*.	30 *March* 1723	1st and 3d *Monday*.

Signs of the Houses.	Dates of Constitution.	Days of Forming.
14. BULL's-HEAD Tavern in Southwark	1 April 1723.	2d Monday.
15. LE GUERRE Tavern in St. Martin's-Lane.	3 April 1723.	1st and 3d Wednesday.
16. SUN Tavern in Lower Holbourn.	5 May 1723.	1st and 3d Friday.
17. MOURNING BUSH Tavern at Aldersgate	- - - 1723.	2d and 4th Friday.
18. SWAN Tavern in Long-Acre, a French Lodge.	12 June 1723.	1st and 3d Monday.
19. ANCHOR and Baptist's Head Tavern Chancery Lane.	4 Aug. 1723.	2d and last Thursday.
20. DOG Tavern Billingsgate.	11 Sept. 1723.	1st Wednesday.
21. HALF-MOON Tavern Cheapside.	18 Sept. 1723.	1st and 3d Tuesday.
22. SWAN and COCOA-TREE in White-cross-street.	- - - 1723.	1st Friday.
23. WHITE HORSE in Wheeler's-street, Spittlefields.	24 Dec. 1723.	2d Monday.
24. FORREST's Coffee-house Charing-Cross, the old Lodge.	27 March 1724.	2d and last Monday.
25. The SASH and COCOA-TREE in Moor-Fields.	July 1724.	1st and 3d Thursday.
26. SUN in Hooper's Square, Goodman's-Fields.	- - - 1724	1st and 3d Monday.
27. SUN Tavern in St. Paul's Church-Yard.	April 1725.	4th Monday.
28. ANGEL and CROWN Tavern White-Chappel.	- - - 1725.	1st and 3d Wednesday.
29. KING's-ARMS Tavern Strand.	25 May 1725.	1st Monday.
30. SWAN Tavern in Long-Acre, an English Lodge.	Sept. 1725.	2d and last Wednesday.
31. SWAN and RUMMER Tavern in Finch-Lane, where there is also a Masters Lodge.	2 Feb. 17$\frac{25}{26}$.	2d and 4th Wednesday.
32. MOUNT Coffee-house in Grovenor-street	12 Jan. 172$\frac{6}{7}$.	1st Thursday.
33. GLOBE Tavern in Fleet-street.	9 Aug. 1727.	1st and 3d Friday.
34. FISHER's Coffee-house in Burlington-Gardens.	31 Jan. 172$\frac{7}{8}$	2d and 4th Friday.
35. HOOP and GRIFFIN Tavern in Leaden-hall-street.	- - - 1728.	2d and 4th Monday.
36. ROYAL-OAK in great Earl-street, Seven Dials.	- - - 1728.	1st and 3d Friday.

37. OLD-MAN's

(187)

Signs of the Houses.	Dates of Constitution.	Days of Forming.
37. OLD-MAN's Coffee-House, Charing-Cross.	- - - 1728.	1st and 3d *Friday*.
38. ANCHOR and CROWN in *King-street, Seven Dials*.	- - - 1728.	1st and 3d *Thursday*.
39. STAR and GARTER in *St. Martin's-Lane*.	15 *April* 1728.	2d and 4th *Wednesday*.
40. ST. GEORGE in *St. Mary-Axe*.	22 *Jan.* 172$\frac{8}{9}$.	2d and 4th *Wednesday*.
41. FOUNTAIN Tavern on *Snow-hill*.	24 *Jan.* 173$\frac{0}{1}$.	1st and 3d *Thursday*.
42. BACCHUS in *Greville street, Hatton Garden*.	- - - 1730	1st and 3d *Friday*.
43. VINE Tavern in *Long-Acre*, where there is also a *Masters Lodge*.	28 *April* 1730.	2d and 4th *Wednesday*.
44. BACCHUS in *Bloomsbury* Market.	22 *May* 1730.	2d and 4th *Monday*.
45. GLOBE Tavern in *Old-Jury*.	26 *June* 1730.	1st and 3d *Monday*.
46. RAINBOW Coffee house in *York-Buildings*.	17 *July* 1730.	2d and 4th *Thursday*.
47. QUEEN's-HEAD in Old Bailey, where there is also a *Master's-Lodge*.	- - - 1730	2d and 4th *Monday*.
48. BLACK-LION in *Jockey Fields*.	11 *Jan.* 173$\frac{10}{11}$.	1st and 3d *Monday*.
49. Two ANGELS and CROWN in Little *St. Martin's-Lane*.	- - - 1731.	2d and 4th *Friday*.
50. THREE TONS Tavern in *Newgate-street*.	21 *Oct.* 1731.	2d and last *Monday*.
51. THREE TONS Tavern in *Smith field*.	17 *Dec.* 1731.	2d and 4th *Wednesday*.
52. OLD ANTWERP Tavern *Threadneedle-street*.	13 *Nov.* 1731.	1st *Tuesday*.
53. FOUNTAIN Tavern in the *Burrough, Southwark*.	24 *Jan.* 173$\frac{1}{2}$.	1st and 3d *Tuesday*.
54. KING's-ARMS Tavern on *St. Margaret's-Hill, Southwark*.	2 *Feb.* 173$\frac{1}{2}$.	3d *Monday*.
55. HORSESHOE and RUMMER Tavern in *Drury-Lane*.	11 *April* 1732.	2d and 4th *Tuesday*.
56. SUN Tavern in *Fleet-street*	12 *April* 1732.	2d and last *Tuesday*.
57. KING's-HEAD in *Tower-street*.	25 *May* 1732.	2d and 4th *Friday*.
58. KING and QUEEN in *Rosemary-Lane*.	21 *June* 1732.	2d and 4th *Monday*.
59. OXFORD-ARMS Tavern in *Ludgate-street*.	29 *June* 1732.	2d and 4th *Thursday*.
60. KING's-ARMS Tavern in *Dorset-street, Spittle-Fields*.	12 *July* 1732.	2d and 4th *Thursday*.

Bb 2   61. KING's-

Signs of the Houses.	Dates of Constitution.	Days of Forming.
61. KING's-ARMS Tavern in Piccadilly.	17 Aug. 1732.	2d and last Thursday.
62. HOOP and GRIFFIN Tavern in Leadenhall street, another Lodge.	18 Aug. 1732.	1st and 3d Friday.
63. CROWN in Upper Moor Fields.	29 Aug. 1732.	2d Tuesday.
64. ROYAL VINEYARD Tavern in St. James's-Park.	5 Sept. 1732.	1st and 3d Saturday.
65. ROYAL STANDARD Tavern in Leicester Square.	8 Sept. 1732.	1st and 3d Tuesday.
66. SALMON and BALL in Wheeler-street, Spittle-Fields	15 Nov. 1732.	1st and 3d Tuesday.
67. TURK's-HEAD Tavern in Greek-street, Soho.	12 Dec. 1732.	3d Thursday.
68. SHIP Coffee-house near the Hermitage Bridge.	2 Feb. 1732/3.	1st and 3d Thursday.
69. THEATRE Tavern in Goodman's-Fields.	17 Feb. 1732/3.	4th Monday.
70. KING's-ARMS in Tower-street near the Seven-Dials.	3 March 1732/3.	1st and 3d Tuesday.
71. FOUNTAIN Tavern in Katharine-street, Strand.	23 March 1733.	2d and 4th Thursday.
72. CROWN in Fleet-Market.	27 Dec. 1733.	1st and 3d Monday.
73. FORREST's Coffee-house Charing-Cross, another Lodge.	1733/4.	2d Wednesday.
74. KING's-ARMS Tavern in Wild-street, where there is also a Master's Lodge.	1734.	1st and 3d Tuesday.
75. MARLEBOROUGH's-HEAD in Petticoat-Lane, White-Chappel.	5 Nov. 1734.	2d and 4th Friday.
76. BELL in Nicholas-Lane near Lombard-street, another Lodge, where there is also a Masters Lodge.	11 June 1735.	2d and 4th Tuesday.
77. STEWARDS LODGE at Shakespear's-Head, Covent-Garden, in January April, July and October.	25 June 1735.	3d Wednesday.
78. BEAR Tavern in the Strand.	26 Aug. 1735.	2d and 4th Tuesday.
79. ANCHOR in Cock-Lane on Snow Hill.	30 Oct. 1735.	1st and 3d Tuesday.
80. ASHLEY's London Punch-house on Ludgate-Hill.	1 March 1735/6.	1st and 3d Thursday.
81. GREYHOUND in Lamb-street, Spittle-Fields.	11 June 1736.	1st and 3d Tuesday.

82. SUN

Signs of the Houses.	Dates of Constitution.	Days of Forming.
82. SUN Tavern on *Fish-street-Hill*	16 *Aug.* 1736.	1st and 3d *Monday.*
83. YORKSHIRE-GREY in *Beer-Lane, Thames-street,* where there is also a *Masters Lodge.*	2 *Sept.* 1736.	2d and 4th *Wednesday.*
84. BLACK-DOG in *Castle-street, Seven Dials,* where there is also a *Masters Lodge.*	21 *Dec.* 1736.	2d and 4th *Tuesday.*
85. BLOSSOM'S-INN in *Laurence-Lane, Cheapside,* where there is a *Masters Lodge.*	31 *Dec.* 1736.	1st and 3d *Thursday.*
86. CITY of DURHAM in *Swallow-street, St. James's.*	24 *Jan.* 1635/7.	1st *Thursday.*
87. CROWN Tavern in *Smithfield*	14 *Feb.* 1736/7.	1st and 3d *Wednesday.*
88. KING'S-ARMS Tavern in *Cateaton-street.*	22 *Feb.* 1736/7.	1st and 3d *Wednesday.*
89. THREE TONS Tavern in *Wood street.*	22 *March* 1736/7.	1st *Monday.*
90. At the Sign of WESTMINSTER-HALL in *Dunning's-Alley, Bishopsgate-street.*	30 *March* 1737.	1st and 3d *Wednesday.*
91. *Whitechapel* COURT-HOUSE in *Whitechapel.*	18 *April* 1737.	2d and 4th *Friday.*
92. THREE TONS Tavern on *Snow-Hill.*	20 *April* 1737.	2d and 4th *Thursday.*
93. KING'S-HEAD in *Old Jewry*	10 *May* 1737.	2d and 4th *Wednesday.*
94. GUN Tavern in *Jermyn street, St. James's.*	24 *Aug.* 1737.	2d and 4th *Wednesday.*
95. BLACK-POSTS in *Maiden-Lane,* where there is also a *Master's Lodge.*	21 *Sept.* 1737.	1st 2d and 3d *Thursday.*
96. KING'S-HEAD Tavern in *St. John's-street.*	8 *Dec.* 1737.	2d and 4th *Tuesday.*
97. FOUNTAIN Tavern in *Bartholomew-Lane* near the *Exchange.*	27 *Jan* 1737/8.	1st and 3d *Monday.*
98. BACCHUS Tavern in little *Bush-Lane, Canon street,* where there is also a *Masters Lodge.*	17 *Feb.* 1737/8.	3d *Wednesday.*
99. KATHARINE-WHEEL in *Windmill-street.*	27 *March* 1738.	1st and 3d *Tuesday.*

100. ANGEL

Signs of the Houses.	Dates of Constitution.	Days of Forming.
100. ANGEL in *Crispin-street*, *Spittle-Fields*.	- - - 1738.	1st and 3d *Tuesday*.
101. GORDON's *Punch-house* in the *Strand*.	16 *May* 1738.	1st and 3d *Friday*.
102. BELL and DRAGON in *King-street*, St. *James's*.	- - - 1738.	last *Wednesday*.
103. SWAN Tavern upon *Fish-street-Hill*.	- - - 1738.	1st and 3d *Thursday*.
104, CHECKER *Charing-Cross* have petition'd to be Constituted.	- - - - -	2d and 4th *Monday*.
105. CAMERON's Coffee-House in *Bury-street*, St. *James's*.	- - - - -	1st and 3d *Friday*.
106. KEY and GARTER Tavern in *Pall-Mall*.	- - - - -	1st and 4th *Friday*.

DEPUTATIONS

Of several *Grand Masters*,

To WALES, the *Country* of ENGLAND, and *foreign Parts*.

I. TO WALES. The Learned of that old Principality can best deduce their own *History* of *Masonry* from the noble antient *Briton* CADWAN the first King of *Wales*, A. D. 589. down to King RODERIC MAWR, who partition'd his Kingdom into 3 *Principalities* among his 3 Sons, which again cemented into one *Principality*, till EDWARD I. King of *England* over-ran

Wales,

Wales, A. D. 1283. When, their *Princes* being flain without Iffue, their Nobles and Gentry willingly fubmitted to the Crown of *England*, till King Henry VIII. united *Wales* to *England*, A. D. 1536. and fo down to thefe Times.

For in *Wales* there are many venerable Remains of moft antient religious Houfes, and many ftately Ruins of the ftrongeft Caftles in the 𝖌𝖔𝖙𝖍𝖎𝖈 Stile. See Part II. Ch. 2.

But now the Augustan *Stile* is as well efteem'd *in Wales* as in *England*, and there alfo the Brethren of the *Royal Art* have coalefced into *Lodges*, as Branches of our Fraternity under our Grand Master.

Thus on 10 *May* 1727.

Inchiquin *Grand Mafter* granted a Deputation to Hugh Warburton, Efq; to be Provincial *Grand Mafter* of *North-Wales* at *Chefter*.

— And another on 24 *June* 1727. to Sir Edward Mansel, Bart. to be Provincial *Grand Mafter* of *South-Wales* at *Caermarthen*.

II. DEPUTATIONS have been requefted from and fent to feveral Countries, Cities and Towns of *England*.

Thus,

— Lovel *Grand Mafter* granted a Deputation to Sir Edward Matthews, to be Provincial *Grand Mafter* of *Shropfhire*.

— Craufurd *Grand Mafter* granted a Deputation to Edward Entwizle, Efq; to be Provincial *Grand Mafter* of *Lancafhire*.

— Another to Joseph Laycock, Efq; to be Provincial *Grand Mafter* of *Durham*.

— Another to Matthew Ridley, Efq; to be Provincial *Grand Mafter* of *Northumberland*.

(192)

These and other *Grand Masters* have also granted 𝔇𝔢𝔭𝔲𝔱𝔞𝔱𝔦𝔬𝔫𝔰. at the Request of some good Brothers in Cities and Towns throughout *England*, for *Constituting* the following *Lodges*, as recorded in the *Grand Lodge-Books*, and in the engraven *List*, who have their *Rank* of *Seniority* at the *Grand Lodge*, according to the *Date* of their CONSTITUTION, viz.

The LODGES at

— NORWICH at the 3 Tons, constituted *A. D.* 1724. and meet every Month on the 1st *Thursday*.

— CHICHESTER, at the *White Horse*, constituted 17 *July* 1724. and meet 3d *Friday*.

— CHESTER at the *Spread-Eagle*, constituted *A. D.* 1724. and meet 1st *Tuesday*.

— DITTO at the *Crown and Mitre*, constituted *A. D.* 1724. and meet 1st *Thursday*.

— CAERMARTHEN at the *Bunch of Grapes*, constituted *A. D.* 1724.

— PORTSMOUTH at the *Vine*, constituted *A. D.* 1724 and meet 1st and 2d *Friday*.

— CONGLTON in *Cheshire*, at the *Red-Lion*, constituted *A. D.* 1724.

— SALFORD near *Manchester*, at the *King's-Head*, constituted *A. D.* 1727. and meet 1st *Monday*.

— WARWICK, at the *Woolpack*, constituted 22 *April* 1728. and meet 1st and 3d *Friday*.

— SCARBOROUGH, at *Vipont*'s Long Room constituted 27 *Aug.* 1729. and meet 1st *Wednesday*.

— LYN REGIS, *Norfolk*, at the *Lion*, constituted 1 *Oct* 1729. and meet 1st *Friday*.

— NORTHAMPTON, at the *George*, constituted 16 *Jan.* 17$\frac{29}{30}$. and meet 1st *Saturday*.

— St. ROOK's-HILL near *Chichester*, constituted *A. D.* 1730. and meet once in the Year, viz. on *Tuesday* in *Easter* Week.

— CANTERBURY, at the *Red-Lion*. constituted 3 *April* 1730 and meet 1st and 3d *Tuesday*.

— LINCOLN, at the *Saracen's-Head*, constituted 7 *Sept.* 1730. and meet 1st *Tuesday*.

— LEIGH in *Lancashire*, at the *King's-Arms*, constituted 22 *Feb.* 173$\frac{0}{1}$.

— BURY St. EDMUND'S, at the *Fountain*, constituted *A. D.* 1731. meet 2v and 4th *Tuesday*.

— MACCLESFIESD in *Cheshire*, at the *Angel*, constituted *A. D.* 1731. meet

BURY St. EDMUND's, at the *Fleece*, constituted 1 *Nov.* 1731. meet 1st and 3d *Thursday*.

— WOOLVERHAMPTON in *Staffordshire*, at the *Bell and Raven*, constituted 28 *March* 1732. and meet 1st *Monday*.

— IPSWICH, at the *White Horse*, constituted *A D.* 1732 and meet 2d and 4th *Thursday*.

— EXETER, at the *New-Inn*, constituted *A. D.* 1732. and meet 1st and 3d *Wednesday*.

— DARBY, at the *Virgin's-Inn*, constituted 14 *Sept.* 1732. and meet

— BOLTON

(193)

— BOLTON LEE MOORS in *Lancashire*, at a private Room, constituted 9 *Nov.* 1732. and meet after every Full Moon, 1st *Wednesday*.

— BURY St. EDMUND's, at the *Seven Stars*, constituted 15 *Dec.* 1732. and meet 2d and 4th *Thursday*.

— SALISBURY, at the *Ram*, constituted 27 *Dec.* 1732. and meet 1st and 3d *Wednesday*.

— BATH, at the *Bear*, constituted 18 *March* 173$\frac{2}{3}$. and meet 1st and 3d *Friday*.

— BURY in *Lancashire*, at the *Red Lion*, constituted 26 *July* 1733. and meet after every Full Moon, 1st *Thursday*.

— STOURBRIDGE in *Worcestershire*, at the *Dog*, constituted 1 *Aug.* 1733. meet each *Wednesday*.

— BIRMINGHAM, at the *Swan*, constituted *A. D.* 1733. and meet last *Monday*.

— PLYMOUTH, at the *Mason's Arms*, constituted *A. D.* 1734. and meet 1st and 3d *Friday*.

— NEWCASTLE upon *Tyne*, at the *Fencers*, constituted *A. D.* 1735. meet 1st *Monday*.

— WARMINSTER in *Wiltshire*, at Lord *Weymouth's-Arms*, constituted *A. D.* 1735. meet 1st *Thursday*.

— BRISTOL, at the *Rummer*, constituted 12 *Nov.* 1735, and meet 1st and 3d *Friday*.

— COLCHESTER, at the 3 *Cups*, constituted *A. D.* 1735. and meet 1st and 3d *Monday*.

— GATES-HEAD in the *Bishoprick* of *Durham*, at the *Fountain*, constituted 8 *March* 173$\frac{1}{6}$. meet

— SHREWSBURY, at the *Fountain*, constituted 16 *April* 1736. and meet 1st *Monday*.

— WEYMOUTH and MELCOMB REGIS in *Dorsetshire*, at the 3 *Crowns*, constituted *A. D.* 1736. meet

— NORWICH, at the *King's-Head*, constituted *A. D.* 1736. meet

— LIVERPOOL, at the *George*, constituted 15 *June* 1736. and meet 1st *Wednesday*.

— BIRMINGHAM, at the *King's-Arms* and *Horshoe*, constituted *A. D.* 1736. and meet 2d and last *Tuesday*.

— BRAINTREE in *Essex*, at the *Horn*, constituted 17 *March*, 173$\frac{6}{7}$. meet on 1st and 3d *Tuesday*.

— SHIPTON MALLET in *Somersetshire*, at - - - constituted 12 *Dec.* 1737. and meet

— LINCOLN *Above-Hill* in the *Baily Wyke*, at the *Angel*, constituted 23 *Dec.* 1737. and meet 1st and 3d *Monday*.

— HEREFORD, at the *Swan* and *Falcon*, constituted 16 *Jan.* 173$\frac{7}{8}$. 1st and 3d *Monday*.

— GLOUCESTER, at the *Wheat-Sheaf*, constituted 28 *March* 1738. meet

— HALLIFAX in *Yorkshire*, at the *Black-Bull*, constituted 1st *Aug.* 1738.

C c   III. DEPU-

III. DEPUTATIONS sent beyond Sea.

Thus

— INCHIQUIN *Grand Master* granted a **Deputation** to some Brothers in *Spain*, for constituting a *Lodge* at **Gibraltar**.

— COLERANE *Grand Master* granted one for constituting a *Lodge* at **Madrid**.

— KINGSTON *Grand Master* granted one to Brother GEORGE POMFRET to constitute a *Lodge* at **Bengal** in *East India*, that had been requested by some Brethren residing there.

— NORFOLK *Grand Master* granted one to Captain RALPH FAR WINTER, to be **Provincial** *Grand Master* of EAST-INDIA at *Bengal*.

— Another to *Monsieur* DU THOM to be **Provincial** *Grand Master* of the *Circle* of Lower SAXONY.

— Another to Mr. DANIEL COX to be **Provincial** *G. Master* of NEW JERSEY in *America*.

— LOVEL *Grand Master* granted one to noble Brother CHESTERFIELD Lord *Ambassador* at the *Hague*, for holding a *Lodge* there, that made his *Royal* Highness FRANCIS Duke of *Lorrain* (now *Grand* Duke of *Tuscany*) an *Enter'd Prentice* and *Fellow Craft*.

— Another to Capt. JOHN PHILIPS to be **Provincial** *G. M.* of RUSSIA.

— Another to Capt. JAMES CUMMERFORD to be **Provincial** *G. M.* of ANDALOUSIA in *Spain*.

— VISCOUNT MONTAGU *Grand Master* granted one for constituting a *Lodge* at **Valenciennes**.

— Another for constituting a *Lodge* at the *Hotel de Bussy* in PARIS.

— STRATHMORE *Grand Master* granted one to eleven *German* Gentlemen, good Brothers, for constituti a *Lodge* at **Hamburg**.

-- **Weymouth**

--- Weymouth *Grand Master* granted one to noble Brother Richmond for holding a *Lodge* at his Castle d'Aubigny in *France*.

--- Another to Randolph Tooke, Esq; to be Provincial G. M. of South-America.

--- Another to Brother George Gordon for constituting a *Lodge* at Lisbon in *Portugal*.

--- Another to Mr. Roger Lacy, Merchant, for constituting a *Lodge* at Savannah of *Georgia* in *America*.

--- Another to Richard Hull, Esq; to be Provincial G. M. at Gambay in *West Africa*.

--- Loudoun G. M. granted one to Robert Tomlinson, Esq; to be Provincial G. M. of New-England in *America*.

--- Another to John Hammerton, Esq; to be Provincial G. *Master* of South-Carolina in *America*.

--- Another to David Creighton, M. D. to be P. G. M. at Cape-Coast-Castle in *Africa*.

--- Darnley G. M. granted one to James Watson, Esq; to be Provincial G. M. of the Island of Montserrat in *America*.

--- Another to George Hammilton, Esq; to be Provincial G. M. of Geneva.

--- Another to Henry William Marshalch, Esq; Hereditary *Mareschal* of *Thuringia*, to be Provincial G. M. of the *Circle* of Upper Saxony.

--- Another to Capt. William Douglas to be Provincial G. M. on the *Coast* of Africa and in the *Islands* of America; excepting such Places where a Provincial G. M. is already deputed.

--- Another to Capt. Richard Riggs to be Provincial G. M. of New-York.

--- CAERNARVON the present G. M. has granted a Deputation to his Excellency William Matthews, Esq; Captain-General and Governor in Chief of his Majesty's *Leeward Caribbee*

Caribbee Iſlands, Vice-Admiral and Chancellor of the ſame, to be **Provincial** G. M. there.

All theſe foreign Lodges are under the Patronage of our **Grand Master** of *England*.

But the *old Lodge* at York City, and the *Lodges* of Scotland, Ireland, France and Italy, affecting Independency, are under their own *Grand Maſters*, tho' they have the ſame *Conſtitutions, Charges, Regulations*, &c. for Subſtance, with their Brethren of *England*, and are equally zealous for the *Auguſtan Stile*, and the *Secrets* of the antient and honourable *Fraternity*.

Thoſe inquiſitive *Europeans* who travel and traffick in Africa and *Weſtern* Asia, have there diſcover'd ſuch beautiful *Remains* of old magnificent *Colonading*, as give much Cauſe to lament the horrid Devaſtations made by the *Mahometans*, and heartily to wiſh for the *Revival* of the *Arts* of *Deſigning* in thoſe Parts, that good *old Maſonry* may alſo be revived there.

The antient Nations of *Eaſtern* Asia, the *Mogulliſtans, Chineſe, Japoneſe, Siameſe*, &c. are ſhy of communicating their Hiſtories and Antiquities to the *Europeans*; yet the *Miſſionaries* and *Merchants* have there diſcover'd many wonderful Monuments of the old Architecture.

We know not much of the Americans before the *Spaniards* came there *A. D.* 1593. and till the *Spaniards* gave us a few Accounts of the two old Empires of Mexico and Peru; where the *Aborigines* had built Cities and Caſtles after their own Manner. But in the *European* Colonies of *America*, true *Maſonry* has flouriſh'd, and will do more and more, along with Commerce and Learning.

But in Europe, even after the Devaſtations made by the **Goths**, and in the darkeſt Ages, while other Parts of *Learning* were lock'd up in *Monaſtries*, Architecture appear'd abroad, tho' in the **Gothick** *Stile*, till the Augustan *Stile* See Part I. was revived in *Italy*. Chap. VII.

Nay, in Proceſs of Time, the *Orders* or Fraternities of the *Warlike Knights* (and ſome of the *Religious* too) borrow'd many ſolemn Uſages from our *more antient* Fraternity that has exiſted

existed from the Beginning: For each *Order* of *Knights* have their GRAND MASTER, or one like him, and other *Grand Officers*, with their *Constitutions, Charges, Regulations,* their peculiar *Jewels, Badges* and *Clothings*, their Forms of *Entrance, Promotion* and *Assembling,* of their *Sessions* and *Processions*, their *Communications* and *Secrets,* with many other such Customs, *&c.* and as they were dispersed over *Christendom,* each *Fraternity* had in divers Places their several Meetings, or particular *Chapters,* or *Lodges* with proper Officers, accountable to the *Grand Chapter* of their respective GRAND MASTER, who was often a *King*, or a Sovereign *Prince,* or some *Nobleman* (as the Prince's *Deputy* 𝕲𝖗𝖆𝖓𝖉 𝕸𝖆𝖘𝖙𝖊𝖗) residing at a certain Place in great State and Magnificence, and who govern'd the *Fraternity* wherever they were dispers'd, supported them in their Undertakings, and protected them in their Privileges, Rights and Possessions, *&c.* as plainly appears from the Histories of those *Knightly Societies,* and from those of 'em that exist in Splendor to this Day.

From the Whole, it must be own'd

That *no other* ART has been so much encouraged by the better Sort of Mankind from the Beginning in every Part of the Earth; as indeed *none other* is so extensively useful: And the MASONS thus countenanced by their *Royal, Princely, noble* and *learned* Brothers and Fellows, did ever separate themselves from the common Croud of *Artizans* and *Mechanicks* in their *well-form'd Lodges* under their proper Officers.

And now the *Freeborn* BRITISH Nations, disengaged from Wars, and enjoying the good Fruits of *Liberty* and *Peace,* the Brothers of the *Royal Art* have much indulged their bright Genius for true antient *Masonry,* in many *particular* Lodges, *quarterly* Communications and *annual* ASSEMBLIES; wherein their *Secrets* and *Usages* are wisely preserved and propagated, the *Science* and the *Art* are duly cultivated, and the CEMENT of the *Lodge* is made so firm, that the *whole Body* resembles a *well-built* ARCH of the beautiful *Augustan Stile.*

Nay

Nay some ROYAL Persons, with many NOBLEMEN, many eminent *Gentlemen*, *Citizens*, *Clergymen* and *Scholars* of most Professions and Denominations, have join'd this amicable *Fraternity*, have strengthen'd and adorn'd the *Lodge*, and have frankly submitted to the *Charges* and wore the *Badges* of a FREE and ACCEPTED MASON; especially from the Time of

𝔊rand 𝔐aster the *Duke* of *MONTAGU*, to our present 𝔊rand 𝔐aster the *Marquis* of *CAERNARVON*.

The APPROBATION of this BOOK of the CONSTITUTIONS.

WHEREAS at the Grand Lodge *on* 24*th* February 173$\frac{4}{5}$. *the* Earl *of* CRAUFURD *Grand Mafter being in the Chair, the Author* James Anderfon, *D. D. having reprefented that a New Book of* CONSTITUTIONS *was become neceffary, and that he had prepar'd Materials for it; the* GRAND MASTER *and the* Lodge *order'd him to lay the fame before the prefent and former* Grand-Officers, *as in the Grand* Lodge-Book.

And our faid Brother Anderfon *having fubmitted his Manufcript to the Perufal of fome* former *Grand* Officers, *particularly our noble Brother* RICHMOND, *and our Brothers* Defaguliers, Cowper, Payne, *and others, who, after making fome Corrections, have fignify'd their* Approbation.

And having next, according to the forefaid Order, committed his Manufcript to the Perufal of the prefent *Grand* Officers, *who having alfo review'd and corrected it, have declared their* Approbation *of it to the* Grand Lodge *affembled in ample Form on the* 25th January 173$\frac{4}{5}$.

This GRAND LODGE *then agreed to order our faid Brother* Anderfon *to print and publifh the faid Manufcript or* New Book *of* CONSTITUTIONS. And it is hereby approved and recommended as the *only Book* of CONSTITUTIONS, *for the Ufe of the* Lodges, *of the* FREE and Accepted MASONS, *by the faid* GRAND LODGE *on the faid* 25th January 173$\frac{4}{5}$. in the Vulgar Year of *Mafonry* 573$\frac{4}{5}$.

DARNLEY, Grand Mafter,
JOHN WARD, *Deputy* Grand Mafter,
ROBERT LAWLEY, } Grand
WILLIAM GRÆME, } Wardens.

John Rebis
Secretary.

Some

Some of the usual *Free-Masons* SONGS.

The 𝔐𝔞𝔰𝔱𝔢𝔯𝔰 SONG, by the *Author* of this Book.

In the first Book it is in 5 Parts, comprehending the History *of* Masonry; *but being too long, the 3d Part is only printed here.*

I.

WE sing of MASONS antient Fame!
　Lo, *Eighty Thousand* 𝕮𝖗𝖆𝖋𝖙𝖘𝖒𝖊𝖓 rise
Under the MASTERS of great Name,
　More than *Three Thousand* Just and Wise.
Employ'd by *SOLOMON* the SIRE,
　And Gen'ral MASTER *Mason* too,
As HIRAM was in stately *Tyre*,
　Like *Salem* built by *Mason*'s true.

2.

The *Royal* Art was then *Divine*,
　The *Craftsmen* counsell'd from above,
The *Temple* was the GRAND DESIGN,
　The wond'ring World did All approve.
Ingenious Men from every Place
　Came to survey the glorious *Pile*;
And when return'd, began to trace
　And imitate its *lofty Stile*.

3.

At length the 𝕲𝖗𝖊𝖈𝖎𝖆𝖓𝖘 came to know
　𝕲𝖊𝖔𝖒𝖊𝖙𝖗𝖞, and learn'd the *Art*
PYTHAGORAS was rais'd to show,
　And glorious EUCLID to impart:
Great ARCHIMEDES too appear'd,
　And *Carthaginian* Masters bright;
Till *Roman* Citizens uprear'd
　The 𝕬𝖗𝖙 with Wisdom and Delight.

5. They

4.

But when proud *Asia* they had quell'd,
   And *Greece* and *Egypt* overcome,
In Architecture they excell'd,
   And brought the Learning all to *Rome:*
Where wise VITRUVIUS *Warden* prime,
   Of Architects the *Art* improv'd
In great AUGUSTUS' peaceful Time,
   When *Arts* and *Artists* were belov'd.

5.

They brought the Knowledge from the *East*,
   And as they made the Nations yield,
They spread it thro' the *North* and *West*,
   And taught the World the Art to build.
Witness their *Citadels* and *Tow'rs*
   To fortify their Legions fine,
Their *Temples*, *Palaces* and *Bow'rs*
   That spoke the Masons GRAND DESIGN.

6.

Thus mighty *Eastern* Kings and some
   Of ABRAM's Race, and Monarch's good
Of *Egypt*, *Syria*, *Greece* and *Rome*,
   True ARCHITECTURE understood.
No wonder then if *Masons* join
   To celebrate those MASON-KINGS,
With solemn Note and flowing Wine,
   Whilst every Brother jointly sings.

Chorus.

Who can unfold the *Royal Art*,
   Or shew its *Secrets* in a Song?
They're safely kept in *Mason*'s Heart,
   And to the antient *Lodge* belong!
      To the KING and the CRAFT.

II. The **Wardens** Song, also by the *Author* of this *Book*.

In the firſt Book it was of 13 *Verſes*, too long: But this laſt *Verſe* and *Chorus* is thought enough to be ſung.

    FROM henceforth ever ſing
     The *Craftſman* and the *King*,
  With Poetry and Muſick ſweet
  Reſound their Harmony compleat,
And with *Geometry* in ſkilful Hand
    Due Homage pay,
    Without Delay,
To great CAERNARVON now our MASTER GRAND.
  He rules the Freeborn *Sons* of *Art*
  By Love and Friendſhip, Hand and Heart.

   Chorus of the **Wardens** Song.

    Who can rehearſe the Praiſe
     In ſoft Poetick Lays,
  Or ſolid Proſe, of *Maſons* true,
  Whoſe Art tranſcends the common View?
Their *Secrets* ne'er to Strangers yet expos'd,
    Preſerv'd ſhall be
    By *Maſons Free*,
And only to the *antient Lodge* diſclos'd;
  Becauſe they're kept in *Maſons Heart*
  By Brethren of the *Royal Art*.

    To the GRAND MASTER.

III. The **Fellow Craft's** Song, by Brother Charles de la Fay, Esq; in the First Book.

1.

HAIL Masonry! Thou *Craft* divine!
 Glory of Earth! from Heaven reveal'd!
Which doth with *Jewels* precious shine,
 From all but *Masons* Eyes conceal'd.

Chorus.
Thy Praises *due who can rehearse,*
In nervous Prose *or flowing* Verse?

2.
As Men from Brutes distinguish'd are,
 A *Mason* other Men excels;
For what's in Knowledge choice and rare
 But in his Breast securely dwells?

Chorus.
His silent Breast *and faithful* Heart
Preserve the Secrets *of the* Art.

3.
From scorching Heat and piercing Cold,
 From Beasts whose Roar the Forest rends,
From the Assaults of Warriors bold
 The *Masons* Art Mankind defends.

Chorus.
Be to this Art *due Honour paid,*
From which Mankind receives such Aid.

4.
Ensigns of State that feed our Pride,
 Distinctions troublesome and vain,
By *Masons true* are laid aside,
 Arts *Freeborn Sons* such Toys disdain.

Chorus.
Innobled by the Name *they bear,*
Distinguish'd by the Badge *they wear.*

5. Sweet

5.

Sweet *Fellowship* from Envy free,
  Friendly Converſe of *Brotherhood*
The *Lodge's* laſting CEMENT be,
  Which has for Ages firmly ſtood.

Chorus.

A LODGE *thus built for Ages paſt*
  Has laſted, and ſhall ever laſt.

6.

Then in our *Songs* be Juſtice done
  To thoſe who have inrich'd the *Art*,
From ADAM to CAERNARVON down,
  And let each Brother bear a Part.

Chorus.

Let noble Maſons *Healths go round,*
  Their Praiſe in Lofty Lodge *reſound.*
To the Deputy GRAND MASTER and **Grand Wardens**.

IV. The *Enter'd* **Prentice's** SONG, by Brother *Matthew Birkhead*, deceas'd, in the firſt Book. To be ſung after grave Buſineſs is over.

1.

COME let us prepare,
  We Brothers that are,
Aſſembled on merry Occaſion;
  Let's drink, laugh and ſing,
  Our Wine has a Spring,
Here's an Health to an *Accepted Maſon*.
  All Charged.

2.

The World is in Pain
  Our Secrets to gain,
And ſtill let them wonder and gaze on;
  Till they're ſhown the Light,
  They'll ne're know the right
Word or Sign of an *Accepted Maſon*.

3. Tis

3.
Tis *This* and 'tis *That*,
They cannot tell *what*,
Why so many great Men of the Nation,
Should Aprons put on
To make themselves one,
With a *Free* and an *Accepted Mason*.
4.
Great Kings, Dukes and Lords
Have laid by their Swords,
Our Myst'ry to put a good Grace on,
And ne're been asham'd
To hear themselves nam'd
With a *Free* and an *Accepted Mason*.
5.
Antiquity's Pride
We have on our Side,
And it maketh Men just in their Station;
There's nought but what's good
To be understood
By a *Free* and an *Accepted Mason*.
6.
We're true and sincere
And just to the *Fair*;
They'll trust us on any Occasion:
No Mortal can more
The Ladies adore,
Than a *Free* and an *Accepted Mason*.
7
Then join Hand in Hand,
By each Brother firm stand,
Let's be merry and put a bright Face on:
What Mortal can boast
So noble a Toast,
As a *Free* and an *Accepted Mason*?

Chorus.

Chorus.

No Mortal can boast
So noble a Toast,
As a FREE *and an* ACCEPTED MASON.
Thrice repeated in due Form.
To all the *Fraternity* round the *Globe*.

The following SONGS are not in the *first Book*, but being usually sung, they are now printed.

I. The *Deputy* Grand Master's SONG.

N. B. *Every two* last Lines *of each Verse is the* Chorus.

1.

ON, on, my dear *Brethren*, pursue your great *Lecture*,
And refine on the Rules of old *Architecture*:
High Honour to *Masons* the *Craft* daily brings,
To those Brothers of *Princes* and Fellows of *Kings*.

2.

We drove the rude Vandals and Goths off the Stage,
Reviving the *Art* of AUGUSTUS' fam'd Age:
And *Vespasian* destroy'd the *vast* TEMPLE in vain,
Since so many now rise in CAERNARVON's mild Reign.

3.

The noble *five Orders* compos'd with such Art,
Will amaze the fixt Eye, and engage the whole Heart:
Proportion's sweet Harmony gracing the Whole,
Gives our *Work*, like the glorious *Creation*, a Soul.

4.

Then *Master* and *Brethren*, preserve your great Name,
This LODGE so majestick will purchase you Fame;
Rever'd it shall stand till *all Nature* expire,
And it's Glories ne're fade till the *World* is on Fire.

5. See

5.

See, see, behold here, what rewards all our Toil,
Inspires our Genius, and bids Labour smile:
To our *noble* GRAND MASTER let a Bumper be crown'd,
To *all* 𝔐𝔞𝔰𝔬𝔫𝔰 a Bumper, so let it go round.

6.

Again, my lov'd *Brethren*, again let it pass,
Our antient firm *Union* cements with the Glass;
And all the Contention 'mongst *Masons* shall be,
Who better can work, or who better agree.

Additional Stanza *by Brother* Gofton, *at the Time when the* PRINCE *was made a* Mason, *and while the* PRINCESS *was pregnant.*

7.

Again let it pass to the ROYAL lov'd NAME,
Whose glorious Admission has crown'd all our Fame:
May a LEWIS be born, whom the World shall admire,
Serene as his *Mother*, August as his *Sire*.

Chorus.

Now a LEWIS is born, whom the World shall admire,
Serene as his MOTHER, *August* as his SIRE.

To our Brother FREDERICK, his *Royal* Highness the Prince of *Wales*.
To our Brother FRANCIS, his *Royal* Highness the *Grand* Duke of *Tuscany*.
To the 𝔏𝔢𝔴𝔦𝔰.

II. The 𝔊𝔯𝔞𝔫𝔡 𝔚𝔞𝔯𝔡𝔢𝔫𝔰 SONG. By Brother *Oates*.

1.

LET *Masonry* be now my Theme,
   Throughout the Globe to spread it's Fame,
And eternize each worthy Brother's Name.
   Your Praise shall to the Skies resound,
   In lasting Happiness abound,
And with sweet *Union* All your noble Deeds } Repeat
  be crown'd. } this Line.

Chorus.

Chorus.

Sing then, my Muſe, to Maſon's *Glory,*
Your Names are ſo rever'd in Story,
That all th' admiring World do now adore ye!

2.

Let Harmony divine inſpire
Your Souls with Love and gen'rous Fire,
To copy well wiſe SOLOMON your SIRE.
Knowledge ſublime ſhall fill each Heart,
The Rules of *G'ometry* t'impart,
While *Wiſdom, Strength* and *Beauty* crown the } Repeat
glorious *Art*.   } this Line.

Chorus. *Sing then my Muſe,* &c.

3.
All Charged.

Let Great CAERNARVON's Health go round,
In ſwelling Cups all Cares be drown'd,
And Hearts united 'mongſt the *Craft* be found.
May everlaſting Scenes of Joy
His peaceful Hours of Bliſs employ,
Which Time's all-conquering Hand ſhall ne'er, ſhall } Repeat
ne'er deſtroy.   } this Line.

Chorus. *Sing then my Muſe,* &c.

4.

My Brethren, thus all Cares reſign,
Your Hearts let glow with Thoughts divine,
And Veneration ſhew to SOLOMON's *Shrine*.
Our annual Tribute thus we'll pay,
That late Poſterity ſhall ſay,   }
We've crown'd with Joy this glorious, *Happy,* } All Sing.
Happy Day.   }

Chorus.

Sing then my Muſe *to* Maſons *Glory,*
Your Names are ſo rever'd in Story,
That all th' admiring World do now adore ye.

To all the *noble* LORDS that have been GRAND MASTERS.

The

III. The 𝕿𝖗𝖊𝖆𝖘𝖚𝖗𝖊𝖗'𝖘 Song.

N. B. The two last Lines of each Verse is a 𝕮𝖍𝖔𝖗𝖚𝖘.

1.

GRANT me, kind Heaven, what I request;
  In *Masonry* let me blest;
Direct me to that happy Place
  Where *Friendship* smiles in every Face;
    Where *Freedom* and sweet *Innocence*
    Enlarge the Mind and cheer the Sense.

2.

Where scepter'd *Reason* from her Throne
Surveys the LODGE and makes us one;
And *Harmony*'s delightful Sway
For ever sheds Ambrosial Day;
    Where we blest *Eden*'s Pleasure taste,
    Whilst balmy Joys are our Repast.

3.

Our LODGE the social *Virtues* grace,
And *Wisdom*'s Rules we fondly trace;
Whole *Nature*, open to our View,
Points out the Paths we should pursue.
    Let us subsist in lasting Peace,
    And may our Happiness increase.

4.

No *prying Eye* can view us here,
No *Fool* or *Knave* disturb our Cheer;
Our well-form'd *Laws* set Mankind free,
And give Relief to *Misery*:
    The POOR oppress'd with Woe and Grief,
    Gain from our bounteous Hands *Relief*.

To all *Charitable* MASONS.

(210)

IV. The Secretary's Song.

N. B. The two last *Lines of each Verse is the* Chorus.

1.

YE *Brethren* of the antient *Craft*,
  Ye fav'rite Sons of Fame,
Let Bumpers cheerfully be quaff'd
  To great CAERNARVON's Name.
Happy, long happy may he be,
Who loves and honours *Masonry*.
  With a Fa, la, la, la, la.

2.

In vain would *Danvers* with his Wit *
  Our flow Resentment raise;
What He and all Mankind have writ
  But celebrates our Praise.
His Wit this only *Truth* imparts,
That MASONS have firm *faithful Hearts*.
  With a Fa, &c.

* That those who hang'd Capt. *Porteous* at *Edinburgh* were all *Free Masons*, because they kept their own Secrets. See *Craftsman*, 16 *April* 1736. Nº. 563.

3.

Ye *British* FAIR, for Beauty fam'd,
  Your Slaves we wish to be ;
Let none for Charms like yours be nam'd
  That love not *Masonry*.
This Maxim *D'Anvers* proves full well,
That MASONS *never kiss and tell*.
  With a Fa, la, &c.

4.

True *Masons!* no Offences give,
  Let Fame your Worth declare,
Within your *Compass* wisely live,
  And act upon the *Square:*
May *Peace* and *Friendship* e'er abound,
And *Great* CAERNARVON's Health go round.
  With a Fa, la, la, la, la, &c.

To All True and Faithful.   V. The

V. The **Sword bearer's** Song.

N. B. The last *two Lines* of each Verse is the **Chorus**.

1.

TO all who *Masonry* despise
    This Counsel I bestow:
Don't ridicule, if you are wise,
    A *Secret* you don't know.
Yourselves you banter, but not it,
You shew your *Spleen*, but not your *Wit*.
        With a Fa, la, la, la, la.

2.

Inspiring *Virtue* by our Rules,
    And in ourselves secure,
We have Compassion for those Fools
    Who think our *Acts* impure:
We know from *Ignorance* proceeds
Such mean Opinion of our *Deeds*.
        With a Fa, &c.

3.

If *Union* and *Sincerity*
    Have a Pretence to please,
We *Brothers* of the MASONRY
    Lay justly Claim to these:
To *State-Disputes* we ne'er give Birth,
Our Motto *Friendship* is, and *Mirth*.
        With a Fa, &c.

4.

Then let us laugh, since we've impos'd
  On those who make a Pother,
And cry, the *Secret* is disclos'd
  By some false-hearted Brother:
The *mighty* SECRET's gain'd, they boast,
From *Post-Boy* and from *Flying-Boy*.
    With a Fa, la, la, la, la.

To all *Masters* and *Wardens* of regular *Lodges*.

VI. An Ode to the FREE MASONS.

N. B. The two *last Lines* of each Verse is the Chorus.

1.

BY MASONS *Art* th' aspiring *Domes*
  In stately *Columns* shall arise;
All Climates are their Native Homes,
  Their learned Actions reach the Skies,
Heroes and *Kings* revere their Name,
While *Poets* sing their lasting Fame.

2.

Great, Noble, Gen'rous, Good and Brave,
  Are Titles they most justly claim:
Their *Deeds* shall live beyond the Grave,
  Which those unborn shall loud proclaim.
Time shall their glorious Acts enrol,
While Love and Friendship charm the Soul.

To the lasting *Honour* of the FREE MASONS.

VII. An

VII. An Ode on MASONRY, by Brother J. Bancks.
N. B. *The two last Lines of each Verse is the* Chorus.

1.

GENIUS of Masonry descend,
   In mystick Numbers while we sing;
Enlarge our Souls, the *Craft* defend,
   And hither all thy Influence bring.
With social Thoughts our Bosoms fill,
And give thy Turn to every Will.

2.

While yet Batavia's wealthy *Pow'rs*
   Neglect thy Beauties to explore;
And winding Seine, adorn'd with Tow'rs,
   Laments thee wand'ring from his Shore;
Here spread thy Wings, and glad these Isles,
Where *Arts* reside, and *Freedom* smiles.

3.

Behold the Lodge rise into View,
   The Work of *Industry* and *Art*;
'Tis Grand, and Regular, and True,
   For so is each good *Mason's* Heart.
Friendship cements it from the Ground,
And *Secrecy* shall fence it round.

4.

A stately Dome o'erlooks our *East*,
   Like Orient *Phœbus* in the Morn;
And *two tall* Pillars in the *West*
   At once support us and adorn.
Upholden thus the *Structure* stands,
Untouch'd by sacrilegious Hands.

5

For *Concord* form'd, our Souls agree,
    Nor Fate this *Union* shall destroy:
Our Toils and Sports alike are free,
    And all is *Harmony* and Joy.
So SALEM's Temple rose by Rule,
Without the Noise of noxious Tool.

6.

As when *Amphion* tun'd his Song,
    Ev'n rugged Rocks the Musick knew;
Smooth'd into Form, they glide along,
    And to a THEBES the *Desart* grew:
So at the Sound of HIRAM's *Voice*
We rise, we join, and we rejoice.

7.

Then may our Vows to *Virtue* move,
    To *Virtue* own'd in all her Parts:
Come *Candour*, *Innocence* and *Love*,
    Come and possess our faithful Hearts:
Mercy, who feeds the hungry *Poor*,
And *Silence*, Guardian of the Door.

8.

And thou ASTRÆA (tho' from Earth,
    When Men on Men began to prey,
Thou fled'st to claim celestial Birth)
    Down from *Olympus* wing thy Way;
And mindful of thy antient Seat,
Be present still where MASONS meet.

9.

Immortal SCIENCE too be near,
    (We own thy Empire o'er the Mind)
Dress'd in thy radiant Robes appear,
    With all thy beauteous Train behind;
INVENTION young and blooming There,
Here GEOMETRY with *Rule* and *Square*.

(215)

10.

In *Egypt*'s FABRICK * Learning dwelt,   * The *Ptolemæan*
   And *Roman* Breasts could Virtue hide: Library.
But *Vulcan*'s Rage the Building felt,
   And *Brutus*, last of *Romans*, dy'd:
Since when, dispers'd the *Sisters* rove,
Or fill paternal Thrones above.

11.

But lost to half of human Race,
   With us the *Virtues* shall revive;
And driv'n no more from Place to Place,
   Here SCIENCE shall be kept alive:
And manly *Taste*, the Child of *Sense*,
Shall banish Vice and Dulness hence.

12.

United thus, and for these Ends,
   Let *Scorn* deride, and *Envy* rail;
From Age to Age the CRAFT descends,
   And what we build shall never fail:
Nor shall the World *our Works survey*;
But every Brother *keeps the Key*!

To ARTS and SCIENCES.

A DEFENCE

A DEFENCE of MASONRY, publish'd *A. D.* 1730. Occasion'd by a *Pamphlet* call'd *Masonry Dissected.*

CHAP. I. AMONG the extraordinary Discoveries of the present Age, nothing has been received with more Delight and Exultation, than a few Sheets, written, it seems, *without Partiality,* call'd *Masonry Dissected.* The *Grand Secret,* which has long withstood the Batteries of Temptation, that neither *Money,* the Master Key of the Heart, nor *good Liquor,* that unlocks the very Soul, nor *Hunger,* that breaks through Stone-Walls, nor Thirst, a sore Evil to a *Working Mason,* could bring to Light; has at last been disgorged *upon Oath,* to the great Easement of a tender Stomach, the eternal Scandal of the *Fraternity,* and the Good of the *Publick* never to be forgotten! The Design was no less then to disburthen a loaded *Conscience,* to acquaint the World, *That never did so ridiculous an Imposition appear among Mankind; and to prevent so many innocent Persons being drawn into so pernicious a Society!*

What could induce the *Dissector* to take that Oath, or the *Magistrate* to admit it, shall not at this Time be decided.

However, I must give the World Joy of so notable a Discovery, so honourable, so circumstantiated! a mighty Expectation was raised, and, without Doubt, is wonderfully gratified by this Course of Anatomy. *It must be this, it can be nothing else: It is as we always supposed, a whimsical* Cheat *supported by great* Names *to seduce* Fools, *who, once gull'd out of their Money, keep the Fraud secret to draw in others.*

I confess, I cannot come into this Method of Arguing; nor is it, in my Opinion, a fair Way of treating a *Society,* to run implicitly with the Cry, without examining whether these Reproaches are founded upon any Thing in the *Mystery* (as now represented) either *wicked* or *ridiculous.* For that stupid Imputation of *drawing in Fools for the Sake of their Money,* can have no Weight in the present Case; since the *Fraternity,* as it now stands, consists principally of Members of great Honour and Distinction, much superior to Views so sordid and ungenerous.

For once then, let this *Dissection* contain *all* the *Secrets* of FREE MASONRY; admit that every Word of it is *genuine* and literally *true,* and that the whole Scheme consists of no more nor no less: Yet under all these Concessions, under all the Disadvantages and Prejudices whatever, I cannot but still believe, *there have been Impositions upon Mankind more ridiculous, and that many have been drawn into a Society more pernicious.*

I would

I would not be thought agitated upon this Occasion, as if I were any Way concern'd whether this *Dissection* be true or false? or whether the Credit of *Free Masonry* be affected by it or not? These Considerations can give me no Trouble. My Design is to address to the sensible and serious Part of Mankind, by making a few impartial Remarks upon this *Dissection*, without contending for the Reputation of *Masonry* on the one Hand, or reflecting upon the *Dissector* on the other.

CHAP. II. THE formidable Objection which has given Offence to the better Part of Men, is the Copy of the *Oath* as it lies in the *Dissection*. It has been a Matter of Admiration, that so many Persons of great Piety, strict Conscience and unspotted Character, should lay themselves under so solemn an Obligation, under Penalties so terrible and astonishing, upon a Subject so trifling and insignificant.

To obviate this Objection, I observe; that the *End*, the *Moral* and *Purport* of MASONRY, as described in the *Dissection*, is *to subdue our Passions, not to do our own Will; to make a daily Progress in a laudable Art; to promote Morality, Charity, good Fellowship, good Nature and Humanity*. This appears to be the *Substance*, let the *Form* or Vehicle be ever so unaccountable.

As for the Terms relating to *Architecture*, *Geometry* and *Mathematicks*, that are dispersed throughout the *Dissection*, it would be strange if a Society of such a Denomination, could subsist wholly without them; tho' they seem (to me at least) to be rather *Technical* and *Formal* (yet deliver'd perhaps by long Tradition) than essentially attached to the *Grand* DESIGN.

Now where is the *Impiety*, where the *Immorality*, or *Folly*, for a Number of Men to form themselves into a Society, whose main End is to improve in commendable Skill and Knowledge, and to promote universal Beneficence and the social Virtues of human Life, under the solemn Obligation of an *Oath?* And This, in what *Form*, under what secret Restrictions, and with what innocent Ceremonies They think proper?

This Liberty all Incorporate Societies enjoy without Impeachment or Reflection: An *Apprentice* is bound to keep the Secrets of his *Master*, a *Freeman* is obliged to consult the Interest of his Company, and not to prostitute in common the *Mysteries* of his Trade: Secret *Committees* and Privy *Councils* are solemnly enjoin'd not to publish abroad their Debates and Resolutions. There appears to be something like *Masonry* (as the *Dissector* describes it) in all regular Societies of whatever Denomination: They are *All* held together by a Sort of *Cement*, by Bonds and Laws that are peculiar to each of them, from the Highest to the little Clubs and Nightly Meetings of a private Neighbourhood. There are *Oaths* administer'd, and sometimes solemn Obligations to *Secrecy:* There are a MASTER, two 𝔚𝔞𝔯𝔡𝔢𝔫𝔰, and a Number of *Assistants*, to make what the *Dissector* may call (if he pleases) a *Perfect Lodge* in the City-Companies. There is the Degree of *Enter'd Prentices*, Master of his Trade, or *Fellow Craft*, and Master, or the *Master* of the Company. There are *Constitutions* and Orders, and a successive, a gradual Enjoyment of Offices, according to the several Rules and Limitations of Admission.

But

But it is reply'd, that the general Design of *Masonry* may be commendable, or at least innocent, and yet be carried on to the same Advantage without the Solemnity of an *Oath*, especially pressed under such dreadful Penalties.

In answer, I observe, t at the *Question* is not whether the Purpose of *Masonry* may as well be served without an *Oath?* But *whether an Oath, in the present Case, be lawful, and may be taken with a good Conscience?* And to solve this Difficulty I shall introduce the Opinion of *Bishop* SANDERSON, the most judicious Casuist that ever treated upon the Subject of *Oaths*;

<small>De Obligatione Juramenti Prælect. 3. Sect. 15.</small>

who says, *When a Thing is not by any Precept or Interdict, Divine or Human, so determin'd; but every Man,* pro hic & nunc, *may at his Choice do or not do, as he sees expedient; Let him do what he will, he sinneth not,* 1 Cor. vii. 36. *As if* Caius *should swear to sell his Land to* Titius, *or to lend him an hundred Crowns: The Answer is brief, an Oath in this Case is both lawful and binding.*

Now I would know what Precept, *Divine* or *Human*, has any way determin'd upon the Contents of the *Dissection?* And whether the general Design of *Masonry*, as there laid down, is not at least of equal Benefit and Importance to the Publick, with the lending of an hundred Crowns to a private Man? The Answers to these Questions are obvious, and the Consequence is equally plain, that *an Oath upon the Subject of Masonry is at least justifiable and lawful.*

As for the Terror of the *Penalty*, the World, upon that Occasion, is commonly mistaken; for the *Solemnity* of the *Oath* does not in the least add to the Obligation; or, in other Words, the *Oath* is equally binding without any *Penalty* at all. The same Casuist has this Expression: *A Solemn Oath of itself, and in its own Na-*

<small>Prælect. 5. Sect. 12.</small>

ture, is not more obligatory than a Simple One; *because the Obligation of an Oath ariseth precisely from* This, *that God is invoked, as a Witness and Revenger, no less in a* Simple Oath *than in the solemn and corporal; for the Invocation is made precisely by the Pronunciation of the Words (which is the same both in the* simple *and* solemn*) and not by any corporal Motion or concomitant Sign, in which the* Solemnity *of the* Oath *consists.*

I write to intelligent Readers, and therefore this Citation wants not to be explain'd.

But further, if the *Oath* in the *Dissection* be taken by *all Masons* upon their Admission, no Member of the *Fraternity*, upon any Pretence whatsoever, dares violate the Obligation of it, without incurring the Guilt of *Perjury*; even supposing that *Masonry* were more trifling and indifferent, than in the *Dissection* it may appear to be. And therefore if the Conduct of the *Dissector* has stagger'd the Conscience of any one of the Brotherhood, concerning the Observation of *that Oath*; and has induced him to trifle and play with the Force of it, I hope he will desist betimes, lest he becomes actually forsworn.

<small>Prælect. 4. Sect. 11</small>

This Case is thus determin'd by the same Casuist, *A Voluntary* Oath *is the more binding for being* Voluntary; *because there is no straiter Obligation than that which we take willingly upon ourselves.* And in another Place

<small>Prælect. 3. Sect. 15</small>

the Casuist is more particular, *Where a Matter is so trivial*

that

that it is not worth the Deliberation of a wise Man, nor matters a Straw whether it be done or not done; as to reach up a Chip or to rub one's Beard; or for the Slightness of the Matter is not much to be esteem'd; as to give a Boy an Apple, or to lend a Pin; an Oath is binding in a Matter of the least Moment: Because weighty and trivial Things have a like Respect unto Truth and Falshood; And farther, because every Party swearing is bound to perform all he promised as far as he is able, and as far as it is lawful: But to give an Apple to a Boy is both possible and lawful; he is bound therefore to perform it, he ought to fulfil his Oath.

CHAP. III. HAVING taken off the Weight of the great Objection, the Design of this Chapter is to remove an Imputation, which has been often urged with great Confidence, viz. *The* Principles *and the whole Frame of* Free Masonry *is so very weak and ridiculous, that it reflects upon Men of the least Understanding to be concern'd in it!* And now, say the merry Gentlemen, it appears evidently to be so by the *Dissection*, which discovers nothing but an unintelligible Heap of Stuff and Jargon, without common Sense or Connection.

I confess I am of another Opinion; tho' the *Scheme of Masonry*, as reveal'd by the *Dissector*, seems liable to Exceptions: Nor is it so clear to me as to be fully understood at first View, by attending only to the *literal* Construction of the Words: And for aught I know, the *System*, as taught in the regular *Lodges*, may have some Redundancies or Defects, occasion'd by the Ignorance or Indolence of the old Members. And indeed, considering through what Obscurity and Darkness the *Mystery* has been deliver'd down; the many Centuries it has survived; the many Countries and Languages, and *Sects* and *Parties* it has run through; we are rather to wonder it ever arriv'd to the present Age, without more Imperfection. In short, I am apt to think that MASONRY (as it is now explain'd) has in some Circumstances declined from its *original Purity!* It has run long in muddy Streams, and as it were, under Ground: But notwithstanding the great Rust it may have contracted, and the forbidding Light it is placed in by the *Dissector*, there is (if I judge right) much of the *old Fabrick* still remaining; the essential Pillars of the Building may be discover'd through the Rubbish, tho' the Superstructure be over-run with Moss and Ivy, and the Stones, by Length of Time, be disjointed. And therefore, as the 𝕭usto of an *old* HERO is of great Value among the Curious, tho' it has lost an Eye, the Nose, or the Right Hand; so MASONRY with all its Blemishes and Misfortunes, instead of appearing ridiculous, ought (in my humble Opinion) to be receiv'd with some Candour and Esteem, from a Veneration to its *Antiquity*.

I was exceedingly pleas'd to find the *Dissector* lay the *Original* Scene of *Masonry* in the EAST, a Country always famous for *Symbolical* Learning supported by *Secrecy*; I could not avoid immediately thinking of the *old* EGYPTIANS, who conceal'd the chief *Mysteries* of their Religion under *Signs* and *Symbols*, call'd 𝕳ieroglyphics: and so great was their Regard for *Silence* and *Secrecy*, that they had

(220)

<small>Vid. Imagines Deorum, a Vincentio Chartario.</small> had a *Deity* call'd HARPOCRATES, whom they respected with peculiar Honour and Veneration. A learned Author has given us a Description of this *Idol*, thus; HARPOCRATES *the God of* Silence *was formed with his* Right Hand *placed near the* Heart, *cover'd with a* Skin *before, full of* Eyes *and* Ears; *to signify by this, that many Things are to be seen and heard, but little to be spoken.* And among the same People, *their great Goddess* Is (*the same as* MINERVA, *the Goddess of* Strength *and* Wisdom, *among the* Greeks) *had always the Image of a* Sphinx *placed in the Entrance of her Temples*; *because their* Secrets *should be preserved under* sacred *Coverings, that they might be kept from the Knowledge of the* Vulgar, *as much as the* Riddles *of* Sphinx!

PYTHAGORAS, by travelling into *Egypt*, became instructed in the *Mysteries* of that Nation; and here he laid the Foundation of all his *Symbolical* Learning. The <small>Vid. JAMBLICHUS, Vit. Pythagoræ. LAERTIUS, Vit. Pythagoræ. PORPHYRIUS. CLEM. ALEX. Strom.</small> several Writers that have mention'd this *Philosopher*, and given an Account of his *Sect* and Institutions, have convinced me fully, that FREE MASONRY, as publish'd by the *Dissector*, is very nearly allied to the old *Pythagorean* Discipline; from whence, I am perswaded, it may, in some Circumstances, very justly claim its Descent. To mention a few,

Upon the Admission of a Disciple, he was bound by a *solemn Oath* to conceal the *Mysteries* from the *Vulgar* and *Uninitiated*.

The principal and most efficacious of their Doctrines were (says JAMBLICHUS) *ever kept* Secret *among themselves*; *they were continued* unwritten, *and preserved only by Memory to their Successors, to whom they deliver'd them as* Mysteries *of the* Gods.

They conversed with one another by Signs, *and had particular Words which they received upon their Admission, and which were preserved with great Reverence, as the Distinction of their Sect*: For (it is the judicious Remark of *LÆRTIUS*) *as Generals use* Watch-Words *to distinguish their own Soldiers from Others, so it is proper to communicate to the Initiated, peculiar Signs and Words, as distinctive Marks of a* Society.

The PYTHAGOREANS professed a great Regard for what the *Dissector* calls the *four* Principles of MASONRY, *viz. A Point, a Line, a Superficies,* and *a Solid*; and particularly held that a SQUARE was a very proper Emblem of the *Divine* <small>Vid. PROCLUS in *Euclid.* Lib. II. Def. 2. & 34.</small> *Essence*; *the Gods*, they say, *who are the Authors of every Thing established in* Wisdom, Strength *and* Beauty, *are not improperly represented by the Figure of a Square.*

Many more Instances might be produced, would the Limits of my Design admit; <small>CLEM. ALEXANDR. Strom. 5.</small> I shall only observe, that there was a *False Brother*, one HIPPARCHUS, of this Sect, who, out of Spleen and Disappointment, broke through the *Bond* of his *Oath*, and committed the *Secrets* of the Society to *Writing*, in Order to bring the Doctrine into Contempt: He was immediately expell'd the School, as a Person most infamous and abandon'd, as one dead to all
Sense

Senſe of Virtue and Goodneſs; and the *Pythagoreans*, according to their Cuſtom, made *a Tomb* for him, as if he had been actually Dead. The Shame and Diſgrace, that juſtly attended this *Violation* of his *Oath*, threw the poor Wretch into a Fit of Madneſs and Deſpair, ſo that *He cut his Throat* and periſh'd by his own Hands; and (which ſurprized me to find) his Memory was ſo abhorred after Death, that his Body lay *upon the Shore* of the Iſland of *Samos*, and had no other Burial than in the *Sands of the Sea!*

The ESSENES among the *Jews* were a Sort of *Pythagoreans*, and correſponded, in many Particulars, with the Practice of the *Fraternity*, as deliver'd in the *Diſſection*. For Example.

When a Perſon deſired to be admitted into their Society, he was to paſs through *Two Degrees* of Probation, before he could be perfect Maſter of their *Myſteries*. When he was received into the Claſs of *Novices*, he was preſented with a *White Garment*; and when he had been long enough to give ſome competent Proofs of his *Secrecy* and *Virtue*, he was admitted to further Knowledge: But ſtill he went on with the Trial of his Integrity and good Manners, and then was fully taken into the Society.

But before he was received as an eſtabliſh'd Member, he was firſt to bind himſelf by ſolemn Obligations and Profeſſions, *To do Juſtice, to do no Wrong, to keep Fait with all Men, to embrace the Truth, to keep his Hands clear from Theft and fraudulent Dealing; not to conceal from his Fellow Profeſſors any of the* Myſteries, *nor communicate any of them to the Profane, tho' it ſhould be to ſave his Life; to deliver nothing but what he received, and to endeavour to preſerve the Principle that he profeſſes. They eat and drink at the ſame Common Table; and the* Fraternity *that come from any other Place are ſure to be received there. They meet together in an* Aſſembly, *and the* Right *Hand is laid upon the Part between the* Chin *and the* Breaſt, *while the* Left *Hand is let down ſtraight by their Side.*

Vid. PHILO de Vita Contemplativa. JOSEPHUS Antiq. lib 8. cap. 2.

The CABALISTS, another *Sect*, dealt in hidden and myſterious Ceremonies. The *Jews* had a great Regard for this Science, and thought they made uncommon Diſcoveries by means of it. They divided their Knowledge into *Speculative* and *Operative*. DAVID and SOLOMON, they ſay, were exquiſitely ſkill'd in it; and no body at firſt preſumed to commit it to Writing: But (what ſeems moſt to the preſent Purpoſe) the Perfection of their Skill conſiſted in what the *Diſſector* calls *Lettering of it*, or by ordering the Letters of a Word in a particular Manner.

Vid. BASNAGE's Hiſt. of the *Jews*, on CABALA. COLLIER's Dictionary on the Word *Cabala*.

The laſt Inſtance I ſhall mention is That of the DRUIDS in our own Nation, who were the only *Prieſts* among the antient *Britons*. In their Solemnities they were clothed in *White*; and their Ceremonies always ended with a good *Feaſt*. POMPONIUS MELA relates of 'em, *that their* Science *was only an Effort of Memory; for they wrote down nothing, and they never fail'd to repeat many* Verſes, *which they received*

Vid. CÆSARIS Comment. lib. 6. SAMMS's Hiſtory of *Britain*, Book I. Chap. 4.

received by Tradition. CÆSAR observes, *that They had a* Head *or* CHIEF, *who had sovereign Power: This* President *exercised a Sort of Excommunication, attended with dreadful* Penalties, *upon such as either divulged or profaned their Mysteries.*

Thus, with reasonable Allowance for Distance of Time, Place, and other intermediate Accidents, the preceding *Collections* discover something, at least, like *Masonry,* if the *Dissection* contains any such Thing.

CHAP. IV. WHatever *Reflections* may attend the few Remarks that follow in this Chapter, arising either from an Overflow of Wit, or ill Nature, I shall be unconcern'd, and leave them wholly to the Mercy of the serious Reader; only desiring them to remember that no more ought in any Case to be expected, than what the Nature of it will reasonably admit. I own freely, I received a great Pleasure in collecting, and was frequently surpriz'd at the Discoveries that must evidently occur to an observing Eye.

The Conformity between the *Rites* and Principles of *Masonry* (if the *Dissection* be true) and the many Customs and *Ceremonies* of the *Antients,* must give Delight to a Person of any Taste and Curiosity; to find any Remains of *Antique* Usage and Learning preserved by a *Society* for many Ages, without Books or *Writing,* by *oral Tradition* only.

I. The *Number* THREE is frequently mention'd in the *Dissection*; and I find that the Antients, both *Greeks* and *Latins,* professed a great Veneration for that Number. THEOCRITUS thus introduces a Person who dealt in secret Arts.

Idyll. B.

'Ες τρις ἀποσπένδω κ᾽ τρις τάδε πότνια Θωρῶ!

Thrice, Thrice I pour, and thrice repeat my Charms!

| *Ovid.* Metam. lib. 7. | Verbaque Ter dixit: *Thrice he repeats the Words.* |

| *Virg.* Ecl. 8. | Necte tribus Nodis ternos, Amarille, colores. *Three Colours in Three Knots unite.* |

Whether this Fancy owes its Original to the *Number* THREE, because containing a *Beginning, Middle* and *End,* it seems to signify *All* Things in the World; or whether to the Esteem the *Pythagoreans* and other *Philosophers* had for it, on Account of their TRIAD or TRINITY; or lastly (to mention no more Opinions) to its Aptness to signify the *Power of all the Gods,* who were divided into *Three Classes, Celestial, Terrestrial* and *Infernal*; I shall leave to be determin'd by Others.

The *Gods* had a particular Esteem for this Number, as *Virgil* asserts.

| Eclog. 8. | Numero Deus impare gaudet. *Unequal Numbers please the Gods.* |

We find THREE *fatal Sisters,* THREE *Furies,* THREE *Names* and Appearances of *Diana.* Tria Virginis Ora Dianæ, *Three different Forms does chaste Diana bear.* Virgil. Æneid. lib. 4.

The

The Sons of *Saturn*, among whom the Empire of the World was divided, were Three: And for the same Reason we read of Jupiter's *Fulmen Trisidum* or *Three-forked Thunderbolt*; and of Neptune's *Trident*, with several other Tokens of the Veneration they bore to this particular Number.

II. A particular Ceremony belonging to the *Oath* (as declared by the *Dissector*) bears a near Relation to a Form of Swearing among the *Antients* mention'd by a learned Author *The Person who took the Oath, was to be upon his bare Knees with a naked Sword pointed to his Throat, invoking the Sun, Moon and Stars to be Witnesses to the Truth of what he swore.* | Alexander ab Alexandro Lib. V cap. 10.

III. A Part of the Masons *Catechism* has given Occasion to a great deal of idle Mirth and Ridicule, as the most trifling and despicable Sort of Jargon that Men of common Sense ever submitted to. The *Bone Box* and the *Tow Line* has given wonderful Diversion: I think there are some Verses in the last Chapter of the Book of *Ecclesiastes*, which in some Manner resemble this Form of Expression: I shall transcribe them with the Opinion of the Learned upon them, without making any particular Application, *viz.*

In the Day when the Keepers of the House shall tremble; and the Grinders cease, because they are few; and those that look out at the Windows be darkned; and the Doors shall be shut in the Streets; when the Sound of the Grinding is low; and he shall rise up at the Voice of the Bird; and all the Daughters of Musick shall be brought low: Or ever the Silver Cord be loosed; or the Golden Bowl be broken; or the Pitcher be broken at the Fountain; or the Wheel broken at the Cistern! | Eccl. xii. ver. 3, 4, 6.

The Expositors upon these Verses are almost unanimous in their Opinion, that they ought to be thus explain'd, *viz.* The **Keepers** of the House are the *Shoulders, Arms* and *Hands* of an human Body; the **Grinders** are the *Teeth*; those that look out at the **Windows** are the two *Eyes*; the **Doors** are the *Lips*; the **Streets** are the *Mouth*; the **Sound** of the **Grinding** is the *Noise* of the *Voice*; the **Voice** of the **Bird** is the *Crowing* of the *Cock*; the **Daughters** of **Musick** are the *two Ears*; the **Silver Cord** is the *String* of the *Tongue*; the **Golden Bowl** is the *Pia Mater*; the **Pitcher** at the **Fountain** is the *Heart*, the *Fountain of Life*; the **Wheel** is the *Great Artery*; and the **Cistern** is the *Left Ventricle* of the *Heart!* | Bish. *Patrick*, Doctor *Smith*, *Forsterus*, *Melanchton*, in locum, &c.

IV. There could not possibly have been devised a more significant Token of Love, Friendship, Integrity and Honesty, than the *Joining* of the Right Hands, a Ceremony made use of by all civilized Nations, as a Token of a faithful and true Heart. Fides or *Fidelity* was a *Deity* among the Antients, of which a learned Writer has given us this Description, *viz. The proper Residence of Faith or Fidelity was thought to be in the Right Hand, and therefore this Deity sometimes was represented by Two Right Hands Joined together; sometimes by two little Images shaking each the Other's Right Hand; so that the Right Hand was by the Antients esteemed as a Thing Sacred.* | *Chartarius* in lib. ut supra.

And agreeable to this are those Expressions in *Virgil, Æneid*. IV.

E t

En Dextra Fidesque! as if shaking by the Right Hand was an inseparable Token of an honest Heart. And Æneid. I.

———— cur Dextræ jungere Dextram
Non datur, & veras audire & reddere Voces?

that is, *Why should we not join* Right Hand *to* Right Hand, *and hear and speak the Truth.*

Vol. I. pag. 251. | *In all Contracts and Agreements* (says Archbishop POTTER, in his Antiquities of Greece) *it was usual to take Each Other by the* Right Hand, *That being the Manner of plighting Faith.* And this was done either out of Respect to the Number *Ten,* as some say, there being *Ten Fingers* on the Two Hands; or because such a Conjunction was a Token of *Amity* and *Concord*; whence at all friendly Meetings they join Hands, as a Sign of the *Union* of their Souls.

It was one of the Cautions of PYTHAGORAS to his Disciples, *Take heed to whom you offer your Right Hand!* which is thus explain'd by **Iambit-**

In Vit. Pythagr. | **chus.** *Take no One by the* Right Hand *but the Initiated, that is, in the Mystical Form*; *for the* Vulgar *and the* Profane *are altogether unworthy of the* Mystery!

V. The *Dissector* frequently taking Notice of the Number SEVEN, I instantly

Pignorius in Mens. | recurred to the old *Egyptians,* who held the Number *Seven* to be *Sacred*; more especially they believ'd that whilst their Feast of *Seven Days* lasted, the *Crocodiles* lost their inbred Cruelty: And **Leo Afer,** in his Description of *Africa,* Lib. VIII. says, *that even in his Time, the Custom of Feasting* Seven Days *and* Nights, *was still used for the happy Overflowing of the* Nile. The *Greeks* and *Latins* professed the same Regard for that Number, which might be proved by many Examples.

VI. The Accident, by which the Body of *Master* HIRAM was found after his Death, seems to allude, in some Circumstances, to a beautiful Passage in the 6th Book of *Virgil's* Æneids. **Anchises** had been dead for some Time; and ÆNEAS his Son professed so much Duty to his departed Father, that he consulted with the *Cumæan Sibyl,* whether it were possible for him to descend into the *Shades below,* in Order to speak with him. The Prophetess encouraged him to go; but told him he could not succeed, unless he went into a certain Place and pluck'd a *golden Bough* or *Shrub,* which he should carry in his Hand, and by that means obtain Directions where he should find his Father. The Words are well translated by *Dryden,* viz.

———— *In the neighbouring Grove*
There stands a Tree; the Queen of Stygian JOVE
Claims it her own: Thick Woods and gloomy Night
Conceal the happy Plant from mortal Sight!
One Bough it bears, but wondrous to behold,
The ductile Rind and Leaves of Radiant Gold;

This

*This from the vulgar Branches must be torn,
And to fair* PROSERPINE *the Present born,
Ere Leave be given to tempt the nether Skies:
The first thus rent, a second will arise,
And the same Metal the same Room supplies.
The willing Metal will obey thy Hand,
Following with Ease.*ㅡㅡㅡ

ANCHISES, the great Preserver of the *Trojan Name,* could not have been discover'd but by the Help of a *Bough,* which was pluck'd with great Ease from the *Tree;* nor, it seems, could HIRAM, the *Grand* **Master** of MASONRY, have been found but by the Direction of a *Shrub,* which (says the *Dissector*) *came easily up.* The principal Cause of ÆNEAS's Descent into the *Shades,* was to enquire of his Father the *Secrets* of the *Fates,* which should sometime be fulfill'd among his Posterity: The Occasion of the *Brethrens* searching so diligently for their *Master* was, it seems, to receive from him the *secret Word* of *Masonry,* which should be deliver'd down to their *Fraternity* in After-Ages. This remarkable Verse follows,

  Præterea jacet exanimum tibi corpus amici,
  Heu nescis!
 *The Body of your Friend lies near you dead,
 Alas, you know not how!* ㅡㅡㅡ This was
MISENUS, that was murder'd and buried *Monte sub Aerio,* under *an high Hill*; as (says the *Dissector*) *Master* HIRAM was.

But there is another Story in *Virgil,* that stands in a nearer Relation to the Case of HIRAM, and the Accident by which he is said to have been discover'd; which is this: PRIAMUS King of *Troy,* in the Beginning of the *Trojan* War, committed his Son **Polydorus** to the Care of *Polymnestor* King of *Thrace,* and sent with him a great Sum of Money: But after *Troy* was taken, the *Thracian,* for the Sake of the Money, kill'd the young Prince and privately buried him; ÆNEAS coming into that Country, and accidentally plucking up a *Shrub* that was near him on the *Side* of an *Hill,* discover'd the murder'd Body of **Polydorus,** Æneid. III. By Dryden.

 Not far, a rising Hillock *stood in View,
 Sharp Myrtles on the Sides and Corniels grew;
 There while I went to crop the Sylvan Scenes,
 And shade our Altar with the leafy Greens,
 I pull'd a* Plant: *With Horror I relate
 A Prodigy so strange and full of Fate!
 Scarce dare I tell the Sequel! From the Womb
 Of wounded Earth, and* Caverns *of the* Tomb,
 A Groan, *as of a troubled* Ghost, *renew'd
 My Fright; and then these dreadful Words ensued:
 Why dost thou thus my* buried Body *rend?
 O spare the* Corps *of thy unhappy* Friend!

The Agreement between these two Relations is so exact, that there wants no further Illustration.

VII. We are told that a *Sprig* of *Caſſia* was placed by the *Brethren* at the Head of Hiram's *Grave*; which refers to an old Cuſtom of thoſe *Eaſtern* Countries of Embalming the Dead, in which Operation Cassia was always uſed, eſpecially in preparing the *Head* and drying up the *Brain*; as *Herodotus* more particularly explains. The Sweet-Wood, Perfumes and Flowers, uſed about the *Graves* of the *Dead*, occur ſo frequently in the old *Poets*, that it would he tedious to mention them. *Ovid* thus deſcribes the Death of the Phoenix.

Metam. lib. 15.

> *Upon a ſhady Tree ſhe takes her Reſt,*
> *And on the higheſt Bough her funeral Neſt*
> *Her Beak and Talons build; then ſtrews thereon*
> Balm, Cassia, Spikenard, Myrrh *and* Cinamon:
> *Laſt on the fragrant Pile herſelf ſhe lays,*
> *And in conſuming Odours ends her Days!*

Brother Euclid's *Letter* to the *Author* Againſt unjuſt Cavils.

BRother Anderson, after Thanks for printing the clever Defence, by the Advice of our Brethren, I ſend you this Epiſtle, to anſwer ſome lying Cavils. But firſt we would acknowledge, that

Indeed, the *Free Maſons* are much obliged to the generous Intention of the unbiaſs'd *Author* of the above *Defence*: Tho' had he been a *Free-Maſon*, he had in Time perceived many valuable Things ſuitable to his extended Views of Antiquity, which could not come to the *Diſſector's* Knowledge; for that They are not intruſted with any Brothers till after dne Probation: And therefore ſome think the ingenious Defender has ſpent too much fine Learning and Reaſoning upon the fooliſh *Diſſection*, that is juſtly deſpiſed by the Fraternity, as much as the other pretended Diſcoveries of their Secrets in publick *News-Papers* and *Paſquils*, all of a Sort; for all of 'em put together don't diſcover the profound and ſublime Things of *old Maſonry*; nor can any Man, not a Maſon, make uſe of thoſe incoherent Smatterings (interſpers'd with ignorant Nonſenſe and groſs Falſities) among bright Brothers, for any Purpoſe but to be laught at; our *Communications* being of a quite different Sort. Next, it is well known,

That the Antiquity and Decorum of our Worſhipful *Fraternity* have been envied by ſome, who, very lately, have coaleſced into Societies, in Imitation of the *Free-Maſons*, and ſome in Oppoſition to them, tho' in vain; as the 𝕲𝖔𝖗𝖒𝖆𝖌𝖔𝖓𝖘, who ſoon diſappear'd, and Others are going.

But

But tho' we envy not the Prosperity of any Society, nor meddle with their Transactions and Characters, we have not met with such fair Treatment from Others; nay, even Those that never had an Opportunity of obtaining any certain Knowledge of us, have run implicitly with the Cry, and without Fear or Wit, have vented their Spleen in accusing and condemning us unheard, untry'd; while we, innocent and secure within, laugh only at their gross Ignorance and impotent Malice.

Have not People in former Ages, as well as now, alledged that the *Free Masons* in their *Lodges* raise the 𝔇𝔢𝔳𝔦𝔩 in a *Circle*, and when they have done with him, that they lay him again with a *Noise* or a *Hush* as they please?

How have some diverted themselves with the wild Story of *an old Woman between the Rounds of a Ladder?* Only they should allow the *Free-Masons* to laugh too in their Turn.

Others will swear to the Cook's *red hot Iron* or 𝔖𝔞𝔩𝔞𝔪𝔞𝔫𝔡𝔢𝔯, *for making the Indelible Character on the new made Mason, in order to give him the Faculty of Taciturnity!* Sure such Blades will beware of coming through the Fingers of the *Free-Masons.*

Some have basely calumniated the *Fraternity* as the *Enemies* of the FAIR SEX, in Terms not fit to be rehears'd, and unworthy of a Reply: But tho' in *Lodge Hours* Masons don't allow of *Womens* Company (like many other Societies of Men) yet they make as good Husbands as any other Men, according to their laudable Charges.

Others wonder *at their admitting Men of all Professions, Religions and Denominations*: But they don't consider that *Masons* are true 𝔑𝔬𝔞𝔠𝔥𝔦𝔡𝔞𝔢, and require no other Denominations, (all other Distinctions being of Yesterday) if the new Brother is a *good Man and True*: For Those of 'em that don't study *Architecture*, are often capable of encouraging the *Craft*, and help to support the poor decay'd Brethren.

Have not some rigid People been displeas'd *at the Admission of some worthless Men?* But if the *Free-Masons* are sometimes deceiv'd about Mens Characters, they are not the only Persons so deceiv'd: Yet when a Brother is obnoxious to Censure, if they don't expel him, they endeavour to reform him. However, the *Grand Lodge* has taken due Care of That.

Others complain *that the* Masons *continue too long in the Lodge, spending their Money to the Hurt of their Families, and come home too late, nay sometimes intoxicated with Liquor!* But they have no Occasion to drink much in *Lodge Hours*, which are not long; and when the *Lodge* is closed (always in good Time) any Brother may go home when he pleases: So that if any stay longer and get intoxicated, it is at their own Cost, not as *Masons*, but as other imprudent Men may do; for which the *Fraternity* is not accountable: And the Expence of a *Lodge* is not so great as That of many a private *Club*.

Some observing *that Masons are not more religious, nor more knowing, than other Men, are astonish'd at what they can be conversant about in Lodge Hours!* But tho' a *Lodge* is not a School of Divinity, the Brethren are taught the great Lessons of their *old* Religion, *Morality*, **Humanity** and *Friendship*, to abhor *Persecution*, and to be *peaceable* Subjects under the Civil Government wherever they reside: And as for *other Knowledge*, they claim as large a Share of it, as other Men in their Situation.   Indeed

Indeed, the *antient Lodges* were so many Schools or *Academies* for teaching and improving the *Arts* of *Designing*, especially *Architecture*; and the present *Lodges* are often employ'd that Way in *Lodge-Hours*, or else in other agreeable Conversation, tho' without Politicks or Party Causes; and none of them are ill employ'd, have no Transactions unworthy of an honest Man or a Gentleman, no personal Piques, no Quarrels, no Cursing and Swearing, no cruel Mockings, no obscene Talk, nor ill Manners: For the *noble* and eminent *Brethren* are affable to the *Meanest*; and *These* are duly respectful to their Betters in *Harmony* and *Proportion*; and tho' on the *Level*, yet always within *Compass*, and according to the *Square* and *Plumb*.

Nor can it be denied, that a *Fraternity* so strongly cemented, is more eligible and safe than most Others; especially that there is no Fear of betraying Conversation: and that since *Masonry* has been so much countenanced by Great Men, there have been more fine *Architects* and more expert *Fellow Crafts* in *Britain*, than, perhaps, in all *Europe* besides.

This appears by the stately and regular *Buildings* throughout these *Islands*, from the first Days of the *Great* 𝕴𝖓𝖎𝖌𝖔 𝕵𝖔𝖓𝖊𝖘, the *English* PALLADIO; nor is the fine Taste abated in this present Reign of *King* GEORGE II. but is rather improved; witness the curious House for the *Bank of England*, the *South-Sea House*, the *Front* of the *East-India* House, the Lord *Talbot*'s fine House in *Lincoln's-Inn-Fields*, the many stately *Fabricks* in the Parishes of St. *George Hanover* and *St. Mary la Bonne*, and many more in and about *London* and *Westminster*, and other Towns and Cities, besides Country-Seats, raised in the *good old* AUGUSTAN 𝕾𝖙𝖎𝖑𝖊; and some also design'd only, or begun, as the *Lord* MAYOR of *London*'s New Palace, the admirable *New Bridge* at *Westminster* cross the *Thames*, &c. all which discover the *English* MASONS *Grand Design* of rivalling fair *Italy* in *Architecture*, even those eminent *Revivers* of the AUGUSTAN 𝕾𝖙𝖎𝖑𝖊 mentioned Part I. Chap. VII.

May the ROYAL ART go on and prosper, and spread itself from *Pole* to *Pole*, from *East* to *West*! As it certainly now does in all polite Nations, in spite of the Ignorant and Malicious. I am

From our *old Lodge*, the HORN, in New *Palace-Yard*, *Westminster*, this 2d *Thursday*, or 9th *Nov.* in the *Vulgar* Year of MASONRY 5738.

Your true and faithful Brother

𝕰𝖚𝖈𝖑𝖎𝖉.

While the BOOK was in the PRESS,

The *Author* was kindly encouraged by the few following *Brethren* and *Lodges*, viz.

Marquis of CAERNARVON the Right Worshipful GRAND MASTER.

—Duke of MONTAGU, \
—Duke of RICHMOND, \
—Earl of INCHIQUIN, \
—Earl of LOUDOUN, } Former Grand Masters \
—Earl of DARNLEY, \
—GEORGE PAYNE, Esq; \
—Rev. Dr. DESAGULIERS,

—MARTIN FOLKES, Esq; \
—WILL. COWPER, Esq; } Former Deputy Grand Masters \
—NATHANIEL BLAKERBY, Esq; \
—THOMAS BATSON, Counsellor at Law,

—Sir ROBERT LAWLEY, Baronet, \
—WILLIAM GRÆME, M. D. } Former Grand Wardens \
—MARTIN CLARE, A. M. and F. R. S. \
—Mr. JACOB LAMBALL, Carpenter.

—Hon. Charles Stanhope, Esq; \
—Hon Edward Montagu, Esq; \
—Capt. Robert Maynard. \
—Sir Hugh Mac Brite, Baronet, of the antient Lodge of *Killwining*. \
—Sir John de Lauze, *Master* of the Fountain-Lodge on *Snow-hill*. \
—Daniel Hopkins, \
—Humphrey Primate, } Esqs; \
—Richard Bowyer, \
—Benjamin Taylor, \
—Mr. Thomas Desaguliers. \
—Mr. William Gofton. \
—Mr. John Glass. \
—Mr. John Banks. \
—Capt. Thomas Burgess. \
—Mr. Samuel Greer \
—Mr. Pat. Ramsay, Chirurgeon.

—JOHN WARD, Esq; D. Grand Master. \
—Lord GEORGE GRAHAM, } Grand \
—Capt AND. ROBINSON, } Wardens. \
—Mr. *John Revis* the Secretary. \
—Edward Hody, M. D. \
—Richard Rawlinson, L. L. D. \
—James Ruck Junior, \
—Fotherby Baker, \
—Samuel Barrington, } Esqs; \
—John Jesse, \
—Thomas Jeffreys, \
—Mr. Benjamin Gascoyn, Wine-Merchant. \
—Mr Henry Prude, Apothecary. \
—Mr. George Monkman, Attorney. \
—Mr. Nath. Adams, Optician. \
—Mr. James Cofin, Attorney. \
—Mr. Samuel Lowman, Merchant, a present *Steward*. \
—Mr. George Garret. \
—Mr. Lewis Philip Boitard. \
—Mr. Charles Hoar, \
—Mr. William Renwick, } Attornies. \
—Mr. John Maddock, \
—Mr. William Dodd, } Vintners. \
—Mr. Richard Skikelthorp, \
—Mr. James Askley, Punch-maker. \
—Mr. Tristram Chambers, Upholder. \
—Mr. Daniel Delander, Watch-maker. \
—Mr. John Baker, Carpenter \
—Mr. Erasmus King, Mathematician. \
—Mr. John Pine the Engraver. \
—Mr. J. Sisson the Instrument-maker. \
—Mr. William Stephenson the Glover. \
—Mr. Thomas Aris the Printer. \
—Messieurs Ward and Chandler, Booksellers, at *London*, *York* and *Scarborough*.

} Former Stewards.

LODGES.

LODGES.

- THE Steward's *Lodge*.
- King's-Arms in the *Strand*.
- Forrest's *Coffee-house*.
- Ditto the Old Lodge.
- Fountain on *Snow-hill*.
- Swan and Rummer in *Finch-Lane*.
- Queen's-Head in Great *Queen-street*.
- Mount in *Grovenor-street*.
- Mourning-Bush near *Aldersgate*.
- King's-Arms in New *Bond-street*.
- King's Arms in *Wild street*.
- King's-Arms in *Piccadilly*.
- Fountain near the *Royal-Exchange*.
- Gordon's *Punch-house* in the *Strand*
- La Guerre in *St. Martin's Lane*.
- Hoop and Gryffin in *Leadenhall-street*.
- Berry's *Coffee house* in *Bridges-street*.
- Key and Garter in *Pall-Mall*.
- Royal Standard in *Leicester-Square*.
- Black Posts in *Maiden-Lane*.
- Vineyard in *St. James's Park*.
- Sun in *Holbourn*.
- Anchor and Crown near the *Seven-Dials*.
- Gun in *Jermyn-street*.
- Gun at *Billingsgate*.
- Globe in *Fleet-street*.
- Globe in *Old Jewry*.
- Bacchus in *Bloomsbury-Market*.
- Turk's Head in *Greek-street, Soho*.
- Bell and Dragon near *Golden-Square*.
- Bell in *Nicholas-Lane*.
- Half-Moon in *Cheapside*.
- Queen's-Head in *Knaves-Acre*.
- Shakespear's-Head in *Marleborough-street*.
- Horn in New *Palace Yard*.
- Crown in *Fleet-Market*.
- Crown in *Smithfield*.
- Three Tons on *Snow-hill*.
- Three Tons in *Smithfield*.
- Three Tons in *Newgate-street*.
- Braund's-Head in New *Bond-street*.
- Checquer at *Charing-Cross*.
- Antwerp near the *Royal-Exchange*.
- Star and Garter in *St. Martin's-Lane*.
- Bear in the *Strand*.
- Fountain in *Katharine-street*.
- Castle in *Drury-Lane*.
- Cameron's *Coffee-house* in *Berry-street*
- Katharine-Wheel in *Windmill-street*.
- Rainbow in *York-Buildings*.
- Daniel's *Coffee-house, Temple-Bar*.
- Queen's-Head in the *Old-Bailey*.
- King's-Head in *St. John's street*.
- Sun in *Fleet-street*.
- Sun in *St. Paul's Church-Yard*.
- Rummer in *Queen-street, Cheapside*.

N. B. An Impression in *Folio* of the *Grand Master's* Sword of *State* (formerly the *Sword* of Gustavus Adolphus King of *Sweden*, and next of Bernard Duke of *Sax-Weimar*, with their Names on the *Blade*) which was presented to the *Fraternity* by our former *Grand Master* THOMAS HOWARD *Duke* of Norfolk, richly adorn'd at the *Hilt* with 𝕮𝖔𝖗𝖎𝖓𝖙𝖍𝖎𝖆𝖓 *Columns* of Massy Silver, and on the *Scabbard* with the *Arms* of Norfolk in Silver, the *Masons Arms*, and some 𝕳𝖎𝖊𝖗𝖔𝖌𝖑𝖞𝖕𝖍𝖎𝖈𝖘, &c. (perform'd by Brother *George Moody* the *Sword-bearer*) all explain'd, illuminated and embellish'd, is to be sold by *Brother* John Pine the Engraver, in *Old Bond-street* near *Piccadilly*. Where also may be had

The small *Engraven List* of the *Lodges*, renew'd annually with their Removals.

FINIS.

Corrigenda.

Page	Line		Page	Line	
8	32.	for Erand read Grand.	110	2.	for Capt. *Joseph Elliot* Mr. *Jacob Lamball*, read Mr. *Jacob Lamball* Capt. *Joseph Elliot*.
16	22.	for A. C. read B. C.			
25	10.	After the Word *Cubits*, make a Comma.			
27.		In the Margin, Line 7. for *thn* read *the*	118.		In the Margin, Line 1. for 1723 read 1724.
29	21.	for *Treos* read *Theos*.			
36	29.	for Wars *ended* read Wars *began*.	125.		In the Margin, instead of
43	28.	for CORACALLA read CARACALLA.		5.	Mr. *William Hopkins*, read
				5.	Mr. *William Serjeant*.
46	9.	for *Cousuls* read *Consuls*.	and for	7.	Mr. *Gerard Hatley*, read
Ditto	18.	*After* MAURICUS read *who* murder'd.		7.	*James Chambers*, Esq;
			132.	3.	for CAERMARTHEN read CAERNARVON.
48	22.	for *in St. Miniate* read *of St. Miniate*.			
			Ditto		in the Margin, for *Gentlemen* read *Esquires*.
58	26.	Instead of *did not at All depart* read *did not All depart*.			
			134.		In the Margin read,
59	8,	for *mind* read *ruin'd*.		9.	*Robert Wright*, Esq;
61	30.	for ETHELBERT read KENRED.	137.		In the Margin read,
75	17.	for 1445. read 1443.		9.	Mr. *Peter Leige*.
77	4.	After CADWAN the First, delete the Comma.	139		in the Margin read
				9.	*Henry Higden*, Esq;
85.		In the 2d Column of the Margin at the End, after the Word *Interview*, instead of a *Punctum* make a *Comma*.		12.	*Harry Leigh* Esq;
			200.		The Reference at the End, instead of 5. *They*, read 4. *But*.
108	16.	for *mostly richly* read *most richly*.			Accurate Reader, pray correct these with your Pen, or any others you find.

Just Published,

By CÆSAR WARD and RICHARD CHANDLER, Bookfellers at the *Ship* juft without *Temple-Bar, London*, and fold alfo at their Shops in *Coney-Street* YORK and at SCARBOROUGH SPAW,

I. A General Dictionary Hiftorical and Critical, including That of the celebrated MONS. BAYLE. The whole containing the Hiftory of the moft *Illuftrious Perfons* of all Ages and Nations. In Ten Volumes Folio. Price 15*l*.

II. A New Abridgment and Critical Review of all the State Trials and Proceedings for *High-Treafon*, from the Reign of King *Richard* II. to the Year 1737. By Mr. *Salmon*. In One Vol. Folio. Price 1 *l.* 10 *s.*

III. The VOCAL MISCELLANY, a Collection of above 800 *celebrated Songs*, many of which were *never* before printed, with the Names of the Tunes prefixed to each Song. In Two Pocket Volumes. Price 6 *s.*
  N. B. *Either Volume may be had alone.* Price 3 *s.*

IV. The *Beauties of the Englifh Stage.* Confifting of all the celebrated *Paffages, Soliloquies, Similies, Defcriptions,* and other Poetical Beauties in the ENGLISH PLAYS Ancient and Modern, continued down to the prefent Time. Digefted under proper Heads in Alphabetical Order, with the Names of the Plays and their feveral Authors referr'd to. In Two Pocket Volumes. Price 5 *s.*

Puriffima mella ftipant. VIRG.

V. *Les Amufemens de Spa*; or, the Gallantries of the SPAW in GERMANY. Intermix'd with many entertaining Hiftories of the *principal Perfons*, reforting thither. Adorn'd with thirteen curious Copper Plates of the Fountains, Walks, Avenues, *&c.* In Two Pocket Volumes. Price 6 *s.* with Cuts, or 5 *s.* without.

VI. MAGNA BRITANNIA ANTIQUA ET NOVA; or, a New Survey of *Great Britain*; wherein, to the Topographical Account given by Mr. *Cambden*, and the late Editors of his *Britannia*, is added a *more large Hiftory*, not only of the *Cities, Boroughs, Towns* and *Parifhes* mentioned by them, but alfo of many other Places of Note and Antiquity fince difcovered; with the Pedigrees of *all our Noble Families* and Gentry, *&c.* In 6 Vols. Quarto, compleat. Price 3 *l.*

Of the faid WARD *and* CHANDLER *Bookfellers, as above-mentioned, Gentlemen may be fupply'd with great Variety of Books in all Sciences at the loweft Prices. Who alfo give Ready Money for any Library or Parcel of Books.*

Bibliographical Note

Anderson's Constitutions have been the subject of a great deal of attention over the years, and a complete bibliographical listing of the material would be a herculean task and would be unduly long. But the major material relating to this subject, together with some general references, is as follows:

Edwards, Lewis. "Anderson's Book of Constitutions of 1738." 46 *A. Q. C.,* (1933), 357-430. Reproduced in full in this volume.

Hewitt, A. R. "Anderson's Constitutions as Source books of Masonic History." 79 *A. Q. C.,* (1966), 1-10.

Miller, A. L. "The Connection of Dr. James Anderson of the Constitutions with Aberdeen and Aberdeen University." 36 *A. Q. C.,* (1923), 86-103.

Newton, Edward. "Brethren Who Made Masonic History." Prestonian Lecture of 1965. 78 *A. Q. C.,* (1965), 130-145.

Robbins, Sir Alfred. "Dr. Anderson of the 'Constitutions'." 23 *A. Q. C.,* (1910), 6-34.

Thorp, J. T. "The Rev. James Anderson and the Earls of Buchan." 18 *A. Q. C.,* (1905), 9-12.

Vibert, A. L. "Anderson's Constitutions of 1723." 36 *A. Q. C.,* (1923), 36-85.

Ward, Eric. "Anderson's Freemasonry Not Deistic." 80 *A. Q. C.,* (1967), 36-57, 271-274.

Crawley, W. J. Chetwode. "The Rev. Dr. James Anderson's Non-Masonic Writings, 1712-1739." 18 *A. Q. C.,* (1905), 28-42.

Calvert, Albert F. "George Payne, 2nd Grand Master." 30 *A. Q. C.,* (1917), 258-262; and 31 *A. Q. C.,* (1918), 188.

Quatuor Coronatorum Antigrapha, Volume 7. Facsimile of the 1738 edition with an introduction by William J. Hughan. 1890.

Anderson's Constitutions of 1723 and 1738. Published in 1977 by Quatuor Coronati Lodge. This is the first time that facsimiles of both editions have appeared in one volume together. The volume also has an excellent foreword by Eric Ward and reproduces an article on the subject by Lionel Vibert and one by William J. Hughan.

Gould, R. F. "Importance of the publication of the 1723 Constitutions." 8 *A. Q. C.,* (1895), 153.

Knoop and Jones, *The Genesis of Freemasonry*. 1949. Good book for background material.

Denslow, William R. *10,000 Famous Freemasons:* Volume 1, pp. 21-22. Biographical sketch of Anderson.

Fisher, W. G. "A Cavalcade of Freemasons in 1731." 74 *A. Q. C.*, (1961), 32-49, especially at p. 41.

Carr, Harry. *The Freemason at Work*. (1976), 130, 215-216, 245, 246-247, 284, 314-315.

Collected Prestonian Lectures, 1925-1960. (1965), 47-48, 142, 160, 162, 187, 299, 302-303, 473.

Coil's *Masonic Encyclopedia*. (1961), 49-50.

Coil, Henry W. *Freemasonry Through Six Centuries*. Volume 1, pp. 5-6, 28, 78, 93, 94, 208-209, 218, 225, 227-228 (being critical on these two pages relative to the 1738 edition.)

COLOPHON

Anderson's Constitutions of 1738

Twelve hundred copies of this limited edition were manufactured by Pantagraph Printing Company and Bloomington Offset Process, Inc. of Bloomington, Illinois, the former doing the composition and binding and the latter the presswork.

The type faces used are of the Linotype Janson and Monotype Garamond families. The facsimile pages were reproduced from Transactions of Quatuor Coronati Lodge, Volume 41 and from Volume Seven of Quatuor Coronatorum Antigrapha from copies supplied by Jerry Marsengill of Des Moines, Iowa, and Harry Carr of London, England.

The text paper is fifty pound basis white Glatfelter Book Antique manufactured by the P. H. Glatfelter Co. The book covers are made of Columbia Mills Riverside Vellum over board and stamped in gold.

All volumes of The Masonic Book Club series are designed and prepared by Louis L. Williams, Alphonse Cerza and Fred A. Dolan.

Related Titles from Westphalia Press

Ancient Mysteries and Modern Masonry: The Collected Writings of Jewel P. Lightfoot, Edited by Billy J. Hamilton Jr.

Jewel P. Lightfoot. Former Attorney General of the State of Texas. Past Grand Master of the Masonic Grand Lodge of Texas. From humble beginnings in rural Arkansas, he worked to become an educated man who excelled in law and Freemasonry. He was a gentleman of his time, well-known as a scholar, public speaker, and Masonic philosopher.

Essay on The Mysteries and the True Object of The Brotherhood of Freemasons
by Jason Williams

This isn't a reprint of a classic. It's a new rendition with new life breathed into it, to be enjoyed both by the layperson trying to understand the Craft and Masonic scholars taking a deeper dive into the fraternity's golden years—when the concepts of liberty and equality were still fresh.

Female Emancipation and Masonic Membership: An Essential Collection
By Guillermo De Los Reyes Heredia

Female Emancipation and Masonic Membership: An Essential Combination is a collection of essays on Freemasonry and gender that promotes a transatlantic discussion of the study of the history of women and Freemasonry and their contribution in different countries.

Freemasonry, Heir to the Enlightenment
by Cécile Révauger

Modern Freemasonry may have mythical roots in Solomon's time but is really the heir to the Enlightenment. Ever since the early eighteenth century freemasons have endeavored to convey the values of the Enlightenment in the cultural, political and religious fields, in Europe, the American colonies and the emerging United States.

Freemasonry: A French View
by Roger Dachez and Alain Bauer

Perhaps one should speak not of Freemasonry but of Freemasonries in the plural. In each country Masonic historiography has developed uniqueness. Two of the best known French Masonic scholars present their own view of the worldwide evolution and challenging mysteries of the fraternity over the centuries.

Worlds of Print: The Moral Imagination of an Informed Citizenry, 1734 to 1839
by John Slifko

John Slifko argues that freemasonry was representative and played an important role in a larger cultural transformation of literacy and helped articulate the moral imagination of an informed democratic citizenry via fast emerging worlds of print.

Why Thirty-Three?: Searching for Masonic Origins
by S. Brent Morris, PhD

What "high degrees" were in the United States before 1830? What were the activities of the Order of the Royal Secret, the precursor of the Scottish Rite? A complex organization with a lengthy pedigree like Freemasonry has many basic foundational questions waiting to be answered, and that's what this book does: answers questions.

The Great Transformation: Scottish Freemasonry 1725-1810
by Dr. Mark C. Wallace

This book examines Scottish Freemasonry in its wider British and European contexts between the years 1725 and 1810. The Enlightenment effectively crafted the modern mason and propelled Freemasonry into a new era marked by growing membership and the creation of the Grand Lodge of Scotland.

Getting the Third Degree: Fraternalism, Freemasonry and History
Edited by Guillermo De Los Reyes and Paul Rich

As this engaging collection demonstrates, the doors being opened on the subject range from art history to political science to anthropology, as well as gender studies, sociology and more. The organizations discussed may insist on secrecy, but the research into them belies that.

A Place in the Lodge: Dr. Rob Morris, Freemasonry and the Order of the Eastern Star
by Nancy Stearns Theiss, PhD

Ridiculed as "petticoat masonry," critics of the Order of the Eastern Star did not deter Rob Morris' goal to establish a Masonic organization that included women as members. Morris carried the ideals of Freemasonry through a despairing time of American history.

Brought to Light: The Mysterious George Washington Masonic Cave
by Jason Williams MD

The George Washington Masonic Cave near Charles Town, West Virginia, contains a signature carving of George Washington dated 1748. This book painstakingly pieces together the chronicled events and real estate archives related to the cavern in order to sort out fact from fiction.

Dudley Wright: Writer, Truthseeker & Freemason
by John Belton

Dudley Wright (1868-1950) was an Englishman and professional journalist who took a universalist approach to the various great Truths of Life. He travelled though many religions in his life and wrote about them all, but was probably most at home with Islam.

History of the Grand Orient of Italy
Emanuela Locci, Editor

No book in Masonic literature upon the history of Italian Freemasonry has been edited in English up to now. This work consists of eight studies, covering a span from the Eighteenth Century to the end of the WWII, tracing through the story, the events and pursuits related to the Grand Orient of Italy.

westphaliapress.org

Policy Studies Organization

The Policy Studies Organization (PSO) is a publisher of academic journals and book series, sponsor of conferences, and producer of programs.

Policy Studies Organization publishes dozens of journals on a range of topics, such as European Policy Analysis, Journal of Elder Studies, Indian Politics & Polity, Journal of Critical Infrastructure Policy, and Popular Culture Review.

Additionally, Policy Studies Organization hosts numerous conferences. These conferences include the Middle East Dialogue, Space Education and Strategic Applications Conference, International Criminology Conference, Dupont Summit on Science, Technology and Environmental Policy, World Conference on Fraternalism, Freemasonry and History, and the Internet Policy & Politics Conference.

For more information on these projects, access videos of past events, and upcoming events, please visit us at:

www.ipsonet.org

www.ingramcontent.com/pod-product-compliance
Lightning Source LLC
Chambersburg PA
CBHW051525020426
42333CB00016B/1778